Introduction Information Security

Introduction to Information Security
A Strategic-based Approach

Timothy J. Shimeall
Jonathan M. Spring

AMSTERDAM • BOSTON • HEIDELBERG • LONDON
NEW YORK • OXFORD • PARIS • SAN DIEGO
SAN FRANCISCO • SINGAPORE • SYDNEY • TOKYO
Syngress is an imprint of Elsevier

Publisher: Steve Elliot
Senior Developmental Editor: Nathaniel McFadden
Editorial Project Manager: Ben Rearick
Project Manager: Mohanambal Natarajan
Designer: Matthew Limbert

Syngress is an imprint of Elsevier

225 Wyman Street, Waltham, MA 02451, USA

First edition **2014**

Library of Congress Cataloging-in-Publication Data
A catalog record for this book is available from the Library of Congress

British Library Cataloguing in Publication Data
A catalogue record for this book is available from the British Library

ISBN: 978-1-59749-969-9

Printed and bound in USA

14 15 16 17 18   10 9 8 7 6 5 4 3 2 1

For information on all **Syngress** publications,
visit our website at *store.elsevier.com/syngress*

Working together
to grow libraries in
developing countries

www.elsevier.com • www.bookaid.org

Contents

Acknowledgments

We are indebted to several wonderful people for the successful creation of this book. Contributing authors Dr. James G. Williams and John Sammons have each made irreplaceable contributions, and we offer them our gratitude.

Dr. James G. Williams graciously agreed to contribute Chapter 10 on change management. Currently professor emeritus at the University of Pittsburgh (Pitt), Jim served as chair of the Department of Information Science for more than 10 years. In his quarter century at Pitt, Jim developed and taught more than 20 different courses, including software engineering, database management, systems analysis and design, network design, and network management. In 1986 he founded the Department of Telecommunications at Pitt. Since his retirement from Pitt, he has been active in the establishment of a graduate program in information science at Siam University in Bangkok where he was recently awarded an honorary doctorate. In addition to his academic appointments, Jim is the president of a software firm that produces software used widely by libraries serving blind users across the United States. For three years he served as CIO of Broadstreet Communications. In addition to more than 100 scholarly articles and books, he served as co-editor of the 42-volume *Encyclopedia of Computer Science and Technology* and the 25-volume *Encyclopedia of Microcomputers*. We have benefited greatly from the experience and wisdom Jim has shared with us.

John Sammons graciously agreed to contribute Chapter 13 on digital forensics. John is an assistant professor at Marshall University in Huntington, WV, and holds an adjunct appointment with the graduate forensic science program. John teaches digital forensics, electronic discovery, information security, and technology in the Department of Integrated Science and Technology. John is the founder and director of the Appalachian Institute of Digital Evidence, a nonprofit organization that provides research and training for digital evidence professionals, including attorneys, judges, law enforcement, and information security practitioners in the private sector. John, a former police officer, still serves as an investigator with the Cabell County Prosecuting Attorney's Office and a member of the FBI's West Virginia Cybercrime Task Force. He is an associate member of the American Academy of Forensic Sciences, the High Technology Crime Investigation Association, the Southern Criminal Justice Association, and Infragard. John is the author of *The Basics of Digital Forensics: The Primer for Getting Started in Digital Forensics* (Syngress, 2012). We are grateful to John for the time and experience he has shared with us.

We received considerable help from several people who reviewed the chapters and provided constructive feedback, namely Jack Alanen (California State University, Northridge), David A. Dampier (Mississippi State University), Thomas Daniels (Iowa State University), Burkhard Englert (California State University, Long Beach), Sidney Faber (SEI, Carnegie Mellon University), Stephen Gantz (SecurityArchitecture.com), Gary Kessler (Embry-Riddle Aeronautical University), and Jean-Philippe Labruyere (DePaul University).

The whole staff at Syngress have been quite helpful throughout this project. Steve Elliot was instrumental in initiating and guiding the process of bringing the book into being. The authors are particularly grateful to the developmental editor, Nate McFadden. His patience and experience with the authoring and reviewing process were invaluable.

Dr. Shimeall thanks his friends and family, particularly his exceedingly patient wife, Shari. Without her organization and encouragement, this work would not have been possible.

Mr. Spring offers thanks to his friends and family for their encouragement and support during this process, especially to his father, as well as Drew and Kael—thank you.

We also must thank our colleagues at the SEI's CERT/CC for providing such a conducive work environment. Many of our colleagues have helped sharpen this work through various hallway conversations. We are especially grateful to Sid Faber for his initial encouragement.

Thanks also to our students at Carnegie Mellon University and the University of Pittsburgh, respectively. They have suffered through our explanations without full benefit of them being written down and organized properly in one place. Their questions have helped clarify our thoughts and the book.

LEGAL ACKNOWLEDGMENTS

The Software Engineering Institute and its CERT® Directorate have kindly permitted us to reprint some figures from their work in Chapter 15 of this book, provided we include the following acknowledgment and attribution:

- This publication incorporates portions of *Defining Incident Management Processes for CSIRTs: A Work in Progress* by Alberts, C., Dorofee, A., Killcrece, G., Ruefle, R., and Zajicek, M., CMU/SEI-2004-TR-015, © 2004 Carnegie Mellon University, with special permission from its Software Engineering Institute.
- Any material of Carnegie Mellon University and/or its Software Engineering Institute contained herein is furnished on an "as-is" basis. Carnegie Mellon University makes no warranties of any kind, either expressed or implied, as to any matter including, but not limited to, warranty of fitness for purpose or merchantability, exclusivity, or results obtained from use of the material. Carnegie Mellon University does not make any warranty of any kind with respect to freedom from patent, trademark, or copyright infringement.
- This publication has not been reviewed nor is it endorsed by Carnegie Mellon University or its Software Engineering Institute.
- CERT® is a registered trademark of Carnegie Mellon University.
- OCTAVE Allegro® is a registered trademark of Carnegie Mellon University.

Timothy Shimeall and Jonathan Spring

Introduction

Organizations find information security and computer security require a lot of attention. As more and more of our lives and livelihoods become digital and interconnected, protecting that information naturally becomes more important. With increasing importance, these fields relate to a wider audience than the technical folks who manufacture, install, and manage computer resources.

Technologists often, naturally, take a technology-centric approach to explaining security. There is so much technology that the reader or listener requires dedicated study to keep track of it all. This attention to detail in turn often leads students to miss the forest for the trees. Retaining the individual technologies' details is difficult enough; the strategic importance of each technology, and how they interrelate, is often omitted or lost. This deficit is a problem for decision makers and leaders, since they need to know what capabilities can be deployed, but do not generally have the time to learn all the technology in detail. It is also a problem for students and young professionals who are technologists and operators, because they inefficiently use the tools they know.

Introduction to Information Security: A Strategy-based Approach was written to partially address this deficit. This book provides a framework for thinking about information security strategically, rather than as a list of technology details. The book introduces each technology as it is relevant to the strategic goals, and in no more detail than is necessary to understand the strategic importance. Additional material for more in-depth exploration, whether as part of a course or as self-study, is provided via the references provided in each chapter (largely linked to online material), and via the companion website for this book.

Professionals and students alike should benefit from this book. The focus on strategy has emphasized certain topics and connections that can be easily overlooked, and even seasoned professionals may be pleasantly surprised at some of the results. Security-related studies are often taught at universities to upper-class undergraduates or at the master's level, however, there are no particular prerequisites to this text besides critical thinking skills. The underlying technologies (e.g., Internet routing) are covered within the text, also with references and companion material for more complete exploration.

Information and computer security, however, are about more than just technology. People have been responsible for the advances in this field, acting as technologists, adversaries, and advocates, shaping the legal environment faced in this field today. The book profiles selected individuals, presenting their contributions and their background. In addition, sidebars throughout describe real-world attacks that motivate the technologies described therein. These profiles and attacks provide an opportunity for students to see the material as relevant to themselves, their careers, and the challenges facing their organizations.

APPROACH OF THIS BOOK

The purpose of this book is primarily to develop a strategic method of thinking about information security. Chapters 1 and 2 motivate the strategic approach and define security-related terms. Chapters 3–15 are organized around a certain type of contribution to a strategic area. The four strategic stages developed are deception, frustration, resistance, and recognition/recovery. The chapter topics are summarized in Table I.1. As each strategy builds on the prior strategies, the most natural way for a reader interested in strategy to proceed is sequentially, perhaps skimming over some of the technical details.

This book can also be used as an introduction to security-related information technology. The reader interested in particular technologies may find it helpful to move through the text by related technologies, rather than sequentially by strategies. Instructors and students should be able to select the chapters that suit instructional needs with the help of Table I.1.

CLASSROOM USE

This book grew out of a series of courses the authors have taught at the Naval Postgraduate School, Carnegie Mellon University, and the University of Pittsburgh over the last 20 years, as well as from experience in working with a group of organizations to improve their security. In a typical course, a selection of technologies is presented, with strengths and weaknesses associated with those technologies. Over time, the analogies to military strategy and the combination of methods associated with those strategies emerged.

The target audience for this book is senior undergraduates and graduate students who need an understanding of information security but are focused

Table I. 1 A Guide to the Technologies Introduced for Each Strategy

Chapter	Strategy	Technologies Introduced
3	*Deception*	Modern Internet history and operations (TCP/IP; BGP)
		Dynamic addressing: DHCP / NAT
4		Proxies
		Honeypots
		Tarpits
		Virtual Hosting
5	*Frustration*	Host-based intrusion detection
		Service Wrappers
		Access Control Lists (ACLs)
		Firewalls
		Proxies
		Dynamic addressing: NAT
		Network design
6		Discretionary Access Control
		Mandatory Access Control
		Security Policy
7	*Resistance*	Passwords
		Security tokens
		CAPTCHAs
		Kerberos
		RBAC
		Phishing
		Password cracking
8		Historic encryption algorithms
		Block ciphers; AES
		Stream ciphers; RC4
		Disk encryption
		Diffie-Hellman key exchange and RSA algorithms
		Key management and PKI
		Hashing algorithms
		PGP
		Asymmetric encryption and digital certificates
		TLS; X.509 certificates
		Steganography
9		Security partitions need to know policy management
10		Configuration management automation systems
		Change management automation systems
		Configuration management databases (CMDB)
		CFEngine and Chef

(Continued)

Table I. 1 (Continued)

Chapter	Strategy	Technologies Introduced
11	*Recognition*	OSI networking model
		Network flow
		Full-packet capture technologies
		IDS
		Human-driven network analysis using various methods
		Suggested blogs for security professionals
12		Intrusion detection systems
		Network-based IDS
		Network behavior analyzers
		Signature-based detection
		Anomaly-based detection
		Wireless IDS
		Intrusion prevention systems
13		MD5 / SHA hash algorithm examples
		Magnetic storage
		Flash storage
		Solid state drive operation
		Common file systems (FAT, NTFS, HFS +)
		Random Access Memory
		Cloning hard drives
14		Hamming codes
		Digital signatures
		Asymmetric encryption
		Hashing algorithms
		Database integrity
		UNIX diff
		GPS and integrity detection
15	*Recovery*	Contingency planning
		Emergency management
		Recovery and response policies
		Incident handling
		After action review and learning lessons
16		Professional certifications and continued learning
		Command-line interfaces

more on the use of security technology than on the development or installation of this technology. Chapter review questions are included with each chapter, to allow the reader to validate their understanding of the important points and terms in each chapter. Chapter exercises are more open-ended, and may require the reader to explore beyond the text content of the book (including reviewing the references provided) to form an appropriate answer. The exercises in this book do not require programming, software configuration, or device configuration. Instead, they are focused on understanding how technologies protect information, and on understanding the trade-offs and supportive relationships among technologies.

SUPPORT MATERIALS

Support materials are available from this books website at http://textbooks. elsevier.com/9781597499699. Any errata will be located there. Instructors will be able to download prepared course materials, including lecture notes, figures from the text, an exam question pool, project ideas, and solutions to the problems at the end of each chapter.

Despite our best efforts, errors also leak into a text. Please let us know about any errors you find while reading the text by emailing InfoSecurityFeedback@ elsevier.com.

Timothy Shimeall and Jonathan Spring

CHAPTER 1

Motivation and Security Definitions

INFORMATION IN THIS CHAPTER

- Information security and its motivation
- Vulnerability, exploits, malware, intrusions, and controls
- Security risk management
- Security strategies and overlapping controls

INTRODUCTION

The role of computer networks as an integral part of daily life makes information security critical for individuals and organizations. The amount of personal and corporate information stored on networks, and the variety of threats to that information, combine to form a pressing need for increased protection of that information. This chapter describes this need and the broad methodology for addressing it, as a foundation for the chapters that follow.

INFORMATION SECURITY AND ITS MOTIVATION

For almost all organizations, information is a critical commodity. The various pieces of information used by these organizations, together with the computers that process those pieces of information, are referred to as *information assets*. Figure 1.1 diagrams some of the information assets and where they fit in an organizational hierarchy. Some of these assets are internal, proprietary information that may not be easily recoverable (without backups) if removed, corrupted, or blocked from the organizations' use. Other assets are information on external entities (including identifying information for customers or business partners, payment-processing information, or records of transactions) maintained as custodial property by the organization—without which, no effective transaction could be undertaken, but limited by the agreements under which the information was provided. Forrester Research, in a 2010 survey of over 300 corporations, found that this custodial data had a mean value

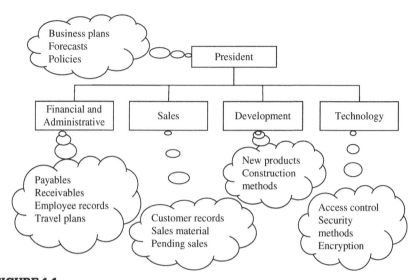

FIGURE 1.1
Organization chart with sample information assets.

of $750,000 per organization (self-evaluated by the senior IT decision makers participating in the study). In contrast, these executives placed more than double this value on the internal information used in the operation of these corporations, including logistics and production information, business plans and new product forecasts, earnings and financial info, and employee information, along with proprietary research and clinical trials [1].

The value placed on this information often does not derive from the cost of gathering or generating the information. In some cases, organizations spend significant investments gathering or generating information, and then ultimately give the information away for free (for marketing, customer support, reputation building, or participation in professional societies, among other reasons). Instead of the initial investment, the value comes from the use the organization makes of the information. Other types of organizations do not measure value in terms of money or effort, but in terms of reputation (particularly in government) or operational advantages (particularly in the military, or in nonprofit organizations, although the advantages sought by these organizations differ greatly). Organizational use is partially determined by the properties of the information, and the protections associated with those properties. Figure 1.2 shows these properties contributing to information security.

In particular:

■ *The information must have a reliable meaning.* This meaning may be protected by assuring the information's *data integrity*—preventing

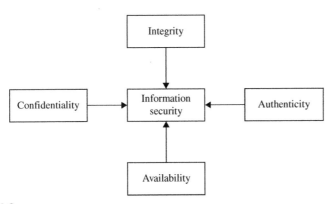

FIGURE 1.2
Information properties and information security.

undesirable and unauthorized changes to the information [2]. By attacking data integrity (i.e., modifying information without authorization), an adversary may block necessary processing, impede other defenses, or disrupt computer-based capabilities. By protecting integrity, the organization assures that the content, format, and semantics of the information remain controlled by the organization, facilitating ongoing reliable use. For businesses, assuring data integrity protects their ability to receive orders, produce quality products, deliver orders to appropriate addresses, invoice the correct parties for payment, and other aspects of business life. For military organizations, assuring data integrity protects their logistics chain, deployment, targeting, damage assessment, and military operations in general. For any organization, assuring data integrity protects general accounting, payroll, internal planning, and other aspects common to virtually all organizations.

■ *The information must provide an advantage to its use, providing a benefit not available to all.* This advantage may derive from the information's *confidentiality*—restricting the knowledge of the information to authorized parties [2]. By attacking confidentiality (i.e., intercepting information without authorization), an adversary may compromise authenticating information, publicize internal planning and forecast information, and disclose personal identifying information (allowing impersonation to other organizations) and other closely held information. By protecting confidentiality, the organization retains control over which parties have access or use of the information, restricting competitors from exploiting this information, and enabling necessary internal planning.

■ *The information must have suitable authority for its use.* This authority is assured by the *authenticity* of the information—protected by nonrepudiation, which is the ability to definitively identify the source of the information [2]. By attacking authenticity (i.e., imitating authorized sources), an adversary may cause false information to be accepted as valid, or fraudulently obtain increased access to computers or data. By protecting authenticity, the organization assures a trace from the responsible individuals to any actions done on the data. This trace enables organizations to audit actions by individuals, reducing the chance that malice or error will corrupt key elements of the organization's information. For businesses, such authority establishes managerial direction over company processes. For the military, such authority enables the chain of command and reduces uncertainty in decision making.

■ *The information must be available when needed by the organization.* The *availability* protections ensure that the information and its processing capabilities are providing service as designed whenever users make authorized requests [2]. Protecting availability involves ensuring the presence of the information, its access rights, usable formatting, and suitable computing resources for handling the information. By attacking availability (i.e., denying service or access), an adversary may block the retrieval, processing, or use of key information supporting an organization's mission. By defending availability, an organization assures that its necessary activities may continue.

There are other properties that may be significant to an organization's information security. Parker, for example, adds utility and possession [3]. However, the four listed here give a sense of the variety of ways that information may be attacked and defended. In later chapters, the defenses will be expanded on further.

While all of these characteristics of information are required for use in organizations, the importance of each characteristic varies from organization to organization. In financial institutions, data integrity is paramount—if an institution loses the reliability of its information, regulators will shut it down. In e-businesses, availability is key—loss of service may lead to large loss of revenue. For many military applications, confidentiality is the most important property—disclosure to the enemy of military plans or operations could be fatal to the personnel involved. In each of these cases, the value of the information (and thus, the corporate value) is increased via the protection of the information and decreased by lack of such protection, as illustrated in Figure 1.3.

Organizations or individuals may choose not to protect some information. Logically, this implies that the organization places no importance on the content, dissemination, originality, and presence of the information. This, in turn, implies that the information is not useful to the organization.

Information security, then, is used in this book as measures that implement services that assure adequate protection for information systems used by or

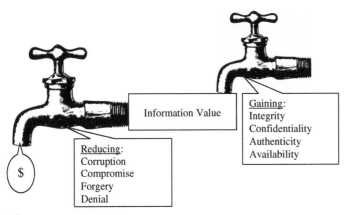

FIGURE 1.3
Gaining and losing value.

SECURITY CASE STUDY: AUTOTOTE INSIDER CASE—COMPROMISE OF DATA INTEGRITY

In early October 2002 [4], Glenn DaSilva placed a "pick four" bet on a local horserace via a phone call to an off-track betting facility operated by Autotote Systems, Inc. His bet was of a form where he picked two specific horses in the first two races, then the field (any horse at all) in the last two races. While this is ordinarily a very poor strategy, Glenn knew his bet would win, whether or not the horses he had marked won. His fraternity brother, Christopher Harn, a senior programmer at Autotote, would make sure of that.

Christopher had learned that, to avoid overloading the track computers, Autotote did not send the off-track bets to the track until 20 minutes after the second race in a four-race exacta, or after the fourth race in a six-race exacta. With Christopher's level of access, that gave him plenty of time. On the day of the race, Christopher arranged to be working. He monitored the races Glenn had bet on, and right after the second race, he ran a program that changed the bet so that the first two actual winners replaced the horses Glenn had bet on. That gave Glenn a guaranteed win, yielding over $100,000 in winnings, which Glenn split with Christopher.

Since no one noticed, the guys grew bolder. Christopher contacted Derrick Davis, another fraternity brother, and in October 2002, Derrick opened an account with Autotote and placed six bets on the Breeder's Cup, a very large national race. Since this was a six-race exacta, Derrick bet on four specific horses in the first four races, then the field on the last two. On the day of the race, Christopher ran his program again after the fourth race, changing the first four bets to reflect the actual winners.

Shortly after that is where things fell apart. The next race was won by a long shot—a horse almost nobody bet on. This was the third long-shot win in the exacta, which gave Derrick the only winning tickets. When the race officials examined the bets, they realized (due to the odd form of the bets, and that the same horses were bet on repeatedly) there was some form of irregularity and started an investigation, which quickly led to the arrest of Christopher, Derrick, and Glenn. Instead of the more than three million-dollar payoff from the bet, they each ended up serving time in prison [5].

hosted within organizations [6]. In this definition, *services* are technical or managerial methods used with respect to the information being protected, *information systems* are computer systems or communication systems that handle the information being protected, and *protection* implies the conjunction

Table 1.1 Selected Legislation with Security Requirements

Short Name	Required Protection	Reference
ECPA	Electronic communications	[7]
Privacy Act of 1974	Government records	[8]
Sarbanes–Oxley	Corporate records	[9]
Fair Credit Reporting Act	Credit records	[10]
HIPPA	Health records	[11]
Gramm–Leach–Bliley	Personal information	[12]

of integrity, confidentiality, authenticity, and availability (although not necessarily in that order). The definition of *adequate* in information security differs between organizations, based on the degree of threat against the organization, management's acceptance of risk, the regulatory climate applicable to the organization, and the mission of the organization, among other factors. Often, what an organization initially elects as adequate protection fails under attack, and more stringent protections are applied. Conversely, where protections interfere with organizational operations, the organization may choose to relax protections to a certain extent and adopt a lower level of protection as adequate. Iteration may occur between increasing and decreasing protections, and this iteration is quite disruptive to many organizations' operations. The selection of services is discussed throughout the remainder of this book, but the level of protection considered adequate must inherently be determined by the personnel in the organization and expressed in the security policy for the organization and its systems.

Organizations are not, however, free to make arbitrary choices about what constitutes an adequate level of protection. In recent years, both legislation and case law have specified some necessary level of information security. While the legal system generally lags the technical innovation of both security compromises and security defenses, the mandated protections do support a "lower bound" for security. Table 1.1 summarizes some major laws that shape this lower bound in the United States.

TERMINOLOGY: VULNERABILITIES OF SOFTWARE, EXPLOITS, MALWARE, INTRUSIONS, AND CONTROLS

The range of protections mandated by legislation and case law are somewhat daunting. Virtually no organization is left without responsibilities in this area. There are several factors that make satisfaction of these responsibilities difficult, including the vulnerability of software and protocols, the

PROFILE: ELOUISE COBELL

Elouise Cobell (1945–2011) was, for 13 years, treasurer of the Blackfoot nation. She was the lead plaintiff in *Cobell v. Salazar*, a lawsuit originally filed (as *Cobell v. Babbit*) in 1996 accusing mismanagement of a $60 billion per year mineral rights trust fund by the Bureau of Indian Affairs (BIA). In late 2010, the government settled the suit for $3.4 billion, about half to go to the more than 500,000 tribe members affected, about half to go to acquisition of tribal lands, and about $50 million to a scholarship fund for Native Americans. As part of this case, the information security of the fund's data processing systems was evaluated by a team of experts hired by the court [13]. The 115-page Special Masters report (issued in November 2001) is a detailed description of data insecurity at BIA. The report found poor or no passwords, no firewalls, no use of data encryption, unauthenticated changes to the payee list, very poor physical security, anonymous funds transfers, poor handling of backups, and insecure document handling, among many other security problems. The BIA data security was so poor that the judge was forced to order BIA and any connected network off of the Internet in late 2001, which resulted in the full Department of the Interior being cut off. At the same time, the judge found that the data insecurity was criminal in nature (the first such finding on record) and initiated criminal contempt proceedings against the Secretary of the Interior and the Assistant Secretary for Indian Affairs [14]. The criminal contempt was overturned on appeal, on the grounds that these individuals were not responsible since they inherited the system from their predecessors.

development practices and priorities, the exploitation of those vulnerabilities via malware and manual methods, and the existence of intelligent adversaries that actively violate information security and attack various organizations. This section explores these factors, and describes, at a high level, how organizations deal with them.

Information security violations arise when an actor takes advantage of vulnerabilities in a computer that handles information. An *actor*, in this sense, is some entity or process that serves as a proximate cause for the violation; an *adversary* is a human actor working against a specific organization. A *threat* is a potential for violation of security, which exists when there is an entity, circumstance, capability, action, or event that could cause harm. A *vulnerability* is a flaw in the system (including its operation) that can be exploited to violate the system's security policy [2]. Vulnerabilities can be introduced throughout the system life cycle, such as:

- A specified lack of authentication in an embedded control system (due to space issues on the device) can be a vulnerability if that system is not fully protected by physical means (e.g., if it is on an open network).
- A design choice for a simple (and weak) form of encryption can be a vulnerability if the encrypted data is available to unauthorized actors.
- A programmer's use of unguarded input (where the length of the input is not restricted to the available storage) can be a vulnerability if an agent can submit arbitrary input, leading to overflow of the storage and corruption of the program's memory.

- A lack of secured storage for backup media can be a vulnerability if unauthorized actors can copy, delete, or steal backups of confidential information.

The breadth of ways that vulnerabilities can be introduced makes them hard to completely eliminate, and has led to them being ubiquitous in current information systems.

One factor that increases the difficulty of eliminating vulnerabilities is that insecure behavior is different from incorrect behavior; often insecure is a subset of incorrect, but occasionally the vulnerability is part of the concept for the system, so the system may be correct but insecure. Indeed, there is a difference in the basic assumptions of developing secure systems and developing correct systems. In conventional software engineering, events breaking the system are normally considered to be unintended or random. The view is that users are annoyed or upset by the cases that break the system. This allows the developers to focus on parts of the system that are frequently executed, and to put the less executed parts of the system at lower priority.

In secure development, breaking the system is considered to be the deliberate intent of an intelligent (and, sometimes, quite persistent and well-resourced) adversary. There are several implications of these adversaries, but one is that any executable portion of the system could be used to break it, whether or not it is frequently executed. Another is that the adversaries may deliberately choose to use inputs to the system that contradict the specified inputs (by length or by content) to break its security. Most system developers are focused on making the system correct (minimizing errors); comparatively, very few know how to make a system secure. Others know how, but fail to include security in their concept or design for their systems. The result is that there are many vulnerabilities in deployed information systems, particularly networked information systems.

Vulnerabilities are discovered in several different ways. Users may accidentally identify a vulnerability in the course of their authorized use of the information system (e.g., in the Harn case [5]). Competitors sometimes find vulnerabilities in competing products [15]. Security firms may identify vulnerabilities using detailed analysis of source code or using system-level testing techniques [16]. Organizations using the vulnerable information systems are notified of vulnerabilities via vendor announcements or popular media, and then fix, or "patch," the vulnerabilities via corrective actions as the organizations choose.

A *vulnerability* is a potential security violation—a doorway that might be entered to violate an organization's security policy. An *exploit* is a process for using a vulnerability to violate such policy (still a potential, not actual, security violation, but directly applicable to real systems). Most exploits are developed after the associated vulnerabilities are known and described—sometimes even after a fix for the vulnerability has been published [17]. Some system developers will only fix vulnerabilities when they have identified exploits for those vulnerabilities. Other developers assess and fix vulnerabilities as they are reported, whether or not an exploit has been identified. Some exploits, however, are for vulnerabilities that have not been previously reported. These exploits, termed *zero-day exploits*, are considered to be especially dangerous to organizations, as there is less time to prepare for adversaries' use of the exploit.

For computer networks, most exploits are implemented as computer software or program fragments to be used within computer software. This malicious software, frequently abbreviated as *malware*, may not necessarily be developed by adversaries intending to violate the security of organizations, but rather may be developed for profit (e.g., by selling it to the affected vendors or to those intending to violate security) or to provide a clear demonstration of vulnerabilities so that they may be fixed. Much malware, however, is developed by those intending to use it to violate security.

There are several types of malware that have been developed, and the terminology will be familiar to many readers:

- A *worm* is a standalone program that copies itself from system to system. Some worms will carry a *payload*, a set of instructions to execute when a set of conditions have been met. Some payloads execute immediately, other payloads execute when the condition that they are on satisfies specific conditions, including when a specific date happens [2].
- A *virus* is much like a worm, except that it is not a standalone program, but rather propagates by modifying some other piece of software. Like a worm, it carries a payload.
- A *Trojan horse* is a program that has a benign public purpose, but hides a malicious payload.
- A *logic bomb* is a program or program fragment set to violate security when accessed using external commands.
- *Spyware* is designed to hide information, gather information, and export that information from the systems on which it executes.
- *Bots* are programs that execute commands in a distributed fashion. Beneficial bots are used in a variety of applications. Malicious bots are designed to hide commands, to receive commands from an adversary, and to execute those commands, exploiting the resources of the systems.

There are other forms of malware, but this list indicates the range of actions and behaviors that have been implemented.

When an exploit is executed, whether manually or via malware, the system's security policy is violated and a *security incident* (hereafter, just referred to as

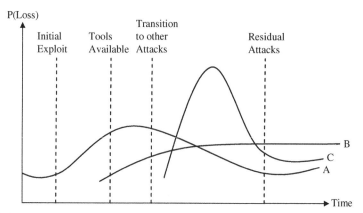

FIGURE 1.4
Incidents and likelihood of loss over time.

incident) occurs. Incidents are occasions that typically involve losses to the organizations involved. These losses (of authenticity, integrity, confidentiality, or availability) have already been described in the initial discussion of the importance of information security. Figure 1.4 describes three common cases of incident activity. Case A, also labeled with events affecting its shape, shows the probability of loss raising and falling as the enabling vulnerabilities have exploits developed and applied against the organizations involved. Case B, the strictly increasing case, is a form of incident in which the associated vulnerabilities either cannot be fixed or organizations choose not to fix them (e.g., if the cost of the fix is larger than the expected loss from the associated incidents). Case C is a common shape for incidents using zero-day exploits, but in this case the incidents are rapidly mitigated. Note that in all of the cases the possibility of loss never vanishes—a new exploit leaves a certain amount of residual risk.

Against vulnerabilities, exploits, and incidents, organizations apply security controls to mitigate their losses. A *security control* is anything done with or to the system that acts in support of the system's information security, passive or active, technical, operational, or managerial. Most of the remaining chapters of this book will detail various security controls and how to use them in an effective fashion. For example, Chapter 8 discusses encryption, which is generally a control for resisting incidents involving confidentiality, integrity, or authenticity, but may actually be a vulnerability with respect to availability. Chapter 15 talks about backups, which are a control for availability, but may be a vulnerability with respect to confidentiality. Using these two controls together properly (i.e., using the strengths of each to mitigate the gaps in the other) may help resist a broad range of incidents, but using them improperly (where the gaps reinforce each other) may make the overall security weaker.

Table 1.2 Overview of OCTAVE Allegro Phases

Phase	Description
1	Define risk measurement criteria
2	Identify information assets
3	Identify storage locations of assets
4	Identify specific threats
5	Construct threat scenarios
6	Apply threat scenarios
7	Score identified risks using measurement criteria
8	Select approach to deal with threats

SECURITY RISK MANAGEMENT

There are two complementary approaches that have helped organizations apply multiple controls effectively: security risk management and security strategies. This section describes the first; the second is described in Chapter 2. Security risk management is any process of identifying, measuring, and mitigating potential loss of information security to reduce the expectation of such loss to a level acceptable to the organization [2]. This section describes a process for risk management, drawn from the OCTAVE Allegro model of the Software Engineering Institute [18], which uses an eight-phase approach to manage risk (as overviewed in Table 1.2). OCTAVE generally is an asset-based risk analysis—it assumes that protecting information assets is a necessary component of protecting enterprise security, although asset protection is not sufficient for enterprise security. Enterprise security must also include site security, personnel security, disaster recovery, and other protections. While the OCTAVE Allegro model has proven useful to several organizations, other methods approach risk analysis differently. As one example, the STAR model [19] uses a five-phase approach and has been applied successfully at a major university. The international standard on risk analysis [20] uses a six-phase approach in a cyclical fashion.

An OCTAVE Allegro risk analysis starts with the definition of measurement criteria to be applied during the analysis. These criteria express the range of impacts that are significant to the organization performing the analysis. Generally, these impacts are those that cause losses related to the essential activities of the organization, such as those that hamper use of information systems or those that interfere with the organization's relationship to its customer base. By defining the measurement criteria, these impacts can be dealt with quantitatively, rather than qualitatively. One example criterion might be using expected hours of system downtime as a measurement of impacts that hamper use of information systems. This model has the organization define its own criteria, reflecting its own concerns over impact, rather than a preexisting set of concerns applied externally.

The second phase is identifying the information assets (people, information, processing systems, or other retainers and processors of information) that are of value to the organization. While most organizations have a general awareness of their information, a detailed inventory is surprisingly difficult to gain, even for modest-sized organizations. This inventory will include where these assets are used by the organization, how the assets are accessed, and who is responsible for the assets. For example, a personnel database is used by the human resources (HR) department to track employees of the organization, and is used only by HR personnel, as validated by their passwords, who have been designated by the organization's director of HR.

The third phase identifies the storage location of each information asset, together with the existing security controls on that storage location. These locations can be internal or external, permanent (archival) or transient (only for the duration of a task). Continuing the database example, the personnel database is maintained on the HR server for the organization, but extracts of the database are often sent via email to executives to support decision making. Both the server and the email system would be evaluated as storage locations, and the security controls for each would be listed.

For each information asset, the fourth phase identifies the specific threats that could negatively affect the asset's security. This phase involves describing the potential impact if the threat occurred, and some conditions that cause that occurrence. In producing this description based on the storage locations previously identified, the organization starts to gain a detailed understanding of where the assets are at risk. Continuing the database example, potential threats include disclosure of proprietary information to unauthorized individuals. While authorized HR personnel maintain the database, IT administrators, who might not be authorized for all content of the database, or even the extracts, maintain the email system.

The fifth phase is to construct threat scenarios with respect to the information assets. A threat scenario includes one or more assets, an actor, a means, a motive, and a list of undesired outcomes. An *actor* can be either natural (a storm, flood, fire, or other disaster), automated (malware), or intelligent (a criminal, activist, or other potentially harmful human). A *means* is a vulnerability and exploit used by the actor against the information asset. A *motive* is the desire or inducement for the actor to apply the means (for natural disasters, this is omitted). An undesired outcome is weakening or damage to the information asset, as identified during the fourth phase. Threat scenarios may be described in a text narrative, but many organizations use a graphical representation, known as a *threat tree*, to show the relationship between the steps

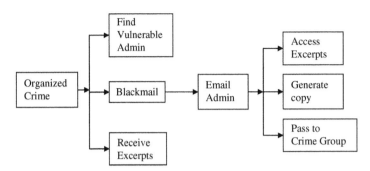

FIGURE 1.5
Threat tree for organized crime scenario.

in the scenario. In the database example, the threat scenario may be that an organized crime group blackmails one of the email administrators, forcing him or her to transparently copy and pass to them the database excerpts being sent to executives. The threat tree for this scenario is depicted in Figure 1.5.

In the sixth phase, the organization applies the threat scenarios to its assets, identifying specific outcomes for the essential activities of the organization. This is the phase where some information related to the potential loss is identified. Continuing the database example, once the data is passed to them, the crime group then uses this information for insider trading, harvesting personal information, or unfair competition with the organization. The impact is loss to the organization's finances and to the reputation and finances of its personnel.

In the seventh phase, the identified risks are scored using the measurement criteria established in the first phase. These scores act to prioritize the risks for mitigation. It isn't always the threats with the highest potential impact that receive the highest scores. Factors that may increase the score for other threats include ease of access by actors, susceptibility to mitigation, and tendency of the mitigation to suit the existing workflows of the organization. In the database example, both the loss and the ease of access by the actors in the threat scenario lead this threat to score high on the organization's measurement criteria.

The eighth and final phase of the OCTAVE Allegro model is to select the approach for dealing with each of the prioritized threats. There are several potential approaches: accept, mitigate threat or impact, transfer threat, or defer. The *accept* approach indicates a decision to take no action on a particular threat and to tolerate the resulting losses. This is generally allowable only for low-impact threats. The *defer* approach indicates a need for more information before a decision can be made to either accept the risk or mitigate it. Sometimes the technology for remediation is relatively immature, or the risk is segmented enough that no solid understanding of its impact is available, in which case the organization may reasonably choose to defer decisions. *Transfer of threat* occurs when the organization chooses to place an asset outside its network and negotiate either a minimum level of security from the hosting provider or insurance against damage from an insurance provider. The *mitigation of threat or impact* is the primary focus of this book, and the methods and strategies discussed in the remainder of the book provide a basis for organizations to determine how to mitigate their threats and the negative consequences resulting from them [18]. To provide some feel for common (but effective) recommended mitigations, the Australian Defence Signals Directorate maintains a list of "top 35" mitigations [21].

In the database example being discussed, one obvious mitigation for the organized crime threat would be to encrypt the database excerpts using a strong encryption technique (see Chapter 8) before sending them through the organization's email. For casual adversaries this might be sufficient, but it is unlikely to be fully successful in this threat scenario. Recall that in this threat scenario, we are dealing with adversaries who have the resources and malice to subvert trusted people in the organization—this is not like dealing with bored teenage hackers (see Kreb's blog [22] for insight on threats like this).

There are several drawbacks to the sole use of encryption as a countermeasure. First, it provides little or no capability to determine whether actors are attempting to compromise this information, so any successful attack will come as a total surprise to the organization. Second, the organized crime group may rapidly recognize the use of encryption, and apply efforts to compromise the encryption system itself or its key infrastructure. Third, the encryption itself might be used against the organization, as the encrypted traffic would naturally be viewed as authentic, and thus false information inserted as encrypted email might be used to manipulate the organization. As such, proper mitigation of the threat may require a comprehensive approach. While this might increase the cost, in this case, the additional investment may be warranted as the negative impacts are severe.

It is in the comprehensive solutions that the security strategies come to the forefront. These strategies will be fully discussed in Chapter 2, but a brief treatment in this example will give some sense of how they may be used. The security strategies work through the various stages of a security compromise, seeking at each stage to progressively deal with the malicious action. The first strategy is *deception*, either fooling the malicious actors as to where to direct their activity or fooling them with respect to the degree of success of their activity. The second strategy is *frustration*, where the initial penetration into the organization is made as difficult as reasonable. The third strategy is *resistance*, where activity following the initial penetration is hampered as much as is reasonable. The final strategy is an *integrated recognition and recovery* from the activity of the malicious actors. These strategies work together to allow improved mitigation of threats and their impacts.

In the database example, the organization may choose to employ all of these strategies to protect their critical personnel information. A deception approach may involve use of false traffic, sending fake excerpts (with all the safeguards of real excerpts) that would cause individuals who attempt to exploit it to act in a very revealing manner. The desired recipients of the real excerpts would know the schedule on which these are generated, and as such would know to ignore off-schedule excerpts, or there could be specific entries in the fake excerpts (e.g., fake excerpts contain names of individuals who are not part of the organization, or a nonexistent branch of the organization) that would flag them to be ignored. A frustration approach may include careful preparation of trusted administrators (and other employees) as to the tactics that resourced criminals use to compromise that trust, and how to report these attempts in a way that will not lead to negative consequences for the employee, so that the blackmail attempts will be forestalled and reported. Encryption can be used as a resistance approach, and in the context of the other approaches its disadvantages may be reduced. Finally, a recognition and recovery approach may involve monitoring for unauthorized data transfers at times associated with the transmission of the excerpts, blocking such transfers, and contingencies for dealing with the compromised data.

HOW TO USE THIS BOOK

This book discusses how to manage security risk using the security strategies to apply security technologies. Several technologies are covered for each strategy. This arrangement gives the reader several options as to how to pursue an introduction to information security.

By Security Strategy

Chapter 2 introduces the security strategies in depth. With this as a basis, the balance of the book goes through each strategy and some associated technologies in depth. Chapters 3 and 4 discuss the deception strategy. Chapters 5 and 6 discuss the frustration strategy. Chapters 7–10 discuss the resistance strategy. Chapters 11–14 discuss the recognition part of the recognition and recovery strategy, with Chapter 15 focusing on the recovery part and how to integrate it with recognition. Chapter 16 provides a concluding summary.

By progressively discussing the security strategies and their associated technologies, the book provides the reader with an understanding of how the technologies can work in a complementary fashion to improve the security of an organization's information systems. The reader is encouraged to view the technologies as progressive hurdles that a malicious agent must overcome to damage the organization. The intent is to discourage adversaries, to render their activity more easily detected, and to reduce the undesired impacts of their activity. All of these reduce risk for the organization's information assets.

By Security Technology

The arrangement of technologies in the book also allows the reader to examine specific technologies of interest. Virtually all of the major information security technologies are discussed, each in an identifiable chapter:

- Chapter 3 explores network configuration and routing from a security viewpoint.
- Chapter 4 discusses honeypots and honeynets.
- Chapter 5 examines host hardening and firewalls.
- Chapter 6 describes formal security models.
- Chapter 7 discusses authentication technologies.
- Chapter 8 discusses encryption.
- Chapter 9 covers policy management.
- Chapter 10 describes patch management.
- Chapter 11 deals with network traffic analysis.
- Chapter 12 examines intrusion detection and prevention systems.
- Chapter 13 discusses host forensics.
- Chapter 14 covers integrity verification technologies.
- Chapter 15 describes backup and restore systems.

The range of technologies in this book allows the reader to explore security controls based on their interest. The reader can pick and choose technologies to learn about. Where useful, the strategy discussion may act as support material for this exploration.

SUMMARY

Information security has become essential to organizations in preserving information of value to them and in providing for continued operations. The principles and techniques of information security have become commonly discussed in popular culture. This chapter provides an explicit listing of these principles and a definition for some of the common terms in this field. These principles aid in the management of information security risks, as described in the risk management model. As the malicious actors in this field have become better resourced and more persistent, simple defensive controls have become less effective. This has given rise to the security strategies briefly introduced here.

Chapter 2 will describe these strategies for implementing or improving the information security in an organization. The following chapters will focus on techniques to implement these security improvements.

REFERENCES

[1] Forrester Research. Value of corporate secrets. San Francisco: RSA Inc.; 2010, March. Retrieved June 15, 2013, from <www.rsa.com/document.aspx?id=10844>.

[2] Shirey R. Internet security glossary. IETF Request for Comment 4949; 2007, August. Retrieved October 10, 2011, from <http://tools.ietf.org/html/rfc4949>.

[3] Parker D. Our excessively simplistic information model and how to fix it. ISSA J. 2010:8(7):12–21.

[4] Plata J. U.S. v. Christopher Harn, Derrick Davis, and Glenn DaSilva, Complaint. 2002, November. Retrieved June 15, 2013, from <http://news.findlaw.com/hdocs/docs/crim/usharn1102cmp.html>.

[5] NTRA and Giuliani Partners Improving security in the united states para-mutual wagering system. New York: NTRA Wagering Technology Working Group; 2003. Retrieved June 15, 2013, from <http://media.washingtonpost.com/wp-srv/politics/documents/WTWG_final_report.pdf>.

[6] ISO 7498-2. Information processing systems: open systems interconnection—Part 2: security architecture. Paris: International Standards Organization; 1989.

[7] 18 U.S.C. Chapter 119. Wire and electronic communications interception and interception of oral communication; 2001, January 7. Retrieved June 15, 2013, from <http://uscode.house.gov/download/pls/18C119.txt>.

[8] 5 U.S.C. Section 552a, 1974. Privacy Act of 1974. Retrieved June 15, 2013, from <http://www.justice.gov/opcl/privstat.htm>.

[9] 15 U.S.C. Chapter 98. Public company accounting reform and corporate responsibility. 2002. Retrieved June 15, 2013, from <http://uscode.house.gov/download/pls/15C98.txt>.

[10] 15 U.S.C. Section 1681. Fair Credit Reporting Act, 2001. Retrieved June 13, 2013, from <http://www.ftc.gov/os/statutes/fcradoc.pdf>.

[11] 42 U.S.C. Section 1320d. Wrongful disclosure of individually identifiable health information, 1996. Retrieved June 15, 2013, from <http://www.law.cornell.edu/uscode/text/42/1320d-6>.

[12] 15 U.S.C. Section 6801–6809. Disclosure of nonpublic personal information, 1999. Retrieved June 13, 2013, from <http://www.ftc.gov/privacy/glbact/glbsub1.htm>.

[13] Markoff J. Hackers find no bar to indian trust files. : New York Times; 2002, February 26. p. 20, Retrieved June 15, 2013, from <http://www.nytimes.com/2002/02/26/us/hackers-find-no-bars-to-indian-trust-files.html>.

[14] NARF. Interior Secretary and Assistant Secretary for Indian Affairs held in Contempt of Court. Native American Rights Fund Legal Review 2002;27(2). Retrieved June 15, 2013, from <http://www.narf.org/pubs/nlr/nlr27-2.htm>.

[15] Lam J. Help your competitor—advise them of vulnerability. Internet Storm Center Diary; 2010, June 24. Retrieved June 15, 2013, from <http://isc.sans.edu/diary.html?storyid=9064>.

[16] Sutton M, Greene A, Amini P. Fuzzing: brute force vulnerability discovery. New York: Addison Wesley; 2007.

[17] Browne H, Arbaugh W, McHugh J, Fithen W. A trend analysis of exploitations. Baltimore: Department of Computer Science University of Maryland; 2000, November. Technical Report CS-4200. Retrieved June 15, 2013, from <http://www.cs.umd.edu/~waa/pubs/CS-TR-4200.pdf>.

[18] Caralli R, Stevens J, Young L, Wilson W. The OCTAVE Allegro Guidebook v1.0. Pittsburgh: Software Engineering Institute, Carnegie Mellon University; 2007, May. Retrieved June 15, 2013, from <http://www.cert.org/octave/download/allegro.html>.

[19] Marchany R. Conducting a risk analysis. In: Lurker M, Peterson R, editors. Computer and network security in higher education. New York: Jossey-Bass Inc.; 2003. p. 31–43. Retrieved June 15, 2013, from <http://net.educause.edu/ir/library/pdf/pub7008g.pdf>.

[20] ISO-27005 Information technology—security techniques—information security risk management. Paris: International Standards Organization; 2011.

[21] Defence Signals Directorate Strategies to mitigate targeted cyber intrusions. Sydney, Australia: Defence Signals Directorate, Department of Defence; 2012. Retrieved June 15, 2013, from <http://www.dsd.gov.au/infosec/top-mitigations/top35mitigationstrategies-list.htm>.

[22] Krebs B. Chasing APT: persistence pays off. 2011, October 27. Retrieved June 15, 2013, from <http://krebsonsecurity.com/2011/10/chasing-apt-persistence-pays-off/>.

Chapter Review Questions

1. Define the following terms and describe their importance to organizations:
   a. Information security
   b. Confidentiality
   c. Authenticity
   d. Integrity
   e. Availability
   f. Vulnerability
   g. Exploit
   h. Malware
   i. Intrusion
   j. Security control
   k. Risk analysis
   l. Security strategy

2. For each of the following, name one type of organization that might find this property (e.g., government, medical, financial, or military) the most critical in information security:
   a. Confidentiality
   b. Integrity
   c. Authenticity
   d. Availability

3. If information security is so important to organizations, why are there so many large-scale violations of security?

4. For each of the following strategies, describe one way in which they could contribute to the protection of information in an organization:
   a. Deception
   b. Frustration
   c. Resistance
   d. Recognition and recovery

5. What are two examples of how natural disasters might become security threats?

6. A local paper reports on a clerk stealing from an organization by issuing false checks. Is this a vulnerability, an exploit, or a security incident?

7. An Internet site starts distributing a program that gets a popular word processor to send a copy of whatever files it produces to be emailed to a specific email address. Is this a vulnerability, an exploit, or a security incident?

8. A programmer discovers a place in a program where it can be made to execute machine-code commands embedded in its input. Is this a vulnerability, an exploit, or a security incident?

9. Which laws specify the protection of your information as a student? Which laws protect you as a private individual? What implications does this have for the university you attend?

Chapter Exercises

1. Assume that you are the chief security officer for Temporary, a company that sets up networks for stockholder meetings and other large-scale meetings where private information may be shared. You contract network service from Infrastructure, a network operations firm. It offers contracted network support as desired by other organizations, including security monitoring and firewall configuration. Security is pretty important to the image of Infrastructure as a reliable network operations firm. Also contracting with Infrastructure is Careless, a network business. Careless has only one firewall (on its T3 connection to the Internet) with contracted support (from Infrastructure). Its access policies include web hosting, unfiltered email in/out, unfiltered file transfer protocol (FTP) in/out, secure shell (SSH) for terminal connection, and corporate dial-in to a networked server. Careless is primarily concerned with taking orders from networked customers via a web-supported catalog (with shopping cart software) and via phone. The acceptable-use policy deals with protecting these services only.
   a. As head of security for Temporary, what vulnerabilities would you be specifically concerned about?
   b. Assuming that there was a security intrusion at Careless, how would this possibly affect the security of Temporary?
   c. What security strategies should you explore to protect against security concerns due to intrusions at Careless?

2. Why isn't it illegal to develop malicious software in the United States?

3. Why might the distinction between various types of malware be important?

4. Based on the description of OCTAVE Allegro and the cited reference of STAR:
    a. How do the phases of OCTAVE Allegro and STAR compare?
    b. Which model would be simpler to apply?
    c. Which model would provide more justifiable results?
    d. Which model would be easier to customize to a specific organization?

5. What are two reasons that using multiple security strategies might be specifically important in dealing with well-resourced, intelligent, and persistent malicious actors?

6. Does the argument for the security strategies suggest that it is never appropriate for organizations to deploy individual security controls?

7. What factors might enter into the decision of how an organization might select controls to mitigate a risk?

8. How does the variation between organizations in the importance of the security properties of information make the task of securing information more difficult?

9. What state or local laws in your area affect the information security plans of local organizations?

Strategies and Security

INFORMATION IN THIS CHAPTER

- Security strategies
- Attack strategies
- Defense strategies
- Security controls

INTRODUCTION

The motivation of adversaries attacking networks changed during the first decade of the twenty-first century. While there are still hobbyist-level adversaries, more and more became self-sustaining financially. During this time, large botnets were accumulated by a number of adversaries, and the selling of use of these botnets lead to one stream of income; another income stream was the emergence of fraud schemes, including phishing and credit card fraud. These self-sustaining adversaries are much more persistent than hobbyists, and protecting networks against these adversaries, or even making a network relatively difficult to compromise, requires understanding the strategies both that they may use to compromise, and that defenders may use to protect information.

This chapter presents concepts of attack and defense strategies. Some basic strategic options are laid out in the next section. Following that, the application of these strategies to security threats is discussed. Example security controls associated with each defense strategy are then covered briefly, and expanded on in the rest of this book. An example security incident and how the defense strategies could have applied are discussed immediately prior to the chapter summary.

SECURITY STRATEGIES

A strategy is defined as a "method or plan chosen to bring about a desired future" [1]. A security strategy is, therefore, a strategy that affects security, either in defense (often, increasing the security of an organization's information) or in attack (often, decreasing the security of an organization's information). Security strategies form the general approaches to security adopted by an organization, and many organizations employ overlapping security strategies to help prevent gaps.

This chapter will discuss both attack and defense security strategies. While the focus of most of this book lies with defense strategies, there is some value in a high-level understanding of security attack strategies as a context for deploying defense strategies. As adversaries have become better resourced and increasingly systematic, the attack strategies they employ have become increasingly diverse.

ATTACK STRATEGIES

One motivation to systematically address information security risk (in addition to the legal requirements described in Chapter 1) is that the threats against information security are growing systematic. The RSA case [2] described in the "Case Study: RSA Attack" sidebar shows how adversaries may target trusted security controls as a means of facilitating later attacks. This shows a degree of attack planning beyond what has been typical of past adversaries. Robert Morris Jr., for example, released his malicious software without plans for follow-on activity (see the following sidebar). The revelations about government-sponsored cyber attacks in the 2007–2011 timeframe [3] have opened discussions about such attacks and their extensive planning and serious consequences for organizations. Pervasive fraud attempts have become a routine warning to business users of the Internet, including the dangers of trusting emailed web references or opening seemingly relevant attachments. As targeted frauds have proliferated, users find it difficult to differentiate legitimate and fraudulent financial web pages, to the detriment of organizational security.

Adversaries may threaten information security on multiple levels simultaneously. They attack individual hosts, exploiting weaknesses in the operating system (e.g., the Windows 95 LAND attack [4]), or in the application software (e.g., the Internet Worm, as described in the following sidebar). They attack via networks, using remote contact methods, or by exploiting the trust within networks to propagate from an initial point of compromise. They attack users, either as malicious insiders (e.g., the Chris Harn case [5], described in Chapter 1), or as malicious outsiders (e.g., using fraudulent email). They attack data that organizations use in essential business processes, including compromise, imitation, or redirection of data sources (e.g., *phishing*), using websites that closely imitate institutions to obtain authentication information used in later frauds [6].

PROFILE: ROBERT T. MORRIS, JR.

Robert Morris grew up in a technical family. His father worked on many of the basic security technologies and is most famous for publishing an analysis of password security. After graduating from Harvard in 1987, the younger Morris entered Cornell as a Ph.D. student and continued research that included network security. In late 1988, he developed a self-replicating computer program, a worm, designed to both measure the size of the Internet and to evaluate the frequency of vulnerabilities in several common network services (remote command execution via email, weak authentication in remote access, and a buffer overflow in *finger*, a user identity service) [7]. He released the program in early November 1988, and it rapidly overwhelmed many of the hosts then on the Internet [8]. His attempts to both shut off the worm and to instruct others on how to block it were both unsuccessful due to a lack of trusted information channels and to blockages caused by the worm itself. Eventually, about two-thirds of the hosts on the Internet were affected to some extent. An ad-hoc group of network administrators and security investigators formed to analyze the worm and successfully blocked it by correcting the vulnerabilities it used. Subsequent investigation pointed back to MIT as the starting point for the worm. Morris was identified as the author and arrested. He was convicted under the Computer Fraud and Abuse Act, and served a suspended sentence involving a fine and community service [7].

Following his sentence, Morris focused on positive developments to computer science including network security. Morris continued his education via Harvard's Ph.D. program. His graduate work included development of network switch technology, and his dissertation work involved modeling and controlling complex networks. Following his graduate work, he was appointed as a professor of computer science at MIT, and was awarded tenure in 1998 for his work on wireless networks, distributed operating systems, and peer-to-peer applications. He is currently continuing this highly respected work as a member of the PDOS group at MIT. Outside of his academic studies, Morris has been active in technology companies, developing e-business software, and partnering in an investment corporation [18].

To illustrate the usefulness of understanding attack (and defense) strategies, this chapter employs a brief continuing example. Consider a small nonprofit organization that has a website, a connection gateway providing external access to internal computers for the use of staff and organizational officers, a file server with shared information, several workstations internally for the staff and authorized volunteers, and an internal office server with human resources and financial information on it. A contract with a service provider supports hosting of the website, external-facing domain name system (DNS) service, and email service for the nonprofit. Figure 2.1 illustrates the organization's logical network structure. After performing a risk analysis, the nonprofit's staff determines the major security concerns are disgruntled staff or volunteers leading to information theft, external adversaries compromising computers as part of their botnet-building activities, and corruption or unauthorized dissemination of financial information.

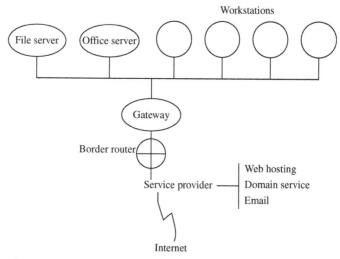

FIGURE 2.1
Logical network structure for strategy example.

An adversary may have diverse malicious goals, including theft of data, misuse of computing time on hosts, consumption of network bandwidth, impersonation of users, and redirection of organization network addresses. Adversaries employ a wide variety of attack strategies to attain these goals. The generic strategies they use include direct attacks, progressive attacks, mass attacks, and misdirection. Most attacks are not launched directly from the host the adversary uses to access the Internet. Rather, adversaries use hosts previously compromised (or acquired legitimately) as launch points for their attacks.

The simplest attack strategy is the direct one. In this case, the adversary strikes against the target from the launch point, without intermediate or third-party hosts involved except in normal traffic routing. Figure 2.2 shows an abstraction of this strategy, where the solid node is the launch point and the patterned node is the target asset (the empty nodes are third-party assets, either hardware, software, or data). This strategy is applied in attacks where the launch point is of little value to the adversary or the probability of being tracked back is low. Some examples of attacks that often use the direct strategy are spam email, cache poisoning, and routing black-hole attacks. In the case of the nonprofit, one attack of concern might be a volunteer making unauthorized changes to the financial information. This is a direct attack, since the attack is entirely local to the office computer. The organization may choose a number of ways to deal with this, including maintenance of an audit chain, use of multiple-entry accounting, and requiring approval by an authorized staff member before changes to the financial information are finalized.

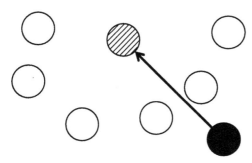

FIGURE 2.2
Abstraction of the direct attack strategy.

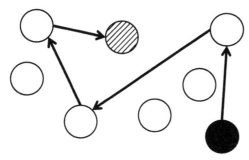

FIGURE 2.3
Abstraction of the progressive attack strategy.

Another strategy is the progressive strategy. In this case, the adversary uses a series of intermediate hosts between the launch point and the target, each of which is compromised using the same set of exploits. In some sense, this is just a generalization of the direct strategy, applying it to successive targets in series, but an organization facing such an attack may find it more difficult to block than a direct attack, since the progressive strategy suggests the adversary has several options for proceeding against the target. From the adversary's point of view, the progressive strategy offers a lot more protection and deniability than the direct attack strategy. Figure 2.3 shows an abstraction of this strategy. There are several variants of this strategy: contracting (possibly black-market) for the intermediate hosts, manual compromise of the intermediate hosts, automated (possibly self-propagating) compromise of the intermediate hosts, and beachhead-lateral attacks.

Adversaries find contracted intermediate attacks attractive since the intermediate nodes may be stable, offering options for later and ongoing use. Adversaries choose manual compromise of intermediate nodes where they wish to carefully diversify those nodes, for example, to spread them between nations

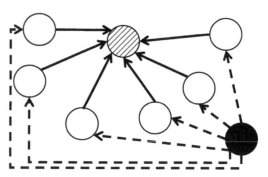

FIGURE 2.4
Abstraction of the massed attack strategy.

without agreements for extradition or mutual cooperation in legal investigations. Adversaries use automated compromise of the intermediate nodes for increased efficiency where they don't care about the identity or placement of these nodes. Beachhead-lateral attacks use an initial compromised host within an organization as a proximate launch point for the compromise of further intermediate hosts within the organization until the attack target is reached. Adversaries find the beachhead-lateral strategy convenient as a means of attack in depth, where many of the hosts a defender might use to detect, diagnose, or recover from the attack are silently under the adversary's control.

A thoroughly discussed example of an attack using the progressive strategy is the "Hanover Hacker" case [9]. In the nonprofit example, one attack of concern might be compromise of a workstation to gain illicit access to the office server. To compromise this workstation, the adversaries might place targeted malicious content on a variety of websites that could be of interest to organization staff. To protect against discovery, this malicious content would be placed from and refer back to computers arranged via a black-market content. The organization would find this scenario difficult to deal with completely, but a combination of browser protections (only allowing downloads to affect browser-specific file space) and content filtering (blocking content from third-party sites of unknown character) may provide some aid.

The massed attack strategy is where the adversary compromises a group of third-party hosts, and uses all of them at once against the targeted host. Figure 2.4 shows an abstraction of the massed attack strategy. In some cases, the group of attacking hosts is compromised solely for one attack, but commonly the group is retained and reused for later attacks. Adversaries find this attractive since it leads to both an ongoing attack capability and to (via black-market rental arrangements) monetary income. Massed attacks have been used for denial of service (particularly, distributed floods of traffic), and for distributed capture of a target's network traffic.

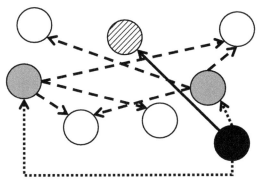

FIGURE 2.5
Abstraction of the misdirection attack strategy.

In the nonprofit example, political activists wishing to impose a specific viewpoint may act as adversaries. As a protest, the activists may choose to flood the organization website, using a black-market rental of a botnet to generate the flood. With such a massed attack, it isn't likely that the sources of the attack could all be blocked, so the response needs to focus on the targets of the attack. Since the website is located along with the nonprofit's email service, this flood attack may block critical communications. The organization may discuss this scenario with their Internet service provider (ISP), possibly shifting the hosting plans to reduce the impact of such attacks.

Adversaries using a misdirection attack strategy generate traffic to confuse or distract the network defenders in dealing with their direct attack. As implied by this statement, there are two main variants to the misdirection attack strategy: masked attack, where the adversaries use cover traffic to confuse the network defenders, and diversion attack, where the adversaries use feints against resources they know the defenders must protect to distract the network defenders. Figure 2.5 shows an abstraction of the misdirection attack strategy, where the adversary first compromises some sources for the feint attacks (dotted lines), then uses those sources to launch the feints (dashed lines), and finally launches the attack against the target (solid line). Adversaries find misdirection strategies useful to ensure that the defenders will likely ignore their attacks against the target, increasing their chance of success.

One example of this occurred in incidents involving the "gameover" variant of the "Zeus" malware, where the adversaries targeted online banking credentials, and used a distributed denial of service to deflect attention from wire transfers involving the compromised credentials [10]. In the nonprofit case, an insider wanting to obtain confidential information from the file server might choose to mount a denial of service attack against the office server as a distraction, since the office server availability would be viewed as more important by the response team, and it would also be more visible than the insider's download and subsequent release of information from the file server.

CASE STUDY: RSA ATTACK

In early March 2011, an email was sent to four employees working at RSA, a security products subdivision of EMC Corporation [2]. This email, which was sent with falsified information to appear to come from a recruiting website and to conceal its actual source, induced the recipients to open an attached Excel spreadsheet. On the spreadsheet was a flash object crafted as a zero-day exploit for a vulnerability in flash rendering. The exploit permitted the attackers to download a tool supporting malicious execution of commands, named Poison Ivy. Once this was installed, the attackers propagated through the RSA infrastructure and extracted information about RSA's widely used security products. The attack was discovered, shut down, and announced in early April 2011. RSA and other security vendors have since published detailed analysis of the attack methods used against it, and strategies for dealing with this form of attack.

This attack used a combination of direct and progressive strategies. The initial false email was crafted to directly appeal to its recipients, in one case fooling a recipient into retrieving the email from the Junk folder to open its attachment. The follow-on activity was quite progressive in nature, propagating through the company's infrastructure until the targeted information was identified and extracted. While the total period of the attack was in the range from a couple of hours to a few days, that was sufficient for the attackers to succeed, despite diligent defenses at the company [2].

Once this attack occurred, the extracted information was reportedly used as a part of security compromises at several customers of RSA. RSA responded by providing revised products to its customers. Additional security protections related to this attack, including signatures for the exploits used, have been deployed by security vendors.

Adversaries may follow multiple strategies as portions of their attacks against organizations. One form of combined strategy is to employ different strategies for various tactical steps: one during reconnaissance, another to exploit vulnerabilities, another for affect, and so forth for the remaining steps. Other adversaries may employ multiple strategies as a means of increasing the effectiveness of their attacks. In either case, the defenders must carefully choose the defense strategies used to counter the attack strategies.

DEFENSE STRATEGIES

To deal with the risks of fire, multiple overlapping measures are taken. Building codes specify fire-containing walls in public buildings, use of fire-resistant materials, elimination of likely fire sources via grounding electrical circuits or venting heating systems, presence of fire alarms, and installation of fire-response systems such as sprinklers, hoses, or fire extinguishers. These measures have been developed over time and provide for redundant and supportive reduction in the risks due to fire. Analogously, to deal with the risks to information security, most authorities recommend multiple overlapping measures. The National Institute of Standards and Technology (NIST), as one example, recommends systems, subsystem, and application security controls (structuring the controls by scope of information processing resources to which they are applied) be employed [11]. This is termed *defense in depth*.

Defense in depth is constructing an information security architecture with layered and complementary security controls, so that if one control is defeated, one or more other controls (that are behind or beneath the first control) still provide protection [12]. Defense in depth implies both assets being protected and multiple controls applied in the protection. A risk analysis, such as the OCTAVE Allegro process described in Chapter 1, identifies the assets to be protected and the form of protection required. Defenders often find the choice difficult to determine which controls to combine to apply this protection. Controls are often developed and described in isolation, or as competing alternatives, when the defender needs to combine them.

In the nonprofit example, protection of the office server, with its content of personally identifying information and proprietary financial information, warrants multiple controls. A simplistic approach would be to find multiple controls already in possession of the organization and just use all of them. The simplistic approach tends to produce uneconomic overprotection with respect to some risks (those already allowed for by the organization, and for which the organization has already acquired controls) and unconsidered gaps with respect to other risks (those that may be specific to the office server). More methodical approaches would be to consider risks to the office server on a case-by-case basis, and identify a limited group of controls that will work together in a supplementary and economically justified fashion.

This section presents a more detailed structure of security strategies than the NIST approach. This structure is loosely based on the military strategies espoused in Sun Tzu's classic text *The Art of War* [13], which describes deception of the enemy, frustrating his or her strategies, resisting his or her advance, along with recognizing and responding to his or her actions. The ordering in this section derives from a functional flow of information defense: hamper identification of targets, then block establishment of an initial compromise, then exacerbate the difficulty of attack progress, and finally facilitate response to identified attacks. This flow is shown in Figure 2.6. The goal in considering the structure of strategies is to support application of multiple security controls that will reinforce each other to protect the organization's information.

Deception

The deception defense strategy is to either make a network attack "no one's problem" or "somebody else's problem." The easiest form of dealing with

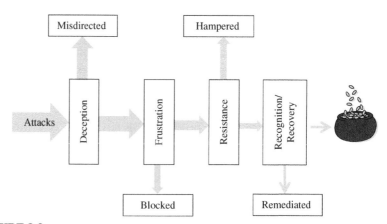

FIGURE 2.6
Defensive flow involving strategies.

an attack is to have it apply to something that does not need defense, and therefore involves minimal effort on the part of the defenders. Sun Tzu states this goal as "Hence that general is skillful in attack whose opponent does not know what to defend; and he is skillful in defense whose opponent does not know what to attack" [13]. In network security, many of the deceptive methods are relatively passive, not requiring continuing action on the part of the defenders. This makes them somewhat attractive as a first line of defense.

To make an attack "no one's problem," the adversary must be acting against an asset that is designed either to be unproductive for attack (i.e., holding content that is not needed by the organization, or structured to be resistant to attack), or that will not provide any advantage to the attacker in compromising the mission of the organization. This implies that the assets attacked by the adversary hold no mission-essential or confidential information, which is most directly provided if the content of the asset is fictitious—that is, provided by the organization only to distract its adversaries. This would be true of a honeypot (a computer that provides virtual machines as false servers to distract adversaries) or tarpit (a computer that responds to network queries with a skeletal and uninformative response as a distraction to adversaries) system, as described in Chapter 4. Another method for making the attack unproductive is to structure the network with redundant servers (computers configured as the real servers, but not used in production or populated with production information) used as indicators of attack, as described in Chapter 3.

To make an attack "someone else's problem," the adversary must be acting against an asset belonging to an organization other than the target organization, and the attack does not impact a service required by the target organization. This could be true of a foreign-hosted service or server (services or computers supported externally via contract, with placement arranged to deceive adversaries) as described in Chapter 3.

In the nonprofit example, the organization has already decided to externally host its web and DNS services through its service provider. However, a flooding attack against these services might interrupt the connectivity of the organization to the Internet by overwhelming the provider. As such, the organization may choose either to provide for backup Internet connectivity, or move the hosting of the web server to another provider, since web servers are a prominent target for adversaries. Either of these controls would provide protection by deceiving an adversary as to the impact (in terms of responsiveness by the organization's network infrastructure) of attacks against these exposed services.

Frustration

The frustration strategy is to deny the initial access necessary for attack. Other than a misdirected attack, the next simplest attack to deal with is one that is stopped before it affects the state of the organization's network. Sun Tzu expresses this as "Thus the highest form of generalship is to balk the enemy's plans" [13]. To frustrate initial access indicates asserting control of either the target of an attack or the medium used for the access. Many of the controls associated with this strategy are passive in terms of security effort, although ongoing maintenance is often required.

To frustrate an attack by asserting control of the target of the attack, the defenders have configured the asset to be unreachable or unassailable to the attack (at least at the time in which the adversary is acting). Many of the classic provably secure systems (combined hardware and operating systems that are developed to provide service only in a secure manner, with protections that adversaries or users cannot evade) work to make assets unassailable, as described in Chapter 6, and also by minimizing the available services on servers (reducing the configuration implemented on servers to those essential for support of the specific services supported by the server), as described in Chapter 5. Making assets unreachable is an approach taken by router access control lists, firewalls, and wrappers (all of which limit response by servers to service requests, either by blocking the receipt of the request to the server or blocking the servers response to received requests), also described in Chapter 5.

In the nonprofit example, one risk of concern might be an external adversary sending a false routing update for the service provider to the border router, corrupting the link between the organization and its service provider. To execute this attack, the adversary would send a crafted packet directly to the border router. The packet (and any basis for subsequent tracing) would be discarded by the router after it incorporates the false information, so the adversary may feel safe in using the direct attack strategy. Considering this attack, the nonprofit may elect to modify its border router configuration to restrict the service provider entries to known addresses.

To frustrate an attack by asserting control of the medium of attack, the defenders have structured the medium such that the adversaries find it difficult or impossible to insert their traffic. One form of such structure is restricting internal connectivity and other traffic-shaping approaches (controls that provide for connection between subsets of the network only via established connection points), as described in Chapter 5. Another form is partitioning the internal and external address space used by the organization (using externally routed addresses only for computers that provide service outside the organization, and private addresses, only routed internally, for the remaining computers on the network), so that external actors cannot directly access assets that are purely internal resources, also described in Chapter 5.

Resistance

The resistance strategy is to make it as difficult as possible for attacks to progress after the initial access, without the necessity of knowledge of the attacks. While this often requires substantial effort, it reduces the damage that would otherwise incur from the attacks. Sun Tzu supports this strategy via the principle that "The art of war teaches us to rely not on the likelihood of the enemy's not coming, but on our own readiness to receive him" [13]. Many of the methods that support the frustration controls will also support the resistance strategy.

Beyond the frustration controls already referenced, resistance strategy methods inhibit progress of the attack by limiting propagation of unauthorized activity on a computer or across the network. To limit propagation on the network, defenders strongly protect the identity of all authorized users, using authentication methods (controls that tie the account on the computer to secrets, identifying tokens, individual physical characteristics, or organizational role of the user), as discussed in Chapter 7, and then leverage that identity by setting up access control identifying allowable and forbidden activity and limiting responses appropriately. To reduce propagation of attacks via exploits that circumvent controls, defenders apply active patch and change management to the configuration of the hosts (controls that limit what changes may be applied to computers in the organization, by whom, and via which processes), as described in Chapter 10, which includes minimization of the services available through the computers. Adversaries might evade these protections, but the protections make computers more difficult for adversaries to exploit in their attacks.

To limit propagation across the network, some resistance strategy methods limit unauthorized activity via encryption (apply codes as a means of limiting the comprehensibility of traffic to authorized computers and users), as described in Chapter 8, blocking unauthorized devices or unauthorized interfaces from communicating on the network. Protections of wireless networks often use encryption in this way. Another approach is to segment the network into security zones (continuing the network structure controls described before as frustration-related controls), as identified by security policy, and then identify what traffic is allowable and what is forbidden between zones. This approach is discussed in Chapter 9. Many corporate networks apply some form of this segmentation.

In general terms, many methods associated with the resistance strategy require active application or maintenance. Authentication information must be protected, which includes refreshing or changing it as required. Host configurations must be updated as patches, new requirements, and new attacks appear. Encryption keys must be updated or replaced on an ongoing basis. Security policy needs to be reviewed and the resultant partitioning modified as necessary. All of this demands substantial effort on the part of the network defenders, a level of effort that will be unsustainable unless applied selectively. One means of selection comes from the risk analysis described in Chapter 1—applying resistance most thoroughly to assets that are most valuable, most exposed, or both. Another means is to scope the application of resistance within the application of deception and frustration strategies, using those strategies to limit exposure to attack before looking at resisting attacks.

In the nonprofit example, the organization might choose to distinguish the workstations permitted to access the office server from those only permitted to access the file server. This distinction would allow different sets of controls to be applied to each group of workstations, and would also reduce the users who can access (or attack) the office server to those who are already permitted to use it. This reduction would allow for increased resistance to attack both by malicious staff or volunteers and by external adversaries.

Recognition and Recovery

The recognition and recovery strategy is to, as rapidly as possible, both identify the attack and reconstruct the attack targets. Experience has shown that reliance on this strategy as the primary defense is unsustainably expensive—it makes information defense entirely reactive, which means accepting damage to the information before acting in defense. As such, this strategy should be the defense of last resort. Sun Tzu describes this strategy as "Therefore the clever combatant imposes his will on the enemy, but does not allow the enemy's will to be imposed on him" [13].

The methods associated with the recognition and recovery strategy are the first that actively focus on individual attacks. These methods work to identify that an attack is underway, diagnose the characteristics (means, purpose, or impact) of the attack, and restore the attacked computers and networks to a secure state [11]. The identification and diagnosis portions of this strategy analyze network traffic and examine the configuration and activity of computers suspected of being attacked. The recovery portions of this strategy work to correct the configuration and restore the activity of these computers.

To recognize an attack from network traffic, defenders compare current network traffic with both an established baseline of authorized activity and with rules or patterns describing attack traffic. Often, attack behavior will be visible on a network before any specific host is affected, so working to recognize attacks from network traffic may allow an opportunity to respond to an attack while damage is small. Network traffic analysis, as described in Chapter 11, focuses on the development and comparison of baseline activity, although some high-level attack patterns are often employed. Network intrusion detection, covered in Chapter 12, deals with rule-based recognition of attack traffic, although some significant departures from the baseline activity (termed *anomalies*) may be used. Together, analysis and intrusion detection provide a balance between awareness of the network usage and focus on specific attack behavior.

Defenders may find that some attacks cannot be recognized from network traffic; for these attacks, the defenders must examine the individual hosts on the network. There are two groups of methods that support host-based recognition of attacks. Chapter 13 discusses digital forensic methods, looking at specific characteristic changes or additions to host configurations related to attacks. Chapter 14 looks at integrity protections and recognition of integrity violations, which either prevent or detect any unauthorized changes to a host's configuration. Together, forensics and integrity work to both find and diagnose attacks, as a basis for recovering from these attacks and resuming normal operations. Both forensics and integrity require software and also an informed analyst to explore the state of the host. As such, these methods require substantial time investment on the part of an organization.

Concurrent with recognition, the defenders move to recover from the attacks and resume normal operations. Commonly, recovery occurs immediately as the attack is diagnosed, although criminal investigation or liability may encourage the defenders to delay and gather further data on the attack to confirm attack diagnosis or identify the specific adversaries involved. The immediacy of the recovery leads to it being considered linked to recognition as a combined strategy, rather than being a separate strategy on its own. Chapter 15 discusses the process of recovery, including use of backup media and the addition of further frustration or resistance measures to inhibit repetition of the attacks. By planning for recovery while performing recognition, the defenders may clarify which recovery actions are required and minimize resources lost due to the attack.

SECURITY CONTROLS

Using security strategies can be costly, particularly if defenders apply their strategies without consideration of the risks associated with various assets. From the risk analysis, defenders should identify their high-priority risks tied to the critical assets. Once this is done, defenders need to decide which strategies are most applicable to each risk. Some organizations have found the security attribute evaluation method [14] a useful method of balancing risks and protections. One graphical tool from this method is a "spider" diagram (shown in Figure 2.7), which provides a high-level view of strategies versus risks. Around the periphery are identified risks for specific assets, in groups of up to eight for each diagram. Along the radius are arranged the defense strategies. Within this space, defenders lay out planned or deployed security controls that act to mitigate each risk, placed to indicate the strategy that the control implements. The resulting chart provides an overview of network defenses, allowing consideration of how deeply layered the controls are for specific risks, where gaps exist, the balance between passive and active strategies, and other security planning issues.

Asset-risk planning at a high level allows organizations to reduce cost in several ways. Where assets are already adequately protected (or overprotected),

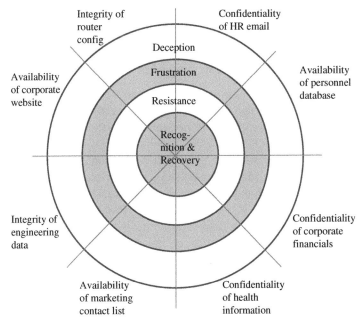

FIGURE 2.7
Nested network strategy.

this planning inhibits unnecessary redundant controls (or facilitates decisions on which controls to remove), saving the associated costs. For example, if protection of the availability of the HR database is protected via an actively maintained honeypot (for deception), router access control (for frustration, since only established authorized hosts may have their traffic reach the database), frequent configuration audits and patches (for resistance), and redundant storage (for recovery), then the cost of protection may exceed the risk to the organization that loss of availability would entail. As a result, management could plan which controls to remove or modify to decrease cost. Where expensive controls are used, the planning helps to identify supplemental (and less expensive) controls that may reduce the frequency of use for the expensive controls (in the HR database example, decreasing the audit frequency due to the protections provided via the honeypot and the router access control), or may provide information that would allow the expensive controls to be used more efficiently, or even replace more expensive controls with less expensive ones (in the HR database example, rather than redundant storage, maintain a transaction log to replay any lost transactions, saving storage). Where critical assets are not protected sufficiently, the planning helps to consider further cost-effective controls.

Strategy-based information security facilitates both reduction in security cost and increase of predictability in those costs. By employing multiple strategies in defense, each strategy provides a context for employing other strategies efficiently, reducing cost. By reducing single points of failure in security, the overlapping controls make violations of security less frequent and more limited in scope, which increases the regularity of security costs (since there is less "drop everything and fix the security breach" going on).

Applying multiple security controls may increase the effort required of an adversary to successfully compromise the security of an organization. The defense strategies described here are not the only concept for selecting multiple controls—one can also apply controls based on anticipated attack strategies. One attack-based method is constructing attack trees and applying controls to inhibit the modeled attacks [15]. The difficulty with this approach is to correctly and completely identify all of the attack strategies that would be applicable to the network; omitting any may leave the network available to adversaries. Another approach is to layer controls based on the assets on the network to which they apply. One asset-based method identifies controls at the network perimeter (connection to the ISP), enterprise, host, application, and data levels [16]. Difficulties with the asset-based method include understanding how to trade off protection of one group of assets against protection of other groups and assuring common protections across assets. Given these alternatives, this book elects to describe layering of security controls via defense strategies.

SUMMARY

This chapter covers security strategies in concept, describing both attack and defense strategies. By learning attack strategies, network defenders can consider potential impacts and aggregate otherwise-unrelated activity into a basis for systematic decision-making on responses to the attacks. The defense strategies provide a means for layering defenses to improve both their effectiveness and cost.

The remainder of this book discusses controls associated with each of the defense strategies. Each of the controls will be described to give an understanding how to apply the control, the advantages and disadvantages of applying it, and its limitations and strengths. The discussion of the controls is grouped by strategy, to facilitate layering of defenses.

REFERENCES

[1] Business Dictionary. What is strategy? Definition and meaning. Retrieved June 15, 2013, from <http://www.businessdictionary.com/definition/strategy.html>; 2013.

[2] Rivner U. Anatomy of an attack. EMC Corporation; 2011, April. April 11, 2011. Retrieved June 15, 2013, from <http://blogs.rsa.com/rivner/anatomy-of-an-attack/>.

[3] Sanger D. Obama order sped-up wave of cyberattacks against Iran. *New York Times*; 2012, June 1. Retrieved June 15, 2013, from <http://www.nytimes.com/2012/06/01/world/middleeast/obama-ordered-wave-of-cyberattacks-against-iran.html>.

[4] M3lt (pseudonym). The LAND attack (IP DOS). Bugtraq mailing list. 1997, November 20. Retrieved June 15, 2013, from <http://insecure.org/sploits/land.ip.DOS.html>.

[5] NTRA and Giuliani Partners Improving security in the united states para-mutual wagering system. New York: NTRA Wagering Technology Working Group; 2003. Retrieved June 15, 2013, from <http://media.washingtonpost.com/wp-srv/politics/documents/WTWG_final_report.pdf>.

[6] Binational Working Group. Report on Phishing. Ministry of Public Safety and Emergency Preparedness Canada and Attorney General United States. 2006, October. Retrieved June 15, 2013, from <http://www.justice.gov/opa/report_on_phishing.pdf>.

[7] Spafford E. The internet worm incident. Technical Report CSD-TR-933. Computer Science Department, Perdue University; 1991, September. Retrieved June 15, 2013, from <http://spaf.cerias.purdue.edu/tech-reps/933.pdf>.

[8] U.S. v. Morris. United States of America v. Robert Tappan Morris. US v. Morris, 928F. 2d 504—Court of Appeals, 2nd Circuit. 1991. Retrieved June 15, 2013, from <http://scholar.google.com/scholar_case?case=551386241451639668>.

[9] Stoll C. The cuckoo's egg. New York: Doubleday; 1989.

[10] FBI FBI denver cyber squad advises citizens to be aware of a new phishing campaign. Denver, CO: Federal Bureau of Investigation; 2011, November 23. Retrieved June 15, 2013, from <http://www.fbi.gov/denver/press-releases/2011/fbi-denver-cyber-squad-advises-citizens-to-be-aware-of-a-new-phishing-campaign>.

[11] Joint Task Force Transformation Initiative Interagency Working Group. Ross, R. (Editor). Guide for applying the risk management framework to federal information systems. National Institute for Standards and Technology; 2010, February. NIST Special Publication 800-37, revision 1. Retrieved June 15, 2013, from <http://csrc.nist.gov/publications/nistpubs/800-37-rev1/sp800-37-rev1-final.pdf>.

[12] Shirey R. Internet security glossary. 2007, August. IETF Request for Comment 4949. Retrieved June 15, 2013, from <http://tools.ietf.org/html/rfc4949>.

[13] Sun Tzu. (c. 500 BCE) The art of war [Giles L, Trans., 1910]. Retrieved June 15, 2013, from <http://classics.mit.edu/Tzu/artwar.html>.

[14] Butler S. Security attribute evaluation method: a cost-benefit approach. 24th International Conference on Software Engineering. Orlando, FL; 2002, May. Retrieved June 15, 2013, from <http://www.cs.cmu.edu/~Compose/ftp/SAEM-%28Butler%29-ICSE_2002.pdf>.

[15] Moore A, Ellison R, Linger, R. Attack modeling for information security and survivability. Technical Report CMU/SEI-2001-TN-001. Software Engineering Institute, Carnegie Mellon University; 2001, March. Retrieved June 15, 2013, from <http://www.cert.org/archive/pdf/01tn001.pdf>.

[16] Ashley M. Layered network security: a best practices approach. StillSecure. 2003, January. Retrieved June 15, 2013, from <http://www.stillsecure.com/docs/StillSecure_LayeredSecurity.pdf>.

[17] Boyd J. A discourse on winning and losing. 1987. Retrieved June 15, 2013, from <http://www.ausairpower.net/JRB/intro.pdf>.

[18] Ycombinator. Ycombinator partners. Retrieved June 15, 2013, from <http://www.ycombinator.com/people.html>; 2013.

Chapter Review Questions

1. Briefly describe one difference between the frustration strategy and the resistance strategy.

2. Briefly describe one difference between the massed attack strategy and the misdirection attack strategy.

3. Define the following terms, and briefly explain their relevance to security:
   a. Adversary
   b. Strategy
   c. Deception
   d. Frustration
   e. Recognition
   f. Recovery

4. How would each of the attack strategies be used to compromise the confidentiality of information?

5. How would each of the defense strategies work to defeat an attempt to compromise the integrity of a private web server?

6. How does the spider diagram work to provide an overview of security controls?

7. Briefly describe how attack-based layering of controls differs from using defense strategy to layer controls.

8. Briefly describe how asset-based layering of controls might be less effective than using defense strategies to layer controls.

Chapter Exercises

1. One strategic view of a number of activities is John Boyd's Observe, Orient, Decide and Act (OODA) loop [17]. Briefly compare the attack and defense strategies described in this chapter to the OODA loop.

2. Sun Tzu [13] describes strategy as an interplay of direct and indirect methods. Briefly profile how the massed and misdirection attack strategies can be characterized in Sun Tzu's terms.

3. Bob's Bank is concerned about online attacks on its business-to-business site. The site is implemented with a front end that supports customer authentication connected to a back end that processes payments, provides account information, etc. Since Bob's Bank is a small local bank, they only have two servers for the business-to-business site. Briefly describe how Bob's Bank might apply each of the defense strategies to protect its business-to-business site.

4. The Tres Rios Electric Service is a small power-generation company located in the southwestern United States. They use a variety of device control systems (SCADA) to optimize performance of their generators and support flexible power distribution. Recently, reports have described vulnerabilities in several SCADA systems, and Tres Rios management has become concerned about malicious manipulation of generation and distribution. Briefly describe two attack strategies that attackers might use to perform such malicious manipulations.

5. The Tartan is a local ISP operating in the mid-Atlantic region of the United States. They support local customer's access to the Internet as a bottom-tier ISP. They have become concerned about attempts to attack their authentication of their customers. Briefly describe two ways in which one defense strategy could aid the Tartan in addressing such attempts.

PART

1

Deception

CHAPTER 3

Deception Strategies: Networks, Organization, and Structures

INTRODUCTION

Deception is a term more commonly associated with network attack than network defense, but, as this chapter presents, several network security controls depend on the adversaries being deceived. Deception is a useful strategy for the defenders of network security since it offers opportunities to distract the adversary away from protected information, misinform the adversary as to the success of the attack, and disrupt the utility of the attack by corrupting the information resulting from it. This chapter discusses techniques that exemplify these opportunities.

After some explanation of how network structures interact on the public network, there are four techniques covered in this chapter. Deceptive network structures work to fool the adversary by standing up extra capacity not used in production, but used to identify incoming attacks. Service outsourcing deceives the adversary by placing servers off of an organization's network so that attacks against those servers will not compromise other portions of the organization's network. Application hosting misdirects the adversary by shifting the flow of processing for isolated applications off of the internal network and into an environment where different defenses apply. Dynamic addressing may cause the adversary to hit the wrong host, since the previous target has shifted addresses and the new occupant of the address will not have received previous steps in the attack. Together these techniques provide network

43

structures that offer some protection against attacks by deceiving the adversary as to targets and locations on the organization's network.

HOW THE INTERNET WORKS

The modern Internet developed from multiple large networks. The earliest of these, and the most influential, was the Arpanet [1]. Arpanet started in 1969 [18] as a major government-funded effort, designed to support communication between computers with varying operating systems and varying information formats, facilitating more rapid research in computer systems.

The Arpanet laid the basic building blocks for getting computers to communicate together. The basic design was as a packet-switched network with a broad public address space. A packet-switched network is one in which the information being transmitted (the *datagrams*) across the network is organized into formatted units (*packets*, which can hold either the entire datagram, or if too large, a fragment of the datagram), each of which contains sufficient information for transmission using a designated protocol [18]. For the Arpanet, this transmission information is stored in the *packet header*, and the Internet Protocol specifies that it contain the source and destination addresses, an identification of the network service being used, the length of the packet, transmission checking, and other fields as required to transmit and receive the packet [2]. Each packet travels individually via multiple steps across the network from its source to its destination. The sequence of steps is referred to as the *route* of the packet, and the decision of which sequence of steps is referred to as *routing*.

At its destination, the packets are reassembled into the datagram, which is processed by the receiving computer to provide the desired network service. A broad public address space indicates that all public nodes on the network may communicate with all other public nodes on the network, without the need to pass through a central control or mediator. This design was later modified into a *catenet*, or interconnected system of packet-switched networks using the Internet Protocol [2], and the Internet was born out of the fusion of previously isolated networks intercommunicating via the Internet Protocol.

Without a central control or mediator, security was planned as a function of the behavior of the individual sites on the network. Figure 3.1 shows a map of the early sites on the Arpanet. With the generalization from the Arpanet to the Internet, the specification of security could, and did, vary from network to network. The communication protocols were designed to accommodate this variation, in a form referred to as *security compatible*. In the early days (prior to 1995), security conflicts or violations were dealt with via communication between known administrators at the various sites, with a last resort of appeal

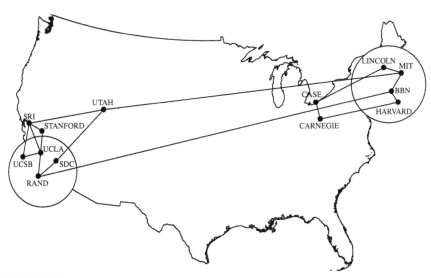

FIGURE 3.1
Arpanet as of December 1970. *(Source: From [1, p. III-81].)*

to the U.S. government authorities running the Arpanet. After 1995, neither option was available: the Internet grew too fast for there to be known administrators, and the U.S. government stopped running the network.

By 2013, the range of threats on the Internet encompassed the groups described in Chapter 1. Symantec's "2013 Internet Security Threat Report" [3] describes analysis of data both from their large sensor network and reports that they monitor. The threat report notes that the primary activity of the threats is violation of information confidentiality. The methods adversaries use include worms, viruses, Trojan horses, phishing, and social engineering (misleading users to fraudulently obtain information). Large-scale data breaches (those involving more than 1,000,000 records illicitly intercepted) were documented in 4 of the 12 months in 2012. Five large malicious networks of bots were identified. Adversaries compromised information in government, large news organizations, large credit card companies, online retailers, and social networks. The information compromise occurred despite the presence of security controls on the computers targeted [3]. Reliance on individual controls is clearly a losing approach, given the variation in threats and attack methods faced by organizations.

The Usenet project [4] started in 1979 as a group of graduate students at two universities deciding to get their computers to phone each other and support discussions between users. The administrative structure of the current Internet has its roots in the Usenet project. This project provided for voluntary passage of communication between sites on the network, with negotiation between sites as to which network services would be allowed (normally remote login, email, or file transfer) and what rate of service would be allowed. Initially, the services were provided over phone lines, with one site literally calling another and communicating in bulk during the call. Between calls, sites would store pending communication locally, waiting for the transfer (termed *store and forward* communication). In some cases, communication between one site and another would require passage through several intervening sites, with communication delays at each site. The Usenet "address" was actually a chain of computer names starting with a well-connected site and ending at the local computer. Some of the more distant Usenet sites could take a couple of days to reach!

In the later period of Usenet, communication was more rapid, replacing phone calls with forwarding information across the Internet. Security on Usenet was largely a social phenomenon, with complaints about specific sites or users handled via social pressures on the administrators involved. There was no central authority to appeal to for enforcement of policy, but the well-connected sites did occasionally act to block traffic moving through them from documented misbehaving sites.

Over time, some sites began to be dedicated exclusively to providing service to other sites, with only limited local users. As Usenet merged into the Internet, these service providers began to keep connections open between each other, allowing for much faster connections (seconds or minutes, instead of days). These connections are via a mix of land-based optical fiber, transoceanic cables, and satellites. Large service providers may use all of these resources to pass traffic to their peers. See, for example, Verizon's map of its communication infrastructure [5]. The providers support these resources by subscription fees based on service levels.

Eventually, a tier structure emerged placing each Internet service provider (ISP) based on its contracting arrangements. Figure 3.2 diagrams this hierarchy. A bottom-tier ISP would have local customers that paid fees to it, and in turn would pay fees to a higher-tier provider for its network service. A mid-level ISP would have lower ISPs that pay for service (termed *transit* relationships), and would pay a higher-tier provider for its service, but in addition it would have voluntary agreements with other mid-tier providers to exchange traffic so that both sides would have improved connectivity. These voluntary agreements are termed *peer* relationships, and can be dropped at any point that either side feels necessary. Top-tier ISPs have only peer relationships and lower-tier contracts, and pay no one for their network access. They own or lease transoceanic cable to support peer relationships with other ISPs. Each ISP sets the terms of the services it provides, including protection of security and responses to security violations. Bottom-tier and mid-tier ISP terms of service are constrained by the contracts under which they receive network

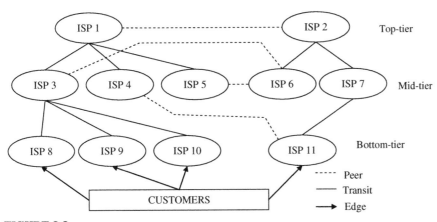

FIGURE 3.2
ISP relationships and tier structure, with peer, transit, and edge connections.

service. Top-tier ISP terms of service are constrained only by the voluntary consensus of their peers and by the governing law of the locale where they do business [6].

This tier arrangement of service provision has several benefits. Many locations have multiple service providers available, competing for customers. This competition encourages providers to provide fast and reliable access and motivates them to offer a variety of network services. As security becomes important to their customers, ISPs improve their security practices to remain competitive. However, compliance with the suite of Internet protocols and security standards is only constrained by market forces and local regulation. For top-tier providers, this compliance becomes largely voluntary.

To keep track of where computers are on the Internet (i.e., which computers have what IP address), the Internet Engineering Task Force (IETF) developed a service called the domain name system (DNS) [7]. The names of Internet computers are arranged in domains, and in a given name, the domains it is part of are arranged from most detailed to most general in a left-to-right fashion, separated by periods. For example, in "myhost.mynet.example.com," "myhost" is the specific hostname, "mynet" is a subdomain for the company, "example" is the company, and ".com" specifies that "example" is registered with the organization handling commercial concerns. To map this to an IP address, a host would make a query on its DNS service. If the host's network communicates with this host frequently, the IP address would be maintained in the DNS server's local cache, and the server would respond immediately. If not, the DNS server would generate a query to one of the 13 top-level DNS servers worldwide, which would respond with the address of the top level server that leads to a chain of references, ending in a server that can identify "myhost.mynet.

example.com" (probably the DNS server for "example.com" or its ISP). The DNS server would then query the referred server, and obtain the address it needs. To map IP addresses to names, the same process is used, except that address blocks are used instead of names. DNS has grown to do more than provide this mapping, including documentation of common network services and contact information for network administration.

To manage the routing of packets across this ISP structure, networks on the Internet use several routing protocols, with the broadest reach being the Border Gateway Protocol (BGP) [8]. BGP's purpose is to exchange information between routers as to the available paths for transmission of packets between groups of routers managed by a single organization, or autonomous system (AS). Each router builds up a set of routing tables that it uses to plan communication to various ASs. Routers send information on the paths that they use via BGP update messages, or "advertisements." These messages include where the router got the information, what AS the information applies to, how long the path to the AS is, and where the path to the AS starts (the "next hop"). Update messages may add, change, or withdraw paths. In classic BGP, these messages carried no authentication, but a Secure BGP protocol has been published that includes provisions for authentication.

To transmit a packet, a router looks at the destination address for the packet, establishes which AS that address belongs to, then consults its tables to find its preferred route to that AS. The packet is then sent to the next hop on that route. If no entry for the AS is found, then the router sends the packet to its gateway, a default next hop. At each step along the path, a field in the header of the packet called "time to live" (abbreviated TTL) is reduced by one. When a router receives a packet with a TTL of zero, it sends an error message back to the source address in the packet's header. The TTL field prevents packets from being endlessly shuttled across the Internet, which could increase the load on the routers to the point of failure.

DECEPTION AND NETWORK ORGANIZATION

The structure of the Internet and its routing methods permit a great deal of deception. Classically, this has been associated with actors that use a variety of attacks against networks (e.g., by sending traffic that purports to come from the internal network, but actually comes from outside, to obtain fraudulent access to information), but more recently defensive deception methods have been identified to blunt network attacks. A report by Erdie and Michael lays out a brief taxonomy of defensive deception for networks [12]. The motivation behind this defensive deception has been to induce the adversaries to strike at the wrong computer or network—those that do not interfere with the organization and provide little advantage to the adversaries. This section

PROFILE: JAMES ELLIS

In the early days following the relinquishment of government control of the Internet, the methods by which vendors would disseminate fixes for security vulnerabilities were a matter of much debate. Some argued for rapid release of such fixes, even if not fully tested or integrated. Others argued for a product release cycle, with associated charges for the fixes. Still others suggested open repositories of such fixes held by third parties, so that administrators could pull what fixes they require. In the end, a quiet voice of consensus moved forward the structure that exists today, where such fixes are maintained by vendors, go through a product development cycle, and are released without charge to the user community. That quiet voice of consensus largely belonged to James Ellis.

James Ellis [9] was a computer scientist who contributed a pioneering vision to the use of computer networks. Shy and quiet as a child, he grew to be an influential voice in discussions that established how organizations would work together to share information and to address information security issues. In 1979, Ellis and his colleague Tom Truscott, both graduate students at Duke University, came up with a way to have computers telephone each other and pass discussions (both technical and general social discussions) between users on various systems—a method that grew into Usenet, one of the key precursors of the Internet.

Ellis and Truscott then published a public "Invitation to a General-Access Unix Network" [10] in which they gave the software implementing their method to anyone interested in using it, and started taking subscriptions (for phone costs, only) for communication. Their software, rewritten twice, is widely noted as the first social application on computer networks, anticipating and motivating modern social networking. Even in its original announcement, handling of information security problems via consensus action was described.

In 1988, the Usenet discussions were a key method of coordinating information for halting and cleaning up the Internet worm, which was the first widespread information security threat on the Internet. In early 1989, Ellis went on to work for Carnegie Mellon's CERT program, coordinating response to security incidents. While there, he was a key participant in discussions on assessing the severity of reported computer vulnerabilities, creating a metric for which vulnerabilities required emergency announcements and that could receive more routine correction. He was an important voice in the discussions that lead to vendor fixes for security vulnerabilities being given away (as opposed to being sold). Colleagues from this period describe how he envisioned and helped to establish a culture by which security would be improved by collaborative response to reported incidents rather than by intrusive probing and coercion [11]. He was also a deeply technical individual, writing software that was important in the coordination of security response.

In 2001, Ellis passed away from cancer, leaving behind his family and a rich legacy of bringing people together over the network to improve its security.

---

discusses defensive deception via the structure of the host network. This allows the defenders to minimize the network footprint of key computers or magnify the footprint of less valuable computers.

One difficulty with using deceptive structures for a network is that productive use of the network must continue unimpeded. Defenders need to carefully plan the deception, and distinguish how the network will appear to outside users and inside users. This variation of view often requires multiple routers (exterior and interior, at least) to present the separate network views, reflected in the entries in their routing tables and in rules that may cause traffic to be blocked to specific portions of the network.

There are several methods for achieving this deception. One is to structure a network such that the valuable servers appear indistinguishable from those

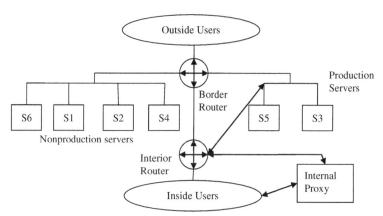

FIGURE 3.3
Defensive server deception.

less valuable. This is done by configuring several identical servers, and providing them with very similar names and addresses. Figure 3.3 diagrams a possible configuration. Only a small subset of these servers are used in production, and any activity on the other servers causes an alert. Any attempt by those servers to establish outbound network connections (either internally or externally) is refused by local routers or computers. For some services, such as file transfer, web hosting, or remote login, this is fairly straightforward. These services are relatively local to the server involved, so standing up redundant servers is not difficult. For authorized users, the specific server to use for production can be specified, and the remaining servers used for deception leading to alerts. The redundancy allows unknowing, automated, or uncaring attackers to be deceived as to which are the production servers, and to have their activity quickly distinguished from benign or productive users. Occasionally, a curious user may contact one of the nonproduction servers, but defenders may distinguish those users via their brief and isolated contact, with no follow-up or attempts to corrupt the server.

As an example, consider an online retailer that is concerned about the security of the shopping cart service associated with their customer website. One option for protecting this service is to implement several redundant shopping cart servers with similar network connections and configurations. An adversary who identifies targets via scanning would find several similar systems, but only a small subset of these would actually be used in production. Attempts to compromise the nonproduction servers would result in an immediate alarm to the network security group, which would then review the production servers to assure that they had not been compromised and to implement further appropriate protections.

Configuring the network's border and interior routers to block any traffic initiated by the nonproduction servers prevents those servers from being used as a basis of attack, either to the local network or other networks. To prevent the nonproduction servers from capturing traffic (including authentication information) from the local network, they may be placed on a network segment of their own, such that the only visible traffic would be other adversaries' attempts to compromise the servers.

For services such as the Dynamic Host Configuration Protocol (DHCP), where the initial contact with the server is done via a broadcast message from the client, having duplicate servers is more difficult. These services require that the first response to the broadcast message be an authoritative one. To ensure such a response, the nonproduction servers might be configured to delay their response to the broadcast message. The difficulty with this is ensuring that the delay is long enough for the production servers to respond first, but short enough that adversaries cannot easily use it to distinguish production and nonproduction servers. Since many of these broadcast protocols are intended only to originate inside the network, another method for achieving initial and authoritative response to the broadcast is to have the broadcasts restricted to the most local segment of the network, and to have a proxy on each segment that will relay both the broadcast request to the production servers and the response from these servers. Unauthorized broadcasts would still reach the nonproduction servers, so an adversary might still be deceived, but legitimate requests would see only authoritative responses. To supplement this protection, the interior router may be configured to drop traffic to and from the nonproduction servers.

One major limitation to deception by network structure is that adversaries who profile the network via traffic analysis prior to their attack will not be deceived, or such deception will not last. These adversaries are those with a goal that involves attacking a specific network and they are both resourced enough and patient enough to prepare their attack for the target network and carefully evaluate the attack to ensure they are hitting their desired targets within the network. While their initial contacts may produce alerts from the nonproduction servers, they will shift operations to only deal with the production servers and such alerts will cease. To deal with these adversaries, other forms of deception (and other strategies) are required.

OUTSOURCING

To protect an organization's internal network from attacks by a persistent adversary, it may be necessary to move particularly public or vulnerable services off of the internal network by arranging them to be hosted by an outside network. The security of these services is then a matter of the contract between the organization and the operators of the hosting network.

There are several characteristics that suggest a service could be successfully outsourced. First, the service needs to be one that is separable from network operations. Services like route management, host virtualization, or device configuration on startup are very difficult to separate from the network structure. Services such as web hosting, external DNS, or email may be easier to outsource. Second, the information involved with the service needs to have a predictable flow from the internal network to the external hosting. Specific internal sources or protocols should be identified. Third, the level of cost (both contact and internal effort) involved in managing the external relationship needs to be less than the cost for maintaining secure hosting internally. If not, then the hosting will not make economic sense. While there are other possible characteristics, these may serve as quick factors for evaluation.

For the organization, such hosting has two security benefits. First, other services on the internal network may be unaffected by attacks against the relocated service. The adversary will be attacking the wrong network and the associate collateral damage will be reduced. Second, the cost of securing the relocated service will be a predictable and contacted amount, rather than a function of the number of attacks against that service. On the other hand, the organization must ensure that the contract includes sufficient levels of security to protect its operations [13]. This may increase the cost of the contract beyond what the organization can support. Also, the organization must arrange for the service to be supported without putting undue trust in the outside network or its operators. Such trust could provide an adversary with a route into the internal network and thus defeat the purpose of the hosting.

Arrangements for securing the service require the organization evaluate the hosting to ensure sufficient staffing and skills to properly secure the service, and sufficient investment in security effort and technology. The organization should examine other services hosted by the outside network and evaluate the availability and integrity maintained by the hosting organization. The specific security methods employed and the service measurements reported need to be included as terms of the contract.

Any internal host acting in support of the relocated service must be carefully configured to protect the network against this support becoming a conduit of attack. Maintaining such configurations will involve further cost to the organization.

However, when such factors can be dealt with, misdirecting the adversaries can be very effective in protecting the network. Adversaries often assume that public and important services are hosted internally, or can be exploited to give access to the internal network or interfere with its operation. Planning for such an assumption and exploiting it to deceive the adversary can be a powerful technique for the network defenders.

OUTSOURCING: 2002 OLYMPIC GAMES

During the 2002 Winter Olympics in Salt Lake City, UT, the Olympic network was used both for the business of conducting the games and for the exchange of data from the sporting competitions. The business end of things involved ticket sales, contracting, venue operations (coordinating the use of buildings and areas for competition), and so forth. The competition data involved event schedules (i.e., who was competing when for which sport), judging, results collection, and results dissemination to news sources and the public. The Olympic network was assembled over more than a year, but was (due to the nature of the games) always intended to be temporary. It was dissembled within a few months after the close of the games.

However, the Olympic organizing committee was quite concerned about security in general (heightened by the terrorist attacks of September 11, 2001, less than six months prior to the games) and about network security in particular [14]. Almost every aspect of the games was supported in some way by the network. The organizers also knew that some services, particularly public web-hosting and external-facing DNS, were popular targets for attack. So they arranged for these two services to be hosted by a commercial ISP outside of the Olympic network. The public-facing DNS information was quite static during the games, and thus no specific internal resources were required. The public web hosting required frequent data transfers as results were disseminated, but these were very similar to the data transfers to news reporting outlets and to the sports federations involved in the games.

The wisdom of this foreign hosting was demonstrated when an American short-track speed skater, Apollo Ono, fell during a final and tripped a Korean skater. This resulted in the Korean not receiving his projected medal, although Ono was able to finish and medal. Numerous Korean protests occurred, and the Olympic public web service was subject to denial of service (flooding) attacks for several days [15]. If the public web hosting had been interior, the level of traffic directed against the service would have seriously degraded the Olympic network. With the external hosting, the ISP was able to shift traffic and continue the web service without degradation, as well as distracting the adversaries away from the internal Olympic network.

APPLICATION HOSTING

In addition to outsourcing network services, it is possible to contract for specific applications that use network services. This is known as *application hosting,* or "software as a service." Organizations often do this for cost reduction, but it does have potential security benefits as well, since particularly difficult to secure or frequently targeted software packages may be moved off of the internal network. As in outsourcing, this reduces the potential for the service to be used as a method of intruding on the rest of the organization's network.

There are several options to implement application hosting [16]. Access to hosted applications is often via secure HTTP, but may use other network services as required (SSH or VPN protocols are common alternatives). In some cases, the hosting service simply takes over an application that the client organization has already licensed from a traditional vendor, moving it to the hosting servers and providing access from the client's infrastructure. Figure 3.4 diagrams a possible configuration. The client saves on operating costs and maintenance costs for the application, since these may be shared with other clients. In other cases, the hosting service offers already-installed software packages to clients to replace existing applications or provide new

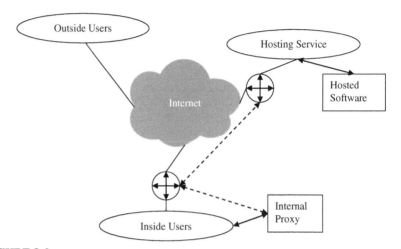

FIGURE 3.4
Application hosting.

applications. Here, the client saves some of the installation costs in addition to operating and maintenance costs. In both cases, management of vulnerabilities related to the hosted applications becomes the responsibility of the hosting service, and the cost is factored into the subscription fee for the hosting. Any security violations in the hosted application are also managed by the hosting service.

Consider the online retail example discussed earlier. One option for protecting the retail network against compromise of shopping cart service is to relocate this application to a hosting service. Shopping cart applications are common enough that a suitable hosting service should not be difficult to find, and suitable contract arrangements can be made. The retailer would modify the flow of processing such that the customer would use the retailer's website to prepare a list of items for purchase, and then be transferred to the remotely hosted application to enter payment information and process the sale. In this way, attempts to intercept payment information by an adversary on the retailer's network would fail, as that information would not go over this network.

There are several characteristics for good candidates for application hosting. First, the hosted application should be one that is common or standard among organizations. While it is possible to host unique applications, there will be less cost savings or security benefit in doing so. The cost savings will be reduced because the hosting organization has less clients to share the costs among. The security benefit is reduced because the hosting organization will have less experience with unique applications and less chance to apply security knowledge, and also since unique applications are not targeted by adversaries as frequently as shared applications.

Second, the hosted application needs to be one that does not require tight binding to the organization's infrastructure. If the application uses a relatively large number of other computers and services, it will be difficult to externally host that application without weakening network defenses. If the application is relatively independent of the organization's infrastructure (e.g., applications that require connection only to already-public computers or services), then it is easier to move it to a hosting service.

Finally, externally hosting the application should provide some identifiable security benefit. The largest security benefits may come from externally hosting applications that are shared both internally and externally to the organization, that simplify access to the organization's data, or that offer ready opportunity for exploiting vulnerabilities.

Conversely, there are several characteristics of applications that would rank low on the list of candidates for external hosting. Little security benefit may come from externally hosting applications that are available only internally to the organization. For these applications, an adversary would already have access to the organization's computers, infrastructure, and probably its data before the application could be attacked, so the additional risk from the application is relatively slight. From a security viewpoint, it may not be worthwhile to externally host applications that provide no additional access to the organization's data. Applications that are used primarily to format data for display, do not deal with confidential data, or otherwise do not give adversaries undue access, would be such low return that adversaries are unlikely to target these applications. Externally hosting these applications would not produce much reduction in the organizations security risk. In addition, if an application is already embedded within nested security protections, or is sufficiently simple and mature that there are very few vulnerabilities in it, then hosting it externally won't change the organization's level of risk significantly.

External application hosting can make the task of the adversary more difficult. Adversaries exploit dependencies between applications and the underlying infrastructure to gain unauthorized privileges. If the underlying infrastructure belongs to a hosting service (with little access to the organization) instead of the targeted organization, then the adversary's attempts to exploit these dependencies will be misdirected. In addition, hosting services are in a better position to detect and respond to effects on their infrastructure from applications, since their business depends on high availability for applications. So attacks misdirected to external hosting services are quite likely to be dealt with rapidly and effectively.

DYNAMIC ADDRESSING

Within the organization's network, addresses for computers (both workstations and servers) may be assigned dynamically from the pool of available addresses. Dynamic addressing methods assign an address to each computer when it first uses the network, and may reassign addresses periodically thereafter, assuming the duration of use is sufficiently long. By assigning addresses dynamically, this method will make address-based attacks more difficult for the adversary.

One of the more common implementations of dynamic address assignment is DHCP [17]. With this protocol, a computer that needs an address sends out *discover* messages (typically, several of them), looking for servers that can provide the address. Figure 3.5 diagrams this interaction. Each available server responds with *offer* messages, identifying potential addresses, along with the terms of use (services, length of address use, and other configuration options). The requesting host then selects one of the offers and sends a *request* message to secure the selected address. It may then use the address for the length of time specified in the offer message. During its use, it may send a request for renewal, to secure a longer use, or a relinquishment, to surrender the address for other computers to use. Some computers on the network may renew their addresses repeatedly, using the same address for extensive lengths of time. Other computers use the network periodically and obtain a new address for each use.

DHCP is mainly intended for computers that use the network periodically, such as workstations that connect during the workday and are shut down

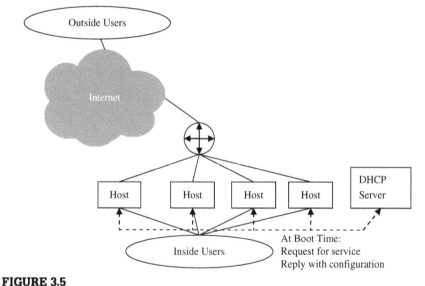

FIGURE 3.5
Dynamic addressing, showing request broadcast.

otherwise. There are at least two advantages to using dynamic addressing on these computers. First, it simplifies (and regularizes) the configuration of these computers. By downloading the address and a number of other networking characteristics, DHCP allows administrators to systematically update these computers rather than dealing with them one at a time. This allows for more even configuration of the networks and fewer mistakes that may lead to configuration vulnerabilities. Second, by varying the address over time, intruders face a somewhat more difficult task in maintaining an attack on a given computer, since some of their attacks are based on the address. On the other hand, since addresses do vary, network traffic analysis of the hosts involved is made a bit more difficult, since tracing activity of a specific computer (to find malware or diagnose an attack) could mean following several addresses.

Computers that provide ongoing service generally don't use dynamic addressing. These servers may use DHCP for configuration (allowing for more regular network structures and security updates), but each server's address is often permanently reserved for that server. The difficulty with using a dynamic address is that if the server shifts addresses, all ongoing communication with it will be disrupted, and only restored by starting the communication over, which will involve (at least) substantial delays and perhaps lost data (or lost customers). Generally, for these servers, other security strategies need to be applied.

SUMMARY

This chapter covers four techniques for improving network security by deceiving the adversary via the structure, services, and addressing on an organization's network. This deception provides the defenders with a chance to misdirect the adversary from an intended target to a less productive (or more obvious) location of the defender's choice. One advantage to this approach is that, since some damage is avoided, the overall cost of security may be reduced.

Chapter 4 continues the discussion of deception as a tool of information security. It focuses on more localized applications of deception to defend specific computers or services. This focus allows for another layer of defense and more difficulties for the network adversary.

Chapter Review Questions

1. Vendors providing security fixes without charge allows for wide distribution of such fixes and application of them without purchase delays, but their cost-free nature also has negative ramifications. Briefly describe two such ramifications.

2. Define the following terms, and briefly explain their relevance to security:
   a. Peering
   b. Transit
   c. Outsourcing
   d. Application hosting
   e. Dynamic addressing
   f. Domain name system

3. How would outsourcing of email help to defeat an email-based virus targeted to a specific organization?

4. What kind of attacks might be wholly or partially defeated by application hosting?

5. How might use of dynamic addressing interfere with an ongoing compromise attempt against a workstation on an organization's network?

6. How would using nonproduction servers as attack alerts help network defenders?

Chapter Exercises

1. While Arpanet and Usenet were two important progenitors of the Internet, they were not the only ones. Describe how the following networks have contributed to the practice of network security on the Internet:
   a. NSFnet
   b. America online (AOL) and prodigy
   c. CERN
   d. Berknet
   e. Decnet

2. Bob's Bank is concerned about online attacks on its business-to-business site. The site is implemented with a front end that supports customer authentication connected to a back end that processes payments, provides account information, and maintains financial services. Since Bob's Bank is a small local bank, they only have two servers for their business-to-business site. Briefly describe two ways that Bob's Bank could use deception to aid in dealing with online attacks on this site.

3. Tres Rios Electric Service is a small power-generation company located in the southwestern United States. They use a variety of device control systems (SCADA) to optimize performance of their generators and support flexible power distribution. Recently, reports have described vulnerabilities in several SCADA systems, and Tres Rios management has become concerned about malicious manipulation of generation and distribution. Briefly describe two ways in which Tres Rios could use deception in preventing or detecting such malicious manipulation.

4. Tartan is a local ISP operating in the mid-Atlantic region of the United States. They support local customers' access to the Internet as a bottom-tier ISP. They have become concerned about attempts to attack their authentication of their customers. Briefly describe two ways in which deception could aid the Tartan in addressing such attempts.

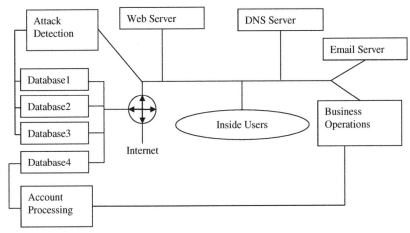

FIGURE 3.6
Bob's Bank logical network structure.

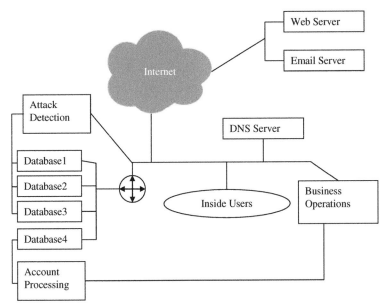

FIGURE 3.7
Bob's Bank new logical network structure.

5. Chris has recently been hired as a network security manager at Bob's Bank, with an initial assignment of reviewing the existing network design to improve security. Some deception is already implemented on the network. Look at the network diagram in Figure 3.6 and identify where deception is already being employed.

6. Terry has just been hired by Bob's Bank, and is proposing a new network plan as shown in Figure 3.7. What features of the new network plan incorporate deception, and what form of deception?

REFERENCES

[1] Heart F, McKensie A, McQuillan J, Walden D. Bolt, Baranek and Newman: Technical Report 4799. Arpanet completion report: a history of the Arpanet—The First Decade. 1978, January. Retrieved June 20, 2013, from <http://www.cs.utexas.edu/users/chris/DIGITAL_ARCHIVE/ARPANET/DARPA4799.pdf>.

[2] Postel J, editor. Internet protocol: DARPA internet program protocol specification. 1981, September. IETF Request for Comment 791. Retrieved June 20, 2013, from <http://www.ietf.org/rfc/rfc791.txt>.

[3] Symantec. 2013 Internet security threat report. Retrieved June 20, 2013, from <http://www.symantec.com/security_response/publications/threatreport.jsp>; 2013.

[4] Truscott T. Usenet interview with Tom Truscott. Giganews Usenet History Project. 2007, April. Retrieved June 20, 2013, from <http://www.giganews.com/usenet-history/truscott.html>.

[5] Verizon. The Verizon global network, 2011. Retrieved June 20, 2013, from <http://www.verizonbusiness.com/ca/about/network/maps/map.jpg>.

[6] Winther M. Tier 1 ISPs: What they are and why they are important. : IDC; 2006. Retrieved June 20, 2013, from <http://www.us.ntt.net/downloads/papers/IDC_Tier1_ISPs.pdf>.

[7] Mockapetris P. Domain names—concepts and facilities. 1987, November. IETF Request for Comment 1034. Retrieved June 20, 2013, from <http://www.ietf.org/rfc/rfc1034.txt>.

[8] Rehkter Y, Li T, Hares S, editors. A Border gateway protocol 4. January 2006. IETF Request for Comment 4271. Retrieved June 20, 2013, from <http://www6.ietf.org/rfc/rfc4271>.

[9] Roddy D. Obituary: Jim Ellis: he helped pave the information highway. Pittsburgh Post-Gazette; 2001, June. Retrieved June 20, 2013, from <http://www.post-gazette.com/obituaries/20010629ellis0629p2.asp>.

[10] Truscott T. Invitation to a general access unix network. Boulder, CO: 1980 Academic Unix User's Group; 1980, January. Retrieved June 20, 2013, from <http://www.newsdemon.com/first-official-announcement-usenet.php>.

[11] Bullard C, Rogers, L. Interviews with the authors on James Ellis; 2012, January.

[12] Erdie P, Michael, J. Network-centric strategic-level deception. Technical Paper 254. Monterey, CA: Naval Postgraduate School; 2005, June. Retrieved June 20, 2013, from <http://www.dtic.mil/cgi-bin/GetTRDoc?AD=ADA464184>.

[13] Allen J, Gabbard D, May, C. Outsourcing managed security services. Pittsburgh: Software Engineering Institute; 2003, January. Security Improvement Module CMU/SEI-SIM-012. Retrieved June 20, 2013, from <http://www.cert.org/archive/pdf/omss.pdf>.

[14] Serrano R, Cart J. Security planners building fortress Utah for Olympics. Los Angeles Times; 2002, January. Retrieved June 20, 2013, from <http://articles.latimes.com/2002/jan/11/news/mn-21969>.

[15] Vamosi R. Explaining the estonian cyberattacks. CNet News; 2007, May. Retrieved June 20, 2013, from <http://www.zdnet.com/news/cyberattack-in-estonia-what-it-really-means/152212>.

[16] Alster N. Software as a service. CFO Magazine; 2005, June. Retrieved June 20, 2013, from <http://www.cfo.com/article.cfm/4077471>.

[17] Droms R. Dynamic host configuration protocol. 1997, March. IETF Request for Comment 2131. Retrieved June 20, 2013, from <http://www.ietf.org/rfc/rfc2131.txt>.

[18] Shirey R. Internet security glossary. IETF Request for Comment 4949. 2007, August. Retrieved June 20, 2013, from <http://tools.ietf.org/html/rfc4949>.

Deception Strategies: Defensive Technologies

INTRODUCTION

Beyond configuring the network to deceive adversaries, there are specific technologies that facilitate deception strategies in defense of computer networks. This chapter introduces four such technologies: proxies/gateways, honeypots/honeynets, tarpits, and virtual hosts. To understand how organizations may use these technologies, it is useful to understand how Internet protocols work, so the chapter starts with a brief overview of common Internet protocols, specifically TCP.

None of these technologies are complete solutions. They all have strengths that may aid organizations, caveats that need to be explored in deciding to deploy, and weaknesses that would need to be supported via other security controls.

INTERNET PROTOCOLS

Information on the Internet is transmitted in segments, often referred to as *packets*, but generically termed *datagrams* when part of the Internet Protocol (IP). The datagrams sent over the Internet have a specific structure, as diagrammed in Figure 4.1(a). The datagrams start with a formatted block of information on how routers are to pass the packet using the IP. This

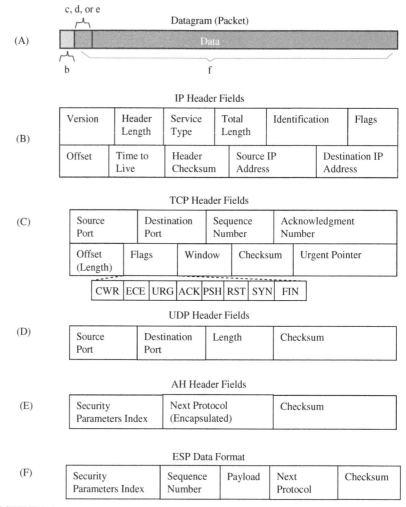

FIGURE 4.1
Selected Internet datagram formats.

block is referred to as the "Internet Protocol header" or, more commonly, "IP header." The IP header contains information as to the source, destination, content of the datagram (i.e., checksum, length, encapsulated protocol, and protocol version), as well as parameters for the Internet routing algorithms (i.e., time to live, which is the number of routers the datagram can go through before it must be dropped, or flags, which indicate options to handling fragmented packets). Following the IP header is a block of information, which often includes another block of formatted information (a second header), the actual information the datagram carries, and, optionally, a final block of information to terminate the datagram (the footer, although footers are much less common in IP datagrams than in the underlying local network protocols). Different encapsulated protocols format the information following the IP header differently (see Figure 4.1(b)–(f)), according to the purpose of each encapsulated protocol.

The most common encapsulated protocols are the Transmission Control Protocol (TCP, see Figure 4.1(c) for its header fields) and the Universal Datagram Protocol (UDP, sometimes referred to as the User Datagram Protocol; see Figure 4.1(d) for its header fields). TCP provides for sequences of traffic, termed segments, grouped in a transmission, allowing for retransmission of any lost portions of the transmission and thus providing for reliable communication. UDP provides for individual datagrams, without retransmission, and thus for service without the overhead required for reliable communication, but with the possibility of lost information.

A TCP transmission starts with a series of three segments that initiate the transmission on both sides (referred to as the "TCP handshake"). One computer sends an initial segment to another with an encapsulated TCP header with the flags field such that only the SYN (synchronize) flag is 1 and the other seven flags are 0. Typically, this segment has no data, merely the IP and TCP headers. The sequence number in the TCP header of this first segment provides the starting point for one side of the communication. The destination port in that TCP header specifies what type of service is requested. The source port in that TCP header is often a high value, and that specifies that the first computer is the one requesting (rather than providing) service. The second computer responds with a segment containing a TCP header with the source and destination ports swapped, its own starting sequence number, and either the SYN and ACK (acknowledgment) flags set to 1, or just the RST (reset) flag set to 1. If the SYN and ACK flags are set to 1, then the second computer is ready to provide service and the sequence number can be used as a starting point for error correction. If the RST flag is set to 1, then the computer is not ready to provide service and the transmission must be abandoned (in practice, busy servers use RST as a quick means to terminate transmissions after passage of data, but this is not part of the documented TCP protocol). The first computer then responds back with a segment containing a TCP header with just the ACK flag set to 1, indicating acceptance of the second host's sequence number, and with the source and destination ports swapped back and a sequence number one greater than the number in the SYN segment (which completes the TCP handshake). The two computers then communicate further as required to implement the service. Each segment acknowledges the preceding portion of the transmission. Often the second computer's response to the ACK segment has data containing a series of values identifying the implementation of the service (referred to as a "service banner").

Most of the common Internet services (Web, email, remote terminal access, file transfer, etc.) are implemented using TCP transmissions. If one of the segments in the transmission is lost or corrupted (indicated by having an inconsistent checksum in it header), no corresponding ACK segment will be received and the sender of that segment will retransmit it. At the end of the transmission, each side will send a segment with a TCP header containing only the FIN (finalize) flag set to 1. When both sides have received and acknowledged FIN segments, then the transmission is terminated.

As referenced in Chapter 3, there are numerous security threats that exploit weaknesses in IP and its encapsulated protocols. To provide for encryption as a control for some of these threats, the Internet Engineering Task Force (IETF) defined an architecture for encrypted connections on the Internet [1], termed IPsec. For an excellent introduction to IPsec, see the summary by Friedl [2].

The Authentication Header (AH) protocol (format shown in Figure 4.1(e)) provides for secure identification of the parties communicating, often followed by the Encapsulated Secure Payload (ESP) protocol (format shown in Figure 4.1(f)), which supports encrypting the body (and much of the header) information in IP datagrams. AH provides for connectionless negotiation of encrypted transmission options. ESP provides for the setup and teardown of encrypted connections. An informational protocol, called Internet Security Association and Key Management Protocol (ISAKMP), is also part of IPsec, used when the communicating computers need more configuration information to support a secure connection. Further exploration of these protocols is left as an exercise to the student (see chapter exercise 1).

When protecting network security, various controls use the datagram-based information. This chapter will refer to several of these controls and how they use this information in support of deception strategies.

PROXIES AND GATEWAYS

A proxy is a process (software, possibly hardware, or, rarely, human) that acts on behalf of a user or client [3]. A proxy receives the network traffic intended for or coming from a group of clients or servers. The term *protected elements* refers to the network clients or servers a proxy acts on behalf of. This traffic is then processed to extract the service-related information (request, response, data transfer, or command, depending on the services involved). This information may be filtered via a set of rules, then passed to appropriate protected elements. Normally, a proxy handles both incoming and outgoing traffic.

Figure 4.2 shows an example of proxy processing. In the figure, each computer's network activity is shown in a separate column, and activity at later times is shown below activity at earlier times. The network's email proxy receives

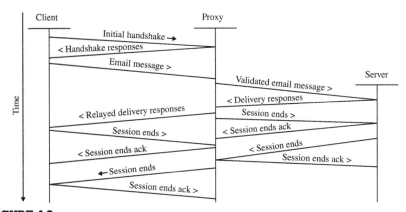

FIGURE 4.2
Example of proxy processing.

the initial service request (in TCP-based services, the datagram with the SYN flag set) and identifies the proper server via the destination port embedded in the TCP header (as in this example), the UDP header, or via the protocol field in the IP header. The source port and source address information in the headers are used internally in the proxy to differentiate multiple requests for the same service. The proxy responds to the initial contact with the TCP handshake, then receives the email header fields and body from the mail handler on the sending network. The proxy processes and validates the incoming message, passing it to the local mail handler since it passed validation, then forwards the receipt response to the sender and shuts down the connection to both mail handlers. A second mail message, however, goes through the same initial contact and processing, but gets dropped (not passed to the receiving mail handler) since it fails validation of the message content (e.g., discussing an internal project inappropriately). When passing either input or responds, the proxy produces new packets with its address (rather than the original client or server), while maintaining an internal table that permits services to be matched with the server appropriately. When the client and server signal the end of their communication (via service messages or flags in a TCP header), then the proxy drops the corresponding table entry.

Computer networks use proxies to either misdirect (deceive) adversaries or frustrate them. Proxies misdirect adversaries by receiving traffic for network clients and services. Proxies have a simpler function than their protected elements: traffic processing, rather than full network service provision or consumption. This simplicity means that proxies possess fewer, or perhaps differing, vulnerabilities than protected elements. Deceiving adversaries into hitting proxies instead of actual clients or servers, therefore, puts the resulting attacks where they are less likely to succeed.

One example of an attack that may illustrate the usefulness of proxies is a web-based attack that uses ill-formatted requests (known as *request splitting*) to corrupt web processing and cause subsequent web traffic to involve the adversary's site rather than a trusted one [4]. In this attack, the adversary is depending on a particular implementation of web request handling to improperly deal with the ill-formatted request. Via a proxy, the request would be received and rejected due to poor formatting. Even if the proxy's information was corrupted using the attack, this corruption would not affect future requests in the way that corruption in a web cache would. Thus, the deception as to where request processing is done would block the attack.

Proxies frustrate adversaries since their processing may block exploits against protected elements. Part of this processing is the application of rules to block interactions with protected elements that violate security policy. This means the rules will drop (and possibly alert on) traffic that the adversary needs for the attack to commence. Even if compromised, the proxy views traffic public on the network rather than accessing internal content used by their protected elements. This difference may impede the initial access required for a network attack.

One vulnerability adversaries use against a network service is a buffer overflow [5]. Carefully crafted messages are sent to the service to supply too much data to an unguarded input operation, causing that operation to overwrite memory including the memory used to keep track of the next operation to perform. The exploits for this vulnerability insert specific instructions in memory locations chosen for a specific implementation of a network service. Since a proxy will provide network service identifying the actual server involved (rather than the proxy), but will process and validate input in the proxy environment (rather than the server), the buffer overflow will end up being attempted against the proxy. The proxy's input validation will likely block the attack, but even if it does not, the instructions embedded in the input will not make sense in the proxy environment and the attack will fail.

A gateway is an intermediate system that connects (acting as a relay or interface) two or more computer networks that have common functions but dissimilar implementations [3]. Gateways may provide one-way or two-way communication among the networks. The dissimilar implementations may be varying network protocols, but often are variations in address usage, network trust level, or network security policies. Gateways receive network traffic, process it to determine the equivalent traffic on the destination network, then send the equivalent traffic on that network. Gateways may run proxies as part of their processing.

Figure 4.3 shows an example of gateway processing. In this example the gateway is running two proxies, one for incoming email and one for incoming

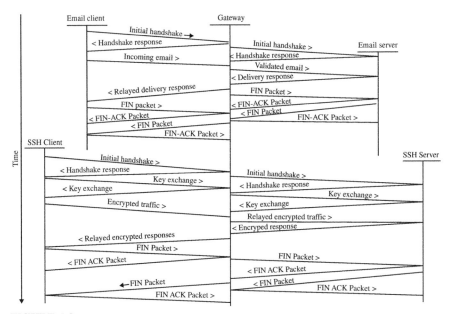

FIGURE 4.3
Example of gateway processing.

encrypted login (secure shell, or SSH). The email proxy acts as the proxy acted in Figure 4.2. The SSH proxy on the gateway needs to be more intrusive in the client-to-server communication. During the setup of the encrypted connection, it separately performs a key exchange with the client and the server, establishing itself as an intermediary. As commands to the server are received, it validates those commands and passes them on to the server. Responses from the server are also validated before passing them to the client. The gateway's proxy does this on an interactive basis, rather than all at once, as is the case with the email proxy. For both sides of the communication, the gateway acts as the corresponding other party for a variety of services, concealing, filtering, and protecting each party. This allows network defenders to deceive adversaries as to the size, scope, and structure of the internal network, as well as allowing the defenders to filter traffic and frustrate adversaries.

Specialized gateways intended to connect networks with differing security policies are referred to as guards. In addition to passing traffic, a major portion of guard functionality is to filter and modify the traffic to comply with the security policy of the destination network. Filtering traffic involves recognizing and dropping packets that involve content, services, sources, or destinations impermissible on the destination network (either due to sources network security policy or destination network security policy). Modifying traffic includes shifting content values or precision to accommodate the differences in security policy between the two networks. Filtering and modification may be implemented via a common set of software that implements rules as to what needs to be modified or filtered out.

In the web request example mentioned earlier, a gateway would receive the request and process it prior to validation. Due to its ill-formatted nature, either the processing would reject it or the subsequent validation would. The gateway itself does not maintain the information the attack seeks to corrupt, so the vulnerability the attack seeks to exploit would not be present. As such, the gateway would block the attack by deceiving the adversary as to what processing environment it implements for the network.

Prior to attacks, adversaries often scan their targets, looking for vulnerable network services [16]. These scans tend to focus either on a single computer, contacting a large number of network services on that computer, or on multiple computers, contacting specific network services across those computers. If the scans are attempting to contact services behind a gateway, the proxies on the gateway will respond to the scan and may deceive an adversary as to how the network services are actually implemented. As such, the adversary may attempt an attack against a service, only to have that attack intercepted and blocked by the proxy.

Proxies and gateways deceptively substitute for organizational servers and the internal network, respectively. They must have sufficient throughput to handle the load required by the organization and its external relationships. The acquisition process needs to assess the actual load required and the throughput provided by the proxies and gateways, ensuring they meet the required load plus a sufficient margin [6]. Rather than assuming vendor figures are accurate and applicable, the assessment needs to involve the actual using environment, or a close approximation. If sufficient throughput is not available, network designers may need to change the proxy and gateway configuration to avoid undesirable bottlenecks in handling service requests.

Proxies and gateways need to be complex enough to receive and process all service requests desired by the organization's business. They need to be simple enough to avoid most of the vulnerabilities in the servers associated with those requests. Achieving both of these properties requires developers and users to strike a balance in complexity. In practice, this will mean that the rules used by a proxy or gateway limit the range of service requests. Organizations must be aware of this, and configure service clients to accommodate this limited range. Conversely, organizations need to choose carefully the rules used by a proxy or gateway to mitigate the operational impact of this limited range. For example, if an email proxy limits use of debugging options in incoming email, the organization should provide an alternate way for authorized administrators to debug incoming email service.

While proxies and gateways provide a number of advantages in network security, their use may offer weaknesses that should be managed. A busy proxy or gateway may generate lengthy log files. While log file analysis tools exist (and will be discussed in Chapter 13), these tools have limits. Even if log analysis tools reduce the effort by 99% on a 10-GB-per-day log file (an optimistic assumption), the administrator still needs to review the equivalent of 100 MB of log information daily (roughly the equivalent of 100 copies of Hugo's *Les Miserables* or Tolkein's *The Lord of the Rings*), seeking the rare entries that alert on an adversary's activity. Many organizations lack the available workforce to maintain this, and so simply delete logs unread after a certain interval. If the authorization rules allowing service via the proxy or gateway get too complex, the performance of the network will suffer as service requests are delayed, possibly to the point of service interruption. If the rules are contradictory or over-encompassing, then they may inadvertently block desired service requests.

Finally, as proxies and gateways mature, a desire for more complete checking and more rapid throughput may motivate adding increased functionality on them, which in turn may increase the number of vulnerabilities that adversaries may use to attack the proxy or gateway itself. A compromised proxy or gateway is a double threat: it allows more direct attacks on targeted servers or clients, and it also decreases the defensive capabilities of the network. While all of these issues can be managed, administrators need to actively manage them.

PROFILE: WILLIAM CHESWICK

For over 35 years, William Cheswick [7] has been passionately involved with improving information security in operating systems and computer networks. His experience has included academic, government, and industrial organizations, but he is most well known for his work with AT&T Bell Labs, where he was a network postmaster, researcher, and network security administrator for many years.

While the security issues in IP networks were well known, the events of the Internet Worm put these issues into sharp focus. At AT&T, Cheswick ran an internal sweep of networked computers and found approximately one-quarter of them had well-known vulnerabilities. While correction of these vulnerabilities could provide a quick fix, Cheswick developed the concept of a proxy [8] and firewall [9] as more systematic solutions. His experience and effective speaking style lead to these methods becoming part of the commonly accepted network security approach.

His later work involves Internet mapping (now available via Lumeta), development of user interfaces, and improvements in password security. He continues his passionate advocacy of practical improvements in the protection of information, but his interests encompass much wider concepts, including science education, medicine, and household technology. He is a frequent speaker at workshops and conferences.

HONEYPOTS AND HONEYNETS

In contrast to gateways, a honeypot is a system or object that exists primarily to attract adversaries [3]. The goal is to entrap these adversaries, distracting them from targeting computers used for organizational operations.

A secondary goal is to expose adversaries, providing an opportunity to study their methods. Often, network defenders assign unused addresses to honeypots, routing all packets addressed to unallocated addresses on the network to the honeypot, so as to make the task of the adversary in differentiating target computers from honeypots that much more difficult. When a network packet initiating a new connection arrives, the router examines its destination address and, if it is in the local address space but not a known host (which does not happen for authorized connections, although defenders may need to make some provision for connections using obsolete information), sends the packet to the honeypot. The honeypot then carries forward the new connection, recording the activity for later analysis.

One key feature of honeypots is that there are no authorized users. The honeypot's only functions are to be attacked, generate an alert of the attack, and profile the activity that constitutes an attack. It has no production or consumer-related use, so all activity on a honeypot is some form of attack. As such, analysis of activity on a honeypot is considerably easier than on a gateway host, as it is all attack activity.

The functionality of honeypots varies widely [10]. *Thin* honeypots respond with an initial packet to connection attempts on a defined set of services, but nothing more. *Moderate* honeypots support prescribed sequences of responses, going beyond the initial contact but permitting little variance in activity. *Thick* honeypots are virtual servers stocked with false (but attractive) information for the adversary to explore. Honeynets are collections of honeypots (and, in some installations, thin clients) designed to offer more complex deceptive interactions.

Thin honeypots provide a certain degree of confusion for the adversary, but repeated contacts will quickly pierce the deception. Often, these honeypots respond to the initial TCP handshake and then, if requested, provide an initial service identification string that indicates a known vulnerable configuration. The honeypot records later packets contacting this service, but does not respond to them. As a result, thin honeypots offer a restricted opportunity to study the adversary's methods; fundamentally, this is nothing beyond the initial contact information: targeted ports and protocols, flag characteristics, packet sizing, whether the adversary continues past the initial response, or the initial form of vulnerability exploit. On the other hand, it also offers the adversary a limited opportunity to subvert the honeypot and use it as a basis for further violation of security. It is both quick to construct and easy to maintain, beyond analysis of logged activity.

Moderate honeypots are a middle-of-the-road option. The scripted interactions allow for more in-depth interaction with the adversary to capture more methodology information, but still offer little option for subversion (although somewhat more than thin honeypots). Differentiating a scripted interaction from a live host interaction is much more intensive than identification of a thin honeypot, often requiring human analysis for the adversary rather than straightforward rules. However, the defenders may expend considerable effort in configuration of a moderate honeypot, maintenance of its capabilities (updating the script to reflect current attacks), and analysis of its logged activity. However, this level of effort is considerably less than thick honeypots or honeynets.

Thick honeypots offer full (but guarded) service configurations for the adversary. The guards limit the outgoing connections through the honeypot, and also the level of exposure of the services on the honeypot. In some cases, the limits deliberately slow the responses from the honeypot to make it less efficient to the adversary. By offering full-service configurations, these honeypots allow defenders to study host-specific adversary behavior in depth. Stocking the honeypots with volumes of deceptive information deepens opportunities for deception of adversaries. However, defenders need to expend a lot of effort designing the configurations, guards, and data to both effectively lure the adversary and proactively limit the utility of the deception in exposing their organization. Log, guard, and traffic information will likely require in-depth human analysis for understanding.

Honeynets offer the fullest opportunities for studying the adversary, but also the largest expenditure of effort and the largest risks of compromise by the adversary. Defenders configure these networks as contained environments in which the adversary may interact with multiple computers, all being monitored, and offering limited interaction beyond the network. Figure 4.4 shows an example network configuration including a honeynet. This configuration allows extensive deception of the adversary, focusing their attention on false information and false infrastructure, away from the production infrastructure and protected information. Even sophisticated adversaries may be deceived by a sufficiently detailed honeynet. Such detailed honeynets, however, require a level of maintenance effort equal to the production network, which involves costs prohibitive to many organizations.

Honeypots (particularly thick honeypots and honeynets) offer a number of deception options. They can deceive the adversary as to the degree of diligence in maintaining security, lulling that adversary with a sense of safety while permitting the network defender to trace, profile, and limit the adversary's activities. These computers can offer false rewards to an adversary, which can both introduce a degree of confusion with respect to real information and distract the adversary from targeting production computers for proprietary information. Honeypots can deceive the adversary as to the deployed operating systems and their vulnerabilities, prompting unproductive and revealing attacks against production computers (running a different operating

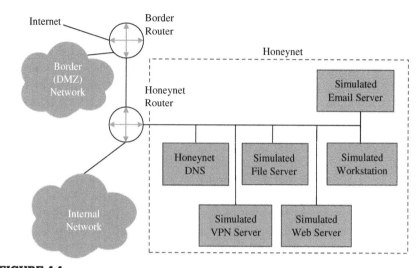

FIGURE 4.4
Example network configuration with a honeynet.

SECURITY CASE STUDY: BERFERD

One early experience with adversary deception began in January 1991 when Bill Cheswick received an alert indicating a persistent adversary on the gateway system at AT&T [11]. For several months, Cheswick interacted with the adversary (whom he dubbed "Berferd," a deliberately insulting pseudonym) via a primitive honeypot (supporting manual interaction with the adversary). Cheswick sent Berferd a series of deceptive files (starting with a fake password file that lead Berferd to the honeypot) and interactions (emulating various network services that Berferd was attempting to use, or introducing limitations on the types of attacks that Berferd could employ due to the simulated configuration), studying the responding activity and profiling the adversary. Early on, Cheswick contacted a number of security experts, alerting them to his study of Berferd and enlisting their aid in both understanding and containing Berferd's activity. One of these contacted experts was Wietse Venema, who was associated with the base network

from which Berferd sent his attacks. From early on in the attack, Venema had identified Berferd's real-world identity and contact information.

Unfortunately, Berferd was outside the jurisdiction of any then-current computer misuse laws. The network that Berferd was using had a liberal usage policy, so his access to this network could not be immediately terminated. As a result, Venema's options in dealing with Berferd (and several other adversaries who were associated with him) were limited. However, Berferd and his colleagues continued to impact a variety of computers on the Internet, and Venema received a continuing stream of complaints on these activities. Eventually, Venema phoned Berferd's home (intending to simply tell him to quit), and ended up talking to his mother. After an extended conversation regarding Berferd's activities, his mother indicated she would handle him, and Berferd's attacks virtually stopped from that point.

system or not configured in such a vulnerable manner). In short, honeypots offer both tactical and strategic deception of adversaries.

Honeypots also have distinct disadvantages. They require some initial effort to configure as believable computers on the network. Installations using default parameters are of little use for deception, as adversaries rapidly identify them and subsequently avoid them. Even carefully configured honeypots (other than intricate honeynets) may be rapidly recognized as honeypots by vigilant adversaries. Therefore, the logged activities on these honeypots will be primarily of scripted attacks or uncaring adversaries. This means that detailed analysis of honeypot activity may produce low return on the analysis effort, since the adversaries profiled in that activity will largely be those who do not intend to make use of the organization's network beyond formulaic methods. A more serious drawback, however, is that a honeypot has a potential to serve as the basis of attacks against third-party networks, putting the hosting organization at increased liability.

One method of attack (known as an *echo attack*) involves the adversary generating packets addressed to the organization's network with a false source address such that responses go to a third-party target computer, with the expectation that the organization will generate responses. A thin honeypot may be exploited by an adversary to support an echo attack. For the adversary, the attack hides the identity of the computer sending the initial packets, since the organization would only see the false-source packet and the victim would only see the organization's response to these packets. Tracing the initial packet to its actual source would require both that the adversary would persist in generating such packets and that the ISPs routing them would cooperate in the trace. Both may be difficult for a victim organization to rely on in the close timeframe of the attack for which relevant logs would be maintained.

Moderate to thick honeypots may be more directly compromised by adversaries and their use coopted to form part of the adversary's attack resources. Honeynets often are closely configured to limit options for coopted use, but they may capture proprietary or personal data on third parties, which again raises the liability of the hosting organization. With these disadvantages (and the counterbalancing advantages) in mind, organizations need to carefully weigh their options in using honeypots or honeynets as a part of network deception.

TARPITS

A tarpit [12] is a computer programmed to return deceptive responses to initial contacts on services and protocols that the organization's network do not implement. If an adversary scans a network before attacking it, to profile potential victim computers on the network and the services that those computers implement, a tarpit will make this process fairly difficult. By generating a response to every initial contact (all addresses, all ports, all protocols), the tarpit will produce a deceptively open profile for the organization's network. Initially, it will look to the adversary like a fully populated network with all potential network services enabled (many more than are currently defined, far beyond those in common use). Sifting through this mass of responses

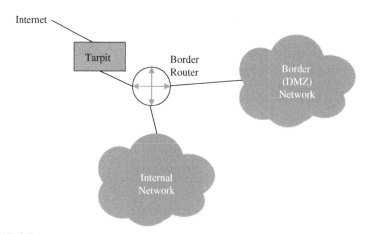

FIGURE 4.5
Example network configuration with Tarpit.

will greatly increase the workload of the adversary. A tarpit is similar to an extremely thin firewall, but often its use is purely deceptive—there is no recognition supported. It isn't a gateway or proxy, since it is not validating traffic; it just generates initial responses and stops there.

To successfully use a tarpit, the organization needs to define the range of addresses, protocols, and ports for deception by the tarpit. Normally, the network administrators define ports and protocols supported elsewhere on the network. A router passes the supported traffic to the appropriate server and all other contacts to the tarpit. This is usually done prior to the organization's border router, both because the organization wants minimal extra network load and to prevent the tarpit responses from overloading the border router. Figure 4.5 shows a sample network configuration for a network with a tarpit. Another form of tarpit [13] monitors network services that identify computers on the network. Unresolved requests are handled by the tarpit.

Tarpits provide a large degree or protection from casual adversaries [13]. By responding to scans, the tarpit produces so many false responses that many casual adversaries will simple break off their attacks. Tarpits are especially effective against programmed attacks, such as network worms [12]. This reduces the risk to the network to those adversaries who have some knowledge of the actual service structure of the network (possibly by social engineering, more often by using the proper network service channels to identify supported services and their servers). Tarpits are easy to set up and require little maintenance and updates. Since tarpits do not actually support any network services, what maintenance is required must be done off the network, via physical proximity to the tarpit's console.

While tarpits may offer significant protection from casual or programmed adversaries, they also have disadvantages that defenders need to consider. Since a tarpit will reply to any contact, it effectively doubles the amount of nonproductive traffic that the organization's network (at least its point of presence) must handle. An adversary might exploit this characteristic in a denial of service (DoS) attack against the organization. To prevent this, several tarpit packages have rate-limiting features that restrict the pace at which the tarpit will generate response packets. Adversaries may also use the tarpit to generate echo traffic, as described earlier with honeypots. This is more difficult to defeat using rate limiting, as the adversary may use multiple networks to echo traffic against the third-party victim. Since the adversary doing the echo traffic attack will generate repeated initial contacts faked to come from the same address, often with the same source and destination points, defenders may look for such repeated contacts and configure the tarpit to limit the number of responses it generates. This would slow or block the adversary's use of the tarpit.

Tarpits, while offering minimal deception, offer some significant protection against self-propagating malware and casual adversaries. These advantages need to be weighed against the level of effort required to configure the tarpit, the extra network load it may generate, and the potential for abuse by adversaries.

VIRTUAL HOSTS

A virtual host is a restricted, simulated computer appearing on a network that is implemented using physical resources that are either part of the network or hosted elsewhere [3]. In concept, virtual hosts are somewhat similar to the application hosting described in Chapter 3, but in detail and implementation there are a number of important distinctions. Where application hosting is focused on providing specific software services, virtual hosts implement complete emulated computer systems with independent operating systems, devices, storage, and applications. Virtual hosts can be virtual clients or virtual servers. One common configuration is for organizations to internally host virtual clients, but to contract with an external network to host virtual servers. This arrangement, diagrammed in Figure 4.6, balances a need for control with the costs of operating virtual hosts.

Network defenders would implement virtual clients to allow internal users to access services known to carry a degree of risk. In operation, the virtual client acts (to the user) simply as an application running on a desktop computer, although with limited access to the data and devices available through that computer. In actuality, the user's request for service becomes a message sent to a local hosting server, which loads a stored image hosting the

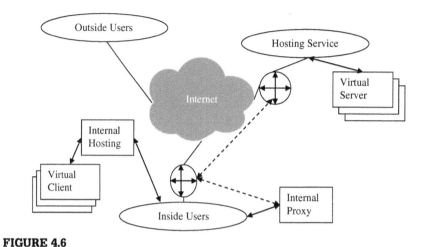

FIGURE 4.6
Example network configuration with virtual hosts.

application and connects that application to the user's computer. The hosting server routes commands to the application and results from the application between the user's computer and the virtual client. The virtual client accesses its own simulated disk storage and devices, rather than using storage and devices on the user's computer. After the application completes running, the hosting server shuts down the virtual client, storing data but no changes to the software.

Network administrators may implement or contract virtual servers for either cost or security reasons [14]. For virtual servers, the users access a local proxy, which establishes a connection with the external hosting computer to support the service request. That computer then connects to an internal image of a server, and handles the request in the context of this image. This image, in contrast to virtual clients, is normally persistent, with the hosting server retaining the image between requests.

Virtual servers are lower cost than physical hosts since a single physical computer can host multiple virtual servers. Since many organizations do not require all the resources of a physical computer to host their services, sharing the computer with multiple servers makes more efficient (and lower-cost) use of resources. Virtual servers may offer security improvement by sharing vulnerability fixes and other common administrative tasks, and also by being rapidly restored to a known clean state if the defenders suspect the virtual server is compromised. On the other hand, if the underlying operating system of the hosting server is compromised, multiple services (and, potentially, multiple organizations) may be affected.

Other than the chance of common compromise, virtual hosts pose few additional security problems for network defenders. Due to the controls placed on the simulated hosts, adversaries find few advantages gained by compromising them, and the restart of these hosts sacrifices those advantages rapidly. There is some contractual and configuration work involved in setting up virtual hosts and using them operationally, and this must be balanced against the gain in security.

SUMMARY

As this chapter shows, there are numerous technologies that can implement specific deception as to service implementations and processing on an organization's network. These technologies work based on the traffic information, using the content of IP datagrams. However, each of these technologies offers only a limited amount of deception, and for specific services or purposes. At some point, this deception will be exhausted and a dedicated adversary may proceed against operational computers on the network. At that point, other security strategies are needed. The first of these other strategies, frustration, is discussed in Chapter 5.

REFERENCES

[1] Kent S, Seo K. Security architecture for the internet protocol. Internet Engineering Task Force. RFC 4301; 2005, December. Retrieved June 26, 2013, from <http://tools.ietf.org/html/rfc4301>.

[2] Friedl S. An illustrated guide to IPsec; 2005, August. Retrieved June 26, 2013, from <http://www.unixwiz.net/techtips/iguide-ipsec.html>.

[3] Shirey R. Internet security glossary. IETF Request for Comment 4949; 2007, August. Retrieved June 26, 2013, from <http://tools.ietf.org/html/rfc4949>.

[4] Klein A. Divide and conquer—HTTP response splitting whitepaper; 2004, March. Retrieved June 26, 2013, from <http://packetstormsecurity.org/papers/general/whitepaper_httpresponse.pdf>.

[5] Cowen C, Wagle, Pu, C, Beattie S, Walpole, J. Buffer overflows–attacks and defenses for the vulnerability of the decade. Proceedings of DARPA information survivability, Conference and Expo (DISCEX); 1999. Retrieved June 26, from <http://ieeexplore.ieee.org/stamp/stamp.jsp?tp=&arnumber=821514>.

[6] Lin Y, Wei H, Yu S. Building an integrated security gateway: mechanisms, performance evaluations, implementations and research issues. IEEE Commun. Surv. 2004. Retrieved June 26, 2013, from <http://speed.cis.nctu.edu.tw/~ydlin/wei.pdf>.

[7] Cheswick W. Bill Cheswick's homepage; 2013. Retrieved June 26, 2013, from <www.cheswick.com/ches>.

[8] Cheswick W. The design of a secure internet gateway, USENIX Summer; 1990. p. 233–8. Retrieved June 26, 2013, from <http://www.cheswick.com/ches/papers/gateway.pdf>.

[9] Cheswick W, Bellovin S, Rubin A. Firewalls and internet security. Reading, MA: Addison-Wesley; 2003. Retrieved June 26, 2013, from <http://www.wilyhacker.com/>.

[10] Honeynet Project. Honeynet project papers; 2013. Retrieved June 26, 2013, from <http://www.honeynet.org/papers>.

[11] Cheswick W. An evening with Berferd, in Which a Hacker is lured, endured, and studied. Winter Usenix Conference; 1992. Retrieved June 26, 2013, from <http://web.cheswick.com/ches/papers/berferd.pdf>.

[12] Bautts T. Slow down internet worms with tarpits; 2010. Retrieved June 26, 2013, from <http://www.symantec.com/connect/articles/slow-down-internet-worms-tarpits>.

[13] Lister T. LaBrea—The Tarpit; 2003. March. Retrieved June 26, 2013, from <http://labrea.sourceforge.net/README>.

[14] Luther M. Virtual private servers explained; 2012. Retrieved June 26, 2013, from <http://www.hostway.com/web-resources/find-web-hosting/virtual-server-hosting/virtual-private-servers-explained/>.

[15] Posey B. The pros and cons of running a virtual server, 2004, August. Retrieved June 26, 2013, from <http://www.windowsnetworking.com/articles_tutorials/pros-cons-virtual-server.html>.

[16] Lakhina A, Crovella M, Diot C. Diagnosing network-wide traffic anomalies. In SIGCOMM, pages 219–230, 2004.

Chapter Review Questions

1. Proxies are widely used to protect network services. Often, firewall vendors offer a variety of such proxies as a part of their products. Identify two network services that might be particularly useful to protect via a proxy.

2. Define the following terms, and briefly explain their relevance to security:
   a. Datagram
   b. Transmission Control Protocol (TCP)
   c. Honeynets
   d. Tarpits
   e. Virtual hosts
   f. Network guards

3. How would use of a gateway facilitate protection of large file storage on an organization's network?

4. What kind of attacks might be wholly or partially defeated by tarpits?

5. How might use of honeynets interfere with an ongoing compromise attempt against a workstation on an organization's network?

6. How would using virtual clients to restrict vulnerability exploits help network defenders?

Chapter Exercises

1. While TCP forms the majority of traffic on the Internet, many secure applications are now being implemented via the AH and ESP protocols [2]. Briefly describe how these protocols may improve the security of an application over the features available in TCP.

2. Bob's Bank is concerned about online attacks on its business-to-business site. The site is implemented with a front end that supports customer authentication connected to a back end that processes payments and provides account information. Since Bob's Bank is a small local bank, they only have two servers for their business-to-business site. Briefly describe two technologies that Bob's Bank could use as deception to aid in dealing with online attacks on this site.

3. Tres Rios Electric Service is a small power-generation company located in the southwestern United States. They use a variety of device control systems (SCADA) to optimize performance of their generators and support flexible power distribution. Recently, reports have described vulnerabilities in several SCADA systems, and Tres Rios management has become concerned about malicious manipulation of generation and distribution. Briefly describe two deception technologies that Tres Rios could use in preventing or detecting such malicious manipulation.

4. Tartan is a local ISP operating in the mid-Atlantic region of the United States. They support local customers' access to the Internet as a bottom-tier ISP. They have become concerned about attempts to attack their authentication of their customers. Briefly describe two ways in which proxies could aid Tartan in addressing such attempts.

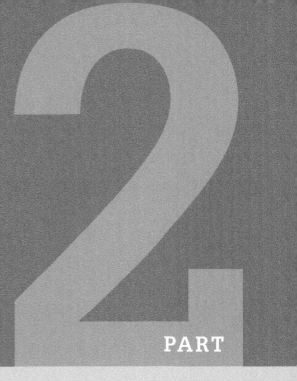

PART

Frustration

CHAPTER 5

Frustration Strategies: Technical Controls

INTRODUCTION

At some point, an adversary will defeat any deception techniques. Implemented correctly, the deception techniques have bought a defender some time from the more dangerous adversaries and caused the most opportunistic of thieves to pass them over as too much trouble. This chapter focuses on the next segment of a successful information security strategy: frustration.

The goal of frustration strategies is to prevent an adversary from successfully targeting the defender's resources. When frustrating the adversary, we assume that the assets of value that will be attacked have been identified already with some accuracy. However, the defender has various tools available that can make it so that the attacker cannot successfully target the desired assets. There are both host-based and network-based frustrations, and, in general, all can be described as some version of reducing the attack surface of a system or systems. There is a lot of literature on attack surface measurement, but the quick definition is "the set of ways in which an adversary can enter the system and potentially cause damage" [1].

MINIMIZATION GOALS AND OBJECTIVES

It is not generally possible to reduce the attack surface to zero. There is an old quip that the only secure system is one that is powered down, unplugged, dismantled, encased in concrete, and dropped to the bottom of a deep-sea trench. The information system will serve benign users, whether internal or external, and such an interaction presents some attack surface. The defenders' goal is to minimize the attack surface, and thus an adversary's entry points for attack. Since there are many types of information technology, there are multiple levels of minimization to frustrate an adversary. Each service and each computer will have minimization applied to it, but in different manners.

Minimization serves two goals. One is to present the smallest possible attack surface to the adversary. This will frustrate the adversary's attempts to compromise the defender's systems. The second goal is not always appreciated—to minimize the cognitive complexity of the system the defender implements. If someone does not know anything about a running service, he or she cannot be reasonably expected to defend it. If the policy rules someone is expected to implement are too many, he or she cannot be expected to understand the importance of a violation. Simplicity has much bigger gains for the defender in the following step of the security strategy as well: a simple system is easier to recognize and remediate errors. The essence of the minimization strategy is captured in a quote often attributed to Albert Einstein: "Everything should be made as simple as possible, but not simpler" [2,3].

This chapter discusses minimization in the context of three aspects of network defense—servers, services, and network protocols—and sums up by discussing how an appropriate network architecture ties it all together. The various strategies are summarized in Figure 5.1 on several relevant axes. These are heuristic estimates, and may not be to scale. Each axis is related to the others, but not necessarily in a linear fashion, so each axis is presented separated with each strategy marked on each axis. Note that no strategy scores well on all axes (desirable computational complexity is low); a complete strategy must use a combination of the available approaches to account for the weaknesses of each.

ASYMMETRY IN INFORMATION SECURITY

The asymmetry inherent in computer network defense makes minimization, and frustration generally, all the more important. This asymmetry is that the

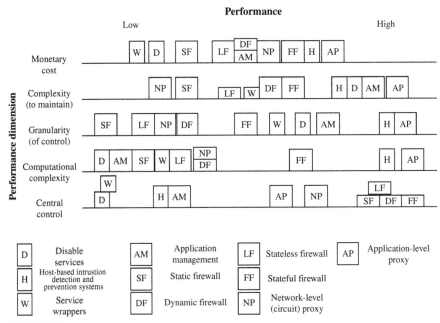

FIGURE 5.1
The frustration strategies discussed in this chapter, roughly displayed by their estimated performance in various dimensions.

adversary only needs to find one of any of the available services to exploit to be successful, whereas the defender needs to equally maintain all of them. This problem can be described in terms of three distinct cases to model the dependability of systems [4]:

- In some cases, it is a sum of efforts where everyone's efforts are aggregated.
- In some cases, it is based on minimum effort where the weakest link in the chain will cause the chain to snap.
- In some cases, it is a best effort where only the high-water mark of the best individual matters.

Unfortunately, program correctness is often a minimum-effort, or weakest-link, activity because it only takes an error from the weakest programmer to compromise the program. Further to the adversary's advantage, compromising that weakness is either a best effort of a skilled individual adversary or, even worse for the defender, a sum of efforts of an organized group of adversaries [5, p. 229].

But do not despair. Although the adversary has an asymmetric advantage in exploitation, the defender has significant advantages as well. Defenders choose what systems to run, how to connect them together, and what policies to implement. Smart decisions on these fronts can frustrate the adversary's advantage. However, the ability to make smart decisions can be hampered by default settings on vendor devices. The vendors, quite reasonably, want their product to work out of the box for the widest number of customers. With all good intentions, the vendor will have enabled quite a few features and services that are not precisely necessary. Thus, the defender must inventory the features that are actually required for the system to function and minimize the set of features to just those. This practice will help frustrate the adversary's asymmetric advantages because fewer features reduces the possible attacks, and it also means management is simpler [1].

HOST HARDENING

Hardening individual hosts has several aspects. The defender can remove services, close ports, use local intrusion detection and prevention services, utilize service wrappers, and generally manage the applications allowed to run on the operating system. In general, host-based security solutions are more sensitive than network-based solutions, since they have access to all the host's information. This is a double-edged sword, however. Since the host-based systems are on the host, a successful compromise of the host may be able to invalidate or otherwise modify the host-based system, which is not possible in the same way in a distributed network-based solution. For appropriate defense-in-depth strategies, both network- and host-based solutions should be applied. The following categories of host-based strategies can also be applied rather granularly to individual hosts with different risk profiles. This also provides some more flexibility than the available granularity to network-based approaches, which, due to their centralized nature, are forced to cover solutions with slightly broader strokes.

Disabling Services

Footprint minimization reaches as far as the basic operating system (OS) functions. Whatever OS the computer is running, there are going to be many system functions that are not necessary. This is true no matter the OS, whether it is Windows, Mac OSX, Linux, BSD, Android, or iOS. It is true about servers and end-user machines, including mobile devices. In an archaic example, many hosts used to listen on port 79 for the finger protocol by default [6]. The finger protocol is designed to provide information about the users on a computer to a remote host that asks about them. Modern OSs no longer open this port by default because the potential information leakage turned out to be too damaging. In general, administrators were not doing their own service minimization on hosts. Especially for high-value assets, OS functions and listening ports should be minimized.

The extent of host service minimization will depend on the risk assessment of the system, as well as the specialization of the system. A very specialized system is easier to pare down. A more valuable system is more important to pare down. The latter should be the driving factor; for example, take Google's OS minimization on its servers that run the virtual machines for the Google API services [7]. The Google virtualization infrastructure is a good example of defense in depth generally, however, in particular the version of Linux that runs the computers is a specialized build that contains only the functions necessary for virtualization and administration. Continuing the finger protocol example, this means more than merely turning off the standard listening port. It means all code that is used to run a finger protocol is deleted from the machine.

Importance of Disabling Services

There are some default services that are important to disable, not due to direct harm to the computer running the service, but from reflected damaged to other computers. One obvious example is domain name system (DNS) servers. The DNS protocol supports the addressing system on the Internet—it allows the computer to find the logical location of, say, *www.example.com* [8]. In this way, it is much like a post office. An envelope addressed "123 N. Main Street, Somewhere, KS, 12345" is taken by the post office, translated into a physical latitude and longitude, and delivered to the right house. For this reason, most computers have a DNS resolver installed by default, so the computer can ask questions. However, many devices come with a DNS server enabled by default also. The metaphor begins to break down, but this is a little like every house coming with a small post office inside, rather than just a postbox to send letters.

The attack scenario goes something like this. The defender and 999 others all have devices running small DNS servers. Let's say there are no known bugs in the servers, but they will answer queries from anyone who asks. As far as this organization is concerned, this is of little importance. The computer doesn't have enough bandwidth to really consume noticeable amounts of resources, and the server doesn't know any information that is sensitive. But the attacker can harm me in this way: the attacker repeatedly asks all 1,000 DNS servers a small question that has a large answer, such as the name servers for the root of the DNS zone. But the attacker lies and says that you asked, which is easy to do, so all 1,000 servers tell you the answer and now you perhaps can't access the Internet. This attack would have two main benefits: the attacker's throughput is multiplied upwards of 20 times because the DNS answers are larger than the queries, and the attack source becomes randomized and hard to block. For a simple illustration, see Figure 5.2. The defender's organization may suffer unnoticeably this time, but the next attack will probably put the crosshairs in a different place.

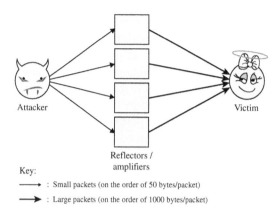

FIGURE 5.2
The amplification and anonymization of a denial of service (DoS) attack using reflection (e.g., with DNS). Many attackers could execute this attack at once against a single target.

The only realistic way to prevent such distributed denial of service attacks (DDoSs) from using reflection and amplification techniques such as the above, is for the Internet community as a whole to band together and have appropriate service minimization policies, such as the IETF best current practices (BCP) document BCP 38. This is similar to the benefits of immunization in promoting public health, which are well documented [9].

Local Intrusion Detection

The line between intrusion detection and prevention is a thin one. In general, the only difference is that intrusion detection systems (IDSs) do not automatically react to a detected intrusion, whereas intrusion prevention systems (IPSs) do. The detection capabilities and strategies of each are roughly the same. However, an IPS is arguably a frustration strategy, whereas an IDS is a recognition strategy. One difference is that the data an IPS can use in real time is more restricted, and that IPS machines are usually more resource intensive and therefore expensive. Furthermore, only detection methods with a high confidence should be allowed to automatically act, otherwise false positives can ruin the user experience and encourage them to circumvent the system. For this reason, we will briefly touch on local IDSs/IPSs here, but a full treatment on host-based IDSs is part of Chapter 13. Similar logic makes the treatment of network-based IPSs in this chapter short, since a full treatment of network IDSs is part of Chapter 12.

IDSs and IPSs are traditionally partitioned into network- and host-based strategies, however, storage system–based IDSs have also been proposed [10]. Host-based IDSs detect changes in local information to detect malicious changes to the system, such as system calls [11]. Some open-source solutions, such as Tripwire, detect changes to files in configurable locations and can be used to log or prevent those attempted changes [12]. High-risk computers, such as public-facing servers like web or DNS servers, or high-value computers, such as domain controllers [13] or Kerberos authentication and ticket-granting servers [14,15], should have local intrusion detection or prevention services installed. This will help frustrate the attacker who will invariably find a way to communicate with such important computers. It is feasible to run IDSs on every computer in an organization, but whether the management or licensing costs of such an endeavor are worth the gains is up to each organization to evaluate. Open-source tools exist that might lower this cost.

Service Wrappers

A Transmission Control Protocol (TCP) wrapper is a tool to add flexibility to the way that a host handles incoming service requests on the network, permitting both monitoring and manipulation [16]. A TCP wrapper functions on network connections, and in that regard is more like a firewall than a host-based IDS. While wrappers are not a replacement for a good firewall policy (see the "Network Devices and Minimization" section), they allow for more fine-grained control and more response options for the services that are permitted through the firewall [17].

On any computer waiting to provide services over the Internet, there is a management process that waits and listens for requests on the network interface. When the server receives a request, this management process starts the appropriate process or daemon to handle the request and then goes back to listening. Each process or daemon would then be in charge of its own access control. However, if the program has a bug or error, the adversary may abuse it. Furthermore, changing the code for all possible services to reflect a consistent security and access control policy would be infeasible anyway [16].

To manage the connection process while making minimum changes to the services themselves, a TCP wrapper inserts itself between the initial management process and the daemons, so the management process calls the wrapper, the wrapper consults the security policy about the requested connection, and then it takes a specified action. This action can be a simple allow or deny, like firewalls, but it can also be any arbitrary command. The action can, therefore, be to gather more information, respond to the request with an error message, send mail to the system administrator, log some information, or most anything else [17].

Service wrappers are a useful layer of frustration against an adversary. They do not replace either network firewalls or host-based protection systems. However, they have some benefits of each. Like network-based strategies, the wrappers use mostly network header information, and require relatively few resources and no modification of host systems. However, like host-based systems, wrappers have added information from sitting on the actual host and added flexibility of a fully functional command line to craft actions. The result is a strategy halfway between a network- and host-based strategy that fills some gaps left by both. Therefore, using a wrapper for more granular access control and logging of necessary services is advisable.

Application Management

In addition to removing default programs, host hardening also means careful management of what additional programs are installed on the computer. This tactic is more relevant to end-user computers, but applies to high-value servers as well. Many organizations' IT departments manage the applications a user is allowed to install for this reason. In an obvious example, if a user receives an email with a malicious Microsoft Office document attached to it, but he or she does not have the office suite of programs installed, he or she is not vulnerable to the attack. While most employees may do document processing, do they need to compose music in GarageBand, which comes packaged with Mac OSX? Or do they need to run a node in a covert peer-to-peer network to make digital phone calls, like Skype [18,19]?

Each program the user installs and uses increases the attack surface. For this reason, it is ideal to have a list of permitted programs rather than attempting to maintain a list of forbidden programs. These concepts are more broadly termed *white lists* and *black lists*. White lists enumerate acceptable elements, with an implicit default action of deny. Black lists are the opposite—they enumerate forbidden elements, with a default policy to accept anything not on the list. The choice of implementing a policy as a white list or a black list is a recurring question in security. In general, white lists are more secure and more troublesome. We will revisit the topic of white and black lists in the context of router ACLs later in the chapter, where for some time the best practice has been to implement white lists. Although it is not as straightforward to implement a white list of permitted, managed applications within an organization, it is the recommended lower-risk strategy and a stronger defensive posture.

The rapid pace of software development makes a thorough analysis of each application update before installing it within an organization difficult. See Chapter 10 for a complete discussion of change and configuration management. To make this task easier, careful thought needs to be given to the applications that will be permitted to run in the first place. Perhaps all peer-to-peer programs are forbidden from the organization, for example, or a nonstandard email client is the permitted client because it has been demonstrated to have much better security properties and the organization has been breached via email before.

PROFILE: ROSS J. ANDERSON, SECURITY ENGINEER

Ross Anderson's current title is professor of security engineering at Cambridge University in the United Kingdom. Some of his work is on the most mathematics-intensive side of security: cryptology. Most significantly, with Eli Biham and Lars Knudsen he designed Serpent, which would nearly go on to become the advanced encryption standard (it lost by only 28 votes to the winning algorithm, Rijndael). But perhaps such mathematical exceptionalism should not be surprising from someone whose academic pedigree (Ph.D. advisor's advisor, that advisor's advisor, and so on back) starts with Roger Needham and runs back to Sir Isaac Newton and Galileo Galilei. However, Ross' unique contribution to how we think about security is not to be found in his peculiar depth on any one subject, but rather in his breadth in tying the seemingly unrelated fields together into the discipline of security engineering.

His professional life began in avionics and passed through a consulting phase that included payment protocol design before attending Cambridge a second time to acquire a Ph.D. His interests range over topics like economics and security, peer-to-peer systems, cryptographic protocols, hardware tamper resistance, signal processing, dependability, public policy, and university governance. Studying such diverse fields is necessary to find the themes that tie all the threads together. When Ross was founding the idea of security engineering—tying up all the subdisciplines that thought they were their own discipline, independent and aloof—it wasn't all thought of as one big system that could be studied. There were OSs for a computer engineer, and biological systems for the psychologists, and monetary systems of compensation for the economists, etc. But the OS folks didn't much talk to the psychologists. A security engineer has to find the way these seemingly disparate aspects of our worlds relate, and use that knowledge to protect them from damage. Specifying these interrelationships has made the field of information security as it exists possible.

There are several exciting developments, such as estimating the cost of cybercrime [20], the problems of user-selected PINs [21], and the resilience of the Internet as a whole [22]. Likely as not there will be more useful research before this book goes to press, though, so it's probably best to check for the most recent information on his website, *www.ross-anderson.com*.

NETWORK DEVICES AND MINIMIZATION

Network-based frustration and minimization are also an important aspect of an information security strategy. Network devices can be used to architecturally reduce information that leaves the organization and to detect or block suspicious traffic. Routers, static and dynamic firewalls, stateful firewalls, network IDSs and IPSs, and various service proxies are the basic logical categories of blocking devices [23]. Many physical devices are comprised of more than one of these categories—it is hard to buy a router nowadays without at least a static firewall embedded in the device. As a rule of thumb, the more complex devices can also mimic the functionality of the less complicated devices. This mimicry is often at a performance cost, so it is often wise to have a layered defense of networked devices as well. For example, a static firewall can be configured to drop blatantly abusive traffic with minimal overhead, which prevents the more expensive devices from wasting time down the line.

This section will give a taste of the important points and complexities of network-based blocking as a frustration strategy. For more in-depth coverage of network issues, see Kaufman et al. [24], and for a discussion focused more specifically on firewall usage and configuration, see Cheswick et al. [23].

Routers and Access Control Lists

Routers direct traffic throughout a network. To do this efficiently, they only inspect the address to which the information is going, and sometimes where it came from. Therefore, any security services installed on a router only have access to this information. When the device begins to inspect information beyond the addressing information, it becomes an IDS, IPS, or proxy.

For the remainder of the chapter we will treat routers and network devices as inert, trusted participants in the network. Before we do that, a quick reminder that this aspect is not to be taken for granted. As routers have become more complicated, they require remote management. In this regard they are just like any other computer, and these remote management interfaces can be compromised. Primarily this is via the Systems Network Management Protocol (SNMP), such as reported in Vulnerability Note #225404 from US-CERT [25]. Furthermore, network devices have their own OSs; Cisco's IOS (not to be confused with Apple's iOS) is one example. These operating systems also can have vulnerabilities, just like any other OS.

Access control lists (ACLs, sometimes pronounced "ackles," as rhyming with "tackles") are the basic way in which routers exert static policy decisions on routing behavior. They are a coarse but centralized method of frustrating the adversary. The rules in the ACL can operate on relatively few attributes of the packet: source and destination IP, IP type (e.g., TCP, UDP, ICMP, etc.), and some attributes based on the protocol type like ports in TCP/UDP and flags in TCP. ACLs usually specify an information pattern and an action. The information pattern is some set of values for the addressing information, specifying a value for one or more source or destination IP addresses (as either a single address or range of addresses), source or destination ports, and TCP flags if applicable. The action is usually one of a small list, such as allow, block, or log, or a combination of two, such as block and log.

Routers have four interface types, which are named in a mildly confusing manner. There are two external interfaces, which connect to routers outside the organization, and two internal interfaces, connecting to computers the organization owns. There are two incoming, or ingress, interfaces that receive messages, and two outgoing, or egress, interfaces that send messages. One internal interface is incoming, taking packets from computers the organization owns, and one is outgoing, sending packets to computers the organization owns that it has processed from the outside. Likewise, one external interface is ingress, and one is egress. These interfaces are always duplexed—the internal ingress interface is connected to the external egress interface, and the external ingress interface is connected to the internal egress interface.

All security policies should be applied at the ingress, or incoming, interfaces. This saves some computing time—the router doesn't have to process the bad packet before it drops it. Therefore, while the outgoing interfaces are important, they are not relevant to security policies. So, when we mention a router interface, if not specified, we will are referring to the ingress interface.

The defender should specify a very different ACL on the external and internal router interfaces. The external-interface ACLs are to frustrate the adversary's ability to get blatantly malicious packets into the organization. The external-interface ACL should also make scanning and reconnaissance more difficult for the adversary. For example, if the organization only has one public DNS server, only that server needs to accept incoming traffic on port 53. The defender can frustrate the adversary's ability to scan for computers listening on port 53 by blocking traffic to any computer but the DNS server on this port. Note that this does not mean a skilled adversary has no chance of scanning an internal network for erroneously configured services on port 53. It just means the adversary needs to compromise or manipulate some computer inside the trusted zone behind the ACL to do so. A successful ACL implementation does not mean that the defender can ignore the host hardening recommendations mentioned earlier in the chapter.

There are several quick wins for external-interface ACLs that will reduce bogus traffic volumes and frustrate an opportunistic adversary. Any packet on the external-ingress interface with a source IP address from inside the organization is spoofed, or forged, and an attempt to deceive some internal host. These should be blocked. There are also some well-known abusive packets, such as a "smurf attack," which involves sending ICMP echo requests to a broadcast address [26]; a "Christmas tree scan" to fingerprint OSs and services, where all the TCP flags are set (so called because the packet is "lit up like a Christmas tree") [27, ch. 15]; and some easily abused services such as UDP echo (port 7) [28], qotd (UDP port 17) [29], and chargen (UDP port 19) [30].

Internal-interface ACLs have different goals from external-interface ones. The external interface will deal with a lot of backscatter—the remnants of attacks elsewhere [31]. While backscatter is annoying, there is not much to be done about it, and so like a loud construction project outside your window, it is best to just close the window and ignore it. However, it would be rather rare for a construction worker to come into someone's office and start jack hammering and pouring concrete—and a serious security breach. Likewise, the internal interface of any network security device should also block malicious outgoing behavior, but instead of ignoring the traffic, rather treat it as evidence of a possible infection inside the organization, namely a recognition strategy. Since these events are less common outbound, an internal interface can also be more strict about what it blocks. This is an example of synergy between different layers in the security strategy, and Chapters 11 through 14 discuss recognition strategies in detail.

Firewalls

A *firewall* is any device that enforces a set of access rules on communications between two networks [32]. A static ACL implemented in a router is an example of a simple network security device, a static firewall. The concepts from the previous section can be expanded and generalized to increase usability and frustrate the more nuanced attacker. Increasing usability may be the more important feature, as an unusable security device or policy will be bypassed by frustrated users and decrease security in practice [33,34]. The increased flexibility is accomplished by either remembering the status of individual communications or inspecting more details about the packets on the network, or a combination.

With a static firewall, certain common ports would need to be permitted through to the clients on the inside simply for the network to be usable, such as ssh (22) [35], DNS (53) [8], and web (80) [36,37]. This provides opportunities to the adversary. He or she can attempt connections to internal hosts on these ports. This is akin to building a wall around a city, but leaving a wide gap open. The gap is necessary for the citizens to get in and out of the city, but all it does when the city is attacked is to force the invading army or flood waters to come in through a known place. As with cities, in the case of the Internet and information security, this approach is not sufficient. Draw bridges and gates are dynamic defenses. Though simple, they can be moved as information about those nearby changes.

A dynamic firewall can be configured with rules that will dynamically make changes to its ACL. This has many advantages. Although we don't want to permit any host on the Internet to communicate with our computers arbitrarily, if a user wants to connect to most any web server, for example, the firewall ought to permit the legitimate connection. This is accomplished by keeping track of what the computers on the internal network ask for and letting legitimate responses come back through the firewall on the external interface [23, p. 188]. The device must have a basic understanding of the IP protocols being used and expanded internal memory resources to keep track of unique connections, defined by the set of [time, source IP, source port, destination IP, destination port]. Dynamic firewall rules usually are of the form that if the device logs a packet going out to a computer A on a certain port from internal computer B, allow a response back in from A to B on the same port. Usually these rules expire after a small number of seconds, to limit the time period where the opening can be abused.

To accurately make rules dynamically, a firewall must remember the status of communications on the network. This process is known as *keeping state*, since the device keeps a record of the state of all the communications. Firewalls that keep state are known as *stateful*. What features of the communication are stored, and for how long, may vary from device to device. A stateful device has more information to make access decisions, since it knows about past communications as well as the present. This comes at some performance cost. Technically, a stateful device does not have to use dynamic rule sets, but in practice almost any stateful firewall is also a dynamic firewall.

The dynamic firewall may keep state, but the term firewall means the device does not inspect the contents of packets. A device that inspects packet contents should be called an IDS, IPS, or proxy. A packet that a dynamic firewall right-fully accepts may have an unexpected payload. There are at least two situations in which this is common. One, if the network is operating a server it must expect unsolicited traffic to that computer. The point of servers is to give services to a relatively unknown set of client computers. On the other hand, even a trusted source may have become untrustworthy. In this case, a client may be tricked into requesting malicious content from the adversary. In one instance of such a case, malicious advertisements were served on Yahoo!'s and Fox's websites [38]. No dynamic firewall would protect the client here—the computer did ask for the Yahoo! web server, it just got much more than it bargained for in return. A defense that inspects packet contents, such as a proxy, would be needed.

Proxies

In general usage, a *proxy* is something that acts on the behalf of someone else [39]. Following this common English usage, as opposed to firewalls, proxies do not allow two hosts to connect directly; rather each host will have a complete connection with the proxy [32]. Proxies are, therefore, more com-plicated, more expensive both monetarily and in computational resources, and allow the defender to implement more detailed defensive strategies. But as Uncle Ben reminds us, "with great power there must also come great responsibility" [40], and so with the added detail power available in a proxy also comes increased upkeep costs and a greater chance the defender will make a configuration error or misunderstand a policy violation. Yet, when implemented properly, a proxy will greatly increase the defender's ability to frustrate, and recognize, attackers.

Proxies disrupt the communication between two computers in a way that firewalls do not. Figure 5.3 demonstrates the effect on a single request and response set of messages. This session duplication is one major computing cost and source of delay in proxies. Since the proxy will establish a new session of the application, the proxy must implement completely whatever application for which it is a proxy. However, there is a significant benefit to frustrating the adversary: only the network address of the proxy is known to the outside world.

Proxies can be divided into network-level proxies, which only translate addresses and ports, and application-level proxies, which proxy a particular

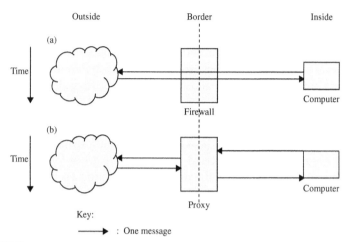

FIGURE 5.3
One message and response transiting (a) a firewall and (b) a proxy service.

application. The most common network-level proxy is the Network Address Translation (NAT) service [41]. One common example of an application-level proxy is a web proxy for HTTP and HTTPS sessions. A common open-source web proxy is the Squid Proxy [42]. Both kinds of proxies can be used to frustrate the adversary when implemented by the defending organization. There are also some frustrating uses of proxies by the adversary of which any defender should be aware.

NAT for Frustration

NAT allows for a large number of computers to advertise only a single IP address to the public Internet. The internal network uses a reserved address space,[1] and the NAT device maintains a table between these private addresses and individual external communications and tags the communications by manipulating port numbers. NAT was initially introduced as a temporary fix for issues of Internet address space depletion and scaling. The primary existing addressing scheme is IP version 4 (IPv4), and its roughly 4 billion addresses are nearly exhausted. The original NAT document also addresses some security and privacy trade-offs of the service [41]. The defender is interested in these security and privacy side effects for frustration purposes, however, keep in mind that these are side effects of NAT, and not a design goal, unlike in some other proxies.

---

[1]The private address spaces for this purpose are the 10.0.0.0/8, 172.16.0.0/12, and 192.168.0.0/16 net blocks [43].

NAT devices provide a simple, application-independent privacy shield for the defender's computers. When a packet leaves the network, it is not immediately obvious which computer issued it. This screen cannot protect public services, such as the web server, since it needs to have a well-defined public address to perform its function. NAT also makes it impossible to address an internal machine directly from the outside. In many cases, this is a desirable security property, however, NAT prevents legitimate usages as well. This shortcoming has led to some interesting methods to circumvent the problem, such as Session Traversal Utilities for NAT (STUN) [44], proving that such security side effects as the privacy screen can be overcome by determined users, and thus determined adversaries. Note that STUN is an official IETF standard for legitimate use, just like NAT itself. It is not realistic for the defender to implement NAT and expect it not to be defeated. It is not a defensive technology and so the Internet community is free to subvert the privacy side effects for usability concerns, such as via STUN.

NAT provides a useful service in frustrating the attacker's reconnaissance of the target network via eavesdropping and counting target IP addresses and mapping observed requests to specific computers. NAT also adds a layer of inconvenience when the attacker attempts to address internal hosts. While these are desirable security services, NAT does not guarantee them. Furthermore, NAT breaks the ability to secure TCP sessions with a protocol such as IPsec, because NAT modifies the TCP header, thereby preventing end-to-end encryption or verification of it [41, p. 7]. A mature organization should implement the IETF-recommended solution for adding IP space, IP version 6 (IPv6). IPv6 has 128 bits of address space, as compared to the 32 bits in IPv4. IPv6 manages the address space depletion issue, and the organization should implement ACLs and internal proxies to provide the desired security services, as described in this chapter.

Application Proxies for Frustration

When the defenders implement a proxy service on a computer on their internal network for use by computers they own, let's call that an internal proxy service. Internal proxy services have several desirable properties. Since they require planning and maintenance, internal proxy services are often implemented for commonly or heavily used services, such as web, email, and DNS. The following discussion will take a web proxy as an example, however, the principles are applicable to a proxy service for any application. Figure 5.4 demonstrates a simplified network map with a web server and web proxy in the recommended conservative configuration, and Table 5.1 lists the simplified access controls to use in this example configuration. This setup is analogous to that for a DNS proxy service or another service.

An internal web proxy will frustrate an attacker in two ways: footprint minimization and protocol enforcement. First, only the web proxy will make web

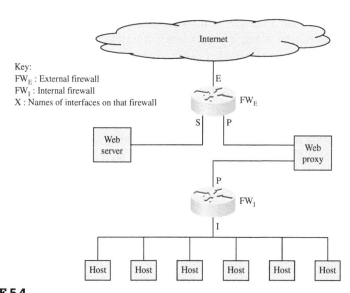

FIGURE 5.4
A simplified network map demonstrating a useful implementation of a web service and internal proxy.

requests to the outside world. Therefore, the attacker will not know which or how many hosts on the defender's network use the web, and will therefore not be able to develop a list of targets by eavesdropping. Second, the proxy must completely implement the HTTP protocol to communicate with each the internal computer and the external web server. If the external server attempts to supply abusive or malicious content, or the internal host simply requests a resource known to be abusive, the proxy should not relay that information back to the internal computer. Since the proxy has a logically separate connection with the internal computer, this is technically relatively easy. The proxy also has access to all information that would go to the host in the same format the host would view it (i.e., reconstructed), and so can make a judgment on the complete package that should not permit the attacker to obfuscate any attacks.

Due to the fact that proxy servers must implement the applications they proxy, they may be vulnerable to errors in the protocols in a way that firewalls are not. Therefore, it is particularly important to harden the application proxy against attacks on that application and keep its patches up to date. The host hardening guidelines in this chapter are a beginning, however, more paranoia is likely justified. Also notice that the proxy is not located on the same subnet as the other internal hosts; this location would be called a demilitarized zone (DMZ). This placement limits potential damage to the internal computers in case the proxy is compromised, and limits the opportunities

Table 5.1 Example Firewall ACLs for Figure 5.4

Device	Interface	Action	Source IP	Source Port	Destination IP	Destination Port	Notes
FW_E	E	Allow	*†	*	Web server	80, 443	External requests to our web server
FW_E	E	Allow	Dynamic	80, 443, 8080	Web proxy	>1024	Allow legitimate replies to requests by the proxy
FW_E	E	Block	*	*	*	*	Default deny
FW_E	S	Allow	Web server	80, 443	Dynamic	Dynamic	Allow the web server to reply to legitimate requests
FW_E	S	Block	*	*	*	*	Default deny
FW_E	P	Allow	Web proxy	*	*†	80, 443, 8080	Allow the web proxy to make reasonable requests
FW_E	P	Block	*	*	*	*	Default deny
FW_I	I	Allow	Internal	>1024	Web proxy	8080, 3128	***
FW_I	I	Block	*	*	*	*	Default deny
FW_I	P	Allow	Web proxy	8080, 3128	Internal, dynamic	>1024	Allow the web proxy to answer requests
FW_I	P	Block	*	*	*	*	Default deny

*is a common symbol for a wildcard, that is "ANY value will pass"
†To be complete this should exclude any private or internal IP addresses.
***Don't run the web proxy as root, and allow the proxy port through (3128 is the Squid default, change as needed).
Note: This is an example, and not production grade.

for compromised internal hosts to attack the proxy and escalate the infection. This location is an example of network architecture for frustration, as described later in the chapter.

Proxies that Aid the Attacker

The attacker can also use proxies external to the organization. In this respect, the attacker/defender roles are flipped, and the attacker is attempting to frustrate the defender. But before terminology gets too muddled, let's just explain an example scenario.

The defender has an ACL rule to prevent internal connections to a particular malicious IP address. The attacker notices the disruption, however he or she is unable to alter the malicious resource's IP address. In the same way an internal proxy service obscures the internal IP addresses using a service, so too would a proxy service external to the organization hide the attacker's IP address. With a new IP address, the attacker will bypass the ACL rule. There are many free, open proxies available on the Internet that could be used for this purpose [45], and the TOR (derived from The Onion Router, although officially the name is no longer an acronym) network would also largely accomplish this goal [46]. Internal users frustrated by strict ACLs may also turn to external proxies to bypass security policies.

If the defender is implementing ACLs as black lists, or lists of resources to block access to, lists of active open-proxy IP addresses should be added to the block list. The most secure and restrictive option would be to only permit users to visit known-benign resources—that is, to use a white list—and to route those users through a web proxy and use firewall ACLs to prevent all other traffic on common web ports 80, 443, and 8080 [37]. This was the tactic in mind for the example in Figure 5.4.

NETWORK ARCHITECTURE AND FRUSTRATION

The physical and logical connections between devices are an important aspect of a security strategy. There are aspects of network architecture that enable effective policies to be implemented, and there are architectures that in themselves contribute to a security strategy.

The first enabling aspect of a network architecture is simply to have it be planned and well documented. It is difficult to make effective access control policy when the defender does not know which networks and subnets contain which resources. This includes both a good logical map or chart of what is connected to what, and physically labeling cable and devices so they can be easily charted. What the labeling scheme is does not much matter, but it must be consistent.

The second enabling aspect of a network architecture is based on the old principle of "need to know," with the general best practices of least access and least privilege in mind [47]. On a local subnet, each computer has unrestricted access to each other computer on the subnet. However, each computer should have unrestricted access to the minimum number of computers that it can while still accomplishing its function. For servers, this generally means placing them in a screened subnet or DMZ, logically separated from the outside world, end-user host computers, and other servers [23, p. 14]. With each important class of computers in their own subnet, useful ACL rules can be written for the devices that control access between the subnets. Just putting a web server on its own subnet doesn't protect it, but properly protecting it without that step is infeasible.

Network architecture can be used as part of the strategy itself. An architecture can frustrate the adversary's ability to do traffic analysis by keeping traffic segregated from the public Internet. For an organization in a single building this may be trivial. But for a larger organization this takes some planning. Furthermore, many organizations find it inefficient to buy or lease a dedicated cable between sites. A more economical option is to deploy a virtual private network (VPN) between two sites. Without a VPN, even if the application contents are encrypted, the adversary could still count the number of users of a service, and profile how often it is used by observing network headers. A VPN eliminates this possibility—all the adversary can know is how much data is transmitted over the VPN. This effect is illustrated in Figure 5.5.

A VPN carves out a logically distinct network cryptographically. More details on cryptography are covered in Chapter 8. VPNs have several distinct uses, and there are a few different implementation strategies, IPsec [48] and SSL/TLS [49] being the most common [50]. To construct a protected connection between two sites, each computer at a site uses a network proxy to connect to the other site. The proxy has a long-standing VPN with a proxy within the other site. The remote proxy terminates the VPN and then the connections can proceed as if they transited private, trusted networks instead of the Internet. Implementing a VPN requires some care; for details on uses see Cheswick et al. [23, p. 236ff], for a comparison of implementations see Rosen [50], for an accessible discussion of IPsec and TLS see Anderson [5, p. 669], and for the details see Kent and Seo [48], Dierks and Rescorla [49], and Kaufman et al. [51].

A VPN can also be used by remote computers to create a trusted connection across the Internet to within the host organization. This is helpful for employees who may travel often. The defender would like to offer them services as if they are in the office, but cannot just open those services to the Internet population at large without serious risks. The employee's computer has a

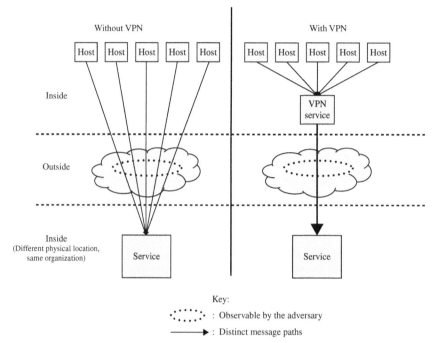

FIGURE 5.5
VPN usage to frustrate traffic analysis by an adversary.

long-standing secret with the VPN endpoint within the organization, which allows the two computers to resume a VPN upon the employee's request. This enables service minimization in general, while still permitting employees to access resources in a reasonable way. Such remote VPNs are fraught with dangers, however. If the employee's computer is connected to the Internet via a second network connection, then that computer has created a bridge between the Internet and the internal network that bypasses the major security mechanisms. Therefore, the VPN endpoint must be treated with the utmost care, and placed in a heavily screened and monitored subnet of its own.

SUMMARY

There are a variety of techniques available to the defender to frustrate the adversary by minimizing various aspects of the IT infrastructure. Broadly speaking, these strategies are either host-based or network-based strategies, with each particular strategy carrying its own benefits and shortcomings. The strategies include such elements as disabling services, local intrusion detection and prevention, service wrappers, application management, access control lists, firewalls, proxies, and network design. An intelligent and comprehensive array of the available strategies is the best defensive strategy, as there is no single solution. This chapter presents frustration strategies in the context of specific available technologies. Chapter 6 continues the discussion of frustration strategies, broadening the context to include formal verification of implementations and strategies.

REFERENCES

[1] Manadhata PK, Wing JM. Attack surface measurement. Retrieved from <http://www.cs.cmu.edu/~pratyus/as.html>; 2012. Retrieved Nov 14, 2012.

[2] Quote Investigator. Everything should be made as simple as possible, but not simpler. Retrieved from <http://quoteinvestigator.com/2011/05/13/einstein-simple/>; 2011. Retrieved Nov 6, 2012.

[3] Calaprice A, editor. The ultimate quotable Einstein. Princeton, NJ: Princeton University Press; 2010.

[4] Varian H. System reliability and free riding. Econ Inf Secur 2004:1–15.

[5] Anderson RJ. Security engineering: a guide to building dependable distributed systems. 2nd ed. New York: Wiley; 2008.

[6] Zimmerman D. The finger user information protocol. RFC 1288; 1991.

[7] Google. Security Whitepaper: google apps messaging and collaboration products. Google, Mountain View, CA; 2011.

[8] Mockapetris P. RFC 1034—Domain names—concepts and facilities. Retrieved from <http://www.ietforg/rfc/rfc1034txt>; 1987, November. Retrieved Nov 24, 2012.

[9] Malone KM, Hinman AR. Vaccination mandates: the public health imperative and individual rights. Law in Public Health Practice; 2003, p. 262–84.

[10] Pennington AG, Strunk JD, Griffin JL, Soules CA, Goodson GR, Ganger GR. Storage-based intrusion detection: watching storage activity for suspicious behavior. Proceedings of the twelth USENIX Security Symposium. Washington, DC; 2003.

[11] Forrest S, Hofmeyr SA, Somayaji A, Longstaff TA. A sense of self for unix processes. 1996 IEEE Symposium on Security and Privacy. p. 120–128.

[12] Tripwire, Inc. Open-source tripwire. Retrieved from <http://sourceforge.net/projects/tripwire/>; 2012. Retrieved Nov 16 2012.

[13] Microsoft. Domain controller roles. Retrieved from <http://technet.microsoft.com/en-us/library/cc786438(v=ws.10).aspx>; 2010. Retrieved Nov 16, 2012.

[14] Neuman C, Yu T, Hartman S, Raeburn K. The Kerberos Network Authentication Service (V5); 2005. RFC 4120. Updated by RFCs 4537, 5021, 5896, 6111, 6112, 6113, 6649.

[15] Stallings W. Network security essentials: applications and standards. 4th ed. Englewood Cliffs, NJ: Prentice-Hall; 2011.

[16] Venema W. TCP wrapper: network monitoring, access control, and booby traps. Eindhoven University of Technology, Eindhoven, Netherlands; 1991.

[17] Rhodes T. 15.6. In: FreeBSD handbook: The FreeBSD Documentation Project. FreeBSD.org; 2012. Retrieved from <http://www5.us.freebsd.org/doc/handbook/tcpwrappers.html>; Retrieved Nov 24, 2012.

[18] Baset SA, Schulzrinne H. An Analysis of the Skype Peer-to-Peer Internet Telephony Protocol. 2004. arXiv preprint cs/041 2017.

[19] Biondi P, Desclaux, F. Silver Needle in the Skype. Black Hat Europe 6:25–47.

[20] Anderson R, Barton C, Böhme R, Clayton R, van Eeten MJG, Levi M, et al. Measuring the Cost of Cybercrime. 11th Workshop on the Economics of Information Security, Berlin; 2012.

[21] Bonneau J, Preibusch S, Anderson R. A birthday present every eleven Wallets? The security of customer-chosen banking PINs. Financial Cryptography and Data Security; 2012. p. 25–40.

[22] Hall C, Anderson R, Clayton R, Ouzounis E, Trimintzios P. Resilience of the internet interconnection ecosystem. ENISA Heraklion, Greece; 2011.

[23] Cheswick WR, Bellovin SM, Rubin AD. Firewalls and internet security: repelling the Wily Hacker. Reading, MA: Addison-Wesley Professional; 2003.

[24] Kaufman C, Perlman R, Speciner M. Network security: private communication in a public world. Englewood Cliffs, NJ: Prentice-Hall; 2002.

[25] Orlando M. Grutzmacher K. HP/H3C and Huawei Networking Equipment H3C-user SNMP Vulnerability. US-CERT, Washington, DC; 2012.

[26] Javvin. Smurf attack and fraggle attack. Retrieved from <http://www.javvin.com/networksecurity/SmurfAttack.html>; 2012. Retrieved Nov 17, 2012.

[27] Lyon GF. Nmap network scanning: the official nmap project guide to network discovery and security scanning. Nmap Project; 2011. Retrieved from <http://nmap.org/book/toc.html>. Retrieved Nov 2, 2012.

[28] Postel J. Echo protocol. RFC 862; 1983.

[29] Postel J. Quote of the day protocol. RFC 865; 1983.

[30] Postel J. Character generator protocol. RFC 864; 1983.

[31] Moore D, Voelker G, Savage S. Inferring Internet Denial-of-Service Activity. In: USENIX Security Symposium. Washington, D.C.; Aug, 2001. Retrieved from <http://www.caida.org/publications/papers/2001/BackScatter/usenixsecurity01.pdf>.

[32] Newman D. Benchmarking terminology for firewall performance. RFC 2647; 1999.

[33] Adams A, Sasse MA. Users are not the enemy. Commun ACM 1999;42(12):40–6.

[34] Cranor L, Garfinkel S. Security and Usability: Designing Secure Systems that People can Use. O'Reilly Media, Inc. Sebastopol, CA; 2005.

[35] Ylonen T, Lonvick C. The Secure Shell (SSH) Transport Layer Protocol. RFC 4253. Updated by RFC 6668; 2006.

[36] Reynolds J, Postel J. Assigned Numbers. RFC 1700. Obsoleted by RFC 3232; 1994.

[37] Reynolds J. Assigned Numbers: RFC 1700 is replaced by an Online Database. RFC 3232; 2002.

[38] Sejtko J. Ads Poisoning—JS:Prontexi. Avast! Retrieved from <http://blog.avast.com/2010/02/18/ads-poisoning-%E2%80%93-jsprontexi/>; 2010. Retrieved Nov 19, 2012.

[39] Collins English Dictionary. Complete and Unabridged. 10th ed. Retrieved from <http://dictionary.reference.com/browse/proxy>; 2012. Retrieved Nov 2, 2012.

[40] Lee S, Ditko S, Kirby J. Amazing Fantasy #15. Marvel Comics; 1962.

[41] Egevang K, Francis P. The IP Network Address Translator (NAT). RFC 1631. Obsoleted by RFC 3022; 1994.

[42] Wessels D. What is Squid? Retrieved from <http://www.squid-cache.org/Intro/>; 2012. Retrieved Nov 16, 2012.

[43] Rekhter Y, Moskowitz B, Karrenberg D, de Groot GJ, Lear E. Address Allocation for Private Internets. RFC 1918; 1996.

[44] Rosenberg J, Mahy R, Matthews P, Wing D. Session Traversal Utilities for NAT (STUN). RFC 5389; 2008.

[45] Proxy org. Proxy.org Frequently Asked Questions (FAQs). Retrieved from <http://proxy.org/faq.shtml>; 2012. Retrieved Nov 17, 2012.

[46] The Tor Project, Inc. Tor: Overview. Retrieved from <https://www.torproject.org/about/over-view.html.en>; 2012. Retrieved Nov 18, 2012.

[47] Saltzer JH. Protection and the control of information sharing in multics. Commun ACM 1974;17(7):388–402.

[48] Kent S, Seo K. Security Architecture for the Internet Protocol. RFC 4301. Updated by RFC 6040; 2005.

[49] Dierks T, Rescorla E. The Transport Layer Security (TLS) Protocol Version 1.2. RFC 5246. Updated by RFCs 5746, 5878, 6176; 2008.

[50] Rosen R. Creating VPNs with IPsec and SSL/TLS. Linux J 2008(165):10.

[51] Kaufman C, Hoffman P, Nir Y, Eronen P. Internet key exchange protocol Version 2 (IKEv2). RFC 5996. Updated by RFC 5998; 2010.

Chapter Review Questions

1. What is the general goal of a frustration strategy?

2. Provide a one-sentence definition of the four host-based frustration strategies introduced in this chapter.

3. Distinguish between the following types of firewalls, without using the words themselves in your answer (static, dynamic, state, stateful, stateless):
    a. Static versus dynamic
    b. Stateful versus stateless

4. Similarly, distinguish between:
    a. Firewall vs. proxy

5. What features of application-level proxies make them more vulnerable to adversaries? Give an example mitigation of these risks.

6. Why is an appropriate network architecture required to build effective ACLs?

7. What types of frustration strategies are best implemented in network-based approaches, and what types in host-based approaches?

Chapter Exercises

1. Let's say that some hacktivist group that shall remain anonymous has decided to target your organization's public web server with a DoS attack. The strategy used is an old one—a TCP SYN flood. Hosts from the Internet are making legitimate connection requests to the web server, but they are not completing the TCP handshake. The web server keeps the port open and the resources allocated to answer the handshake until the handshake times out, which takes several seconds. This quickly exhausts one particular resource of the web server—the number of TCP port numbers that it can keep open at one time. Legitimate users cannot access the web server. Without expanding the web server's resources, what are some strategies that you could implement to frustrate the attackers? Describe at least two host-based and two network-based strategies.

2. Describe the security and privacy features that NAT happens to provide, and then try to describe how these features could be more reliably provided, using some combination of host-based, network-based, and network architecture–based frustration strategies.

3. Not all frustration strategies are technology based. In what ways could you train average users to make themselves more resistant to social engineering attacks, such as phishing? (For a definition of phishing, see Chapter 7.)

4. Draw a network diagram, similar to Figure 5.4, but instead for a secure DNS service. The service must provide resolution of names for use by internal hosts (e.g., the web proxy) to hosts in the organization, and the service must provide resolutions of public names (e.g., the web server) to the Internet. Also, create a table similar to Table 5.1 with the general ACL rules that should be implemented to secure the services on your diagram.

CHAPTER 6

Frustration Strategies: Formal Verification

INTRODUCTION

Most security defenses are based on best practice. These defenses work by improving the relative security of the systems involved (in comparison to other possible configurations), rather than by providing a fundamentally trustable infrastructure on which to produce, process, and disseminate information. For many applications, this is sufficient—for example, where adversaries are unlikely to expend the resources to determine and evade security measures. For especially critical systems, where high-value information is stored, best practice may not be sufficient. A frustration strategy in such systems may include application of a formally secure computing system, even though such systems may be somewhat difficult to apply and use.

The implementation of a formally secure computing system starts with development of a formal model of security—defining security before building it. In a technical sense, the word "formal" refers to working from a basis of explicitly defined aspects of a system, and then expressing properties using those aspects and a restricted set of explicitly defined operations, based on rules of mathematics [1]. This chapter starts with an explanation of how these explicit definitions are presented. Over the last several decades, a number of formal security models have been developed and applied [2]. This chapter describes the more common formal models of security. It ends with a discussion of the limits of formal models when applied to common security needs.

SECURITY CASE: KERNEL HACKING

The most commonly implemented method of security is reactive: wait for a vulnerability to be identified (or a security penetration to occur) and then do a minimal correction (a "patch" in technical jargon) to deal with the vulnerability—a process often termed *penetrate and patch* security. One difficulty with this process is that it is extremely labor-intensive, as vulnerabilities are constantly identified, leaving the manufacturers constantly developing patches and the users constantly applying them. Another difficulty is that this process does not address fundamental aspects of the system that are insecure: when the insecurity of an operating system comes from the structure of the system itself, rather than from details of how the operating system is implemented.

As an example, consider a commonly used structure when implementing an operating system: the kernel. Kernels are small, trusted parts of a system that provide services on which the other parts of the system (including resource allocation, object control, or the program interface) depend [1]. When the kernel structure of an operating system is shown to be vulnerable, it may be a systemic vulnerability that cannot be fully addressed by minimal changes.

There are a number of methods to exploit the kernel structure, which has been applied against both Windows [3] and Linux operating systems [4]. There are a variety of basic approaches taken in these exploit methods: corruption of the kernel (e.g., via feeding information to the kernel that causes overwrite of the kernel executable instructions), augmenting the kernel (e.g., replacing pieces of the kernel with code from the attacker, done via a device driver or other normal augmentation method), man-in-the-middle (e.g., intercepting calls to the kernel from the application software and inserting calls to malicious code in its place), and augmentation of the application (e.g., exploiting kernel operations that set up for program execution to insert malicious code to be executed at the program user's privilege level) [5]. All of these attacks work by identifying vulnerabilities in the kernel, in the configuration methods, and in the interaction between the kernel and either the operating system or the programs being executed by the user.

Dealing with these systemic vulnerabilities demands a more thorough approach than is currently practiced. While specific malicious attacks can (and are) patched, the underlying insecurity remains. The kernel itself needs to be designed to be secure in its internal operation and updates, and to assure interactions between the kernel and the operating system. The secure design requires a detailed and unambiguous expression of secure action, which implies a formal security model.

FORMAL MODELS AND MODEL VERIFICATION

Formally secure operating systems are designed and implemented in compliance with formal security models. A security model is a schematic description of a set of entities and relationships by which a specified set of security services are provided by or within a system [1]. The description provides an unambiguous and consistent definition of secure processing within the system. Several examples of these formal security models will be given later in this chapter. The model itself does not specify any processing, but rather provides a set of properties that must be present for any secure processing.

Formal models are often expressed mathematically, since the regularity of mathematics (where the same rules always apply) provides a means of expressing things without the ambiguity of natural languages. Two of the most common forms of mathematics used for this expression are high-level algebras and mathematical logic. A high-level algebra defines objects with explicit operations, then uses those operations to express desirable properties [6]. For example, a model may define algebraic objects "file" as a tuple $F = \{C,o,p,s\}$ where C is the content, o identifies the owner, p is a permission, and s is a file state (open, closed, read, modified, and others if needed by the specification). A permission, in turn, would be described as a mapping between users and rights. Using these descriptions, the model can define grant(i, (u,q), F) (indicating the user i is granting user u a permission q with respect to the file F). An algebraic formal model may then express that users may grant write access if they are the owner of the file by the property:

$$grant(x,(y,\text{write}),F) = \{F.C,F.o,F.p + (y,\text{write}),F.s\} \text{ if } x = F.o; F \text{ otherwise}$$

This property states that a user x is providing a user y with permission to write on a file F if x is the owner of F; if not, F is unchanged, which in this case means y is provided no new permissions on F. This property allows for the case where y already has write permissions on F, but x is not the owner and tries to grant y write permissions redundantly—x's attempt to add permissions would fail, but y would retain the permissions previously granted.

A mathematical logic describes properties in terms of predicates—combinations of statements asserted to be true [7]. These predicates are mathematical expressions of characteristics of the system. A logic-based security model may express that a file F has an owner o as $o = O(F)$ and that y's permissions for F contain w (for write) as $w \varepsilon P(y,F)$. Then we can express that users may grant write access only if they are the owner of the file as $g(x,y,F,w) \leftrightarrow x = O(F)$. In contrast to the algebraic semantic, the logical semantics simply state the granting—they provide no model of how such a grant is accomplished. However, the redundant (and unauthorized) grant described earlier could also be handled via the logical statement, in that while x's unauthorized grant would violate the principle (and should be blocked by security controls), a prior authorized grant would be unaffected by the attempted grant (since the statement of the property does not describe denial of permissions previously granted).

Once the initial definitions are laid out, further properties may be described in the formal model using the operations of the underlying mathematics. While such constructions may become difficult to read, they do follow regular structures and can be manipulated in a systematic manner. The regularity of structure yields unambiguous statements, which allows for consistency in design and implementation, and may make the resulting property descriptions suitable for formal proof.

As system developers construct security models, they also apply those models to verify and validate the security of the systems being developed. Verification is the process of examining information to establish the truth of a claimed fact or value [1]. In security, claimed facts or values are expressions of the security properties of the system, and are verified with respect to the security model.

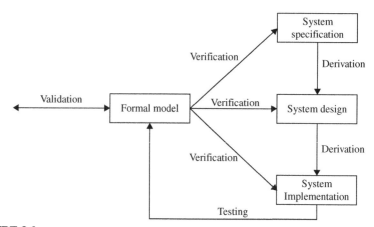

FIGURE 6.1
Formal models, verification, and validation.

This is done in several ways, as diagrammed in Figure 6.1. In the construction approach the developers progressively derive the design and implementation of the system from its specification while establishing that each stage in the derivation is consistent with the security model [8]. In the proof approach, the developers establish the consistency of each portion of the design or implementation with the security model via application of mathematical proof techniques [9]. In the testing approach, the developers identify test cases from either the elements of the security model or the assumptions present in it, then apply those test cases to establish consistency between the model and the system implementation (or, less commonly, the system design) [10].

Validation is the process of establishing the soundness or correctness of a construct [1]. In security, the developers validate that the approach taken in construction of the security model is sound with respect to the intended security environment for the system under development. In contrast to verification, which establishes truth in terms of consistency between the system and the model, validation establishes truth between the model and the application environment (i.e., the real world). But while verification will hold for any environment that meets its assumptions, validation will only hold for the specific class of environments to which it is applied. Still, the unambiguity and regularity of the security model provides for a far more complete validation than do informal methods for security.

DISCRETIONARY MODELS

Formal models may apply to describe multiple aspects of the information system security, including security policies. One division of these policies is into mandatory and discretionary policies, particularly for access control. Discretionary access control is defined as an access control service that (1) enforces a security policy based on the identity of system entities and the authorizations associated with the identities, and (2) incorporates a concept of ownership in which access rights for a system resource may be granted and revoked by the entity that owns the resource [1]. This definition implies that different users may or may not apply security consistently to similar objects, and that a single user may or may not apply security consistently to different objects that they own. The advantage to a formal discretionary access control is that the mechanisms for securing objects are defined clearly, as are the dependencies between access rights.

Mandatory access control is an access control service that enforces a security policy based on comparing (1) security labels, which indicate how sensitive or critical system resources are, with (2) security clearances, which indicate that system entities are eligible to access certain resources [1]. In contrast to discretionary access control, mandatory access control policies are enforced by the system, not the user, and are applied consistently across users and the objects that they own. However, as will be seen in the next two sections, mandatory access control models cover more restricted issues in security than discretionary access control models.

One simple model for discretionary access control is access groups. An access group is an algebra on the relationships between users and owners (self, collaborators, and other users on the computer), on which security controls can make access decisions based on the rights that the owner gives to various relationships. In the Unix/Linux access groups, users are assigned to groups, based on the roles they assume in the processes supported by the information on the computer [11]. More details on the applications of access controls are covered in chapter 7.

A single user may be assigned to one or more groups, and groups are defined with zero or more users. A group with zero users is a placeholder for a role not currently associated with the users on the computer, although it may be associated with programs. Each file is associated with one group. Figure 6.2 diagrams this access control method. Explicit access rights are granted on each file by the owner to each of these groups (often using the default settings configured for the owner), and access decisions are enforced by the operating system based on these access rights. The operations implemented to set, modify, and retrieve access rights can be modeled by algebraic rules, but informally, they correspond to access rights that can only be retrieved by individuals with read rights on the directory in which the file is stored. They are initially set to the default access rights configured by the owner of the file as part of his or her login environment. They can only be modified by the owner of the file or by individuals with write access to the directory in which the files are stored. While there have been proofs of selected security properties of this model [8], those properties tend to be somewhat weak, due to the vagary of the grouping of the relationship.

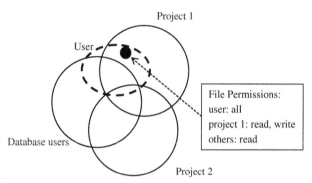

FIGURE 6.2
Group access control.

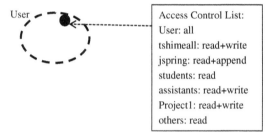

FIGURE 6.3
Access control list.

An access control list (ACL) is a mechanism that implements access control for a resource (e.g., a file, device, or area of memory) on the computer by enumerating the users or agents who are permitted to access the resource and stating, either implicitly or explicitly, the permissions granted to each user or agent [1]. Figure 6.3 diagrams an ACL for file protection. As an operational convenience, users are often enumerated by establishing groups, but this does not change the formal semantics of the ACL. Formally, this forms an algebra of tuples coupling users with privileges related to the object. The operations on this algebra identify allowed actions similar to the preceding access group discussion [12]. Generally, ACLs are tightly associated with the objects they protect, which means that analysis of all of the rights that an agent has requires polling of all of the objects on the computer. This level of indirection limits the generality of the properties that can be proved from ACLs.

An access matrix is a rectangular array of cells, with one row per subject and one column per object. The entry in a cell—that is, the entry for a particular subject–object pair—indicates the access mode that the subject is permitted to exercise on the object [1]. This extends the semantics of ACLs by allowing semantics across objects and across agents. One formal model expressed in

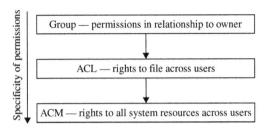

Specificity of permissions

Group — permissions in relationship to owner

ACL — rights to file across users

ACM — rights to all system resources across users

FIGURE 6.4
Discretionary access models.

terms of access control matrices is the Graham–Denning security model [13]. This model defines eight explicit rules for secure manipulation of the access control matrix. Developers may apply these rules as a formal means of verifying the security of the access control mechanisms, and then use these mechanisms for discretionary protection of information.

Figure 6.4 illustrates the relationships in models for discretionary access control. Taken together, these models offer defenders several options to control the access rights to files, devices, and other objects on defended computers. Many implementations of these access controls exist for a variety of operating systems. However, due to the nature of discretionary protection (users may or may not follow policy), it is insufficient to verify protections to information, which need mandatory access control.

CONFIDENTIALITY MODELS

Confidentiality, as described in Chapter 1, is one of the core properties on which security is based. If an organization cannot prevent unauthorized disclosure of information, then it is difficult for that organization to retain control over the use of that information. When the information is critical enough, a clear and unambiguous structure for the analysis of confidentiality becomes useful. This section describes two such structures: Bell–LaPadula, and Chinese Wall.

The Bell–LaPadula model [2] has both mandatory and discretionary components for expressing confidentiality properties in computer systems. Each object in the system has a label expressing its degree of confidentiality, and this label may not be changed or removed from the object (the "tranquility principle"). Each subject has both a clearance level and a current confidentiality level, which may not exceed the clearance level, and is no lower than the maximum confidentiality of the information that has been read. Bell and LaPadula express algebraic semantics in a state-machine form, then define a

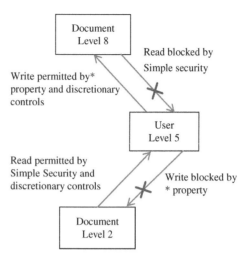

FIGURE 6.5
Bell–LaPadula properties.

number of security axioms. Figure 6.5 illustrates these axioms. For mandatory access control, the two most important axioms are the:

- *Simple security property:* No subject has read access to an object with a classification level higher than the clearance level of the subject.
- **-property ("star property"):* No subject may write to an object with a classification level lower than the current confidentiality level of the subject.

The first property prevents an actor from reading information at a level the subject isn't cleared for (or, colloquially, "no read up"). The second property prevents an actor from declassifying information for unauthorized dissemination (or, colloquially, "no write down"). The discretionary portion of the Bell–LaPadula model uses access control matrices similar to the Graham–Denning model, but with increased stringency to support the two central properties. The Bell–LaPadula model was successfully applied to several secure developments, including secure Xenix [8]. It forms the basis for many of the criteria used for certifying confidentiality, including the common criteria.

The Chinese Wall security model [14] is a formal logic model that takes a different approach to confidentiality than Bell–LaPadula. In the Chinese Wall model, the set of objects on a computer system is partitioned into conflict classes, where a conflict class is defined to be objects that relate to information from competing sources. For example, if an organization is receiving bids from multiple vendors, then the information on a given vendor is bound into

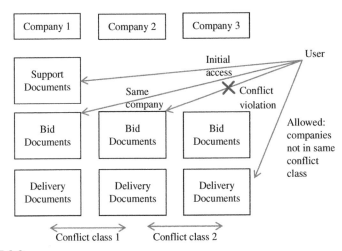

FIGURE 6.6
Chinese Wall security model properties.

a company subset, and the collection of company subsets for a given contract form a conflict class. If a subject may access multiple company subsets for the same contract, then the potential for information leakage (violating the competition) may occur. The model allows for sanitization of information, which involves transformation such that the source of the information may no longer be deduced from the information.

The Chinese Wall security model provides properties preventing such violations:

- Once a subject has accessed any object in a conflict class, then the subject may only access objects that belong to the same company subset, or that belong to an entirely separate conflict class. This implies that a subject may at most have access to one company subset in each conflict class and that if, for some conflict class X, there are at least Y company subsets, then at least Y subjects are required to process X.
- A subject may write to an object if the subject has accessed only information in compliance with the preceding property, and if no object containing unsanitized information has been read in another company subset in the same conflict class. This implies that unsanitized information remains contained in the company subset, but sanitized information may be processed freely.

Figure 6.6 visualizes these properties. The Chinese Wall security model has been incorporated in a number of audit models and applied to commercial data processing systems. Figure 6.7 contrasts the Bell–LaPadula and Chinese Wall confidentiality models.

	Bell-LaPadula	Chinese Wall
Basis	Algebraic	Logic
Goal	Privacy of objects	Information disclosure
Method	Rating of objects and subjects	Company subsets and conflict classes
Application	OS security	Financial security

FIGURE 6.7
Bell-LaPadula contrasted to Chinese Wall.

PROFILE: ROGER SCHELL

Roger Schell was born in the 1930s in eastern Montana [15]. He grew interested in electronics working on radios at an early age, which grew into an academic career in electrical engineering with graduate degrees at Washington State and MIT. In the course of his graduate studies he was more and more involved with computers, eventually working on the development of MULTICS while at MIT. Exposure to some prominent formal methods professors lead him to experiment and master formal derivation approaches, although formal security models did not exist at the time.

After his Ph.D., he returned to the U.S. Air Force and eventually became interested in computer security. He developed the concept of the security kernel, and used that as a basis for making formal statements about the security of an operating system. This design approach, in turn, lead him to experience in developing security models and evaluating operating systems. This experience eventually allowed him to spearhead the development of the influential "Trusted Computer System Evaluation Criteria," colloquially known as the "Orange Book" for the brightly colored covers given it in production.

After leaving the U.S. Air Force, Schell became active in industry, leading companies that build trustable computing systems. He currently remains active in such efforts.

There are a number of other confidentiality models that have been developed (see, for example, the military need-to-know model described in Chapter 9). However, these should provide an insight into how such models constrain the flow of information in a computer system to provide verifiable confidentiality.

INTEGRITY MODELS

Integrity is the property that data has not been changed, destroyed, or lost in an unauthorized or accidental manner [1]. This implies both that control is exercised over the content of information in the system and over modifications made to that information. The primary formal model of integrity, the Biba model that extends the Bell–LaPadula model, incorporates both of these aspects.

The Biba model focuses on mandatory integrity policies [2]. It specifies integrity labels on each object in the system, which cannot be modified by any operation on the data (although a new copy of the object with a different integrity label is possible). Each subject has an integrity class (maximum level

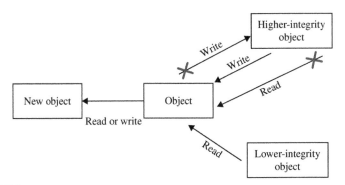

FIGURE 6.8
Biba model properties.

of integrity) and an effective integrity rating (taken from the integrity of information sources that have been read, and no higher than the integrity class), shown in Figure 6.8. In contrast to Bell–LaPadula, most Biba applications have had only a small number of integrity levels (e.g., just "user" and "administrator"). The model then defines a simple integrity policy that a subject may not read sources of lower integrity than his or her effective integrity rating, and a * property that a subject may only write objects that are of his or her effective integrity rating or lower.

LIMITS OF FORMAL MODELS

While formal models are a powerful tool for the improvement of security, there are a number of significant factors that limit their utility. These range from limitations on the basic properties that they depend on, to limitations in the realism of the underlying mathematics, to limitations on the implementation of trust, to difficulties in using the resulting system. This section explores these limits, and their implication for formal model techniques.

The basic preconditions of some formal models may be unrealistic for many organizations. For example, the Bell–LaPadula and Biba models depend on labeling governed by the tranquility constraint—the labels, once set, cannot change (although some interpretations allow for shifts outside of data access, but doing so may lead to potential violations of the security properties). In practice, the confidentiality level of a piece of information changes. Sales plans may be highly confidential prior to the sales campaign, but not at all confidential thereafter. Financial records may be highly confidential, until the period of required disclosure to stockholders and regulators. This shift in confidentiality cannot be captured without invalidating the security models—the change would open numerous opportunities to break the security of the resulting system.

The underlying mathematical system supporting the model provides a regularity and clarity of semantics, but is also a subject of concern when applying security models. There are many factors (e.g., wear, hardware failures, or chip manufacturing issues) that are extremely difficult to include in a formal model. The regularity of the mathematics makes it difficult to model the irregularity of the real world [16]. Attempts to include such irregularities yield a formal model of unwieldy size and complexity, which makes use with security extremely difficult.

As the system is developed, the derivation or verification operations on the implementation also make assumptions. Full validation is not possible, as there are always variations in manufacture and operation. At some point, the developers must make assumptions, which are always a source of challenge, and occasionally a basis of attack.

These factors produce theoretical limits on the application of formal models, but often the dominant limitations are usage factors. To support knowledge or level limits, users must often explicitly gain or relinquish privileges frequently while using these systems. This tends to make the system cumbersome to use in comparison to general computer systems. Common software is not developed securely, and may not support the trust operations required to comply with secure systems. As such, formal systems are likely to remain confined to a specific niche of operations—one that does not demand frequent user interaction or as a general-purpose computer system.

SUMMARY

When considering the frustration strategy, the ultimate in frustration for an adversary is a system that possesses known security properties that cannot be evaded. There are few technologies that offer the possibility of providing known security properties in the system, but among those is formal modeling for derivation or verification. This chapter discusses this technology and several of the common models associated with it. While there are several factors that limit the utility of this technology, its advantages make it useful to understand in considering how to improve organizational security.

Chapter 7 initiates the discussion of resistance, which hampers the ability of an adversary to propagate through the system once an initial foothold has been gained. Several resistance technologies will be discussed as a means of improving the security of organizations.

REFERENCES

[1] Shirey R. Internet security glossary. IETF Request for Comment 4949. Retrieved October 10, 2011, from <http://tools.ietf.org/html/rfc4949>; 2007, August.

[2] Landwehr C. Formal models for computer security. ACM Comput Surv 1981;13(3):247–78.

[3] Crazylord (pseudonym). Playing with Windows /dev/(k)mem. Phrack 2002;11(59), Phile 16. Retrieved April 18, 2013, from <http://www.phrack.org/issues.html?issue=59&id=16>.

[4] Palmers (pseudonym). Sub proc_root Quando Sumus (Advances in Kernel Hacking). Phrack, 2002, February;11(58), Phile 6. Retrieved April 18, 2013, from <http://www.phrack.org/issues.html?issue=58&id=6>.

[5] Palmers (pseudonym). 5 Short Stories about execve (Advances in Kernel Hacking II). Phrack 2002, 11(59), Phile 5. Retrieved April 18, 2013, from <http://www.phrack.org/issues.html?issue=59&id=5>.

[6] Ehrig H, Mahr B, Classen I, Orejas F. Introduction to algebraic specification. part 1: methods for software development. Comput J 1992;35(5):460–7. Retrieved April 18, 2013, from <http://0-comjnl.oxfordjournals.org.library.hct.ac.ae/content/35/5/460.full.pdf>.

[7] Nielson F, Nielson H, Hankin C. Principles of program analysis. Berlin: Springer; 1999.

[8] Gligor V, Burch E, Chandersekaran G, Chapman R, Dotterer L, Hecht M, et al. On the design and on the implementation of secure xenix workstations. IEEE security and privacy symposium. Oakland, CA; 1986, May. p. 102–17. Retrieved April 18, 2013, from <http://www.cs.washington.edu/research/projects/poirot3/Oakland/sp/PAPERS/00044466.PDF>.

[9] Gligor V. Analysis of the hardware verification of the honeywell SCOMP. IEEE security and privacy symposium. Oakland, CA; 1987, May. p. 32–43. Retrieved April 18, 2013, from <http://www.cs.washington.edu/research/projects/poirot3/Oakland/sp/PAPERS/00044529.PDF>.

[10] Gligor V, Chandersekaran G, Cheng W, Jiang W, Johri A, Luckenbaugh G, et al. A new security testing method and its application to the secure Xenix Kernel. IEEE security and privacy symposium. Oakland, CA; 1986, May. p. 40–58. Retrieved April 18, 2013, from <http://www.cs.washington.edu/research/projects/poirot3/Oakland/sp/PAPERS/00044455.PDF>.

[11] Tutorialspoint. UNIX-File permissions/Access Mode. Retrieved April 18, 2013, from <http://www.tutorialspoint.com/unix/unix-file-permission.htm>; 2013.

[12] Gruenbacher A. POSIX access control lists on Linux. Retrieved April 18, 2013, from <http://users.suse.com/~agruen/acl/linux-acls/online/>; 2003, April.

[13] Graham G, Denning P. Protection—principles and practice. Proceedings of the 1972 Spring AFIPS Joint Computer Conference. Anaheim, CA; 1972, May. p. 417–29.

[14] Brewer D, Nash M. The Chinese Wall Security Policy. IEEE Security and Privacy Symposium. Oakland, CA; 1989, April. p. 206–214. Retrieved April 18, 2013, from <http://www.cs.washington.edu/research/projects/poirot3/Oakland/sp/PAPERS/00044340.PDF>.

[15] Yost J. An interview with Roger R. Schell. Computer security history project, Retrieved December 8, 2012, from <http://conservancy.umn.edu/bitstream/133439/1/oh405rrs.pdf>; 2012, May.

[16] Denning D. The limits of formal security models. National Computer Systems Security Award Acceptance Speech. Retrieved April 18, 2013, from <http://faculty.nps.edu/dedennin/publications/National%20Computer%20Systems%20Security%20Award%20Speech.htm>; 1999, October.

[17] Denning D. A lattice model of secure information flow. Commun ACM 1976;19(5):236–43. Retrieved April 18, 2013, from <http://citeseerx.ist.psu.edu/viewdoc/download?doi=10.1.1.84.5776&rep=rep1&type=pdf>.

Chapter Review Questions

1. Briefly explain one reason each for why clarity and unambiguity are important in formal models.

2. Define the following terms, and briefly explain their relevance to security:
   a. Logical semantics
   b. Algebraic semantics
   c. Access control list
   d. Access control matrix
   e. Tranquility principle
   f. Verification
   g. Validation

3. How would the Bell–LaPadula model hamper the ability of a rogue system administrator to release information held in a computer based on this model?

4. What kind of attacks might be wholly or partially defeated by systems based on the Biba model?

5. How might use of the Chinese Wall security model interfere with attempts to pass data regarding a competitive bid using a workstation on an organization's network?

6. Which of the limiting factors on formal models would be of greatest importance to organizations considering application of these models to improve their security?

Chapter Exercises

1. How might use of an access control matrix aid in restricting indirect release of information on a computer system?

2. Bob's Bank is concerned about online attacks on its business-to-business site. The site is implemented with a front end that supports customer authentication connected to a back end that processes payments and provides account information. Since Bob's Bank is a small local bank, they only have two servers for their business-to-business site. Briefly describe how use of a formal model of the financial transactions might aid in protecting the validity of the back-end system. Explain why such a system is more closely related to the Bell–LaPadula model or the Biba model.

3. Tres Rios Electric Service is a small power-generation company located in the southwestern United States. They use a variety of device control systems (SCADA) to optimize performance of their generators and support flexible power distribution. Recently, Tres Rios management has become concerned about attempts to shut down the SCADA control network by repeated transmission of valid requests. Briefly explain how a formal model might be constructed to aid management in analyzing the control network with respect to this concern, and what factors might make such a model difficult to apply.

4. Tartan is a local ISP operating in the mid-Atlantic region of the United States. They support local customers' access to the Internet as a bottom-tier ISP. They have become concerned about attempts to attack their authentication of customers. Briefly describe two ways in which the Biba model could aid Tartan in addressing such attempts.

5. How would virtual images be used to support a system based on the Bell–LaPadula model?

PART

Resistance

Resistance Strategies: Authentication and Permissions

INTRODUCTION

The previous chapters described deception and frustration strategies, which respectively aim to hide resources from an attacker and prevent the attacker from targeting any discovered resources. Good frustration strategies should have turned away most opportunistic attackers. However, at some point a determined attacker will evade even the best frustration strategies; the next step is to resist the attacker at the point of attack.

The goal of resistance strategies is to prevent the adversary from successfully exploiting a resource that has been successfully targeted. Resistance strategies are numerous, because there are so many different types of resources that are targeted. This chapter, as well as Chapters 8, 9, and 10, considers various resistance strategies commonly available to the defender. This chapter

125

focuses on strategies for controlling access to resources via authentication and permission, which are agent-centric resistance strategies. Other strategies focus on information (Chapter 8), preventing abuse by authorized persons (Chapter 9), and systems (Chapter 10).

AUTHENTICATION AND PERMISSION GOALS AND OBJECTIVES

Authentication has to do with verifying that an entity is in fact the entity that it identifies itself as. This is a separate issue from permissions, which has to do with granting legitimate parties access to the correct resources. Consider passports in the physical world. My passport contains my name and other identification information, as well as my photograph. When I'm holding the passport, I can show airport staff that I am who I say I am, because the passport serves to authenticate that my name and my picture are linked. This authentication works because a trusted party, here the U.S. Department of State, has bound my name and photograph to the information therein. However, whether or not I am authorized to get on the plane, or through immigration, is another matter entirely. And although my identity doesn't change—I only even need to renew my passport every 10 years—I may only be permitted to visit a foreign country (i.e., access the resource) for 30 days without renewing my permissions.

This chapter discusses systematic methods for authenticating users or services, as well as determining what resources those entities are authorized for—that is, permitted to access. For this chapter, assume the attacker is not a genuine user of the system. Authentication mechanisms should prevent the attacker from pretending to be a genuine user of the defender's system. Permission mechanisms will then prevent the attacker from accessing protected resources, since only genuine users have permission to do so. There are two general categories of authentication: humans authenticating themselves to computers, and computers authenticating to other computers. Often, computer–computer authentication is one computer on behalf of its human user. Since humans are comparatively slow and unreliable with processing large numbers, it makes sense to offload authentication procedures to computers as much as plausible.

AUTHENTICATION METHODS

An authentication method is some process for determining whether an entity is what it claims to be. There are three factors by which one can base authentication methods: what the subject knows, what the subject has, and what the subject is [1]. The subject is the entity that needs to be authenticated. The quintessential example of something known is a password. Possession of an object is an authentication method used often in the physical world, such as a house key or student ID card. Authentication can also be based on inherent physical details of the subject that are intricate and not easily changed, such as human faces or fingerprints (e.g., when greeting friends, people subconsciously authenticate who they are by their face or voice).

Authentication can be made significantly more rigorous by combining multiple factors. However, the improvement only occurs when using two different factors, not just two different instances of one factor [1]. If a website asks for a password, and then asks for the user's mother's maiden name to verify, the website has not added a factor. It has asked for something the subject knows, and then asked for something else the subject knows. This does not significantly increase resistance to attackers. Two-factor authentication is more secure because the different types of factors require entirely differently sorts of channels to be subverted, and the difficultly for the attacker is subverting the channel. If the attacker can eavesdrop on the channel, the subject will reveal any answers to tests about what is known—it doesn't matter if there is one or six questions. But no amount of eavesdropping can steal a physical item, so to obtain that second factor—a possession—would require coordination of a separate attack.

One simple example of two-factor authentication is common when withdrawing money from a bank. The customer must be in possession of his or her ATM card and know the PIN to make a withdraw at the ATM. The card is something the customer has; the PIN is something the customer knows. If the customer did not need a PIN, then losing the ATM card would be much more damaging because anyone who found it could withdraw money.

The following sections detail one example of each of the three factors usable for authentication. Passwords are something one knows, security tokens are something one has, and biometrics are something one is. Refer to the last section of the chapter for possible attacks on and common misuses of these methods.

Passwords

Passwords are a classic authentication and access control mechanism, although the people implementing passwords in the 1820s probably did not think of it in this way. The term *password* was coined around 1815 [2], but the general idea of a secret word that grants the speaker access requires no technology, and is an ingenious method for scaling access control so that each guard or gatekeeper does not need to know the face of each person who is to be admitted (face recognition would be a form of biometric authentication, discussed later in this chapter). Passwords are suitable for situations with minimal technology, for example, in J. R. R. Tolkien's *Lord of the Rings* series, the mines of Moria have a password—the Elven word for "friend." However, one might claim the password is not the secret in this single-factor, knowledge-based authentication scheme. "Friend" is written over the door—the knowledge factor is that the subject must know how to read the Elven language (which is presumably beyond orcs' capabilities) [3]. Passwords in the modern conception are a bit more specific than requiring someone to read a language.

The most important item to know about passwords is they alone should be considered insufficient to protect any important system. This section will elaborate details, and the "Attacks" section later in this chapter should drive that point home. Several banks and militaries have come to this conclusion years ago [4,5, p. 72], but it would be doing the reader a disservice to state this fact in any uncertain terms.

Passwords are natural for people to remember—we are pretty good at remembering language. This made passwords one of the first authentication mechanisms for identifying a human to a computer. If the human supplies a name and matching password, the computer considers the human to be the genuine owner of the account name. It is first helpful to understand a little bit about how computers make this verification. There are several methods that have been implemented over the years, some to better effect than others.

Password Verification Mechanisms

The computer must store some information to match against the user-supplied password. In the first implementations, this was simply a file with one column for the user name and one column for the matching password, in plaintext. This makes checking passwords a trivial operation—the computer just checks if the input password matches the column in the password file. However, there are some obvious problems with storing passwords in plaintext. Even if only privileged users of the system have permission to read the file, those users will know everyone's passwords. Furthermore, if any malicious user gains such privileges, the attacker instantly gains everyone's password.

On Linux and Unix systems there was incremental improvement. The password verification information was stored in /etc/passwd and was readable by everyone, but it was obscured. It was obscured using the Data Encryption Standard (DES), the standard algorithm at the time. The action was to obscure, not encrypt; there is a technical difference between those two words. Encryption using DES means that the information is recoverable, or that the process is reversible, given the key. However, in the Unix password system, the user's password was the key, and the starting text was known: a string of all zeros. To verify the user's password, the computer would encrypt this string using the password as the key, and if the resulting string matched the contents in the /etc/passwd file, then the user was considered authentic.

This is a one-way function—an attacker cannot recover the password by reversing some function of the resulting string using the "key." If the attacker can, it doesn't matter, because that is the password, which is the critical piece of information anyway. One-way functions are not encryption—there is no "key" in the same way. Encryption is a two-way function. One-way functions are called hash functions. Hash functions have many uses in information security. Encryption is covered in Chapter 8; hashes are touched on in Chapter 8 as well and explored more in Chapter 14.

There are severasl shortcomings with this approach, which became apparent as computing speeds increased and internetworking exposed more computers to attacks. First, due to the features of the DES algorithm, the key is only 56 bits long. This amounts to 8 ASCII characters. Anything longer was thrown away when calculating the password match. For example, if my password were "hippopotomonstrosesquipedaliophobia," an attacker could gain access to my account by just typing "hippopot" at the password prompt.

Furthermore, password guessing became easier with faster computers. Since the /etc/passwd file was readable, anyone with system access could try to guess the password that would result in the hashed string stored in the file. The original Unix password system took this into account. First, when hashing the password and checking user credentials, DES is actually run 25 times, instead of just once. This does not add extra randomness or further obscure the text or key. It just takes longer. This is not noticeable to a regular user—it is the difference between a couple hundred microseconds and a couple milliseconds. However, it makes it significantly harder to go through guessing millions of passwords.

Second, the passwords were salted. A salt is a number that changes the configuration of the password verification algorithm, so that two users with the same password will not produce the same hashed text. This is important, because if the obscured text is the same, then the password used to generate it is the same, and so without additional obscurity all users with the same password would know who shares their password. The salt bits are appended in plaintext to the hashed string. They do not add security to an individual user, but to a group of users. Due to the features of the DES algorithm, there were 4,096 (2^{12}) possible salts. Therefore, if one system had fewer than 4,096 users, the system could guarantee that no two users would have the same entry in the /etc/passwd file.

As will be explained in the "Attacks" section, both the 56-bit password and the 12-bit salt are too small on modern systems, with millions of users [6] and supercomputers available for rent [7]. The mathematics behind how a password is sufficiently large is unintuitive when many users are involved, because the adversary often only needs access to one account to escalate privileges. As more users are involved, the chances that someone picked a weak password is nearly certain.

Despite modern computational shortcomings, conceptually the Unix approach to storing and checking passwords is valid. Namely, store the result of a one-way function of the password and salt the function; one adjustment though: do not allow any user to read the results. The /etc/passwd file is still in use today, but with different parameters, and different algorithms used to hash the password. The hashes are stored in /etc/shadow, which only the superuser can read [8]. This does not mean that all systems use a robust checking or storage mechanism. Several million-user web companies were found not to have salted their password files, as described in the "Attacks" section.

The Problem with Passwords

Passwords just are not long enough to be secure any more. Once they are long enough, people generally cannot remember them. This is not to mention that people can only remember so many distinct passwords, and users have more and more distinct accounts that ought to have distinct passwords. There may be different resistance strengths against different kinds of attacks, but a general estimate to protect against an offline brute-force attempt to guess a password or secret key is that the secret should have about 90 bits of information [9]. A brute-force attempt is the least sophisticated kind of attack—the attacker just keeps trying every possible input until the correct answer is guessed. Offline means the attacker can make attempts on his or her own resources, off the target system, at speeds only limited by hardware, and is not subject to the defender's password-checking rate limits or attempt maximums.

A common QWERTY keyboard produces 94 possible characters. If users could truly randomly select from them, 14 characters would provide 90 bits of information ($2^{90} \approx 94^{14}$). Thus, a password like ";M%aa~+g\p42? E" might be safe. But users do not make passwords like this. What about English words? The *Oxford English Dictionary* estimates English contains about 250,000 distinct words [10]. If the user actually selected randomly from all of these, then 5 words would be sufficient ($2^{90} \approx 250,000^5$), which would yield passwords such as "anopisthograph inclined yukata verandas jassid." However, in common written usage the average information per word is only 2–3 bits [11]. This is due to redundancy in the language that restricts words to certain combinations of letters, sentences to certain patterns of words, and so on. Assuming Shannon was correct, it would take about 57 words of written English to reach 90 bits of information ($2^{90} \approx 3^{57}$), or the first three sentences of this section.

So, the sorts of things that people can remember are now easy for computers to guess quickly. And the sorts of things that are hard for computers to guess are nearly impossible for humans to remember. This is the gist of the problem; the last section describes some attacks that make the situation even worse. Thus, authentication using simply one factor—something the subject knows—should be considered insufficient. If passwords are used, a second factor should probably be implemented to reduce risk.

A Brief Note on Cryptology

This book does not endeavor to teach cryptology (the study of both making and breaking methods for encoding information, which are called cryptography [making] and cryptanalysis [breaking], respectively), however, some concepts are essential to understanding information assurance strategies. For a complete discussion, see Katz and Lindell [12] or Stallings [13, chs. 2–10]; for a shorter discussion, see Anderson [5, ch. 5]. For details on symmetric encryption as a resistance strategy, see Chapter 8.

In a cryptographic system, the key is a secret between two parties that want to communicate privately. The key is a relatively short piece of information, on the order of hundreds of bits. System architects generally follow what is known as Kerckhoffs principle: the system itself must not be secret; system design details must be able to fall into the hands of the enemy without trouble [14].

In modern cryptography the system is broken up into two parts: the algorithm and the protocol. The algorithm does the hard math of obscuring bits using the secret key. The protocol is the method for communicating the information, the design decisions on what algorithm is applied to what information, and so on.

There are a few ways for an attacker to defeat a cryptographic system. The algorithm itself could be broken—either it was poorly designed and is not as random as was believed, or new developments in mathematics make the computationally hard parts of the algorithm easier practically. Currently, publicly available cryptographic algorithms have been rigorously tested, and algorithmic failures are rare. Alternatively, the protocol for communicating the secret information could have a flaw. There are several common flaws that permit replay or middle-person attacks, for example, and will be discussed later. The final possibility is that the secret key could be discovered. The key could be disclosed by trickery, such as social engineering or brute-force guessing, both discussed in the "Attacks" section.

The most widespread damage and risk is caused by an algorithmic break, then a protocol break, and finally by a key break. This is due to the number of agents and sessions using each part unchanged. There are relatively few algorithms, so if one is broken, many things are at risk. Each algorithm is used in a variety of protocols, and fewer agents use any one given protocol. Finally, a key should be unique to an agent or a communication, causing the least widespread damage; there are actually different kinds of keys as well—some designed to be secret for years and some for only seconds, which cause correspondingly less damage upon disclosure.

There are two broad types of encryption algorithms: symmetric and asymmetric. Symmetric algorithms use the same key for encryption and decryption. In asymmetric encryption, there are two keys, or a key pair: one is for encrypting and one is for decrypting. The mathematics of the algorithms usually center around discrete logarithms, or elliptic curves in discrete fields—a completely different type of algorithm than those used for symmetric encryption [12]. One key is called the private key, because only one entity should know it. The other key is called the public key, because anyone can know it. The use cases for each type are quite different; the basic advantages and uses of each are introduced throughout the rest of this chapter and in Chapters 8 and 14.

Security Tokens

Security token is a broad term, but every security token serves as a "something you have" element in an IT authentication system. Just like elements of physical systems, such as house keys, IT security tokens contain some piece

PROFILE: WHITFIELD DIFFIE

The Asymmetric Key Revolution

Whit Diffie, along with his collaborator Martin Hellman, initiated a sea change in cryptography when they presented their key exchange method in 1976. The Diffie–Hellman key exchange is still widely used today, with minor adjustments for defense against a middle-person attack and increases in the key size to resist brute-force attacks. The key exchange is the first published instance of asymmetric key cryptography, in which the two parties need not share a secret to begin with to decide on a secret that, provably, only those two parties know. This ability is nothing less than required for widespread use of cryptography, and the feature was missing until the Diffie–Hellman key exchange.

Diffie has certainly led a colorful life. Born in 1944 and raised in Queens, NY, he reportedly did not bother with reading until he was 10 years old. However, only a few months later he was introduced to ciphers by his public school teacher, and asked his father, a City College of New York history professor, to check out every book from the New York Public Library that had to do with cryptology. Whit promptly forgot about crypto throughout high school and university at MIT and his work for MITRE through the Vietnam War. Not until 1970, when he took a position at Stanford in John McCarthy's artificial intelligence (AI) lab, did he return to the field that would shape his life, and that he would shape for the rest of his [15].

With how pervasive cryptography is on the Internet now, it is hard to imagine the culture around cryptography when Diffie was working on it. He, and anyone else working on new cryptography methods, essentially worked under the threat of prosecution from the U.S. government. Cryptography was held in the same regard as other high-tech implements of war under the International Traffic in Arms Regulations (ITAR). As late as 2000, the U.S. government still rather heavily restricted the export of implementations of cryptographic technology [12, p. 324].

The fact that Diffie has been subtly bucking the administration for so long probably has a lot to do with his current roles. He has been a critic of bad cryptography policy—during the formation of the DES [16] and during the infancy of the web [15]—and continues to maintain a public stance on many such issues. However, he does so with a charisma, respect, and goodwill that some of his would-be opponents have found surprising. After a long tenure at Sun Microsystems, Diffie took a position with ICANN (Internet Corporation for Assigned Names and Numbers) in 2010. He still maintains a signature full beard and long white hair, which is now almost iconic of the irreverent technocrat, just as Albert Einstein's disheveled hair worked its way into the cultural ethos as a symbol of the scatterbrained genius-scientist.

of secret information that identifies the item as authentic. The item also has some properties that are difficult to reproduce without the appropriate equipment. With house keys, the information is contained in the pattern of ridges on the key. However, just having a picture of the pattern won't suffice to open a door—an attacker would also have to have a machine for making keys. These two features are true, in some way or another, about security tokens in IT systems as well.

With security tokens, the secret information is usually just a relatively short string of bits, which serves as the key in a cryptographic system that can prove the identity of the device. It is wise for an organization to implement authentication using tokens because, as noted earlier, passwords can no longer be considered sufficient to resist attackers' attempts to subvert authentication mechanisms. In this way, tokens are just like house keys. If everything goes well, only someone with a token can access the electronic resources. Of course, tokens can be lost or stolen. So a good resistance system will require not only the token, but that the user of the token verify they are the valid owner of the token with something they know—a password.

A section on how security tokens work would be lengthy, because that is too broad. A token system can use almost any protocol or algorithm to authenticate the validity of the token to the home system. Furthermore, some of the popular token systems use proprietary algorithms and protocols. RSA's SecurID token is one example, and this disregard for Kerckhoffs principle has occasionally caused the company difficulty in maintaining the security of their token system [17,18].

At a high level, there are several methods for designing a token authentication system. The protocol can be a simple assertion, or a challenge-response protocol [5, p. 66ff]. The keys stored in the devices could be for asymmetric or symmetric encryption. Some systems are more simple than others. At some point, complexity is the enemy of security and so simple is better, but in some places simplicity is a euphemism for laziness in system design. An assertion protocol is more simple than a challenge-response protocol, and key management in symmetric cryptography systems is probably more simple than managing asymmetric keys.

If a token simply asserts its identity, it presents an identify for itself along with a proof-of-identity. This proof is an encrypted set of data with some special properties to demonstrate the token is authentic. At a minimum, the data encrypted is the identifier for the device, and a nonce, or a number used only once. The properties of the nonce are important. It can be a simple counter, a timestamp, or a random number, and each of these choices has ramifications for the cryptographic system. However, the basic purpose of the nonce is to prove freshness—that is, to prevent an attacker who has observed a previous communication from trivially replaying it to defeat the system. The identifier and the nonce are bound together and encrypted by a key that only the device contains. Therefore, if the plaintext and enciphered identifiers match, and the message is fresh, the authenticator will admit the device.

Assigning the keys is important. One possible method is that the authentication service has its own master secret key, and every token's internal secret key is just a function of the master secret and a device identifier, like the serial number. This way, the authenticating computer doesn't have to remember a whole lot. The computer is presented with a token's ID, and the computer looks up its serial number, computes its key, and uses that key to verify its assertion of identity by decrypting the proof-of-identity and comparing it with the asserted identity. Of course, this is also dangerous because there is a single point of failure—if the master key is compromised, it becomes trivial for the attacker to discover the secret key of any device. The attacker just has to know its serial number. This appears to be the method used by RSA's SecurID, because after the company was compromised in 2011, one of the recommendations was that customers under no circumstances reveal the serial numbers of their tokens [18].

There are at least two different key management schemes possible. One is for each device to still use symmetric encryption, but for the key to actually be randomly assigned instead of derived using a single secret. This table of device IDs to secret keys would then have to be stored at the authentication computer, and so it is still a single point of failure. However, it would make it so that the attacker could only gain secret keys up to the time of compromise, unlike the previous derived secret key method where once the attacker learns the master key, any key for any device in the future can be derived without repeated compromise. Of course, the manufacturer could change the master key with the same effect, but it does require the manufacturer notices their key has been stolen.

The second option is to use asymmetric, or public key, encryption, which makes key distribution simpler. Additionally, by using the public and private keys wisely complex assertions of identity can be proven and no central repository of keys is necessary. This removes the single point of failure in the case of a compromise. However, public key cryptography is computationally more intensive than symmetric cryptography, so tokens or devices to use it will be more expensive to manufacture.

More robust tokens would use asymmetric cryptography to identify the tokens. The security token would contain the only instance of its private key. The authentication system would contain a list of token IDs to public key mappings. The proof-of-identity supplied by the token in the exchange would be its ID, as well as several pieces of information to prove its authenticity and freshness of the message encrypted with its private key. To verify the message, the authenticating system would look up the public key, and check that only the private key on the token would be able to create a message matching the known public key.

An even more robust token protocol could be constructed. A simple assertion might be sufficient when the token is in close physical proximity to the authenticator, such as an RFID (radio-frequency identification) fob to enter a building. However, a challenge-response protocol is more robust when the authentication is remote. Although the token can sufficiently prove its identity, we may want the system to which it is authenticating to prove itself. The basic idea is that to authenticate, the authentication system provides a challenge, and the token computes and returns the appropriate response. The challenge could simply be a number, and the response could simply be to add one to the number and send it back. Using the features of the proof-of-identity previously discussed, this can be constructed simply to ensure both parties are assured of the authenticity of the other. The authentication system will also have a key pair, so it can encrypt the challenge with its private key. As long as there are timestamps to prevent replay of old requests, since the authentication system's private key encrypted the challenge the token can verify the correct system sent the challenge. Then the token can generate the appropriate response, and encrypt it with its private key and send it back, completing this simplified authentication. An analogous challenge-response protocol can be written using symmetric cryptography as long as both parties share a single secret key.

Desirable Features of Security Tokens

If you are designing or managing the resistance strategies for an organization, there are some basic types of features in tokens to consider before purchasing and implementing one. Whether the token is hardware or software, whether the hardware is wired to a USB or sealed or wireless, and other physical features of the token are more dependent on the intended use of the device than security concerns. However, the cryptographic choices effect any token system. Ask about the algorithms used; secret algorithms should be suspicious, because if the manufacturer cannot reveal the algorithm then it is not following best practices for algorithm design, namely Kerckhoffs principle [14].

Also ask about key management and generation. If the key space (number of possible keys) is too small, then the tokens have the same problem as passwords—there are not enough to prevent the attacker from guessing them. "Small" varies if the algorithm is symmetric or asymmetric, but the equivalent of 128 bits of information is the lowest reasonable amount that should be sufficient for the near future [9, sec. 5.6.2]. If keys are generated from device identifiers like serial numbers, then there need to be enough possible serial numbers that the generated key space is not too small, which means randomly assigning the serial numbers in a space at least 2^{112} large. Key management also should avoid a central point of failure or compromise, if authentication is remote (as opposed to fob access to a door, which is local), which probably means using public key cryptography.

Biometrics

Biometrics is a commonly used factor for "something you are." As the etymology of the word implies, biometrics refers to measuring aspects of biological systems or entities. It has had this broad usage since the early 20th century, developed in places such as the scholarly journal *Biometrics*. Only relatively recently has the term acquired the specialized sense of identification of individuals via differentiation within specific biological traits, especially for the purpose of identification and authentication to computers [19].

However, that this term usage is new may be misleading—authenticating a subject's identity by what they are is perhaps the oldest form of authentication. Facial recognition seems to be as old as history, and identifying a person by his or her signature or handwriting has been a common practice for hundreds of years. However, the scientific research to demonstrate that other physical characteristics were sufficiently unique for identification purposes took some time. Fingerprints were demonstrated to be unique and persistent through a human lifetime in the late 19th century [20], and other characteristics have followed (e.g., iris or voice patterns).

Authentication via biometrics is attractive in security for several reasons. Unlike passwords or tokens, your fingerprints can't be forgotten or lost. Biometric details also are not transferable (easily), and so where multiple humans may share a single account password, making attribution to a single individual difficult, biometric details should always identify one individual. Security also has a lot to do with deterrence and legal frameworks, and since fingerprints and handwritten signatures have a longer history, they have a legal standing that, while perhaps not directly relevant to biometric technology, at least people are used to the idea of these aspects of subjects being used for authentication. For example, even though handwritten signatures are relatively easy to forge, the banking system works reasonably well using them and authenticates billions of dollars of transactions with little practical loss, due to the legal framework surrounding the verification system [5, p. 458ff].

There are a wide variety of aspects of human beings that have been tried for automated, computerized biometric identification, with varying levels of success. In 2001, the National Physical Laboratory (NPL) in the United Kingdom tested six different human characteristics for authentication: facial recognition, fingerprints, hand geometry, iris patterns, hand vein recognition, and voice recognition [21]. Retina scans (the inside of the eye, rather than the iris on the outside) have also been used, but are more invasive than iris scans [22]. All of these examples are physical biometrics. There are also behavioral biometrics, which are characteristics of behavior that are deemed both unique and relatively static across a lifetime. Examples include keystroke typing patterns and the pattern and speed of pen strokes and lifts while hand writing a signature. Although it may seem surprising, keystroke biometrics have lower error rates [23] than some physical biometrics, such as automated facial recognition [5, p. 463].

Despite these benefits, biometric identification systems are not as widely implemented as the other two factors. Perhaps because they require specialized equipment and have relatively high error rates, both in false positives and false negatives. A false positive is when a system incorrectly attributes a result or attribute to a subject, for example, identifies an innocent person as the criminal. A false negative is when the system fails to attribute a test characteristic to a subject, for example, a fingerprint examiner fails to identify a set of prints as belonging to a criminal.

The impact of a false positive or a false negative varies depending on the application. In some situations it is more important to minimize one or the other. For example, in medical tests it may be considered more important to accurately identify a disease if it exists (minimize false negatives) than to reduce the number of healthy patients who are wrongly diagnosed (false positives). For further discussion of false negatives and positives, and some counterintuitive interplay between the two, see Chapter 12.

CAPTCHAs

CAPTCHAs are another example of testing what the subject authenticating is. In this case, the test tries to check whether the subject is a human or a machine. The term CAPTCHA (Completely Automated Public Turing Test to Tell Computers and Humans Apart) was coined in 2000 at Carnegie Mellon University [24]. These are images of distorted text that are keyed on difficult problems for AI to solve but are generally easy for humans. As AI improves, CAPTCHAs have to become more difficult. With reCAPTCHA, the tests come directly from old digitized books that the optical character recognition (OCR) could not understand, and the results are used to improve that very process [24]. Figure 7.1 demonstrates some basic CAPTCHAs.

CAPTCHAs are generally used on sites that want to make sure a genuine human is doing something, but do not care who. This is an effective anti-abuse measure for things like free account generation or sending messages. If a computer could do it, the volume of unwanted events would be overwhelming.

FIGURE 7.1
Some examples of text-based CAPTCHA styles.

AUTHENTICATION SYSTEMS

There is really only one system in use for distributed authentication of entities within an enterprise: Kerberos. Certainly other systems have been described, but practically speaking, essentially all organizations use Kerberos internally, whether they know it or not. Microsoft's Active Directory domain services use Kerberos for authentication [25]. There are other authentication systems in use over the Internet, such as X.509 certificates with certificate authorities, but an understanding of Kerberos will provide the major concepts in authentication systems generally, as well as the practical usefulness that Kerberos is common. This section will explain the conceptual details of Kerberos, but will abstract away from technical details such as precise message contents. Kerberos makes use of passwords and tokens, methods described in the previous section, however, for details on the composition of the tokens and messages see Stallings [26, p. 99ff], or for the authoritative, complete details see the RFCs [27–31].

Kerberos is organized into domains. One domain contains all the human users and servers that can be authenticated to one another. The steps in a Kerberos authentication are displayed in Figure 7.2. The first step in a Kerberos authentication is that the human must authenticate him- or herself to the local workstation, usually using a password. The local workstation can then process the remaining requests on the user's behalf. The first request is to an authentication server. The authentication server verifies the user is permitted to use servers within the domain. The authentication server then grants a digital ticket to the user. Kerberos tickets function as a "something

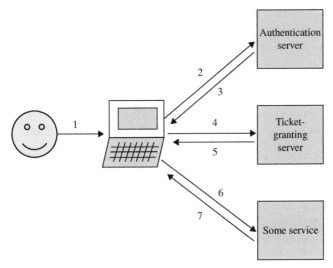

1: User authenticates to work station using password
2: Work station provides proof-of-identity from user, requests ticket for TGS
3: Ticket for local TGS
4: Request for service-granting ticket for some service
5: Ticket for some service
6: Request some service, includes ticket for some service
7: Access to service, server identifies itself to workstation

FIGURE 7.2
The basic, abstract flow of a Kerberos authentication. Steps 1, 2, and 3 only happen once per user logon. Steps 4 and 5 are repeated for each service to which the user requests access during that logon. Steps 6 and 7 are repeated for each session between the user's computer and the server, for as long as the ticket is valid.

you have" kind of authentication for future exchanges. This first ticket is for a special kind of server—the ticket-granting server (TGS).

The TGS is a special server in Kerberos because it can grant access to any other server in the domain. Using the ticket from the authentication server, the user can request access to other servers within the domain from the TGS, which will then provide a separate ticket granting access to the desired server. It is also possible to establish relationships between two domains in Kerberos version 5, if the TGS in domain A has a relationship with the TGS in domain B. This just adds one more set of tickets the users in domain A need to obtain before getting access to the services in domain B.

Kerberos minimizes the number of times a user must input a password, and is therefore a very usable system. To achieve this design goal, the contents of the tickets contain a lot of information to prevent replay of tickets and ensure they are fresh. The system is also scalable and reliable, which requires some abstraction of the roles of computers in the service and ticket contents, to make sure it is sufficiently modular to supply these design goals. The system is generally considered to be well designed, which means that as long as the Kerberos server is secure, the authentication service is secure [26]. What this really means is that if the attacker wants to defeat your resistance strategies of requiring all users to authenticate, the attacker will go after the Kerberos server by whatever means necessary. This computer should, therefore, be monitored very closely, on a separate subnetwork, as well as housed in a locked room or cabinet to which the access is tightly controlled.

The only service that Kerberos provides is authentication of the user to the end-system. It does not determine if the user has permission to access all or part of the services to the end-system. Permissions are the responsibility of each individual system. Role-based access control and agent-based permissions, including file permissions, are common methods of determining authorization, as described in the following sections.

PERMISSIONS AND ACCESS CONTROL

Assuming the security system authenticates everyone accurately, one still must ensure that the authentic entities only perform the actions that they are permitted to perform. This restriction is particularly important for systems that are designed to allow anonymous access to a resource, such as web servers. It may seem simple—just do not permit users or their processes to do things that they are not allowed to do. However, once the security manager gets into the details of what each user should be permitted to do, what all the possible actions are, and what the possible targets of the actions are, the sheer volume of options can become overwhelming. This management difficulty presents practical problems for a security manager.

When the "Orange Book" was published in 1983, it contained only two models of access control, and these seemed to be the only two available [32]; namely, mandatory access control (MAC) and discretionary control (DAC). These two formal models were introduced in chapter 6. MAC is generally associated with highly trusted systems for processing classified or sensitive proprietary information, whereas an example of DAC is the file protections on Linux or Windows operating systems. These were the only two models for nearly a decade, when role-based access control (RBAC) was introduced and the concept demonstrated to be irreducible to either MAC or DAC [33]. Both MAC and DAC assign permissions on the level of individual agents, whereas RBAC is more general: RBAC assigns permissions to roles, and roles to agents. This is not to say that the idea of roles for access control was completely new in RBAC; MAC has a sense of roles via the concept of compartments, further discussed in chapter 9, but agents are not assigned roles based on job function, which is the key contribution in RBAC.

The following sections build up to a description of RBAC. Where possible, the description avoids the rigorous set theory and access control matrix notation that is used to formally describe access control mechanisms in favor of natural language descriptions. For a formal description, see Osborn et al. [34]. The following subsections first describe the Unix file system permissions as an example, then the more modern access control lists (ACLs). The final subsection will consider the benefits and difficulties of RBAC as a resistance strategy.

Agent-based Permissions

The traditional Unix file permissions and ACLs are both agent-based permission management methods. An agent is an individual user or software process. The methods are termed agent-based because access to every file is based on the identity of the agent requesting access. There is a set of permissions allowed to each agent for every file on the system. This complete description of agents to file can be represented in one access control matrix (ACM), however, this is often impractical to implement, although attempts have been made [35]. With traditional Unix file permissions, as well as ACLs, each file is marked with its permissions and ownership information.

File Permissions

File permissions control what user is permitted to perform which actions on a file. File permissions form a crucial part of a resistance strategy. On public systems, only part of the system is public. The system files, at least, need to be protected from wanton modification by attackers. Furthermore, on internal systems, file permissions help support the best practices of least privilege and least access, and therefore reduce damage from attacks by insiders.

File permissions are a construct developed on multi-user systems, namely Multics and all the *nix operating systems. Microsoft's Windows did not have a concept of file permissions until Windows NT, more than 20 years after the Unix method was determined. The two methods for describing file permissions are the traditional Unix method and ACLs. Either method is a form of DAC—users are permitted to change file permissions, at least on files they own. In the traditional method, files have attributes describing the owner of the file and the group the file is in, as well as permissions for the owner, group, and everyone else.

On a *nix system, every object is treated as a file (including directories and network devices), and so every object has file permissions. There are three possible permissions, which can be granted in any combination. These are read (r), write (w), and execute (x) [36]. These can be granted independently to each of three mutually disjoint sets of users: the owner (u), the group (g), and other (o), which means anyone on the system [36]. Additionally, there is a single special-purpose 1-bit flag that can be on or off called the sticky bit, or restricted deletion flag.

The meaning of the permissions changes slightly depending on the type of object. For files, the permissions have their common English meanings. If a user has read permission, he or she can read but not modify the file. A user needs write permissions to modify the file. To run the file as a compiled program, the user needs execute permissions. However, with the proliferation of powerful scripting languages like Python and Perl, to name just a couple, it is important to note that scripts only need to be read to be run by the interpreter, and so do not need execute permissions themselves. The sticky bit promotes behavior that helps the file load more quickly (to stick in memory) [36].

For directories, read, write, and execute have slightly different meanings. Read allows the indicated users to view the names of files in the directory. Write permission is needed to add or remove files from the directory. However, unless the sticky bit is set, properly called restricted deletion flag on directories, a user with write access to a directory can delete any file in that directory, regardless of whether he or she owns it. If the restricted delete flag is set, a user with write access in a directory can only delete files that he or she owns. Execute permissions for a directory permit the user to work from that directory.

*nix systems have a variety of users and groups by default. Many users are human users of the system, but many are also software agents such as the web server, DNS server, or the process that controls writing to the network interface. By making these specific processes owners of the files they need, but no more, file permissions can help resist an attacker who compromises the web server process in the same way as an attacker who compromises a user account. The end goal for an attacker is usually superuser access, sometimes called the root user, because that user can read and modify all files on the system, including the ones that maintain file permissions and group access.

The system maintains a file of what users are in what groups (often /etc/group), which allows for a very rudimentary role-based kind of access. There are lots of default groups for various purposes. This is also configurable. For example, if the administrator puts all the human users who are full-time employees in one group, then all of them can be given access to certain resources without worrying about exactly who has been hired recently. A user can then also share results with colleagues, easily, but without giving the interns access to data that perhaps they should not have.

Access Control Lists

In practice, each file can have an ACL associated with it, and this ACL permits more detailed permission control than the traditional Unix file permissions. On Unix-like systems, the ACL permissions granted are the same as the traditional operations—read, write, and execute—however, there is more fine-grained control over which users have these permissions [37]. This need not be the case. On Windows systems ACLs are the only access control, and they often contain a fourth basic operation for which rights are controlled: delete. This can be misleading, because it only is permission to remove a file. A user with write permission could still overwrite the file contents to make it empty [38]. This is similar to a directory in a Unix-like system with the restricted delete flag set, however, the attributes are only connected to the file.

Role-based Access Control

In RBAC, permission for operations is not based strictly on the identity of the agent performing the operation. Each entity, termed a subject, is assigned some number of roles, and each role has some number of permissions. A subject acting in a particular role has permission to do actions permitted to that role. Roles are usually somewhat abstract, such as "full-time technical employee" or "HR manager." In this way, roles can be assigned across the organization, and implemented on each of the specific computer systems. The permissions assigned to each role will vary on each computer system, as well as the technical implementation of the controls to enforce the permissions.

RBAC is more abstract than either of the agent-based methods, and this abstraction helps security folks manage permissions in larger organizations. Roles can also inherit permissions from other roles. If all employees have some permissions, then there could be an "employee" role. If there is a "database manager" role and a "contracts management" role, both of those can inherit permissions from "employee," which promotes clarity in the rules and simplifies the interpretations for the humans who have to set the whole thing up. Managing permissions in a large organization is still labor-intensive, but RBAC provides the most sane method of doing so.

Figure 7.3 demonstrates all the elements of an RBAC policy and their relationship to one another. One organization can have many roles. Each role can itself inherit attributes from many roles in the role hierarchy. Roles are assigned to subjects in "user assignment," and this process is limited by formal user/role constraints. A common example of a constraint is any user who may authorize a transaction also may not order the transaction. This would prevent a user from easily embezzling funds, by ordering transactions to themselves and then authorizing them right away. If there is separation of duties, such abuses of privilege are less likely.

One subject can have many sessions, which might be on different machines or across time, to which their roles are applied. No session can have more than one subject, so the subject–session relationship is one-to-many. This is denoted by the asterisk (*) on the line to the session, but no such mark next to the subject. We see that most of the relationships in RBAC are many-to-many, which is one of the reasons it is so flexible. Roles are assigned permissions in a many-to-many fashion, so each role can have zero or more

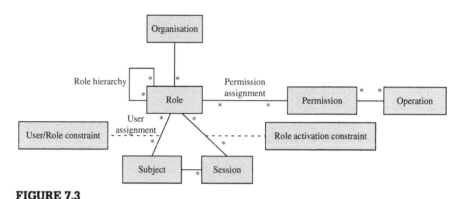

FIGURE 7.3
The relationships between the various entities described by RBAC.

permissions, and each permission can be assigned to zero or more different roles. Likewise with the mapping between permissions and individual operations.

ATTACKS

There are several attacks possible on any system. The attacks discussed here are by no means an exhaustive list. However, social engineering and brute-force attacks are particularly dangerous because they are not based on exploiting errors in the technology or the protection strategies, but rather attacking the assumptions defenders make about what they are defending. If authentication and permissions systems are working properly, only a human with valid credentials can access a system. If the organization is managing its credentials properly, then the attacker should be resisted and should not be able to get a foothold within the organization. However, social engineering attacks the human users, rather than the technology, to bypass the technological resistance strategies.

Brute-force attacks on passwords and cryptographic keys bypass a different elemental assumption. Cryptography generally does not provide what is known as perfect forward secrecy, which is a guarantee of secrecy going forwards forever in time so long as the key remains secret. This is because to provide this, the key has to be the same size as the data protected, and this is impractical [12, ch. 2]. The reason for this has to do with the amount of information an adversary can gain from the protected data, and as long as the key is shorter than the data, the adversary can gain some additional information thath theoretically eventually breaks forward secrecy [39].

Therefore, protection has generally been satisfied with computational security. Computational security is based on practical assumptions about computational speed and resources, as well as the mathematics of the algorithm not having shortcuts. The general idea is while a defender cannot have perfect secrecy, one can select a large enough random key that it would take many times the age of the universe to compute all possible keys, given current technology [12, ch. 3]. If any of these assumptions change or are subtly violated—randomness of the key, size of the key, computational resources available, strength of the algorithm, etc.—computational security may not last as long as the defender expects.

Social Engineering and Phishing

Social engineering is a general term for extracting credentials or other security-relevant information from legitimate human users by trickery and subterfuge. Military-grade interrogation is generally not included, however, the term is more broad than merely the ubiquitous phishing email. Attackers have been known to use phone calls, paper mail, or just casually walk past security guards to obtain useful information, to name a few [40]. There are also plenty of other scams that can use email. We will focus on phishing because a phishing attack is often designed to provide credentials to an adversary that can be used to gain further access into the organization, whereas plan scams are not.

Phishing requires relatively little work by the attacker, and still returns reasonable results. A phish is an email that is sent to the victim. The email purports to be from a trusted organization, however, it is a forgery. A distinguishing characteristic from other abusive or unsolicited email is that phish asks the recipient to divulge their personal information, such as user name and password, credit card credentials, social security number, etc. Figure 7.4 shows an example.

Figure 7.4 highlights some distinguishing aspects of phishing attempts, besides that it was tagged as spam by the web-mail provider. Most obviously, it asks for user ID and password. It also contains a from address with a completely different domain than the reply-to address; this discrepancy is also suspicious. Of course, it is asking about university web-mail at a noneducational email address. It also contains some subtle typos—no spaces after the commas. And finally, a common phishing tactic seems to be to implore the recipient to take immediate action or some consequence will happen very shortly. This was a dangerous social engineering email because it is in plaintext, with no attachments or HTML, and therefore the email is not technologically dangerous and more easily evades automated scanning and blocking systems.

Phishing is relatively successful, and quite prevalent. Between 2009 and 2012 the number of unique websites hosting phishing attacks rose from about 30,000 to 60,000 [41,42]. However, the number of emails sent as lures to these websites is much larger. Although the purpose of the abusive mails is not specified (phishing or some other purpose), in general, abusive mail consistently accounts for about 90% of all email [43].

@Gmail.com>

Dear Webmail Account Owner,

Webmaster Alert <uni_webmaster@w.cn>   Tue, Jan 1, 2013 at 2:38 PM
Reply-To: uni_webmast@aim.com

Dear Webmail Account Owner,

This is our second message to you from the University Webmail Messaging Center to all email account owners.

We are currently carrying out scheduled maintenance, upgrade of our web mail service and we are changing our mail host server,as a result your original password will be reset.

We are sorry for any inconvenience caused.

To complete your webmail email account upgrade, you must reply to this email immediately and provide the information requested below.

****
CONFIRM YOUR EMAIL IDENTITY NOW
E-mail Address:
User Name/ID: **Suspicious!**
Password:
Re-type Password:
****

Failure to do this will immediately render your email address deactivated from the University Webmail.
****

This E-mail is confidential and privileged. If you are not the intended Recipient please accept our apologies; Please do not Disclose, Copy or Distribute Information in this E-mail or take any action in Reliance on its contents: to do so is strictly prohibited and may be Unlawful.

Please inform us that this Message has gone astray before deleting it.

Thank you for your Co-operation.

Copyright ©2011 University Webmaster. All Rights Reserved

FIGURE 7.4
An example phishing email that one of the authors received at a Google mail address, with some hallmarks of phishing attacks annotated.

The attacker's basic idea in a phishing scheme is that it is too difficult to break the authentication system, so it is easier to simply acquire valid credentials to use on the system by asking for them. "Ask" is a flippant description, but it is accurate insofar as the attacker is taking nothing by force, nor exploiting vulnerabilities in an email client or web browser to gain these credentials. Granted, phishing sites are not usually run by upstanding members of society, so there is often also malicious code on the sites. But at the heart of it, the user is simply tricked and gives the credentials away. There is no technological defense for this. A relatively strict (but recommended) approach to email would be to strip all attached files, and to only allow plaintext (no executable code such as HTML). However, even with this approach, phishing could succeed almost unchanged.

Phishing is common enough that it has developed subcategories. Generic phishing generally refers to mass emails, sent to as many addresses as possible, asking for credentials from common brands such as Bank of America or PayPal. These are the easiest to spot. They often have spelling and grammar errors, and don't look particularly like emails a company would send. However, they are still sufficiently effective. The tagline is commonly something that requires urgent attention, such as a locked account or missed delivery on a package, to rush the recipient in to action (divulging the password) without thinking. If the attacks are more targeted, the metaphor with "fishing" is stretched and the attacks are called *spear phishing*. In this case, the attacker probably actually knows who the target is by name, and can address the email appropriately and asks for something relevant to the target's profession or recent activity. For anyone who regularly receives email from unknown persons, such as HR staff or professors, these can be difficult to detect. Stretching the metaphor to its breaking point, if the target of the attack is a high-profile person in an organization, such as the CEO, then the attack is called *whaling*.

Although there is no complete technological defense against phishing, that does not mean there are no defenses. Technical defenses can limit, but not eliminate, user visits to suspicious web pages and receipt of suspicious mail. An appropriate resistance strategy must also consider the human element of the organization and train employees appropriately, as well as provide sufficient technological resources and protections. There are training approaches specifically for phishing that go beyond simple briefings. Some systems send benign phish to employees, and not only keep statistics on how many employees were tricked, but present educational material to the employee on what went wrong instead of stealing their data [44,45].

Technologically, the best defense against the threat of malicious email is sharing among organizations. This is a resistance strategy, as the phishers are successfully targeting the organization's employees. For the phish (as well as other scams and malicious code sent via email) that are mass-mailed to organizations indiscriminately by the attackers, if the defending organizations can share effectively, then the attackers cannot reuse the same messages to attack each organization. It may hit the first few organizations that see it, however if they share, then the next 100 or 1,000 organizations can prevent the attack easily. Information sharing is also the only way to discover if an attack is a spear phish, or in general if the attack is targeted at one organization, because no other organization in the sharing network will report it.

Organizations often object to information sharing of this sort because there is a culture of not cooperating with direct economic competitors. It may not be surprising, therefore, that the most successful instance of such sharing of attack data is within the research and higher-education space, by the REN-ISAC (Research and Education Network Information Sharing and Analysis Center), and their open-source Collective Intelligence Framework (CIF) [46]. However, if other sectors expect to not all fail together, other organizations will have to figure out how to work together. In some sectors, such as defense contractors, the U.S. government has identified this shortcoming and has attempted to fund and construct a sharing network among the companies [47].

Password Cracking

Earlier in this chapter, some of the problems with passwords were discussed. However, there are multiple styles of attacks on passwords, and the requirements to resist each type are different. The primary attack types are online and offline. There is also an important difference from password cracking as described in the early 1990s, which is the scale of computer and password usage today. Two high-profile breaches provide evidence, using a bit of statistics, of the new problem, which has more to do with human psychology than computers.

An online attack on a password means the attacker is making guesses about the password to the live verification system. In an offline attack the attackers have some means of checking if the right key or password has been guessed independently, and can make the guesses at their leisure. An online attack is defensible while it is in progress. The verification system should include resistance measures, such as limits on password attempts for one account, and perhaps, more importantly, should make each guess relatively slow. If the verification system enforces a half-second wait time, then the amount of time for the attacker to make 10,000 guesses will be much longer than if the system verifies the passwords as fast as possible. A human will not likely notice the difference between a hundredth of a second and half a second, however, when the attacker wants to make 10,000 guesses, that increases their attack time from 1.7 minutes to 83.3 minutes. This difference adds up, as upwards of a million guesses is feasible.

To conduct an offline attack, the attacker must obtain some piece of information that permits verifying their guesses. For passwords, this is commonly the password file for the operating system. Even large web services have an equivalent file, although it may or may not follow the best practices in the

Unix-like password verification system. Once the information is obtained, offline attacks are often successful. The defender has no further defenses once the password file is stolen, the attacker can calculate with only the physical limitations of their machines. And several optimizations are possible. Previously in this chapter, it was noted that a safe passphrase might need to be over 50 common English words long. This is to resist an offline attack.

Part of the reason offline attacks are so successful is due to a feature of humans. As it turns out, we all often tend to pick the same passwords. This has likely been true for a while, however, it has become painfully obvious with large-scale breaches of RockYou and Gawker, in 2009 and 2010, respectively [48,49]. For example, with the RockYou breach, 32 million accounts had their details (account name and securely encoded password) leaked. Only 116 unique passwords were needed to open approximately 1.6 million of the accounts. These included passwords like "123456" and "password," but there are some more surprising commonalities. In the Gawker leak, the most common password was "monkey." Figure 7.5 demonstrates these common password selection patterns.

So what does a poor attacker do, since no one has the computational resources to try every possible password? The attacker makes a dictionary of common passwords, including common English words, simple substitutions, and additions of numbers and special characters. The dictionary is the plain-text password paired with its securely stored version that would be in a password file. Then, instead of attempting to guess what password would make the obscured text in the password file, the attacker simply looks in the dictionary to see if he or she has the obscured text. If the lookup is successful, then the attacker knows that password was used to generate the obscured text, and saves a lot of work. This is called a dictionary attack [50], and they can be quite successful. In the RockYou breach, 6.4 million out of 32 million accounts could have been accessed in this way, or 20% [48].

It may seem impossible to protect against this human predictability. However, the defender actually has a somewhat simple solution, even though it may frustrate users. If it is so trivial to crack a password that is in a dictionary, when a user is selecting a password for the organization it should be checked against some common password dictionaries (which are freely available online now). If the password is in a dictionary, then the user should not be allowed to select it. Conveniently, the attackers have even already gone through the trouble of collecting the list of common passwords for us, since the dictionaries used in attacks today are freely available on the Internet.

There has been another important event in the password-cracking landscape in the 2010s. It used to be very expensive to purchase and maintain 10 or 100 parallel computers. However, in 2009, some security researchers realized that

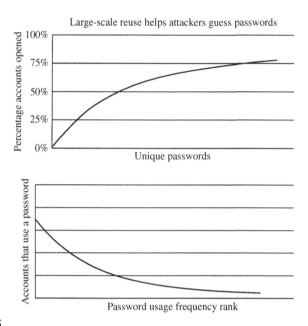

FIGURE 7.5

Although exact numbers may vary, the distribution of passwords among many users generally takes this shape. There are very few passwords that are popular, and therefore will open a rather large percentage of accounts.

Amazon was renting just such a resource at quite a reasonable price. They could try 9.36 billion keys an hour for only 30 cents per hour [51]. Jumping on this idea, a year later wireless router passwords using Wi-Fi Protected Access (WPA) an up-to-date standard, could be broken in about six minutes using Amazon's resources [52]. Defenders must take this lesson to heart—if you are targeted, the password can be broken using rented resources very quickly, even if one has taken care to avoid such simple mistakes as being vulnerable to a dictionary attack.

SUMMARY

This chapter discusses resisting attackers by authenticating users and only giving them the appropriate minimal permissions. Each of authentication and permissions has various methods and implementations appropriate for different situations. Some attacks against authentication methods were also discussed: social engineering and password cracking. These methods are some of the strategies for resisting attackers; further methods are discussed in the following three chapters. Authentication and permissions resist attackers from accessing computing resources. Chapter 8 discusses symmetric encryption, a resistance strategy for protecting information, whether it is on the defender's computing resources or not.

REFERENCES

[1] Authentication in an Internet Banking Environment. Federal Financial Institutions Examination Council, Arlington, VA; 2011. <http://www.ffiec.gov/pdf/authentication_guidance.pdf>. Retrieved Sept 20, 2013.

[2] Collins English Dictionary: Complete and Unabridged 10th Edition. Retrieved from: <http://dictionary.reference.com/browse/password> ; 2012, December.

[3] Tolkien JRR. The fellowship of the ring: being the first part of The Lord of the Rings. Boston: Houghton Mifflin Harcourt; 1954.

[4] Brewin B. CAC Use nearly halves DOD network intrusions, Croom Says. Federal Computer Week 2007, January 25. <http://fcw.com/articles/2007/01/25/cac-use-nearly-halves-dod-network-intrusions-croom-says.aspx>. Retrieved Dec 16, 2012.

[5] Anderson RJ. Security engineering: a guide to building dependable distributed systems. 2nd ed. New York: Wiley; 2008.

[6] Fowler GA. Facebook: one billion and counting. Wall Street Journal; 2012, October 4.

[7] Amazon. Amazon EC2 FAQs. Retrieved from <http://aws.amazon.com/ec2/faqs/>; 2012. Retrieved Dec 5, 2012.

[8] Red Hat, Inc. 6.3.2. In: Domingo D, editor. Red Hat Enterprise Linux 4: introduction to system administration for Red Hat Enterprise Linux 4; 2008. Retreived from <https://access.redhat.com/knowledge/docs/en-US/Red_Hat_Enterprise_Linux/4/html/Introduction_To_System_Administration/s2-acctsgrps-files.html> Retrieved Dec 5, 2012.

[9] Barker E, Barker W, Burr W, Polk W, Smid M. Recommendation for key management—Part 1: general (revision 3). NIST Special Publication 800–57; 2011.

[10] Pearsall J, editor. How many words are there in the english language? Oxford University Press. <http://oxforddictionaries.com/words/how-many-words-are-there-in-the-english-language>. Retrieved Dec 12, 2012.

[11] Shannon CE. Prediction and entropy of printed English. Bell System Tech J 1951;30(1):50–64.

[12] Katz J, Lindell Y. Introduction to modern cryptography: principles and protocols. Baco Raton, FL: Chapman & Hall/CRC; 2008.

[13] Stallings W. Cryptography and network security. 5th ed. Upper Saddle River, NJ: Pearson Education, Inc.; 2011.

[14] Kerckhoffs A. La cryptographie militaire. J des sciences militaires 1883, IX:5–38.

[15] Levy S. Prophet of privacy: Whitfield Diffie took cryptography out of the hands of the spooks and made privacy possible in the digital age by inventing the most revolutionary concept in encryption since the renaissance. Wired vol. 2, no. 11; 1994, November.

[16] Gilmore J. DES (Data Encryption Standard) Review at Stanford University; Stanford, CA: Stanford University; 2005. Available from: <http://www.toad.com/des-stanford-meeting.html>.

[17] Mudge and Kingpin. Initial cryptanalysis of the RSA SecurID algorithm. @stake; 2001. <http://www.linuxsecurity.com/resource_files/cryptography/initial_securid_analysis.pdf>.

[18] Messmer E. RSA's SecurID security breach: what should you do? Network World; 2011, March 18. <http://www.networkworld.com/news/2011/031811-rsa-securid-breach.html>. Retrieved Dec 5, 2012.

[19] The International Biometric Society. Definition of biometrics. Retreieved from <http://www.biometricsociety.org/about/definition-of-biometrics/> ; 2012. Retrieved Dec 7, 2012.

[20] Galton F. Finger Prints. New York: Macmillan; 1892.

[21] Mansfield T, Kelly G, Chandler D, Kane J. Biometric product testing final report. National Physical Laboratory, Teddington, UK; 2001.

[22] Hill R. Retina identification. In: Jain A, Bolle R, Pankanti S, editors. Biometrics. New York: Springer; 2002. p. 123–41. Retrieved from <http://dx.doi.org/10.1007/0-306-47044-6_6> Retrieved Dec 15, 2012.

[23] Killourhy KS, Maxion RA. Comparing anomaly-detection algorithms for keystroke dynamics. In: Dependable systems and networks, DSN'09. IEEE/IFIP International Conference on IEEE; 2009. p. 125–34.

[24] Carnegie Mellon University. The Official CAPTCHA S. <http://www.captcha.net/>; 2010. Retrieved Dec 20, 2012.

[25] Microsoft. About active directory domain services. Retrieved from <http://msdn.microsoft.com/en-us/library/wind <ows/desktop/aa772142(v=vs.85).aspx>; 2012. Retrieved Dec 6, 2012.

[26] Stallings W. Network security essentials: applications and standards. 4th ed. Englewood Cliffs, NJ: Prentice-Hall; 2011.

[27] Neuman C, Yu T, Hartman S, Raeburn, K. The Kerberos Network Authentication Service (V5). RFC 4120. Updated by RFCs 4537, 5021, 5896, 6111, 6112, 6113, 6649; 2005.

[28] Zhu L, Jaganathan K, Hartman S. The Kerberos Version 5 Generic Security Service Application Program Interface (GSS-API) Mechanism: Version 2. RFC 4121. Updated by RFCs 6112, 6542, 6649; 2005.

[29] Zhu L, Leach P, Hartman, S. Anonymity support for kerberos. RFC 6112; 2011.

[30] Emery S. Kerberos version 5 generic security service application program interface (gss-api) channel binding hash agility. RFC 6542; 2012.

[31] Astrand LH, Yu T. Deprecate DES, RC4-HMAC-EXP, and other weak cryptographic algorithms in kerberos. RFC 6649; 2012.

[32] Brand SL. DoD 5200.28-STD Department of Defense Trusted Computer System Evaluation Criteria (Orange Book). United States Department of Defense. Arlington, VA; 1985.

[33] Ferraiolo DF, Kzzuhn DR. Role-based access controls. In: Proceedings of the fifteenth National computer security conference. Baltimore, MD: National Institute of Standards and Technology; 1992. p. 554–63.

[34] Osborn S, Sandhu R, Munawer Q. Configuring role-based access control to enforce mandatory and discretionary access control policies. ACM Transactions on Information and Systems Security 2000, 3(2):85–106. Retrieved from <http://doi.acm.org/10.1145/354876.354878> Retrieved Dec 14, 2012.

[35] Sandhu RS, Samarati P. Access control: principle and practice. IEEE Commun Mag 1994;32(9):40–8.

[36] MacKenzie D, Meyering J. chmod(1)—Linux main page. Free Software Foundation. Retreived from <http://linux.die.net/man/1/chmod>; 2010. Retrieved Dec 14, 2012.

[37] Gruenbacher A. ACL—Ubuntu Main Page; 2010. <http://manpages.ubuntu.com/manpages/precise/en/man5/acl.5.html>. Retrieved Dec 19, 2012.

[38] Stanek WR. 13. In: Microsoft Windows 2000 Administrator's Pocket Consultant. Microsoft, Redmond, WA; 1999.

[39] Shannon CE. Communication Theory of Secrecy Systems. Bell System Tech J 1949;28(4):656–715.

[40] Johnston R. Proving voltaire right: security blunders dumber than dog snot. In: Cylab seminar series. Pittsburgh: Carnegie Mellon University. Retrieved from <http://www.cylab.cmu.edu/news_events/events/2011/e_johnston_1_31_11.html>; 2011. Retrieved Dec 15, 2012.

[41] Rasmussen R, Aaron G. Global phishing survey: trends and domain name use in 1H2009. Anti-Phishing Working Group, Boston; 2011.

[42] Rasmussen R, Aaron G. Global phishing survey: trends and domain name use in 2Q2012. Anti-Phishing Working Group, Boston; 2012.

[43] Email metrics program: the network operators' perspective. Messaging Anti-Abuse Working Group, San Francisco; 2009. p. 15.

[44] Kumaraguru P, Cranor LF, Mather L. Anti-phishing landing page: turning a 404 into a teachable moment for end users. Sixth conference on Email and Anti-Spam; Mountain View, CA. July 16–17, 2009.

[45] Wombat Security Technologies. Helping organizations combat cyber security attacks. Retrieved from <http://wombatsecurity.com/research-publications>; 2012. Retrieved Dec 20, 2012.

[46] Young W. Security message standardization: the beginning of the end. 5th Annual REN-ISAC Member Meeting. Retrieved from <http://www.ren-isac.net/docs/ren-isac_ses_rimm_2011.pdf>; 2011. Retrieved Dec 20, 2012.

[47] United States Department of Defense. DOD Announces the Expansion of Defense Industrial Base (DIB) voluntary cybersecurity information sharing activities. Retrieved from <http://www.defense.gov/releases/release.aspx?releaseid=15266>; 2012. Retrieved Dec 19, 2012.

[48] Vance A. If your password is 123456, Just Make It HackMe. NY Times; 2010, January 20; p. A1.

[49] Seward ZM, Sun A. The Top 50 Gawker media passwords. Wall Street Journal; 2010, December 13.

[50] Shirey R. Internet Security Glossary. RFC 2828. Obsoleted by RFC 4949; 2000.

[51] Goodin D. Amazon's EC2 brings new might to password cracking. The Register; 2009 November 2. <http://www.theregister.co.uk/2009/11/02/amazon_cloud_password_cracking/>. Retrieved Dec 19, 2012.

[52] Rashid FY. Amazon EC2 used to crack password encryption on wireless networks. eWeek; 2011, January 10. <http://www.eweek.com/c/a/Security/Amazon-EC2-Used-to-Crack-Password-Encryption-on-Wireless-Networks-490541/>. Retrieved Sept 20, 2013.

[53] McConnell J. National Training Standard for Information Systems Security (INFOSEC) Professionals; Fort Meade, MD: United States National Security Agency; 1994. NSTISSI-4011.

Chapter Review Questions

1. What is the difference between authenticating an entity and an entity's permissions?

2. What are the three distinct factors that may be used to authenticate an entity?

3. What are the benefits of a token or something you have versus authentication methods like passwords or something you know?

4. What are the benefits of passwords or something you know versus authentication methods like a token or something you have?

5. Regarding key management, specifically in security tokens, what does it mean for a key space to be small, and why is a small key space a problem?

6. How does RBAC simplify assigning permissions to subjects?

7. Why is phishing and social engineering generally difficult to address or prevent with technological controls?

Chapter Exercises

1. Find a phish that you received recently. How would you know it was a social engineering attempt without help from your email service? If you had received a phishing email, report it to Phish Tank (*http://www.phishtank.com/*). If you are extremely lucky and haven't received one recently, go to Phish Tank and look at one phish that has been recently submitted.

2. Consider the security services of confidentiality, integrity, and availability as described in the seminal NSTISSI whitepaper [53]. Which of these services does managing permissions support, and how?

3. Find a password-guessing dictionary on the Internet. How many of the passwords that you use are in the dictionary? For those passwords that are not in the dictionary, about how long would it take to brute-force find the password? The section "The Problem with Passwords" has some values for password elements if they are random characters, random words, or random common words. Common substitutions, like 3 for E or 0 for O, add about 1 bit of information per possible substitution place. Don't use the value for random characters if the password is actually a word followed by numbers and punctuation (or numbers followed by a word). This is a common enough pattern to treat it as a word, possibly with substitutions, followed by 1 of 10 digits and 1 of 22 punctuations.

4. Rigorously describe the authentication and permissions methods you use when you are in your house and you receive a knock at your door. Explain how you would navigate several scenarios, such as receiving a friend you were expecting, girl scouts selling cookies, your postal worker delivering a package, a police officer, and a stranger late at night when you are expecting a friend to visit. How do you authenticate these people? What permissions do you give them? What possibilities, if any, do you see for these methods to be subverted? What similarities, if any, do you see to the technical protocols discussed in this chapter?

CHAPTER 8

Resistance Strategies: Symmetric Encryption

INTRODUCTION

This chapter continues the discussion of resistance strategies with the discussion of encryption and modern cryptography. Cryptography may be defined as *the study of rigorous scientific methods of obscuring information from those who are not meant to read it*. This is a more colloquial definition than other authors may use. For example, modern cryptography has also been defined as "the scientific study of techniques for securing digital information, transactions, and distributed computations" [1, p. 3]. Encryption and decryption are the two sides of cryptography. Encryption obscures information, and decryption recovers the information. Cryptography is a subset of the scientific field of cryptology, which also includes the study of attacking and breaking encryption, called cryptanalysis. A discussion of cryptanalysis is beyond the scope of this book. Additionally, although the history of cryptography goes back over 2,500 years, past ancient Rome, this book focuses on modern cryptography. "Modern" in cryptography begins about 1980[1] [1].

Cryptography is an extremely useful tool in securing computers and networks. It is not, however, a panacea or a solution to all problems. Encryption is a particularly useful tool for resisting an adversary who has the ability to read the defender's data, either on the network or on a computer. The first section discusses the general principles of cryptography, as well as some limitations. It also discusses cryptography in contrast to a related but distinct field: steganography, the hiding of information. The older kind of encryption in modern cryptography is symmetric encryption, which the second section focuses on, as well as various methods for using it. The newer cryptographic method, asymmetric encryption, is discussed next. Asymmetric encryption is particularly important in the discussion of key management. The final section briefly covers host identification.

ENCRYPTION CONCEPTS

Cryptography is a specialized field, and the use of some special terms to describe it is unavoidable. The following list captures these terms. The definitions given sacrifice some rigor to provide a more colloquial understanding of the important kernel ideas. More rigorous readers will hopefully forgive this expedience, and may find more expansive definitions in either Katz [1] or Stallings [2], and the officially recommended definitions are found in Shirey [3]. The goal of the list ordering is that reading from the top, you will not encounter any special term that has not been previously defined.

- *Cryptography:* The study of rigorous scientific methods of obscuring information from those who are not meant to read it.

---

[1] A prerequisite of calling cryptography "modern" is the scientific undertaking, which in turn requires wide publication of results for peer review and a sense of a methodological, repeatable, and empirical critique of results. Until the mid-1970s, cryptography was the unique purview of militaries, which almost by definition do not publish their results widely, and what was published had no systematic method for evaluation. So before this it is not considered modern, although this is not to say that World War II and following did not see a tremendous amount of work on cryptology. The publication of and public attention surrounding Data Encryption Standard (DES) and public key cryptography in the late 1970s provided the final springboard into the modern era.

- *Cryptographic algorithm:* A set of step-by-step instructions that can be used to obscure information or recover obscured information. It is often implemented by a computer, but need not be.
- *Key:* A secret. The key is used in a cryptographic algorithm to vary the way in which the information is obscured. Therefore, if everything goes as it is designed, properly managing the secrecy of the key, and only the key, keeps the obscured information from being read by those who are not supposed to read it.
- *Encryption:* Applying a cryptographic algorithm to information to obscure it. Encryption requires a key as input, as well as the information to encrypt.
- *Plaintext:* The original, readable information (but not the key) input during encryption.
- *Ciphertext:* The information output from encryption, in obscured (enciphered) form.
- *Decryption:* Restoring the obscured information (ciphertext) to its original, readable form (plaintext). The cryptographic algorithm used to decrypt the ciphertext may be the same or different from the one used to encrypt the information, but for the sake of simplicity, the design goal is usually that it is the same algorithm. Likewise, cryptographic algorithms differ as to whether the same key is used for encryption and decryption or not.
- *Hashing algorithm:* A set of instructions that takes in a piece of data of any length, and outputs a fixed length of data. Any change to the input produces a large, unpredictable change in the output—that is, the function is sensitive to input changes. Hashing algorithms share this property of sensitivity with cryptographic algorithms; however, hashing algorithms are fundamentally different from encryption because there is no intended way to recover the input data from the data that is output. That is, there is no equivalent decryption function to a hashing algorithm.
- *Hash:* The output of a hashing algorithm.
- *Cipher:* A cryptographic algorithm that can be used for both encryption and decryption.
- *Symmetric key:* A type of cryptographic algorithm or cipher in which the same key is used for encryption and decryption.
- *Asymmetric key:* A type of cryptographic algorithm or cipher in which the same key is *not* used for encryption and decryption. Such a cipher employs two mathematically related keys, where one key is used for encryption and the other key is used for decryption. For an introduction to one of the inventors of asymmetric key cryptography, see the sidebar in Chapter 7.
- *Key management:* The process for handling keys during the period of time for which they exist. This includes making the keys, and storing, protecting, distributing, and archiving the keys. Importantly, key

management also includes destroying keys when they should no longer exist, and accounting for keys and the parties who are responsible for each step in the process.

- *Key lifetime:* The amount of time in a key management process between when a key is created and when a key is destroyed. Also sometimes called a *cryptoperiod*. The longer the key lifetime, the more time an adversary has to attempt to guess the key.

- *Cryptosystem:* The system made up of both a set of cryptographic algorithms and a key management process that can be usefully implemented to achieve the goal of obscuring information from adversaries, as well as ensuring those authorized to view the information can recover it.

These definitions should be sufficient to begin the conversation. Note that the goal is generally to build cryptosystems, and that encryption is only a piece of such a system. Cryptography without adequate key management is not terribly useful. However, choosing the appropriate cryptographic algorithms for the system is also vital to resisting the adversary. To this end, parts of this chapter provide some description of how algorithms work, at least in the abstract. If the defenders have no idea how any algorithms work, they will be hard-pressed to choose the appropriate algorithms and cryptosystem.

Utility and Failings

The utility of cryptography is in the ability to protect information from unauthorized access. This property can be used to provide a wider variety of services than it may appear at first glance. If it can be assured that only one entity possesses a particular key, then information encrypted by that key can be trusted to have originated from that entity. Likewise, the integrity of information can be checked using hashing algorithms in conjunction with cryptographic algorithms. Asymmetric key algorithms can also be used by two entities to agree on a single key without worrying about eavesdropping by an adversary, which is a tremendously important step in key management.

However, there are several services and strategies that cannot be fulfilled using cryptography or cryptosystems. Authentication mechanisms can be aided with cryptography, but the essential act of linking an identity with a key cannot be done without account management and the authentication factors discussed in Chapter 7. Partitioning information also must be done independent of cryptography. Like authentication, mechanisms for partitioning information may use cryptography, but they need not, and the essential aspect of partitioning is the organizational policy on which individuals have the need to know certain information and which do not. If that policy is inadequate, then the wrong individuals will access information regardless of any cryptographic controls. Partitioning as a resistance strategy is discussed in Chapter 9.

Change management, the resistance strategy discussed in Chapter 10, also can fail despite the best applications of cryptography. If the defender is running the wrong or otherwise out-of-date software, it is probably vulnerable to attack. Important tactics used in the other security strategies are also independent of cryptography, but are still necessary for a complete defense.

Several defensive mechanisms that fail regardless of cryptography resistance strategies are policy decisions. Here, *policy* quite broadly means an abstract set of rules for humans to guide system design and operation. Firewall rule sets (a frustration strategy) enact a policy, for example, regarding what traffic is allowed in or out of an organization. User password choices are also governed by a policy, although they have to be enforced by procedures. The organizational response to an incident, discussed in Chapter 15, is also largely driven by policies. An organization's risk tolerance is a complex policy choice that affects many aspects of operation. These are just a few examples, but most other chapters of this book describe aspects of security that cryptography cannot help with. Therefore, while cryptography is the technical crux of modern computer security, it should be clear that there are a myriad of other aspects of a complete security strategy that must also be adequately addressed.

SYMMETRIC ENCRYPTION

Symmetric encryption is the oldest kind of encryption, in which the same key is used both for encryption and decryption. There are two basic functions used to obscure the plaintext in symmetric encryption ciphers: substitution and transposition. Modern cryptographic algorithms use both in rather labyrinthine fashion; the first subsection will briefly discuss some classical cryptography to more simply present each of these functions. Symmetric ciphers can also operate either on chunks of input or on each bit of input serially. If the cipher operates on chunks, or blocks, of input as one unit, it is creatively called a *block cipher*, whereas if it operates on each bit serially, in a stream, it is called a *stream cipher*. These types of ciphers are discussed in the next two sections. The main difference is that stream ciphers have performance and energy consumption advantages over block ciphers, and are easier to implement in hardware, however, stream ciphers are much more vulnerable to certain attacks, and so are generally only used when this performance enhancement is absolutely necessary. The final subsection discusses an example implementation of symmetric encryption: disk and file encryption.

Historic Ciphers

For almost as long as people have wanted to keep writing secrets there have been ciphers. Many of these are very simple by modern standards. However, the principles of substitution and transposition are still the only building blocks in modern symmetric key algorithms. When asymmetric key cryptography was introduced in the 1970s, discussed later in this chapter as well as briefly in Chapter 7, it was the first novel cryptographic algorithmic building block in over 2,000 years. Therefore, understanding the principle of how historic ciphers work is still relevant to a general understanding of cryptography, although this book will not explore the gritty details of modern symmetric algorithms. First, substitution ciphers will be discussed, in which each symbol in the plaintext is substituted for another to create the ciphertext. Then transposition ciphers are tackled, in which the plaintext is rearranged to produce the ciphertext.

Substitution Ciphers

Substitution ciphers encrypt the plaintext by swapping each letter or symbol in the plaintext by a different symbol as directed by the key. Perhaps the simplest substitution cipher is the Caesar cipher, named after the man who used it. To modern readers, the Caesar cipher is perhaps better known through the Captain Midnight Code-O-Graph and secret decoder rings that even came inside Kix cereal boxes [4]. Technically speaking, the Caesar cipher may be differentiated from other, more complex substitution ciphers by terming it either a shift cipher or a mono-alphabetic cipher; both are correct.

Let's take a look at an example. Since case does not matter for the cipher, we can use the convention that plaintext is represented in lowercase letters, and ciphertext in uppercase. Spaces in the ciphertext are just added for readability; they would be removed in a real application of the cipher to make attacking the ciphertext more difficult.

Plaintext: speak, friend, and enter

Key: E

Ciphertext: WTIEOD JVMIRHD ERH IRXIV

This cipher's method of combining the plaintext and the key is actually addition. Each letter of the alphabet is assigned a number—that is, A is 0, B is 1, and so on, through Z at 25. The set of letters used can be more complex. This example also uses the comma character as the final character of the alphabet, 26. The spaces in the plaintext are ignored, for now. For each letter in the plaintext, it is converted to its number, then the value for the key is added, and the resulting number is converted back to a letter: S is 18 and E is 4. So the result is 22, or W. This is repeated for each character in the plaintext. Decryption is simple—the inverse of addition is just subtraction, so the key is subtracted from the ciphertext to get the plaintext back. Of course, 22 − 4 = 18.

There are obviously lots of problems with this. To decrypt the message, one could quickly try all 26 keys. The number of possible keys is called the *key space*.

If the key space is small enough that an adversary can try all possible keys in a "short" amount of time, then it doesn't matter what the algorithm is, it is essentially useless. This is known as the *sufficient key space principle* [1, p. 11]. "Short" is in quotes because the exact length of time depends on the use of the key in the cryptosystem and the risk model that the defender has for how long the communication needs to be secret. However, if the adversary can try all of the keys in a day or a week, then the key space is generally too small for general commercial use. On modern computer systems, about 2^{80} keys can be tried in a "short" amount of time, so any algorithm employed by the defender to resist attack should have a key space at least this large. However, if the defender does not want to have to change the cipher relatively soon, we suggest a rather larger key space, and so does NIST (National Institute of Standards and Technology) [5].

In this simple shift cipher, the key space is small. The best case for a mono-alphabetic cipher does not have a small key space, however. If A is randomly assigned to one of the 26 letters, B one of the remaining 25, C to one of the remaining 24, and so on, we create a table for the key that looks like this:

Plaintext character: a b c d e f g h i j k l m n o p q r s t u v w x y z

Key character: X F Q G A W Z S E D C V B N M L K J H G T Y U I O P

This is called a mono-alphabetic substitution cipher. For this cipher, there is no equivalent addition for encrypting the plaintext. The key is the whole table, and each letter is substituted by the key character. Decryption uses the same key, but you look up the ciphertext character on the bottom row and substitute the top-row character. The previous plaintext, "speak, friend, and enter," becomes HLAXCWJEANGXNGANGAJ, ignoring commas and spaces. The whole key space is quite large. There are $26 \times 25 \times 24 \times 23 \times \ldots \times 2 \times 1$ possible keys. This is written as 26!, read "twenty-six factorial." 26! is about equal to 2^{88}, which is large enough to resist brute-force attacks that try all the possible keys; that is, it satisfies the sufficient key space principle. But that does not mean the algorithm resists all attempts to subvert it.

The mono-alphabetic cipher is subject to frequency attacks or guessing. The ciphertext has just as many 'A' characters as there are 'e' characters in the plaintext. Anyone trying to attack the ciphertext could use a table of the frequency of letters in the English language to make some smart guesses about which ciphertext characters are which plaintext characters. This succeeds relatively easily. Humans can do it, rather slowly, once they have about 10 words, sometimes less. This is a relatively common puzzle in newspapers, so it should not be surprising it's easy to break. Computers can also do it reliably when they have at least 150 characters [6, p. 131].

Frequency attacks are not limited to single letters. The problem applies to modern systems as well. If a bank begins every transaction with the same

10 characters, then an adversary would rightfully guess that that string is more frequent. Modern algorithms try to be robust against this in a variety of ways, which will be discussed later. However, sometimes the best course of action for the defender to resist such frequency attacks is for the defender to modify the contents of the actual message, before encryption, to remove these regularities. If that is not possible, regularities in the plaintext should be minimized.

One method of frustrating frequency attacks on the underlying plaintext is to increase the block size of the cipher. The block size is how many units (in our example characters) are encrypted at once. Both the Caesar cipher and the mono-alphabetic substitution have a block size of one—only one character is encrypted at a time. A different defense is to use a key that changes per element of plaintext, whether or not the block size increases. The number of changes in the key per element of plaintext before the key repeats is called the *period of the key*; both preceding cipher examples have a key period of 1 as well as a block size of 1. Block ciphers are ciphers with a block size greater than 1, and they will be discussed in more detail in the context of modern encryption in the section "Block Ciphers". However, before moving to the discussion of transposition ciphers, we will discuss one more substitution cipher: one with a key period of arbitrary length.

The Vigenère cipher, or polyalphabetic shift cipher, was invented in 16th-century France, and for many centuries was considered unbreakable. Instead of choosing a single letter as the key, we choose a word or random string of letters. The encryption per character is the same as the Caesar cipher—letters are converted to numbers and added. When the final letter of the key has been used, the algorithm loops back to the beginning of the key and starts again, and so on, until it reaches the end of the message. For example:

Plaintext: speak, friend, and enter

Key: FRODO

Ciphertext: XFSDYE WELSSUN DAI VAWSW

To encrypt, use the first letter s + F = X, the second letter p + R = F, the third letter e + O = S, and so on. On the sixth character we reach the end of the key, and so go back to the beginning of the key to compute , + F = E, followed by f + R = W, and so on. The cipher is conceptually like using multiple different mono-alphabetic cipher keys in sequence.

In this example, the letter e in the plaintext is variably encrypted to S and V, and in the ciphertext W is, in different places, the result of a plaintext f, t, and r. This variability makes attacking the ciphertext by the frequency of letters in English much more difficult. Note a feature of the math here that did not arise in the previous example. The letter P is 15, R is 17, and so 15 + 17 = 32.

However, 32 is greater than the value of a comma, 26, the last character in our alphabet. To bring 32 back into our ring of numbers, we subtract by the number of characters we have (27) and then convert the answer to the letter F. What mathematicians use to be rigorous about this is the modulus operator, which uses the "mod" symbol, %. So we write 32 % 27 = 5, read "32 modulo 27" or "32 mod 27" for short. The operation is technically to divide by 27 and then take the whole number remainder that is left. It comes up a lot in cryptography, but that is all that needs to be said about it for now.

The Vigenère cipher is still breakable, although it is harder. If the adversary knows the key period, frequency attacks are possible on each unit that uses the same key. And in the mid-19th century a robust method for discovery of the key period of the cipher was developed. This problem persists to this day. The Vigenère cipher is an example of a stream cipher. Modern stream ciphers are discussed in a following section. However, the general method for avoiding this problem has simply been to make a key period that is long enough that it essentially never repeats, and if it does repeat, to start using a new key. There is no good algorithmic way around the problem of short key periods—once it starts to repeat, the cipher is breakable.

Transposition Ciphers

Transposition ciphers are the other primary type of cipher that can be used. Unlike substitution ciphers, which change the content of the plaintext, transposition ciphers change the order of units in the plaintext but leave the values unchanged. The first example of a transposition cipher is also taken from ancient Mediterranean military use, probably by the ancient Greeks, although the first complete description we have is from the Roman historian Plutarch [7]. The key in this example is a stick of wood. Two identical sticks, called scytale, must be produced. A strip of parchment one letter wide is then wrapped around the scytale and the message is written along the length of the scytale. A scytale with writing wound around it is shown in Figure 8.1. When the parchment is unwound the letters are transposed, and the message is not readable. Only the person with the other scytale can read the message. By wrapping the parchment around the other, identical stick, the message is decrypted—that is, unscrambled.

Throughout history people thought of more clever methods of scrambling messages. The difficult part is to make the method reversible but also easy enough to do that human error does not disrupt the process. One example, published in 1902 by a retired French colonel and the cipher's namesake, is Myszkowski transposition [8]. The message is written horizontally across columns, and the columns are numbered based on a keyword. The key must have at least two letters that repeat for the cipher to work as intended. The letters in the key are numbered according to their relative order in the alphabet;

FIGURE 8.1
A simple scytale. The word "gust" would be legible when the leather is wound around the stick, but when the leather is unwound the message is not readable.

duplicate letters have the same number. Using a quote from Mark Twain as the plaintext (ignoring punctuation and truncating the last two letters, "ly" so the columns are the same size), and "samclemens" as the key, we would write:

Key:

7 1 5 2 4 3 5 3 6 7

Plaintext:

i o n c e s e n t a
d o z e n o f m y f
r i e n d s a t e l
e g r a m s a y i n
g f l e e a t o n c
e a l l i s d i s c
o v e r e d t h e y
a l l e f t t o w
n i m m e d i a t e

To obtain the ciphertext, we read columns in the order they are numbered. If the column has a unique number, it is read straight down. Any columns that share a number are read in sequence horizontally before moving to the next line. So the ciphertext from the preceding would be the following, with spaces inserted for readability: OOIGF AVLIC ENAEL RLMSN OMSTS YAOSI DHFTD AENDM EIEEE NEZFE ARALT LDETL TMITY EINSE OTIADF RLENG CECOY AWNE. To decrypt the message, you would need the keyword and then just fill in the columns in the order prescribed by the keyword and reconstruct the plaintext.

The transposition is not vulnerable to frequency attacks in quite the same way that substitution ciphers are. The letters in this ciphertext are already in the same proportion as letters in English, because the cipher does not change the letters. However, this is also a major weakness. Word scrambles are also a popular newspaper challenge, and humans are naturally fairly good at unscrambling words. In general, just transposition is not sufficient to resist an attack on the ciphertext.

PROFILE: CLAUDE SHANNON

Father of Information Theory

Claude Shannon was born in 1916 in Petoskey, MI. After graduating from the University of Michigan, he attended MIT and worked with such luminaries as Vannevar Bush. By the age of 21, he had completed his master's thesis at MIT. His paper, "A Symbolic Analysis of Relay and Switching Circuits," has been called one of, if not the most, important master's theses of the 20th century [9]. This idea of electronic circuit switching underlies almost all digital communications and computing that occur today.

It is difficult to adequately describe how much influence Shannon had with his work. Not only did he begin the conversion of cryptography from an art to a science, but the very concept of digital computing and digital telecommunications would not be possible without his contributions [notably 10–12]. This includes the first prominent mention of mathematically encoding information to transmit it successfully. This idea seems trivially obvious now, but when Shannon started there essentially was no concept of information as a mathematical construct. Much of this work was done in the heat of the WWII effort from 1941–1945, during which time Shannon worked at Bell Laboratories in New Jersey. As if cryptography and computing were not enough, Shannon also did important work on ground-to-air defense systems that helped protect England during the Blitz. He continued to be affiliated with Bell Labs until 1972.

Given his technical prowess, one might expect a taciturn or unapproachable personality. This was not so. Among other frivolities, Dr. Shannon was known to ride the halls of Bell Labs on a unicycle, juggling three balls. He also had some more whimsical inventions, such as a mechanical mouse that could navigate a maze [9].

Dr. Shannon continued to teach at MIT until 1978. He passed away in 2001, at the age of 84, in a Massachusetts nursing home. The interested reader should consult Gallager [13] for a more detailed account of Shannon's life and his influence on the modern world.

Modern Ciphers

Modern symmetric key ciphers can be broken down into two broad categories: block ciphers and stream ciphers. While the use cases for each type varies, the design principles behind each are largely similar. Katz and Lindell identify three principles of modern cryptography [1, p. 18]. The principles can be cast in the light of resistance strategies as follows:

1. *Principle 1:* Before attempting a solution, precisely what is meant by *security* must be rigorously and precisely defined. At a minimum, this means exactly what kinds of adversary are being resisted, what the resources and access abilities of the adversaries are, and for how long they need to be resisted.

2. *Principle 2:* All assumptions must be completely and precisely stated. There are bound to be some unproven assumptions, however, stating them precisely and explicitly is necessary to manage risk from those assumptions. Since assumptions carry some risk, assumptions should be minimized.

3. *Principle 3:* There ought to be a rigorous proof of the security of any piece of a cryptosystem. The proof should demonstrate that the definition from principle 1 is obtained, given any assumptions stated from the process described in principle 2.

These principles are valuable not just for cryptosystems and resistance via encryption, but for security strategies generally. Cryptography is one part of the strategy that is most suited to rigorous proof, and so fewer assumptions may be needed here than elsewhere. But all strategies would benefit from a precise statement of assumptions and how those assumptions interact with the level of security that is desired.

Modern symmetric key ciphers have two primary functional components: some substitution steps and some transposition steps. These two components are conceptually the same as in historic ciphers. By using both substitution and transposition, the conceptual weaknesses of substitution can be supported by the strengths of transposition, and vice versa. The functions are more sophisticated than the historical examples, and according to the preceding principles, they have been much more rigorously tested. But the concepts of what is done to the plaintext to produce the ciphertext and then decrypt it again has not changed as much in symmetric key ciphers as one might expect.

Information Theory

In discussing modern cryptography, we must briefly introduce a special use of the term *information*. Without this numerical definition of information rigorous proofs of cryptography do not seem possible. In fact, without Shannon's work on quantifying information, networked communication as we know it, including the whole Internet, probably would not be possible. The seminal work is Claude Shannon's article "A Mathematical Theory of Communication" [10], which was published in 1948 and expanded into a textbook published the following year [12]. These works are the foundation of a broad field now called information theory.

The only aspect of information theory with which we will be concerned here is Shannon's definition of information. Since Shannon is formulating a theory for engineering communications systems, he is only concerned with the information provided by signals on the wire. He goes on to formalize a mathematical notion of information. The information in a message is based on the statistical likelihood of a message given all possible messages. The unit

0000	0100	1000	1100
0001	0101	1001	1101
0010	0110	1010	1110
0011	0111	1011	1111

FIGURE 8.2
All the possible combinations of 4 binary digits. This string is equal to 4 bits of information, because there are 16 possible combinations and $4 = \log_2 16$.

of information, as far as we are concerned, is *bits*, short for binary digits. Bits, and later the playfully named byte, that are stored and transmitted on modern digital computers are named after this information theoretic unit, which at the time of Shannon's publication was primarily an abstract unit rather than something one buys trillions of at the store.

Bits on a computer disk are represented by a string of 1's and 0's. The number of combinations of 1's and 0's in a string N binary digits long is the number of possible messages. For example, there are 16 possible combinations in a string of 4 binary digits, as demonstrated in Figure 8.2. The maximum amount of information is the same as the length of the string, namely N.[2]

It is in this numerical sense that *information* is used for the remainder of this discussion. In this sense, increases and decreases in information are explicitly calculable. Such calculations are extremely useful in robust proofs of security concepts and cryptosystems, as recommended by principle 3. We will not, however, delve into any such mathematical proofs in this chapter.

Perfect Secrecy

The concept of *perfect secrecy* was first defined by Claude Shannon in 1946, although the work was not declassified and published until three years later [11]. This paper is one of the foundational works of modern cryptography; perfect secrecy is only one of the contributions. The definition of perfect secrecy is based on statistics and probabilities. A ciphertext maintains perfect secrecy if the attacker's knowledge of the contents of the message is the same both before and after the adversary inspects the ciphertext, attacking it with unlimited resources. That is, the message gives the adversary precisely no information about the message contents.

---

[2]This is because the amount of information is based on the logarithm of the possible messages. A logarithm is the inverse of exponentiation. Logarithms, in this binary (base 2) system of 1's and 0's, are a mathematical function where the output increases by 1 when the input doubles. When the length of the string of bits increases by 1 bit, the number of possible combinations doubles. Since the base-2 logarithm of a binary string happens to be equal to its length, the length of the shortest string of bits that can encode a message is also the maximum information carried in the message.

The result of working through what would be required for perfect secrecy is that there must be as many possible keys as there are possible ciphertexts. Therefore, the key material must be as long as the ciphertext, when both are represented in bits. This is generally considered impractical. The only cipher that meets this requirement is known as the one-time pad, which was invented before Shannon's formalization of the problem by either 30 or 65 years, depending on how credit is distributed for the cipher and realizing its value [14]. The one-time pad is rather simple. It is a Vigenère cipher, as described earlier, where the key period is at least as long as the message, it never repeats or is reused, and the key is truly random. Shannon proves the one-time pad is perfectly secure, and that the key material for any other perfectly secure cipher must have the same properties as keys in one-time pads [11].

Perfect secrecy is impractical to implement. There are enough potential operational difficulties that provide the adversary an attack vector that the defender's effort is often better spent on something besides the one-time pad key management problems. Therefore, modern cryptography suffices with what is called computational security. The symmetric cipher might use a 256-bit key, which does not provide perfect secrecy if the message is more than 256 bits. Most messages are. However, as long as the cipher is well designed, the adversary must try all the keys—actually, half the keys on average—to break the encryption. For a random 256-bit key, this would currently take all the computing resources of the world running for more time than the universe has existed so far. This is generally considered sufficient.

Block Ciphers

Block ciphers, if used properly, are an effective method for resisting adversarial attempts to read data, either data stored on disk or in transit on the network. A block cipher is one of the two common modern symmetric cipher types. It is distinguished from a stream cipher, because a block cipher performs operations on a chuck of data at once, whereas a stream cipher can operate on a single bit of plaintext at a time. The foremost example of a modern block cipher is the Advanced Encryption Standard (AES) [15]. AES is the primary cipher approved for use by the U.S. government to protect electronic data. It was certified in 2001, and has been something of a de facto standard cryptographic algorithm worldwide. It replaced the aging DES, also a block cipher, which was issued in 1977 [16]. There are too many block ciphers to list them all, but DES and AES are the two most famous examples.

A block cipher maps each possible input block of plaintext to an output block of ciphertext. For a cipher with 64-bit inputs and outputs, to write down this complete mapping would take about 2^{69} bits [17, p. 60], or about 74 exabytes of memory. This is too much. But as we saw with historical substitution ciphers, a "short" block size makes breaking the cipher too easy. To efficiently use large enough input blocks without using infeasible amounts of memory, ciphers are used. A well-designed cipher will map an input value to an output value using the key in such a way that the mapping appears random unless one knows the key. Modern block ciphers tend to have block sizes of 128 bits or larger, because if the block size is too small there is the same problem as a small key space as described previously—the adversary can enumerate all the possible options and thus undermine the algorithm.

This book will not describe in any detail the operation of AES or DES. Briefly, each is composed of rounds. A round is a substitution phase followed by a transposition phase, each of which is conceptually the same as the substitution and transposition ciphers historically used. In this regard, the ciphers are quite simple. However, there are plenty of subtle mathematical attacks to defend against. This defense requires rigorous design of the algorithm in sometimes surprising ways. Designing a sound algorithm is extremely difficult for this reason. The general recommendation is that no modern organization should try to design its own cryptographic algorithm. AES is freely available and quite safe. Ten years after it was certified by NIST minor inroads were made against the algorithm, yet the paper itself states the advances "do not threaten the practical use of AES in any way" [18].

Just because the defender is using a secure block cipher does not mean it is automatically operated in a secure manner. Although each block of input is 128 bits, the message is almost certainly longer than that. There are multiple modes of operation with which to adapt the cryptographic algorithm to this situation [3]. Most have some interaction between the blocks in a message. For example, the value of the block i is combined with the key material used to encrypt block $i + 1$, cryptographically linking the blocks to be in that order. This is preferable because it links the blocks together both as part of the same message and in the correct order.

To see why this is necessary, imagine a bank that sends its transactions encrypted via AES. If the account numbers are 128-bit numbers, and are always in the same place in the message, there can be trouble. If block 6 contains the account number to withdraw money from, and block 8 contains the account to deposit the money in to, then an adversary could make a deposit into someone's account and wait. If he or she sees the transaction go out, the adversary could modify the message by swapping blocks 6 and 8. The adversary does not need to know the key used in the encryption to do this. As long as the blocks do not depend on each other, everything will decrypt properly and the victim's account will likely be debited for the amount that the adversary asked to deposit.

In most computing equipment, block ciphers are the preferred symmetric encryption cipher. The ability to ingest blocks of data, perform both substitution and transposition, and then use the appropriate mode of operation to link the blocks together is a robust method for protecting data and resisting attacks. However, there will always be devices with resource constraints. Small devices such as embedded sensors and RFID (radio-frequency identification) tags lack the memory, computing power, and/or electrical power reserves for a block cipher. In these cases, it is advisable to use a stream cipher.

Stream Ciphers

Stream ciphers are good for fast implementations with low resource consumption. These two features help the defender implement resistance strategies in devices that may not have the resources for a block cipher implementation. Stream ciphers are also useful for encrypting wireless signals, which more naturally fit a streaming model than transmitting data in larger, fixed-size chunks. For example, the A5/1 stream cipher is used in GSM phones [19], and the RC4 stream cipher has been used in the security system for wireless local area networks (WLANs) [20]. The simplicity of stream ciphers is both a blessing and a curse. It appears to be more difficult to adequately include stream ciphers in cryptosystems. For example, the implementation of RC4 in Wired Equivalent Privacy (WEP) for WLAN security was a failure, even though the RC4 cipher itself was not broken—it was just implemented badly [20]. Specifically, the implementation artificially shortened the key period; the technical reason this is a problem will be explained shortly.

Stream ciphers can be broadly classified into those that work better in hardware and those that work better in software. A5/1 is an example of a cipher better suited to hardware. It is one of a class of algorithms called linear feedback shift registers (LFSRs), which are easy to construct with a little electrical engineering knowledge. RC4 is an example of a cipher suited for software, but optimized for low resource usage. It only requires less than 1 kilobyte of memory and simple array-based operations.

Stream ciphers use conceptual tools similar to block ciphers. Substitution is the primary tool: each bit or byte of plaintext is combined with the key material by an exclusive-or (XOR) operation to substitute the plaintext bit into the ciphertext bit. Binary XOR is quite simple. There are only two possible values, 1 or 0, and if the two inputs are the same the result is 0, otherwise it is 1. A small table of these results is presented in Figure 8.3.

Since stream ciphers cannot do transposition per se, as the cipher cannot cache one block of input and transpose the contents, successful stream ciphers create a feedback system where current key material depends on the previous operation of the system. Therefore, one rather short key can initialize the system to produce a pseudorandom stream of key material that does

Plaintext	Xor	Key	Result
1	$\oplus$	1	0
1	$\oplus$	0	1
0	$\oplus$	1	1
0	$\oplus$	0	0

FIGURE 8.3

A simple example of the XOR operation on a single bit of input from two sources—plaintext and a key—to produce the ciphertext.

not repeat for quite a long time. Due to the XOR operation, once a stretch of key material has been used it can never be used again. This is a common mistake in stream cipher implementation, and was one implementation error in WEP [20].

This attack is possible because the XOR operation is its own inverse. Any number $+2 - 2$ equals itself because addition and subtraction are inverses. Likewise, combining two ciphertexts encrypted with the same key eliminates the key, since it is XOR'd with itself. In this case, when the key is eliminated the two plaintexts remain. They are still XOR'd together, but from this information, statistical methods like those used to defeat the mono-alphabetic substitution cipher, described earlier, can be used to recover each plaintext without much difficulty.

To demonstrate the danger of this graphically, see the process in Figure 8.4. In this case, black and white are used instead of 0 and 1, respectively, but otherwise the XOR operation is the same. When either image is XOR'd with the key, it is adequately protected by the encryption. However, if the same key image is reused, the two source images are quite starkly and easily recovered when the two ciphertexts are XOR'd.

Due to the preceding problems, stream ciphers must be used carefully. However, they serve a useful role in the defender's resistance strategy. Encrypting network traffic resists the adversary's efforts to eavesdrop on the traffic or modify it. For details on how a stream cipher can be successfully implemented, consult explanations of the Wi-Fi Protected Access (WPA) protocol, for example, in Stallings [22, ch. 6]. However, note that in WPA the preferred mode of operation is to use AES to create a key stream, rather than RC4 [6, p. 667]. One viable mode of operation for block ciphers is to encrypt a counter with the key to create a stream of key bits to XOR with the plaintext stream. In this way, a block cipher can be used like a stream cipher. It does not have the resource savings that RC4 has, however, the algorithm and mode of operation are more robust and certified by NIST for use on U.S. federal government systems. Since computing power has become cheaper, wireless

FIGURE 8.4

An example of why key reuse is dangerous when encryption with XOR is used. Black and white pixels are treated as 0 and 1 bits, respectively. The two initial images are each adequately protected on their own, but since the key was reused the two ciphertexts can be XOR'd, canceling out the key and revealing the two plaintexts XOR'd. This example was inspired by Smith [21].

access points have enough processing power to perform these AES computations without trouble.

There are three modes of data that need to all be protected: data in motion, data at rest, and data being processed. Encrypting data on the network is protecting data in motion. Block ciphers are commonly used to protect data at rest, such as on file systems. Protecting data at rest is the topic of the next section. Unfortunately, there is currently no common practice for protecting data while it is being processed. It is very difficult to process data without knowing what the contents are. Solutions to this problem have been proposed [23], but are currently considered infeasible. Therefore, it is notable that encryption, either with block or stream ciphers, does not help protect data while it is being processed. This fact is important to consider in a comprehensive resistance strategy, especially when considering cloud computing, in which data processing is outsourced [24,25].

File and Disk Encryption

File encryption and disk encryption are complementary technologies for resisting the adversary's access to data at rest. File encryption is the more granular technology, whereas disk encryption has broader coverage but is less precise. Disk encryption is best for resisting the threat of media being physically stolen—it functions best when the computer is powered off. A computer that is powered on has access to read the disk on-the-fly, otherwise performance would suffer unacceptably, so an adversary who can issue commands to a powered-on machine may bypass disk encryption. File encryption only permits access on a per-file basis, and so is better suited to protect particular files of interest from being read even if the adversary has access to the machine. But the logistical overhead of encrypting individual files makes it unsuitable for encrypting all the files on a computer, a task that disk encryption does quite easily.

File Encryption

Individual files on a computer can be encrypted to resist the adversary's attempts to read the contents of the file. This is useful for particularly sensitive files on a computer, but is also useful for application-level transfer of files across an insecure channel such as email. Any suitably secure modern symmetric cipher can be used as part of a file encryption mechanism. Some common mechanisms for file encryption are PGP (pretty good privacy) and GPG (GNU privacy guard), both of which are implementations of OpenPGP as described in RFC 4880 [26]. The RFC gives a good concise description of the system purpose: "OpenPGP software uses a combination of strong public-key and symmetric cryptography to provide security services for electronic communications and data storage."

Public key cryptography is synonymous with asymmetric key cryptography, as discussed briefly in Chapter 7 and in more detail in the following section, "Asymmetric Encryption". Asymmetric cryptography supports, among other services, entity authentication. This feature is not necessary for understanding file encryption; however, it is important and is discussed in the section on Asymmetric Encryption as well.

File encryption usually uses block ciphers. The process is best accomplished in the following order. The file is compressed using a program like winzip or gzip. When a file is compressed, common long strings in the file are replaced with an encoding that shortens the file. These encodings are likely different for each file. Therefore, this step is both for efficiency—the file is smaller so less encryption rounds are needed—and for security—eliminating long, repeated strings makes frequency analysis more difficult. The compressed file must be padded with extra bits to make sure the length is a multiple of the block size. The file is then encrypted, with AES, for example.

Generating the secret key for file encryption is an important step. It can use a user-supplied password, but this subjects the file encryption to all the human problems with passwords. Note that encryption without any form of authentication (described in Chapter 7) is not useful. For this reason, the recommended PGP behavior is to generate a random key for symmetric encryption, called the session key, and then encrypt the session key with an asymmetric key that can authenticate an entity. This method is particularly useful when encrypting email contents, as then only the recipient can decrypt the session key, and thus the message.

Database encryption is related to file encryption, but is not exactly the same. Databases are, at some level, files on the system, and so can be encrypted to protect them. However, many database systems provide more granularity on what particular contents can be protected with encryption. Individual tables, columns, or records might be protected. Implementation details vary by database provider, but the concepts are no different from file encryption using PGP. A symmetric key is used to encrypt the desired data, and that key is protected and stored using a key or password related to users authorized to view the data.

Disk Encryption

Disk encryption prevents a disk drive, such as a hard drive in a laptop computer or a portable USB storage device, from booting up unless the user inputs valid authentication data. The standard process for booting up an operating system is that the first section of the disk, called the master boot record, instructs the system where to read the first file that begins the instructions for loading the operating system. There are then no special instructions needed for interpreting the contents of the disk—files are in plaintext by default. Installing a disk encryption technology modifies this process.

When disk encryption is installed, the contents of the disk—except the master boot record and a small system that it loads—are encrypted using any suitable modern symmetric cipher by a secret key. The master boot record is modified to first load this small system, which can validate authentication information from the user. If the user authenticates successfully, the encryption key is unlocked. This small system, which varies per implementation, contains the master key for the device encrypted to one or more keys based on the authentication information, which can be a password, a fingerprint scan, a public key–based token, etc. When the valid authentication information is read, it can decrypt the master key. This master key then remains in the computer's memory for the duration of power-on so that the operating system can first read itself from the disk to boot up, and then any other disk contents the user requests during operation of the computer.

There are a variety of implementations of whole disk encryption. One open-source implementation is Linux Unified Key Setup-on-disk-format (LUKS;

http://code.google.com/p/cryptsetup/), which is the standard for most flavors of the Linux operating system. Hardware-based disk encryption technologies also exist, in which the disk drive itself contains the small authentication system as part of its firmware or device driver [27]. Software solutions such as LUKS are flexible and allow the defender to encrypt existing disks that are not specially built. Intuitively, there seems to be greater possibility for user misconfiguration of software solutions because of this added flexibility, which is a potential problem. But in general, there are two weak points of disk encryption solutions:

1. If the computer is powered on, including in sleep mode, the disk encryption keys are available to an adversary who can access system memory.
2. It is only as strong as the authentication method used, and human users are known to select poor passwords if they are permitted to do so.

These weak points are not serious. They simply demonstrate that full disk encryption, like any other security strategy, is not sufficient in itself to protect data. Other strategies can be used in coordination with disk encryption to provide a more comprehensive strategy. In particular, file encryption as discussed earlier and strong user authentication as discussed in Chapter 7 directly address these two weak points and help to formulate a comprehensive resistance strategy.

ASYMMETRIC ENCRYPTION

Asymmetric encryption uses completely different elementary pieces and methods than symmetric encryption. There are no substitution and transposition steps. The methods are "asymmetric" because there are two different keys: one for encryption and one for decryption. This creates lots of good opportunities. There are two keys: the public key and private key. These are kept secret as the English meaning of their names implies: everyone can know the public key, and no one should know the private key but the owner. The two related keys together are known as a key pair. Public key cryptography was initiated by Diffie and Hellman [28], although the RSA algorithm was the first to implement the concepts. The Diffie–Hellman key exchange soon followed, with their own implementation.

Use of a key pair permits some interesting and useful implementations and properties that are not available with symmetric key cryptography. If no adversary interferes, there are primarily two properties. First, a message encrypted by the private key can be read by anyone, but it demonstrates that only one entity—the owner of the private key—authored the message. Second, anyone can encrypt a message with the public key, but only the owner of the private key can read it. These two features enable robust statements about authentication without the complicated and fragile logistics that would be necessary to accomplish the same level of authentication with symmetric key encryption.

Asymmetric encryption is more resource-intensive than symmetric key encryption. For this reason, it is common to encrypt only a small piece of information with the relatively expensive asymmetric operation. This small piece is a symmetric key that can be used to encrypt and decrypt the bulk of the information; it is usually called a session key. This method permits the computer to generate a strong random key for use with the symmetric encryption. A further beneficial property is that each operation can use a different session key, and therefore if one section of data is compromised by cryptanalysis, the other parts or files are encrypted with a different key and so are not. Of course, if the asymmetric key pair is compromised, all the session keys could still be discovered. But compromise by attacking the key pair is essentially impossible when the plaintext is random strings such as session keys. The key management cycle (see the next section) is the more vulnerable target.

Asymmetric encryption is based on operations in mathematics that are hard to reverse. There are a couple different candidates. The original method devised by Diffie and Hellman in the late 1970s is straightforward, even though the mathematics were obscure at the time [28]. We have already introduced the basics in another context. All available asymmetric key algorithms rely on the modulus operator, which we encountered in our discussion of the Vigenère cipher. The modulus operation forces the result to be a whole number (no decimals or fractions), and also to be restricted to a certain range. So it creates a sort of unique set of numbers on which to do operations. For example, the only numbers that can result from anything mod 7 are the numbers 0, 1, 2, 3, 4, 5, or 6.

The Diffie–Hellman method involves the difficulty of finding inverses for certain mathematical operations on these novel sets of numbers. For example, addition and subtraction are inverses. In the mod 7 example, $1 + 6 = 7$, but 7 is not a possible number; $7 \bmod 7 = 0$, and so 1 and 6 are inverses for the addition operation. In the common set of numbers that are not restricted, 1 and -1 are inverses. This result in mod 7 is different, but not hard to find.

Diffie–Hellman takes advantage of a different operation, raising numbers to an exponent, for which there does not seem to be any method to find the inverse except to try most of the possible options.[3]

---

[3]The inverse of exponentiation is the logarithm: $2^3 = 8$ and $\log_2 8 = 3$. Further, $\log_b(b^x) = x$. Logarithms are well defined in sets made up from a modulus—there is an answer. Diffie–Hellman just takes advantage of the fact the answer is "hard" to calculate.

For example, $2^3 \bmod 7 = 8 \bmod 7 = 1$, but knowing that the base is 2 and the answer is 1, there is no known method to find the power was 3 without just guessing until the correct answer is found. There are a few careful aspects of how you select the numbers involved in the system, which are beyond the scope of this book. The interested reader may consult Katz and Lindell [1] or Stallings [2] for such details on how these mathematics can be used to create and exchange keys.

Other examples of asymmetric key cryptographic algorithms include elliptic curve, El Gamal, Digital Signature Standard (DSS), and RSA (for its inventors, Rivest, Shamir, and Adleman). Diffie–Hellman is the basis for El Gamal and DSS; the others use related but different mathematical problems. El Gamal and RSA can be used for encryption in their own right, rather than just key exchange. In practice, though, what they are usually used to encrypt is a symmetric key that protects the data of interest.

KEY MANAGEMENT AND DISTRIBUTION

All cryptography rests on one assumption: the key is secret. The beautiful thing about cryptography is that a huge amount of information can be kept secret if only a small key is kept secret. This is also a danger, and the operational considerations of getting and sharing a secret key are significant. And unlike other aspects of cryptography covered so far, we will not come to some seemingly magical mathematical function in which we can place our trust. Key management and distribution are process management exercises. Although there are some cryptographic tools that can assist the process, in the end the policy on key management must be aligned to the organization's risk tolerance and enforced with human involvement.

Key distribution is concerned with transporting a key from where it is generated to where it is used in a cryptographic algorithm. This might involve a key distribution center (KDC), which actually creates the keys, or a key translation center (KTC), which merely serves as a trusted broker for keys that are generated elsewhere. Key management is a larger process that includes the whole life cycle of each key used by the organization. Key management is generally considered to have several steps, including "ordering, generating, storing, archiving, escrowing, distributing, loading, destroying, auditing, and accounting for" keys [3]. Certain functions, such as escrow, need not be performed at all. NIST publishes more detailed standards for key management that are binding for U.S. government executive branch organizations, but can also serve as a good reference for best practices more generally [5,29].

Two essential lessons from the NIST documentation are about key usage purposes and duration. For anyone designing a key management system, it is recommended you read the whole document. Please. However, for the general audience these two lessons get at the heart of the way to think about resisting the adversary using encryption.

Keys can be used for many purposes, including encryption itself, but also authentication, key transport, random number generation, and others. A single key should only be used for a single purpose [5, p. 45]. Using a key for more than one purpose can weaken the security services provided by one or both of those services by increasing the adversary's ability to attack the key. Furthermore, the damage done if the key is compromised is greater because the key had multiple purposes. Finally, different key purposes should have different durations of time the key is active for legitimate use. Using keys across different purposes disrupts this duration-management task.

The duration of time that a key is available to users for valid use is called the cryptoperiod of the key. Keys used for different purposes should have different cryptoperiods. The length of time a key is in valid use is influenced by a number of factors, including [5, p. 46]:

- The strength of the algorithm being used to resist attacks.
- The expected adversary access to the operating environment.
- To the volume of data encrypted.
- How long the data needs to remain protected from disclosure.
- The purpose of the key.
- The robustness of the process to install new keys.
- The human cost of the process to install new keys.

A stronger algorithm means the key can be used for longer time periods. More access by the adversary means the key should be replaced more frequently. Larger data volumes likewise require shorter key lifetimes. Shorter cryptoperiods increase security, in general, so the longer the data needs to remain protected the shorter the cryptoperiod should be. In this manner, each piece of data that needs to be protected for a long time may have its own key, so that compromise of one key does not compromise much data. Short cryptoperiods can be counterproductive, however. If the rekeying process is not robust but rather a manual, human-intensive process, operator error may be a much more serious concern to key integrity than anything else [5, p. 47].

There are several models for key distribution and several methods or tools for doing so. The primary cryptographic tool that enables large-scale key distribution is asymmetric key cryptography. Although key distribution can certainly be done without asymmetric key algorithms, it is impractical to do key distribution on the web or any other large system without such algorithms.

The primary models for the key distribution architecture are either a centralized, oligarchical, or distributed architecture. Key distribution and management on the Internet relies on a public key infrastructure (PKI). A PKI is comprised of all the hardware, software, people, and policies needed to manage keys. PKI is usually used to refer to the management in a centralized or oligarchic model, and usually includes a method of binding keys to identities using digital certificates, described shortly.

In a centralized architecture, users trust one computer or entity to negotiate and distribute keys on their behalf. This one entity is a single point of failure, and in general, this makes centralized architectures fragile, which is dangerous. An oligarchical model divides up this authority among a small number of entities with different areas of responsibility; however, authority is still vested in a few hands that have significantly different responsibilities than the average user. The way that Transport Layer Security (TLS) certificates are managed for host identification on the Internet follows an oligarchical model. This infrastructure is described in more detail in the following section. In a distributed key distribution model, no user has more authority to negotiate keys than any other. PGP is a common example of this type of architecture. In both the TLS architecture and PGP, asymmetric key algorithms are used to distribute a symmetric key for the session.

In PGP, users trust other users based on a network of trust relationships. If Alice knows Bob, she can make this known by signing Bob's PGP key and then publishing this. Keys happen to live on key servers that generous organizations run for everyone's benefit, but these key servers have no special authority. All the data about Bob's key is self-contained within the key format. If Bob trusts Charlie, Bob can sign that key and publish it. Charlie can do the same for Dan. If Alice wants to send Dan a file, she can decide if she trusts Dan based on her policy about how far away Dan is from a key Alice has signed and trusts. In this example, Dan is three degrees away. Alice's decision as to whether to trust him is based on her risk tolerance for the data she wants to send; there is no categorically correct answer as to whether or not she ought to.

COMPUTER IDENTIFICATION

An important task in the functioning of the Internet, or any large network, is to verify that the computer the defender is communicating with is the correct one. Early in the development of the Internet, this identification was implicitly asserted with the IP address. Even though there was no formal method protecting the IP address from modification or hijacking in the operation of the IP protocol, in the 1970s the network was a research network shared by a small enough number of people that they all could call one another on the phone. In this environment, it was adequate to know who the operation of an IP address was assigned to in order to trust that the connection was to that computer. This implicit assumption worked its way into several early remote tools, such as rlogin and rcp (remote copy).

Implicit computer identification caused several security problems once the Internet grew large enough. The older remote-access programs (rcp and telnet) have been replaced by programs with more robust authentication that replicate the function, such as scp (secure copy). However, at the most basic level, the IP protocol has not been updated. It is too ingrained in the operation of the network to be easily changed. Efforts have been made, namely IPsec, to improve this situation, however, they have not been adopted on a large scale. In this environment, host identification is an important service that needs to be provided independent of the IP protocol.

Secure Socket Layer (SSL), the new version of which was renamed Transport Layer Security (TLS), is a common distributed computer identification protocol in use on the Internet. The original SSL protocol was developed privately by web browser pioneer Netscape [30], however, it was later standardized publicly by the IETF (Internet Engineering Task Force) as TLS [31]. When a URL (uniform resource locator) begins with https://, rather than just http://, this means "HTTP over SSL/TLS."

TLS provides a number of security services besides computer identification, and the protocol does not require the parties perform the identification step. However, in practice, most of the services provided by the protocol require at least one computer to identify itself [31, p. 3]. The identification uses asymmetric key cryptography. The crux of the work is done by a network of digital certificates. A discussion of computer identification would be incomplete without an understanding of the digital certificates. In some ways, the digital certificate infrastructure is the keystone of the system, and TLS is just a flexible specification for utilizing the certificates.

Digital Certificates

Digital certificates can come in many forms, but the most common is the X.509 certificate. The X.509 format is an ITU (International Telecommunication Union) standard, but the implementation for use on the Internet for identifying computers is standardized by the IETF [32]. This section will focus on the X.509 implementation for any details, but certificates are conceptually rather simple. A certificate links certain information together. The most important fields are a public key for use in asymmetric cryptography, a domain name, and an expiration date.

The fields in a certificate are all linked together because they are signed by the private key of some certificate authority (CA), which verifies the certificate as genuine. Anyone can use the CA's public key to verify the certificate. Anyone with a certificate can use their private key to sign other certificates, which users can verify as long as they can verify the matching public key. Users can do this so long as a chain of certificates leads back to a CA. To ground the system, CA public keys come preinstalled in web browsers. The way Microsoft, Google, or Mozilla determine what CAs are preinstalled involves internal policies idiosyncratic to the browser author, but it usually involves the CA paying a recurring fee.

These CAs are then authorized to issue certificates (i.e., sign them with their private key) for other people or organizations. There are no official rules about how these certificates are issued. It is generally done by private companies, and market forces drive the competition among them. Incentive for cost-cutting is not always a good motivator for secure practices. If there is a valid chain of signed certificates back to a CA, a website is considered secured. All this really means is that a person with access to the email address that was used to register the domain name for the website agreed to let someone pay for a certificate to be issued, and the computer who served the website has that certificate. Some companies used to force applicants to show up in person, or receive mail at a physical address. However, this rigor is not required. This is not an awful model, but it has several opportunities for subversion.

A useful exercise is to investigate the number of CAs preinstalled in your browser. There are about 100, which is far more than most users need for their daily browsing. This has caused significant trouble in the past. The security of everyone browsing the Internet is the result of the weakest link among these CAs. Weakest-link efforts are dangerous to rest security on, as compared to sum of efforts or best efforts, as discussed in Chapter 5 and Anderson [6, p. 229]. Even if a relatively obscure CA that mostly only provides services to Dutch users has the CA's private key compromised, browsers in Iran or Washington, DC, can be redirected to a perfect forgery of any website by an adversary.

This is precisely what happened when DigiNotar's private key was compromised in 2011 [33]. The adversary was able to issue his or her own certificates as if they were DigiNotar. Unless the user noticed by a stroke of pure luck that DigiNotar had signed their Google login page instead of Thawte, the valid CA for the site at the time, there was no warning of the forgery. This permitted the adversary to steal credentials from users for a number of sites, since the users did not notice the forgery and input their credentials as if they were logging in to the real site.

Forged certificates were issued for over 500 organizations, from Google to the intelligence agencies of the United States, United Kingdom, and Israel. All these organizations possibly had user credentials stolen. Further exacerbating the situation was that DigiNotar certificates could not be universally revoked—the company had legitimately signed several sites used by the Dutch government to deliver critical services to its citizens. Revoking the DigiNotar certificate would invalidate these legitimate certificates at the same time as the forgeries. To give the Dutch enough time to provide alternatives, there was a browser patch issued to try to block the DigiNotar certificates being used on known-forged sites, and eventually the certificates were revoked. The company went bankrupt not long after, but the damage to many unwitting Internet users had been done.

Many of the CAs that come preinstalled in browsers will never be used by a user. This is because many of them specialize in business in one geographic area or for speakers of a particular language. One mitigation for attacks on CAs is to remove as many of the defaults as is feasible. However, this only reduces the risk, it does not eliminate the fundamental problem. Security based on a weakest-link architecture such as this gets weaker the more entities are added [6, p. 229], and as the Internet grows more, CAs are inevitable.

Transport Layer Security

TLS makes use of digital certificates in the *handshake phase* of the protocol. When the handshake is completed, the server should have presented a valid certificate to identify itself. The client computer can also be required to present one, if the server requests it. At the end of the handshake the two computers have also agreed on a symmetric key cipher to use to protect the session, as well as a session key to use. TLS guarantees that only the two computers in the communication know the session key, and the selection of the session key cannot be influenced by a middle-person attack [31].

There are not any glaring problems with TLS itself. It can also be used by any application, not just web traffic, with relatively little modification to the application. This makes it a flexible solution to provide encryption and entity authentication for applications that are otherwise security-agnostic.

All of these items—CAs, TLS, certificates—as well as the policies and people that implement them, make up the PKI of the Internet. The technology is sound, but without accurate certificates to identify the endpoints, a secure connection is not of much help in resisting attacks. Namely, an encrypted connection to the adversary instead of the intended target does not help. For this reason, a robust public key infrastructure that adequately ties public keys to real identities is extremely important. The existing PKI has shown weaknesses, not in the technologies themselves, but via attacks on CAs.

STEGANOGRAPHY

Steganography is the study of hiding messages [3]. This is quite different from cryptography, although related through the fact that both fields have been used by spies for espionage. Where cryptography secures a message from being read by someone without the key, steganography hides the very existence of a message. Modern steganography does this by subtly manipulating bits with computers. There is a long history of steganography, just like there is for cryptography. Interested readers should consult Kahn [34] for the historical methods.

Much of modern steganography takes advantage of the fact that digital formats for media files tend to contain more detail than the level at which human senses can perceive differences. Since these media, usually audio or images, are just stored as numbers, those numbers can be manipulated to store information in addition to information about the audio or picture [35]. But it need not. For example, readers of the print book will have a hard time reading this white-on-white message, however, anyone with a digital copy can highlight the text to read the message:

A secret message, photo, or letter to your mother or a web-browsing program are all encoded the same way in the end: in bits. These are written as a string of eight 1's and 0's, for example, 190 is 10111110 and 191 is 10111111. Letters are also represented this way; capital J is 01001010. So only using the green color, if we have a string of eight green pixels, all the same color, say green 190, we can encode a J by manipulating the low-order bits. Low-order bits are the ones that change the color the least—that is, the ones to the right of the string, and the ones that differentiate between green 190 and 191. Instead of the picture having eight pixels of green 190 in a row, the steganographer would change the eight pixels to green 190, 191, 190, 190, 191, 190, 191, 190. This changes the image very little, but hides the character J in the low-order bit of these pixels.

There are various further ways to hide and obscure the message. It can be encrypted or compressed first, so it doesn't immediately look like a message in case some computer program is trying to find messages in pictures. The pixels in which the message is hidden can also be scrambled, so only the receiver knows how to reconstruct the message. But this is the gist. Audio steganography works similarly—the human ear cannot discern between 1 millisecond of sound at 10,000 hertz and 1 millisecond at 10,001 hertz. Any steganography relies on the fact that the cover file (picture, audio, etc.) is much larger than the message to be hidden. A mouse may be able to hide behind a tree, but an elephant cannot.

Steganography is not a particularly good resistance strategy for most modern use cases. Hospitals are not trying to hide the existence of patient records, they are trying to make sure only authorized personnel read them. Banks are not trying to hide the existence of transactions (regulations generally forbid that), but to prevent unauthorized modifications to transactions. And so on with most items for business uses. Furthermore, it is not generally possible to provide a mathematical estimation of how difficult a steganographic technique is to discover. It is possible to calculate such difficulties for cryptography, the preferred resistance strategy for keeping information private. This provides a much better ability to anticipate and plan for risk than steganography does, which is the most compelling reason to prefer cryptography.

SUMMARY

Encryption is a broad topic in security that can support a variety of security services. This chapter introduces the basic terminology and concepts, described methods for hiding information that is not ciphers, and introduced the function of modern ciphers by way of their historical predecessors. In a broader security strategy, encryption as resistance is best suited for resisting adversarial attempts at unauthorized access to data, whether that data is at rest or in transit. Negotiating and distributing keys is particularly difficult for symmetric encryption, however, asymmetric encryption provides an irreplaceable tool to facilitate key distribution. The tool needs to be used well and appropriately; there is no silver bullet and administrative errors can still undermine the benefits of cryptography. Finally, some of the uses of cryptography that support remote authentication are discussed, building on the concepts of authentication for resistance introduced in Chapter 7.

REFERENCES

[1] Katz J, Lindell Y. Introduction to modern cryptography: principles and protocols. Baco Raton, FL: Chapman & Hall/CRC; 2008.

[2] Stallings W. Cryptography and network security. 5th ed. Upper Saddle River, NJ: Pearson Education, Inc.; 2011.

[3] Shirey R. Internet Security Glossary, Version 2. RFC 4949. 2007.

[4] Stephen A, Kallis J. Captain midnight and decoder rings. Retrieved from <http://www.mwotrc.com/rr2005_08/decoders.htm>; 2005. Retrieved February 14, 2013.

[5] Barker E, Barker W, Burr W, Polk W, Smid, M. Recommendation for key management—Part 1: General (Revision 3). NIST Special Publication 800-57; 2011.

[6] Anderson RJ. Security engineering: a guide to building dependable distributed systems. 2nd ed. New York: Wiley; 2008.

[7] Plutarchus, Lysander, Sulla. In: Perrin B, translator. Plutarch's Lives. London: W. Heinemann; 1918. ch. 19.

[8] Myszkowski ÉVT. Cryptographie indéchiffrable: Basée sur de nouvelles combinaisons rationelles. Paris: Societé Française d'imprimerie et de librairie; 1902.

[9] MIT Professor Claude Shannon Dies; Was founder of digital communication. MIT News; 2001, February 27. <http://web.mit.edu/newsoffice/2001/shannon.html> [access date is 11.09.13].

[10] Shannon CE. A mathematical theory of communication. Bell System Techn J 1948;27(3):379–423.

[11] Shannon CE. Communication theory of secrecy systems. Bell System Technical J 1949;28(4):656–715.

[12] Shannon CE, Weaver W, Blahut RE, Hajek B. The mathematical theory of communication, vol. 117. Urbana: University of Illinois Press; 1949.

[13] Gallager RG, Claude E. Shannon: a retrospective on his life, work, and impact. IEEE Trans Inf Theory 2001;47(7):2681–95.

[14] Bellovin SM. Frank Miller: inventor of the one-time pad. Cryptologia 2011;35(3):203–22.

[15] Daemen J, Rijmen V. Advanced Encryption Standard [(AES) (FIPS 197)]. National Institute of Standards and Technology; 2001; <http://csrc.nist.gov/publications/fips/fips197/fips-197.pdf>.

[16] Bronstad DK, editor. Data encryption standard, federal information processing standards publication (FIPS PUB) 46. Washington, DC: National Bureau of Standards; 1977.

[17] Kaufman C, Perlman R, Speciner M. Network security: private communication in a public world. Englewood Cliffs, NJ: Prentice-Hall; 2002.

[18] Bogdanov A, Khovratovich D, Rechberger C. Biclique cryptanalysis of the full AES. Advances in Cryptology—ASIACRYPT; 2011. p. 344–371.

[19] Biham E, Dunkelman O. Cryptanalysis of the A5/1 GSM stream cipher. Progress in Cryptology—ÑINDOCRYPT; 2000. p. 43–51.

[20] Stubblefield A, Ioannidis J, Rubin AD. Using the Fluhrer, Mantin, and Shamir attack to break WEP. In: Network and Distributed Systems Security Symposium (NDSS); 2002 <www.internetsociety.org/sites/default/files/Download_PDF.jpg>.

[21] Smith R. Stream Cipher Reuse: a graphic example. Cryptosmith Blog. Retrieved from: <http://www.cryptosmith.com/archives/70>; 2008. Retrieved Feb 1, 2013.

[22] Stallings W. Network security essentials: applications and standards. 4th ed. Englewood Cliffs, NJ: Prentice-Hall; 2011.

[23] Ahituv N, Lapid Y, Neumann S. Processing encrypted data. Commun ACM 1987;30(9):777–80.

[24] Spring J. Monitoring Cloud Computing by Layer, Part 1. IEEE Secur Priv 2011;9(2):66–8.

[25] Spring J. Monitoring Cloud Computing by Layer, Part 2. IEEE Secur Priv 2011;9(3):52–5.

[26] Callas J, Donnerhacke L, Finney H, Shaw D, Thayer R. OpenPGP message format. RFC 4880. Updated by RFC 5581; 2007.

[27] Computer Weekly. Assess your software- and hardware-based full disk encryption options. TechTarget. Retrieved from <http://www.computerweekly.com/feature/Assess-your-software-and-hardware-based-full-disk-encryption-options>; 2009, February. Retrieved Feb 20, 2013.

[28] Diffie W, Hellman M. New directions in cryptography. IEEE Trans Inf Theory 1976;22(6):644–54.

[29] Federal Information Processing Standard Publication #140: Security Requirements for Cryptographic Modules. Washington, DC: US Department of Commerce, National Institute of Standards and Technology; May 25, 2001. FIPS 140–2. http://csrc.nist.gov/publications/fips/fips140-2/fips1402.pdf.

[30] Freier A, Karlton P, Kocher P. The secure sockets layer (SSL) protocol version 3.0. RFC 6101; 2011.

[31] Dierks T, Rescorla, E. The transport layer security (TLS) protocol version 1.1. RFC 4346. Obsoleted by RFC 5246, updated by RFCs 4366, 4680, 4681, 5746, 6176; 2006.

[32] Cooper D, Santesson S, Farrell S, Boeyen S, Housley R, Polk W. Internet X.509 public key infrastructure certificate and certificate revocation list (CRL) profile. RFC 5280; 2008.

[33] Hoogstraaten Hans, editor. Black Tulip: Report of the Investigation into the DigiNotar Certificate Authority Breach. Fox it 2012. the Netherlands: Ministry of the Interior and Kingdom Relations; 2012. <http://www.rijksoverheid.nl/bestanden/documenten-en-publi-caties/rapporten/2012/08/13/black-tulip-update/black-tulip-update.pdf>.

[34] Kahn D. The Codebreakers: the story of secret writing. New York: Scribner Book Company; 1996.

[35] Johnson NF, Jajodia S. Exploring steganography: seeing the unseen. IEEE Comput 1998;31(2):26–34.

Chapter Review Questions

1. Differentiate between symmetric and asymmetric key encryption.

2. Draw the relationship between the elements in a cryptosystem for which terms are defined in the section "Encryption Concepts."

3. What are the elements of key management?

4. What is a session key? Why do session keys improve security?

5. What is a brute-force attack?

6. What are the differences between file encryption and disk encryption? How are they similar?

Chapter Exercises

1. What is the difference between a code and a cipher? Which term, if either, does steganography fall under?

2. Find the list of certificate authorities preinstalled in your browser (in Firefox this is under something like Edit→Preferences→Advanced→Encryption→View Certificates). In your browser history, figure out which sites used HTTPS. Then figure out how many certificate authorities you have relied on during the browser history. Would it be sensible to remove some of the certificate authorities from your browser?

3. Attack the following ciphertext and discover the message: ENJ,NWXBRWBN,NAB NMRWBQNOJLBBQJBBQNK,JRWQJABQNLXWARABNWLGXOLXUMYXRMPNIJ UJWBC,RWP. See footnote[4] for answer.

---

[4]Answer: "We are not interested in the fact that the brain has the consistency of cold porridge, Alan Turing."

CHAPTER 9

Resistance Strategies: Partitioning and Need to Know

INTRODUCTION

The previous resistance chapters have discussed methods for authentication and for increasing the resistance of networks from attacks via encryption. This chapter covers how limitations on internal information flow can aid in reducing the effective attacks against networks. In general, there are two approaches to controlling information: restricting usage and restricting availability.

Restricting usage in information systems generally relates to restrictive information formats, content, or encryption. Restricting availability involves ensuring that even authorized individuals have access to only the information and services required to perform their assigned functions. This restriction of information involves understanding what information and services are required for various job functions, and ensuring that the network traffic related to that information is segmented, but remains useful for the business processes that demand it. The restriction of information also demands an understanding of the threats to the information, even threats from persons either currently or recently given authorized access to the network or the information stored on the network.

This chapter starts with a discussion of adversaries, especially internal threats, covers management of these threats via technical and managerial means, and closes with discussion of the support for these means in an organization's information security policies. Organizations find it difficult to manage persistent and knowledgeable adversaries, particularly when those adversaries are already allowed some access to the infrastructure. Knowledge of the characteristics of these threats and balance in the approach taken in handling them provides options to address the difficulty.

OMEGA ENGINEERING VERSUS TIMOTHY LLOYD

On the morning of July 31, 1996, an employee of Omega Engineering, a parts manufacturing company, started one of the company's production servers to download the tooling programs to the manufacturing systems. Instead of the normal startup messages, the computer reported a "fixing" message, and then it crashed. Employees rapidly discovered that all of the software on that server, including all of the custom tooling programs used by Omega, had been deleted and purged. When employees searched for a backup tape, none could be located. Subsequent data-retrieval efforts were unsuccessful—these critical programs were simply and thoroughly gone [1]. Suspicions quickly lead to a former network administrator who had been fired approximately three weeks earlier, Timothy Lloyd.

Timothy Lloyd was a self-taught administrator who had started with Omega Engineering as a machinist, and worked to learn and improve his skills progressively during his employment. At one time, he was the key administrator and developer for Omega, responsible for implementing the production network. As Omega expanded, Lloyd had become increasingly displaced by individuals with higher qualifications. Eventually, Lloyd was relegated to managing the network backups, a low-status job. This caused significant tensions between Lloyd and his managers, to the point where Lloyd was terminated [1].

Investigators eventually pieced together clues confirming the suspicions against Lloyd. Backup tapes were found marked with his name and key dates, but reformatted to remove any contents. Investigators linked to Lloyd fragments they retrieved from the damaged server of a short program designed to destroy its contents. Lloyd eventually was tried and convicted for the damage he caused, but this did not reduce the millions in lost revenue and permanent loss of market share experienced by Omega Engineering.

OUTSIDER AND INSIDER THREAT

An insider is any individual (including an employee, contractor, customer, or vendor) who currently or recently has authorized direct access to private capabilities on a computer network or set of organization-owned computers. An insider threat is an insider who intentionally misuses or exceeds this authorized access in a manner that damages the organization that owns the network [2, p. 2]. An outsider is any user of the network resources that is not an insider—that is, a user who has only access to public capabilities or has no authorized access to capabilities.

Dealing with insider threats is both difficult and necessary. It is difficult, as insiders, by the authorization provided them, already possess the means to employ paths past most defenses of the organization's information. Deception is largely inapplicable, since they have valid authentication information, and they may have valid access to the encryption keys protecting the information. Defenses must not interfere with proper business activities by authorized insiders. Managing insider threat is necessary, as all adversaries will seek to act as insiders during some part of their attacks against the organization. Improving the resistance of the organization's network to the progress of the adversary's attacks, therefore, aids in managing adversaries as insiders.

Managing insider threats also involves positive management. Malicious insiders rarely act without warning. Managers need to be alert to threatening statements (even if expressed as theory or in humor) and to follow up on such statements by direct interaction with the individuals involved. Often expressing that such statements have been recognized as a potential threat is enough to head off further action, since now the individuals will know they are at the attention of management. Without such follow-up, many cases lead to initial experimentation with activities damaging to the organization, including small compromises, minor actions designed to "slip under the radar," or brief escalation of privileges. If those experiments do not lead to identification, the insiders tend to grow bolder, and shift to more damaging actions. This cycle of progressively more damaging action continues until either the insider quits the organization, or the damage becomes so obvious that the organization must act against the insider. Once the cycle reaches this point, the organization has experienced significant loss. Positive management and consistent follow-up help to break the cycle before it reaches the point where termination (and/or prosecution) is required.

People act in many roles in an organization. A given person, particularly in a small-to-medium-size organization, may propose acquisition of a piece of equipment, participate in the approval of the purchase, place the order, receive the equipment, configure it, and employ it in his or her daily work. While this combination of roles is natural, it poses problems in combating insider threats. To fulfill all those roles, an insider requires broad access to the services of the organization, and to the data handled via those services. The breadth of access increases the number of ways an insider may both damage an organization and conceal this damage. To manage access, organizations need to plan restrictions on the roles that an employee may perform, segmenting the chain of processing for critical actions so that separate individuals are deliberately involved. An example segmentation is diagrammed in Figure 9.1.

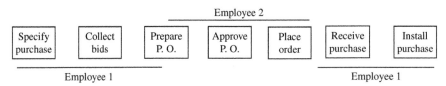

FIGURE 9.1

Separation of roles.

PROFILE: DAWN CAPPELLI

Until 2013, Dawn Cappelli was a technical manager and founder of the CERT Insider Threat Center at the Software Engineering Institute of Carnegie Mellon University [3]. This center has explored a large number of case studies of malicious insiders, looking at both technical and behavioral indicators of their malicious activity, including prior to the activity (spotting the lead up), during the activity (assessing the damage), and after the activity (dealing with the consequences). From this, the center has proposed a variety of security controls, including both technical and behavioral measures, to combat insider threats. The technical controls include reinforcement of separation of roles and need to know in information systems. The behavioral controls include active management of technical personnel, and specific threat indicators, although not constructing a fixed profile of a malicious insider.

After graduating with a B.S. in computer science from the University of Pittsburgh, Dawn worked for Westinghouse for eight years developing software for nuclear power plants. Following that, she worked at the Software Engineering Institute (SEI) as an information technology manager, moved to the Carnegie Mellon University's computing services as a manager of web development projects, then

shifted to the Carnegie Mellon Research Institute (CMRI). While at CMRI, she headed a team that developed a diverse selection of security-critical systems, including information sharing on weapons of mass destruction, public epidemiology, and a collaboration portal for teachers and educational consultants of special-needs children. It was during this time, realizing how important security was to such portals, that she began to be systematically interested in information security. After CMRI, she moved to the SEI as a manager, eventually focusing on the prevention, detection, and response to insider threats.

Dawn is an extremely outgoing individual who has a productive management style, combining multiple viewpoints to focus on various aspects of complex problems. She has been instrumental in the publication of numerous papers and reports on insider threats, and coauthored *The CERT Guide to Insider Threats: How to Prevent, Detect, and Respond to Information Technology Crimes (Theft, Sabotage, Fraud)*, published in 2012. She has also served on the program committee of numerous conferences and technical boards. Dawn is quite passionate about her work, focusing on the importance of dealing proactively and effectively with adversary actions.

Separation of roles is achieved by examining the sequence of operations required to conduct transactions critical to the organization and deliberately arranging permissions so that no single individual—however trusted—has sufficient access to perform all of those operations on a transaction. In the purchasing example, the organization may choose that an individual who proposes equipment acquisition may not approve that acquisition or actually place the order. Separation of roles requires having multiple individuals who can perform each role within the organization, limiting the access of individuals with respect to transactions, and monitoring the sequence of operations to ensure that the limits are maintained [2]. One method of limiting access involves partitioning the flow of operations on the organization's network.

INTERNAL SECURITY PARTITIONS

Partitioning a network means logically or physically separating the computers on a network into disjoint groups. Each of these groups is called a network partition. Partitioning an organization's network to secure the flow of operations works by localizing both the data required for a transaction and the access to the operations that process that data [4].

Localizing the data means establishing a required storage location for the data, and placing the processing resources that use that data within the same network partition. In the purchasing example, an organization may localize the accounting data required to place an order by maintaining it on a dedicated accounting server. Only resources that can retrieve the accounting data may issue a debit against those accounts. To localize the data, both the storage server and the retrieval resources must be in the same network partition. One method of localizing the data uses a packet filter between the network partitions to limit data moving between the separate partitions [5].

Partitioning the organization's network to separate the flow of operations involves localizing access to these operations, as well as to the data processed by them. This localization may take the form of only permitting key software to be installed on particular servers, then restricting access to those servers. This may involve blocking of shared authentication across network partitions, restricting network file sharing, monitoring or limiting data transfers, and establishing an audit trail of information processing that can be used to identify the roles in which individuals process information and track or block separation of roles by an individual. There are several forms of journaling systems that can be used for this audit trail. In some cases, automated decisions about when an individual may be allowed to execute software may be determined by previous actions with the data. For example, having developed a purchase request against a particular account, an individual may be blocked from issuing expenditure approvals against that account until the request is approved or denied by other parties. The audit trail would tie the individual to the purchase request, and application proxies would consult the audit information before allowing approvals to be issued.

Partitioning the network does little good, however, without partitioning the trust that the elements of the network have in each other. If the trust remains global on the network, then adversaries may abuse the functional relationships between computers to spread through the network unimpeded. A trust boundary is a network partition that blocks shared functional relationships between computers in the separate partitions. Partitioning trust has several elements [6]: authentication, privileges, object spaces, communication paths, and delegation.

Partitioned authentication requires explicit reidentification for actors employing resources across the trust boundary. For example, a user accessing a computer on one side of the trust boundary from the other side must provide authentication information (possibly via a one-time-password scheme) to the target computer; this authentication does not use any identity on the originating side. Partitioned privileges require explicit assumption of access rights when crossing the trust boundary, including relinquishment of privileges on the originating side that might form an unprotected path to the receiving side. These privileges are revoked at the end of the communication, and require reestablishment for each contact. Similarly, the trust partition also requires partitioned object spaces, in which device, file, and program identification are not shared across the partition. Where objects must pass the partition, a specialized import/export process, known as a network guard, inspects the object and establishes its suitability for passage. In some cases, this guard may modify the attributes of the object to clear its suitability. For example, if shipping and receiving are partitioned from each other, and an outgoing order requires receipt of certain components, then the guard may permit information about the receipt status of the components to be communicated to the shipping partition, but not the purchase order, price, and shipment information from the receiving partition.

Partitioning communication pathways involves providing for separate physical links, or separate logical paths, through the network for each partition, with the logical paths often reinforced by encryption with separate key spaces. Communication partitioning reinforces several of the previous properties, and makes leakage across partitions more difficult. Partitioning delegation requires that operations on one side of the trust boundary may only make requests to the other side of the trust boundary if explicitly authorized by an authenticated party on both sides of the partition. This prevents leakage across the trust boundary via covert channels. Figure 9.2 diagrams a computer network with trust partitions.

It is somewhat rare that all of these aspects of a trust boundary are fully enforced, but doing so provides for maximum protection against threats that propagate across the organization's network. On the other hand, the redundant infrastructure and management effort that such partitioning requires makes it quite expensive, and as such, it is only warranted in critical conditions.

NEED TO KNOW

Shirey defines *need to know* as "the necessity for access to, knowledge of, or possession of specific information to support official duties" [7]. Need to know involves each piece of controlled information having a designated guardian who accepts requests for information and makes determinations on the need before releasing the information to the requesting individual. This system enforces separation of roles, as guardians require need to know (approved by a separate individual) prior to acting as guardians. Guardians

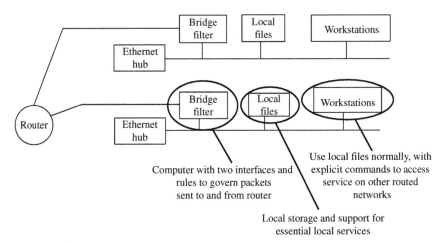

FIGURE 9.2
Trust partitions.

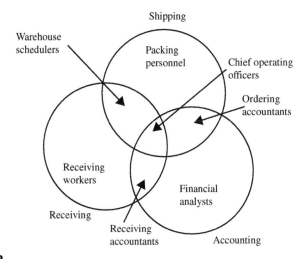

FIGURE 9.3
Need to know.

are also responsible for monitoring changes to the information and assuring appropriate integrity and availability of that information [8, p. 5-3-4].

To support need to know, organizations need to define key groups of information used by employees in their specific duties. These groups are specific to operations involved in those duties, rather than broad groups. For the example shown in Figure 9.3, the need to know for purchase requests may be determined separately from the need to know for invoices. Purchasing and receiving personnel may require access to approved purchase requests, but may not require access to invoices. Sales and shipping personnel may require access to invoices for shipment addresses and verification, but may not require access to purchase requests. Accounting personnel may require access to both invoices and purchase requests. Once the groups of information are determined, then the organization maps groups to individuals dealing with the information, and appoints guardians for each group responsible for enforcing need to know.

Need to know is systematically enforced in the military security model, used by multiple military organizations worldwide. In the military security model, individuals are investigated to determine a personal clearance level. The clearance level documents the sensitivity level with which the individual may be trusted: only general information, information critical to one organizational mission, or information critical to multiple organizational missions. In military terms, "critical to" is often defined as "possibly threatening loss of life and resources required for military operations." In addition to the initial investigation establishing personal clearance level, individuals are reinvestigated when they require access to more sensitive information, and periodically thereafter. Then, for the individuals' specific official duties, their need to know determines which groups of information (in military terms, compartments) they require access to.

Access is reviewed and approved by the guardian for the compartment. Before access, the guardian informs the individuals explicitly of the permissible operations on the information, and with any special processes involved in handling the information (a process referred to as *read-in*). When access is no longer required (due to a shift in responsibilities, change in position, or leaving the organization), the guardian informs the individuals explicitly of the termination of their access, required ongoing protections after access, and explicitly denied operations unless need to know is reestablished (a process referred to as *read-out*). Current authorized access to compartments is documented and tracked by the guardians involved [8].

POLICY MANAGEMENT

Policy, in information security terms, refers to detailed statements of what is allowed and prohibited with the organization's information, along with statements of purpose and decisions as to what organizational positions are responsible for interpreting and enforcing these statements. In more general terms, policy may also be used for "documentation of security decisions by the organization" [9], but this section will tend toward the more specific definition. In principal, information security policies are broadly similar to policies designed to deal with other sorts of threats to the organization (e.g., threats to finances, logistics, or physical security). These policies are used to guide implementation and modification of the organization's security infrastructure, allowing the organization to manage its risks. As risks change, policy must also change, but Chapter 10 deals with that topic as an aspect of change management.

Since policy provides the opportunity for systematic decision making, all security should be developed from policy. NIST defines three levels of information security policy [9]:

- *Program (or enterprise) policy* covers the broad scope of information protections across the organization.
- *Issue-specific policies* focus on protections related to specific security threats or types of information.
- *System-specific policies* specify protections related to specific processing or storage assets within the organization.

Together, these policies, with their implementing procedures and mechanisms, need to provide an organization with a flexible but enduring structure for protecting their information.

In general, a policy statement covers four aspects of a security decision: purpose, position, responsibility, and compliance:

- *Purpose* covers the need and motivation for the policy statement, although this may be shared across multiple policies.
- *Position* identifies the scope of the statement (to whom and what it applies) together with characterization of the mechanisms and procedures used to implement the statement.
- *Responsibility* establishes who in the organization is responsible for interpreting, implementing, enforcing, and revising the statement.
- *Compliance* describes acceptable and unacceptable practices associated with the statement, together with consequences (vetted by the organization's legal and human resources departments) for infractions, along with other remediation actions.

In the example of information related to purchasing, a policy statement (issue-driven, in this case), might look something like the following:

> To ensure appropriate use of organizational funds, all departments shall define and enforce a purchasing process for acquisition of information technology computers and software. This process shall mandate separate individuals acting to recommend and specify an acquisition, to approve the acquisition, and to receive, install, and configure the acquisition. No fewer than two individuals, acting separately, shall be mandated for these actions. Acquisition documentation and audit

journals shall be used to document the execution of the process and identify the individuals acting in the process. This documentation and audit journal content shall be reviewed by and found acceptable to the financial audit committee chair. The chief operating officer shall review and approve all department purchasing processes and the implementing mechanisms. In cases where this multiple-individual process is violated, the acquisition in question shall either be voided, or the acquisition costs shall be taken from the individual's compensation, unless variance from the chief operating officer or chief executive officer is granted. Any such variances shall be reported to the board of directors for their review.

In this example (although admittedly generic), the purpose is briefly given in the opening clause. The position is given by the remainder of the first sentence and the three sentences that follow. The responsibility description starts with "The chief operating officer," the compliance section starts with "In cases where" and covers the rest of the clause. Together, these sections lay out a clear statement of protection, while providing both for reasonable variation within the organization and modification of processes over time as needs arise.

A generic policy life cycle is shown in Figure 9.4. Enterprise policies generally are introduced and refined as an organization is established and matures. Issue-specific policies are defined when new threats or capabilities are introduced. System-specific policies are introduced along with the assets to which they apply. Often, such policies codify previous practice or record decisions consistent with such practice. Practices tend to be modified as conditions demand. Enterprise policies are retired when there is a major shift in security posture due to mergers or significant shifts in mission. Issue-specific policies are retired when the issue is no longer significant to the organization or when

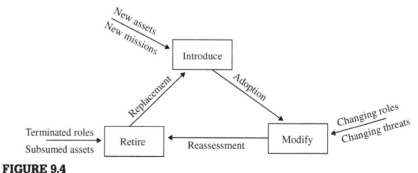

FIGURE 9.4

Policy management life cycle.

one issue is subsumed by another. System-specific policies are retired when the system itself is retired.

Two factors largely drive the policy management life cycle: cost of policy change and risk to the organization. Changing policy can cost the organization significant effort and lead to confusion of employees. Old policies and their supporting mechanisms need to be retracted or modified. New procedures need to be instituted with the attendant training and mentoring. In some cases, the corporate culture of the organization needs to be modified to support the new policy. On the other hand, insider and external risks can also cost the organization large amounts of funds. Policy offers a roadmap to dealing with such risks, and the mechanisms and processes that implement the policy provide for systematic risk management. In some cases, particularly insider cases, dealing with the risk without a clear directive policy may itself be a risk to the organization, as incomplete or biased attempts to deal with the risk may leave the organization exposed and yet prevent management from recognizing this exposure.

SUMMARY

This chapter discusses a number of aspects for dealing with persistent and knowledgeable adversaries. Understanding these adversaries and the importance of resistance as a responsive strategy are key starting points. Use of separation of roles, network partitions, and need-to-know information structures provides for resistance, and may support other strategies like recognition. The coverage of recognition starts in Chapter 11, which discusses how network traffic may be examined to identify actions by adversaries. Policy support, particularly when assessing remediation or punishment actions to be taken against individuals, is also a significant issue. Taken together, this chapter provides a broad basis for increasing the resistance of the organization to malicious actions by persistent and knowledgeable adversaries.

REFERENCES

[1] Gaudin S. Case study of insider sabotage: the Tim Lloyd/Omega Case. Comput Secur J 2000;16(3):1–8.

[2] Sitowash G, Capelli D, Moore A, Trzeciak R, Shimeall T, Flynn L. Common-sense guide to managing insider threat. 4th ed. Technical Report SEI/CMU- 2012-TR-012. Software Engineering Institute, Carnegie Mellon University; 2012, December. Retrieved March 3, 2013, from <http://www.sei.cmu.edu/library/abstracts/reports/12tr012.cfm>.

[3] Software Engineering Institute. Dawn Cappelli. Retrieved from March 3, 2013 <http://www.sei.cmu.edu/about/people/profile.cfm?id=cappelli_13037>.

[4] Cisco Systems, Inc. Deploying firewalls throughout your organization. CISCO Tech Report C11-377025-00; 2006, November. Retrieved March 3, 2013 from <http://www.cisco.com/en/US/prod/collateral/vpndevc/ps5708/ps5710/ps1018/prod_white_paper0900aecd8057f042.html>.

[5] Chapman D, Zwicky E. Building internet firewalls. Sebastopol, CA: O'Reilly and Associates; 1995. Retrieved March 3, 2013 from <http://docstore.mik.ua/orelly/networking/firewall/ch04_04.htm>.

[6] Blaze M, Feigenbaum J, Ionnadis J, Keromytis A. The role of trust management in distributed system security. In: Vitek J, Jensen C, editors. Secure internet programming: security issues for distributed and mobile objects. Lecture notes in computer science, vol. 1603. Berlin: Springer; 1999. p. 183–210. Retrieved March 3, 2013 from <http://cs-www.cs.yale.edu/homes/jf/BFIK-SIP.pdf>.

[7] Shirey R. Internet security glossary. IETF Request for Comment 4949; 2007, August. Retrieved March 3, 2013, from <http://tools.ietf.org/html/rfc4949>.

[8] Department of Defense. National industrial security program operating manual. DoD 5220.22-M. March 2013 (change); 2006, February. Retrieved April 15, 2013 from <http://www.fas.org/sgp/library/nispom/nispom2006.pdf>.

[9] Guttman B, Roback E. An introduction to computer security: The NIST handbook. National Institute for Standards and Technology. Special Publication 800-12; 1995, October. Retrieved March 3, 2013, from <http://csrc.nist.gov/publications/nistpubs/800-12/>.

Chapter Review Questions

1. Briefly define the following terms:
   a. Insider
   b. Need to know
   c. Network partition
   d. Trust boundary
   e. Network guards
   f. Need-to-know guardians
   g. Information security policy
   h. Policy life cycle

2. What are two reasons that managing insider threats requires both technical controls and managerial follow-up?

3. What three protections to information does need to know (and the associated guardians) enforce?

4. What are two reasons why it is useful to define need to know in terms of small groups of information (e.g., invoices, purchase requests, sales contacts, production schedules, or assembly instructions) rather than in terms of larger groups of information (e.g., accounting, engineering, sales)?

5. What are two ways in which having a clear information security policy helps manage costs to an organization?

Chapter Exercises

1. Examine the network in Figure 9.5 and identify three of the partitions present.

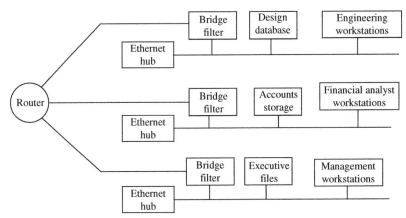

FIGURE 9.5
Network for exercise 1.

2. Sales-O-Matic, a maker of online sales support software, has become concerned about the security of its product development plans. The accounting division is currently sharing cubical space with the programming staff, and the sales staff is working remotely. All of the company files are stored in a central cluster, with access rights given out on request by the programming staff administrative secretary. The company does have a firewall, but it does not currently cover the VPN traffic from the sales staff.
  a. What are three risks that you think this company is taking?
  b. How should the network be restructured to allow Sales-O-Matic to address its risks?
  c. What are three policy statements that need to be made to support addressing its risks?

3. Examine the network in Figure 9.6 and redraw the diagram to support partitioning the network.

4. Explain which of the following might be indicators of illicit insider behavior:
  a. The main file server spontaneously reboots, but comes up fine.
  b. Unexplained large email messages are sent to a web-based public email.
  c. Files associated with a core product development are encrypted with an unknown key.
  d. Large amounts of network scanning activity are detected.
  e. Organizational routers stop communicating.
  f. Organizational competitors start approaching key customers with underbids on contracts.
  g. Unexplained files are downloaded to organizational servers, but not corrupted or replaced files.

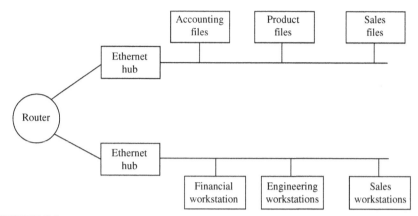

FIGURE 9.6
Network for exercise 3.

5. What are three items that are missing in each policy statement?
   a. Based on reported threats, the chief operating officer shall communicate a statement of threat to the board of directors, together with an estimate of potential loss associated with such threats.
   b. The information security officer shall be responsible for specifying an approved file-import policy for the organization that shall be used for all data downloads.
   c. To comply with email retention regulations, the information security officer shall identify a retention solution that the chief operating officer shall implement and apply to the email of all company officers. Any email not participating in such a retention solution shall not be delivered or passed through the organization's network.

6. What are three problems with the security of the following organization as described here: LazyLaxSec.com, a low-cost network application service, implements regular weekly backups of all storage. It offers SSL-encrypted connectivity as well as password-protected file transfers. All applications are regularly checked for viruses. A current set of IDS signatures is maintained to screen traffic on the company network. All user concerns are routed to the chief of engineering for evaluation and resolution.

CHAPTER 10

Change Management

James G. Williams
University of Pittsburgh, Pennsylvania, USA

INFORMATION IN THIS CHAPTER

- Change management versus configuration management
- Why use change and configuration management
- Change management process
- Minor or insignificant change process
- Automation of the change process
- Change management and security-related issues
- Change management and software control issues
- Change management documentation
- Patch management
- Configuration management system
- Software configuration management
- Configuration management and information assurance
- Configuration management and system maintenance
- Automation of configuration management
- Network configuration management system
- Configuration management database
- Certification for configuration management

INTRODUCTION

Change management is the process by which changes to an installation are implemented in a systematic manner following a well-defined set of procedures. The process applies to all hardware and software including network components. The procedures are typically based on a change management model or framework, such as ISO [1]. There are also models for the related, but distinct, field of configuration management, such as PMI [2].

Organizational security technologies typically include intrusion detection, intrusion prevention, firewalls, event management systems, network access control, identity management, anti-virus software, security policies and procedures, and security standards. These common topics are covered in various other chapters, and change and configuration management impact the operations of all of them. However, change and configuration management are rarely prominently considered. Change management and its associated process of configuration management are usually ignored as part of security measures and risk analysis [3].

In the real world, change management may range anywhere from an informal process, such as an email involving only some advance notifications of the intention to make a change, to a formal process that requires a change request form to be input and submitted to a change control committee that reviews and ultimately approves or disapproves the requested changes [4].

Effective change management allows organizations to introduce change into an information technology (IT) environment quickly and with minimal service disruption and minimal security risk. Change management is responsible for the process of making changes in technology, systems, networks, applications, hardware, tools, documentation, and processes, as well as changes to roles and responsibilities. The primary goal of change management is to ensure that everyone affected by a particular change to an IT environment understands the impact of the impending change and to ensure that security and the operating environment are not negatively impacted. Since most systems and networks are heavily interrelated, any change made to one component of a system or network can have a major impact on other systems, networks, or parts of the same system or network. Change management attempts to identify all affected systems, networks, users, and processes before the change is implemented so that adverse effects, especially those related to security, can be eliminated or held to a minimum. Providing an effective change management process is one of the most challenging aspects for IT and network management.

The closely associated activity of configuration management is the process of handling changes to the configuration of a system or network so that it maintains its integrity over time. Configuration management implements the policies, procedures, techniques, and tools as required to manage change, evaluate proposed changes, track the status of changes, and maintain an inventory of system and support documentation as the system changes. Configuration management systems and associated plans provide both technical and administrative procedures for the development, implementation, procedures, functions, services, tools, processes, and resources required to successfully develop and support a complex IT environment.

During system development, configuration management allows program managers to track requirements throughout the program life cycle, including acceptance, design, implementation, operations, and maintenance. As changes are inevitably made to the requirements and design of any system, they must be approved and documented, thereby creating an accurate record of the system status. Ideally, the configuration management process is applied frequently throughout the system life cycle. Although there are several system life-cycle models, the major components of most of them are composed of the following phases:

1. *Conceptual system design phase:* The identified need is examined, requirements for potential solutions are defined, potential solutions are evaluated, and a system specification is developed.
2. *Preliminary system design phase:* Subsystems that perform the desired system functions are designed and specified in compliance with the system specification. Interfaces between subsystems are defined, as well as overall test and evaluation requirements.
3. *Detail design and development phase:* The development of detailed designs that bring the preliminary design work into a completed form based on the specifications. This work includes the specification of interfaces between the system and its intended environment, and a comprehensive evaluation of the systems logistical, maintenance, and support requirements.
4. *Production and construction phase:* The product is built or assembled in accordance with the requirements specified in the product, process, and material specifications, and is deployed and tested within the operational target environment.
5. *Utilization and support phase:* The system is used for its intended operational role and maintained within its operational environment.
6. *Phase-out and removal phase:* When continued existence of the operational need and meeting operational requirements and system performance is no longer feasible, the system is phased out and removed assuming the availability of alternative systems.

Change and configuration management may be utilized in all the life-cycle phases to minimize system and service disruptions, as well as security risks.

CHANGE MANAGEMENT VERSUS CONFIGURATION MANAGEMENT

Many project managers are not sure about the difference between a configuration management system and a change management system. Most project managers know about a change management system, and change control, but most of them are neither aware of nor have used a configuration management system. Configuration management is primarily a version control system for the products of a project or system. These products are referred to as configuration items, such as software modules, hardware devices, database tables, etc. A configuration is the identified and documented functional and physical characteristics of a product or service, or components of a system such as hardware devices and software modules. The work that is done as part of a project such as programming is considered a process. The change management system oversees how any change to the processes related to a project should be done. The configuration management system oversees how any changes to a product's configuration should be performed.

The following is an example of the difference between a configuration management system and a change management system. Suppose a software product has been designed as a two-tiered set of software modules. This would be the configuration aspect of the software product and would come under configuration management. The actual process of writing code, testing, integrating modules, making changes, etc. would be the process of making the product and would come under the control of change management. If it was decided to change the product from a two-tiered set of modules to a three-tiered set of modules, this would come under the configuration management system since it is a change to the product configuration in terms of adding an additional component to the structure and relationships within the project.

WHY USE CHANGE AND CONFIGURATION MANAGEMENT SYSTEMS

Change in the IT world is inevitable because technology changes, businesses and services change, laws and regulations change, and users change (both productive users as well as hackers). Therefore, it is essential for any IT organization to have a change management plan and a configuration management plan in place and functioning. A change management plan documents how changes will be monitored and controlled. It defines the process for managing changes to a product like an accounting system. A configuration management plan documents how configuration management will be performed. It defines those items that are configurable, those that require formal change control, and the process for controlling changes to such items. Basically, a change management plan is a generic plan that guides the project manager in terms of making any kind of change to a product, especially the ones that can impact the baselines (scope, time, security, cost), whereas a configuration management plan guides an IT organization in making changes that are specific to a project or service configuration [5].

Why are change and configuration management important for system, network, and information security?

1. New sources of risk or elevation in the severity of identified risks frequently accompany changes in software or hardware. Changes in an application, utility program, or operating system software can easily result in coding errors, as well as new functions that compromise security.
2. Changes in the configuration of systems and network devices can result in new paths of attack. For example, opening a Transmission Control Protocol (TCP) port on a firewall to help a colleague get access to a host within the internal network increases the likelihood of successful attacks via this port.
3. Without change control in effect, a system can be left open for attack since any person can make any desired change. Inconsistency in settings, code substitutions and revisions, and other areas increases attackers' ability to gain entry since all an attacker has to do is discover and take advantage of an inappropriate setting or lines of code.
4. Change and configuration management decisions are the outcome of deliberations by multiple individuals who generally are chosen to be on a change control committee or board because they possess the necessary technical and management knowledge and skills that typically result in better change and configuration management plans than that of a single individual.
5. Change and configuration management also help prevent fraud by those inside an organization. Fraud is almost always performed by an individual changing something in a system, network, or application to allow some illegal action. Change detection processes implemented as part of a change management plan will discover the fraud changes and report them and lead to the identification of the fraud attempt.
6. Change and configuration management usually result in traceability that enables an organization to determine why a configuration is the way it is, or why certain changes were made and when the decision that resulted in the change was made. This is because change management and configuration management decisions are normally documented and archived. Traceability and good documentation can lead to better decisions about security measures.
7. Change and configuration management should be part of good information security governance.

It is becoming more commonly known that change and configuration management are important in minimizing security risks. As a result, organizations are creating more internal documentation related to information security policies and standards. Automated change management systems are not new to the IT community. Change management systems like BMC Remedy, HP

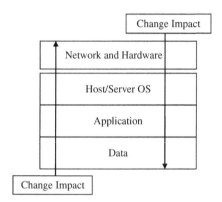

FIGURE 10.1
Four layers of change and configuration management.

Service Manager, and AlgoSec's FireFlow have been around for many years, and standards like Information Technology Infrastructure Library (ITIL) and ANSI-649-B-2011 [6] that include frameworks for change management are also available. The ITIL-process security management documentation describes how the structure of information security fits into the management of an organization. ITIL security management is based on the code of practice for the information security management system (ISMS) now known as ISO/IEC 27002.

Change and configuration management are concerned with four layers within an IT environment as shown in Figure 10.1. The network layer includes all the devices within a domain or organization and how they are connected. The host/server OS layer includes the operating system and associated utilities. The application layer includes all the application programs including those developed in-house and from third-party vendors. The data layer includes all files and databases within the IT environment. A change in any layer can have an impact on any of the other layers both in terms of security as well as services and functionality. For example, a change to a database can have an effect on how an application program functions, the performance and security of a host/server operating system, or the performance and security of a network depending on the configuration of the IT environment and the process of making changes. Likewise, a change in a host/server operating system can have an impact on a network as well as a functioning database.

Many organizations do not have an adequate process for managing change requests. Change requests are often received via emails and even at coffee-break conversations. When existing change management systems are used, they are limited in their capabilities to enforce a workflow based on a request. That is, person 1 performs something based on a change request and the change request is then forwarded to person 2 who performs another part of the change request, and the change request is passed to others who make changes based on the request. In many cases, these individuals have no understanding of firewall rule sets, network topology, or the company's security policy and procedures, which leaves security operational teams with a lot of manual and error-prone work that needs to be done, such as:

- Understanding which firewalls need to be modified to fulfill a specific change request that may be business related.
- Analyzing the security and compliance implications of making the requested change, such as whether the organization still is payment-card-industry compliant if they make the requested change.
- Designing the change in an optimal manner, such as making use of existing firewall objects as opposed to creating duplicate objects that add even more complications to the system.
- Ensuring that changes are performed as requested, and in some cases discovering changes that are performed without a formal request.

The goal of the change management process is to introduce change into the IT environment quickly, correctly, securely and with minimal disruption. In addition, such changes should be justified and approved. A basic component of IT operations is to accept change and control it correctly. A good change management plan and associated processes should include a process for quickly implementing urgent changes required to quickly restore IT services. Change management should be a core and regularly utilized part of all IT operations, not simply for a major upgrade. Configuration management should make sure that only authorized components are used in the IT environment and that all changes are recorded in a configuration management database. Effective change management allows an organization to introduce change into their IT environment quickly and with minimal service disruption. Change management attempts to identify all affected systems and processes before a change is implemented so that adverse effects and risks are minimized.

CHANGE MANAGEMENT PROCESS

To effectively manage change within an organization, the types of changes that might occur need to be categorized [7]. The types of changes might include:

- Applying service packs
- Adding new servers
- Adding new users
- Adding new administrative groups

- Changing routing group topology
- Changing backup and restore procedures
- Modifying and applying security policies
- Changing a process or script utilized to administer servers
- Adding new application programs
- Modifying existing software modules (patches)
- Adding network components
- Adding new IP addresses
- Changing firewall settings
- Changing database management systems

These changes can be categorized as follows:

- *Application changes:* Changes to any application code that is running on or linked to any hardware or software in the IT environment. These changes are typically made to enhance functionality or performance or to fix a known error in the IT application environment.
- *Hardware changes:* All IT equipment installations, discontinuances, and relocations are controlled by the change and configuration management.
- *Visual image changes:* Changes to the "artistic" presentation of web pages are not required to make entries into the change management system. Changes to "active" areas of the web page are required to use the change management procedure.
- *Software changes:* The criteria for entering software changes into the change management process are based on the effect that the changes may have on IT resources. If the changes affect the system, users, or support staff, there is a requirement to enter it into the change management process. If the change is made for the exclusive benefit of the requester and if failure could not affect anyone else, that change would be exempt from the change management process. For example, a change made by a programmer affecting a procedure or a program under development on a test application requires no entry. However, when standalone test time is required on a production system, a request for change (RFC) form is required. Typically, software changes would include changes to the operating system, vendor-supplied program products (e.g., Visual Studio, Java, etc.), or common application support modules.
- *Network changes:* All installations, discontinuances, and relocations of equipment used for IT teleprocessing communications are entered into the change process. This includes all routers, switches, and telephone lines, as well as personal computers if they are connected to the network.
- *Environmental changes:* Environmental changes normally involve the facilities associated with the IT Installation. These facility changes include items such as air conditioning, chilled water, raised flooring, security,

motor generators, electricity, plumbing, and the telephony system for voice and data.

Changes can be categorized into four general groups, each requiring a different type of change management process [7]:

- *Major change:* Widely impacts the entire IT environment, and requires major resources to plan, build, and implement the change (e.g., upgrading all server hardware or network routers).
- *Significant change:* Requires a large amount of resources to plan, develop, and implement the change (e.g., upgrading to a new database management system).
- *Minor change:* Requires no significant resources and doesn't have a large impact on the IT environment (e.g., applying a service pack).
- *Insignificant change:* Follows a well-documented procedure that is not expected to affect the IT environment at all (e.g., adding a new user).

Some organizations and standards categorize requests for change as:

- Level 1 (minimal risk)
- Level 2 (low risk)
- Level 3 (medium risk)
- Level 4 (high risk)

These categories respectively match the insignificant, minor, significant, and major categories.

By thoroughly documenting as much of the IT environment and how changes should be made, it should be possible to maximize the number of changes that are categorized as minor or insignificant, and thus decrease the costs and impact associated with major hardware and software changes [7].

Change management involves the following activities:

1. A RFC is initiated.
2. The impacts (technical and business) of making the changes are assessed, which should include extensive testing and risk analysis.
3. The change is authorized or denied by teams and committees established by the organization to assess the change request and perform an impact analysis of making the change.
4. The change is given to a release management team for implementation.
5. The change is evaluated, verified, and documented.

A number of different personnel should be involved in change management. The following phases of change management demonstrate how organizational personnel would be involved [7]. The example phases that follow are based on a major change, such as upgrading all servers with new software.

Phase 1: Request for Change is Submitted to a Change Manager

Everyone in an organization should be authorized to submit a RFC. In most major change situations, the RFC has probably come from a member of the IT staff. Other change sources include IT staff responsible for systems and networks, service-level managers who are planning to sell new services or upgraded levels of existing services, programmers who need to make a change to an application, or a third party who has changed their software, hardware, etc.

Phase 2: Change Manager Assesses the RFC

The change/project manager receives the RFC and records it in the change management database. The manager examines the RFC, making sure it is a complete and practical proposal. The manager also determines the technical feasibility of the proposed change and the impact it will have on the current IT environment including security vulnerabilities. In some organizations a cost-benefit analysis is performed as part of this phase. If the request is considered unsatisfactory, it is returned to the person who submitted the RFC (known as the requestor or initiator) with colored marks and comments indicating problem areas. Even if the change request is approved, the change manager may pass it back to the requestor or others (e.g., system engineer/designer, software engineer/implementer, a manager/customer/user) for further analysis and further documentation.

When the change request is determined to be satisfactory, and adequate information is gathered, the change manager prioritizes the change. Changes can be prioritized as urgent, high, medium, or low, which determines how soon the change will be made:

- *Urgent:* Changes that must be performed immediately and are quickly transferred to the urgent change process.
- *High priority:* Changes that must be performed quickly to maintain system availability to a significant number of users.
- *Medium priority:* Changes that are necessary to resolve problems, but are not of immediate importance, or only affect a small number of users.
- *Low priority:* Changes that can typically wait until the next major release of software or hardware to resolve the problem.

Next the requested change needs to be categorized. In this case, a change such as upgrading all servers with new software would be judged to be a major change. The change manager will make a record of this prioritization and categorization in the change management database. During this phase, if the RFC is assessed as a minor or insignificant change, the change manager may pass the RFC directly to the change implementers responsible for implementing the change. If the RFC is considered to be a significant or major change, it will be passed to an appointed team or committee that will prepare implementation details for consideration in the next phase.

Phase 3: Change Request is Forwarded to an IT Executive Committee for Approval

An IT executive committee should have the responsibility of approving major changes in an organization. It will typically consist of senior members of the IT staff in an organization. It will decide if the change should proceed or not based on the information gathered in phase 2.

Phase 4: Change Request is Passed to the Change Advisory Committee for Scheduling

The change advisory committee should consist of a knowledgeable group of personnel who are familiar with organizational and business requirements, the user community, IT system and network technology, and the IT organization's application development, testing, and support staffs. Typically, the change advisory committee includes the release, capacity, configuration, network, security, and systems administration managers. In addition, the change manager may appoint others who have expertise relevant to a particular RFC and representatives from the group affected by the change. In this case, expertise with software and hardware is very important. The change advisory committee determines the upgrade schedule, according to the IT executive committee recommendations. The change advisory committee is also responsible for monitoring the change and ensuring that all authorized changes are coordinated and scheduled to eliminate the possibility of one change negatively affecting another change.

Phase 5: Change Request is Passed to the Change Implementers

The change implementers are responsible for planning and implementing the change once it has been approved and scheduled by the change management process. The change implementers will provide feedback to the change advisory committee, the change manager, and in some cases the requestor during the implementation stage. However, the change manager remains involved at this stage, monitoring what the change implementers are doing and recording it in a database. After the change is complete, the change implementers will help the change manager and requestor assess the impact of the change.

This may appear to be a complicated process, but this ideally describes a major change to the IT environment. Minor and insignificant changes could pass through a simpler path, primarily involving the change implementer.

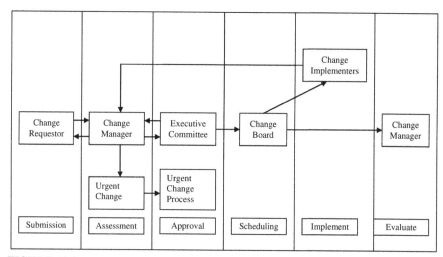

FIGURE 10.2
Change management process.

Phase 6: Change Process Evaluation

After the change is implemented, the entire change management process from receipt of RFCs through implementation must be evaluated. This is done by conducting personnel interviews and reviewing documentation. The main objective is to evaluate the effectiveness of the change process. Unsuccessfully implemented changes should also be evaluated so that problems can be identified and corrected before additional changes are initiated.

Figure 10.2 illustrates the change management process, with the personnel responsible for each stage of the process. The process moves from left to right starting with the submission of an RFC, which is then assessed by the change manager as to technical feasibility, service impact, security risks, and cost benefit. The change manager may pass the RFC back to the requestor for additional explanation or information. In some cases the change manager may deny the change. If the change manager determines that it is an urgent change it is sent through an urgent change process, otherwise it is sent to the IT executive committee for approval. If the executive committee approves the change request, it is sent to a change advisory board/committee for scheduling. The change advisory board/committee then passes the change request to those who will be responsible for actually implementing the change.

MINOR OR INSIGNIFICANT CHANGE PROCESS

The advantage of minor or insignificant changes is that individuals with less authority can be preassigned permission to perform them. This is a reasonable policy, because the changes are not likely to cause significant problems when implemented. The change manager, and in some cases the change advisory committee, will need to decide whether a particular change is minor or insignificant. However, once this is done and the nature of the change is documented, the change implementers can be preauthorized to perform the change [7].

A typical example of an insignificant change is the addition of a new user to a system. This type of change can be anticipated in advance, so the change manager should have already preauthorized the change implementer to be responsible for this change. The change should be adequately documented with appropriate settings for factors such as disk quotas, password renewal intervals, etc.

PROFILE: ALAN TURING

Father of Computer Science, and Information Warrior

Alan Turing (1912–1954) was a British mathematician. He studied and worked at King's College, Cambridge, from his undergraduate studies in 1931 until the British entry in WWII, when he began working full time for the U.K.'s Government Code and Cypher School (GCCS). At Cambridge, Turing no less than founded theoretical computer science. And at Bletchley Park, the GCCS headquarters, Turing's cryptanalysis of German communications proved absolutely essential to the British victory.

Turing was a mathematician by training. There was no such field as computer science in 1936 when he proposed the concept of a "universal machine" that would read and follow simple instructions from a ticker tape. Turing was able to prove that this construction—just the set of instructions and the tape to read and write to—was sufficient to simulate any possible computation. This conception is now called a universal Turing machine. All modern computers are Turing machines. This concept provided the first foundations of computer science.

Not only did Turing revolutionize the world, he also saved it. At Bletchley Park, with a jumpstart from the Polish Cipher Bureau, Turing and his colleagues Dilly Knox and Gordon Welchman invented a machine to break the German Enigma cipher. The machine to break the Enigma was called the bombe, first developed in the spring of 1940. The German navy used the cipher to send messages to submarines patrolling the ocean attempting to disrupt shipping to the British Isles. The British had no technical answer to the superior German U-boats. However, the Enigma messages decoded by the bombes told the British where the U-boats were, so they could be avoided. Without this information, the Isles probably would have been cut off, sieged, and starved out. From 1940 to the end of the war, the German navy had no idea Turing and Bletchley Park were reading their messages. Turing also had four other major cryptanalytic breakthroughs after the bombe.

Turing was eccentric. During the war, he was known to run the 40 miles from Bletchley Park to London for meetings at a pace a marathon runner would respect. When there was not enough funding for the bombes, he and his colleagues wrote directly to Winston Churchill for funding. In 1950, he developed the concept of the Turing test, still relevant to artificial intelligence studies today, which proposes a method for testing whether machines can think or not. He studied biology, and wrote a chess program for computers that did not exist when he wrote it.

Sadly, Alan Turing's promising life and career was cut short. Homosexuality was illegal in the United Kingdom in the 1950s, and in 1952 Turing was convicted of "gross indecency." He was embarrassed, stripped of his military clearance, prevented from pursuing most of his previous work (he now did not have the clearance to read his own papers), and subjected to hormone treatments. Eighteen months later, he committed suicide. Only recently, in 2009, has the British government acknowledged this mistreatment of one of the country's biggest war heroes. The prime minister issued an official apology for Turing's mistreatment in September 2009.

AUTOMATION OF THE CHANGE PROCESS

Although both minor and insignificant changes may not take very long, they are among the most frequent and repetitive tasks and, therefore, the ones most likely to benefit from automation. To further reduce the amount of time spent on any of these change-related tasks, it may be more efficient to use automated tools. Using the example of creating a new user, the change advisory committee may have previously categorized users according to the type of user and established a set of parameters for each type. Administrators could then use a tool to create users by specifying their type.

Over time, the change management team could build or acquire a set of tools that are used to administer minor or insignificant changes. Similar tools could be used for implementing both major and significant changes as well. If change management tools and procedures are considered configuration items, then controlling their changes demonstrates the relationship of change and configuration management.

CHANGE MANAGEMENT AND SECURITY-RELATED ISSUES

An important and not always recognized part of effective change management is the organizational security infrastructure. Without careful control of who has the authority to make certain changes, the organization will have undocumented or unauthorized changes occurring. The organization should ensure that only authorized personnel have the capability to perform tasks that they have been specifically authorized to perform. It is well known that a number of system violations occur as a result of individuals inside an organization making unauthorized changes. These unauthorized changes are typically either to avenge what an insider considers as being treated unfairly or simply greed for financial gain. But regardless of the reason, the change management system must be able to recognize such change possibilities and protect against them occurring.

CHANGE MANAGEMENT AND SOFTWARE CONTROL ISSUES

Updating software represents a major change since it can have an impact on a large number of users. As a result, software updates should be carefully planned so that any update has an insignificant impact on users. Changes to operating systems have significant impacts, especially changing from Windows to UNIX, for example.

At times a change may be required immediately, and the change management teams and committees will not have time for planning as carefully and thoroughly as desired, but they should plan as much as possible. In an organization with distributed administration and technical personnel, a major challenge is to ensure that software updates are distributed with as little disruption as possible to users.

CHANGE MANAGEMENT DOCUMENTATION

Linking all of the change management phases together is needed for up-to-date, complete, and accurate documentation. Without complete and accurate documentation, the benefits of change management will not be useful to an organization. Complete and accurate documentation when implementing recurring changes makes the process more efficient and effective. One of the major benefits of thorough documentation is that it can make a major or significant change seem more like a minor or insignificant change. Many changes are major or significant simply because they have never been made previously. But if there are documented standard procedures and a record of prior changes, as well as a thoroughly documented and up-to-date system and network configuration, it will allow the organization to avoid downtime and intervals of poor performance. It may allow the IT executive committee or change advisory committee to preauthorize certain changes for the future, thereby reducing the number of steps required to make the change the next time it occurs.

An organization should ensure that the entire process of change is properly documented in the change management database tables. The database should contain information about the change, including RFC status, schedule information, and work orders. It is the responsibility of the change requester, change manager, and change implementers to make certain that the organization has complete documentation about the change. Change management should also work closely with configuration management to ensure that all changes to IT components are properly documented in the configuration management database, which is used to track the status of all components of the IT environment. It is not only necessary to have the change and configuration management data available, it needs to be readily accessible by those who need it, it should be easy to search and retrieve data, and it should follow a standard form and format.

Two primary tools are used to manage the change request process. The RFC form is used to forward requested changes to the change manager as well as record the impact, resolution, and approval decision. The change manager uses a change request database to track the status of change requests. Figure 10.3 is an example of a RFC form. This could be a paper form (to be avoided if possible) or an electronic form that the requestor is required to complete and submit. An electronic form and associated database is the

Project Change Request Form		
Change Request Number	Requested By	Date Requested
Change Request Description		
Change Description (Include impacted obectives, deliverables and any new objectives and deliverables)		
Business or Technical Justification For Change Request		
Priority ☐ Top ☐ High ☐ Medium ☐ Low Impact Of Not Matching The Change		
Change Impact Analysis		
Impact on Project Requirements ☐ In Scope ☐ Out of Scope		
Impact on Project Risk		
Impact on Project Schedule		
Impact on Project Budget Projection		
Impact on Project Configuration		
Alternatives		
Recommendation		
Change Request Resolution		
Change Request Decision ☐ Approved ☐ On Hold ☐ Denied	Decision Date	
Decision Made By ☐ Project Manager ☐ Project Sponsor ☐ Executive Sponsor ☐ Other		
Reason for Decision		

Change Request Tracking (updates to project baseline)					
Requirement Document	Yes	N/A	By	Date	Comments
Schedule (WBS)	Yes	N/A	By	Date	Comments
Risk Mgt. Plan	Yes	N/A	By	Date	Comments
Configuratin Mgt. Plan	Yes	N/A	By	Date	Comments
Communication Plan	Yes	N/A	By	Date	Comments

FIGURE 10.3

Sample Change Request Form using Washington State format.

preferred context for documenting the data related to change and configuration management [8].

The change request database is used to track the progress and status of a requested change. Figure 10.4 illustrates what a change request log printout might look like [8].

PATCH MANAGEMENT

A patch is software designed to fix problems with computer programs at the system and application level or its supporting data. This includes fixing

Project Change Request Log

No.	Requestor	Date	Change Request Description	Impact and deliverables affected	Priority Top, High, Medium, Low	Status	Status Date	Assigned To	Comment/Resolution

FIGURE 10.4
Change request log using Washington State format.

security vulnerabilities, other bugs, and improving the usability or performance of the software. Change management is critical to every phase of the patch management process. As with all system modifications, patches and updates are performed and tracked through the change and configuration management systems. It is not likely that a patch management program can be successful without being integrated with the change and configuration management systems. Patch applications should be submitted through change management and must have contingency and back-out plans in place. In addition, information on risk considerations for patches should be included in the change management system.

Patch management is an important part of change management, but has become increasingly important because of the increase of worms and malicious code targeting vulnerabilities of unpatched systems, and the resulting cost incurred. Also, the regulatory compliance issues related to such things as HIPAA and Sarbanes–Oxley has caused organizations to provide better control over their information assets. The main objective of a patch management program is to ensure that software updates or fixes that are inevitable in modern applications are introduced expediently but also effectively, and minimize the disruption to the system or other unintended consequences. A patch management system must also create a uniformly configured environment that is protected against known vulnerabilities in the operating system and application software. Managing updates for all the applications and operating system versions used in an organization is complicated, and becomes even more difficult when additional platforms, systems and application availability requirements, and remote locations and personnel are involved [9].

Security and Patch Information Knowledge

A key component of patch management is the acquisition and analysis of knowledge and related information about security issues and patch releases, because IT personnel must know which security issues and software updates are relevant to the organization's environment. Organizations should have personnel responsible for keeping up to date on newly released patches and security issues that affect the systems and applications in its environment. These personnel should be part of the change management process and should take the lead in alerting administrators and users about security issues or updates to applications and systems the organization supports and uses. A comprehensive and accurate configuration management system can help determine whether all existing systems are accounted for when researching and processing information on patches and updates. Ideally, an organization should have contacts with their operating system, network devices, and application vendors to keep up to date on the release and distribution of information about product security issues and patches.

Establishing Patch Priorities and Scheduling

Scheduling standards and implementation plans should exist as part of a patch management program and should include patch cycles. A patch cycle should be generated that guides the application of patches and updates to systems. This patch cycle is not specifically concerned with security or other major updates. It is intended to implement the application of standard patch releases and updates. This cycle can be time or event driven. Another patch plan cycle can deal with major security and functionality patches and updates. A number of factors are routinely considered when determining patch priority and scheduling. Vendor-reported criticality (e.g., high, medium, low) and known intrusions by malicious code are important variables for calculating a patch's significance and priority.

Patch Testing

Patch testing starts with the acquisition of the software updates and continues through acceptance testing. The initial component of patch testing is the verification of the patch's source and integrity. This ensures that the update is valid and has not been intentionally or accidentally altered. Digital signatures or some form of checksum or integrity verification should be a part of patch validation. Once a patch has been determined valid, it can be placed in a test environment. Many organizations use a subset of production systems as a test environment using department-level servers and IT programmer systems. The actual mechanics of testing a patch vary widely by organization. The approach taken to perform in-depth patch testing will be determined by system criticality, system availability requirements, available resources, and patch severity level.

Patch Installation and Deployment

Installation and deployment of patches is where the actual work of applying patches and updates to production systems occurs. The most important technical factor affecting patch deployment is the choice of tools that are utilized. In the past, many organizations have created custom solutions using scripting languages combined with available platform tools to distribute and apply patches. As the demand for automated updates has increased, tools have become available to help manage the patch application process. Many existing system management tools have the capability to perform software and system updates.

While applying patches they must be made in a controlled and predictable manner. The type of controls will be determined by organizational policy, such as restricting user rights (who has the authority to apply updates) and network-based access controls in terms of whether the system can access the resources needed to perform an update.

Patch Audits

Regular audits should be performed to assess the success of the patch management program. The patch audit phase of the patch management program determines what systems need to be patched for any given vulnerability and whether the systems that were scheduled for patching were actually updated. System discovery and auditing should also be part of the audit process. This will aid in identifying systems that are out of compliance with organizational guidelines. To supplement the audit process, controls should be in place to determine whether newly deployed and rebuilt systems are up to specifications in terms of patch levels. All patches and updates that are approved and installed should be integrated with the change and configuration management systems, providing an audit trail to determine if they followed procedural guidelines.

CONFIGURATION MANAGEMENT SYSTEM

Configuration management is a process for establishing and maintaining the status of a product's functional attributes, physical attributes, and performance along with its related requirements, design, and operational status throughout its life cycle. Configuration management verifies that a system performs as intended, and is documented at an adequate level of detail to support its planned life cycle, which requires detailed recording and updating of information that describes an organization's hardware, software, and network components. This information typically includes the versions and updates that have been applied to installed software packages and the locations and network addresses of hardware devices. Special configuration management software is commercially available. When a system requires a hardware or software upgrade, IT personnel can access the configuration management software and database to determine what is currently installed for the system. The IT personnel can then make a more informed decision about the impact of the upgrade.

The configuration management process is intended to facilitate the management of system changes for such purposes as to enhance user and system capabilities; enhance applications, system, and/or network performance; improve reliability; support changes to the system (maintenance); extend the system's life; reduce risk and liability; and correct system defects (fix bugs). The return on investment (ROI) of implementing a configuration management system by an organization is reduced cost due to down time and the resources needed to make changes. The lack of a configuration management system, or its low-quality implementation, can be expensive for an organization and possibly have catastrophic consequences like a complete failure of system components.

Configuration management documentation is primarily concerned with the functional relationships among parts, subsystems, and systems for controlling system change. It supports verifying that proposed changes are systematically analyzed to minimize adverse effects. Changes to a system are proposed, evaluated, and implemented using a standard process that should ensure consistency and requested changes are evaluated in terms of their expected impact on the entire system. Configuration management documentation verifies that changes are implemented as prescribed and that documentation of objects and systems reflects their specified configuration. A complete configuration management system includes provisions for the storing, tracking, and updating of all system information on a component, subsystem, and system basis [10].

A well-structured configuration management process ensures that documentation for objects, such as requirements, design, test, and acceptance, is accurate and consistent with the actual physical and logical design of the system objects. Without configuration management, the documentation may exist, but it may not be consistent with the object itself. Because of this, engineers, contractors, and management are sometimes forced to develop documentation reflecting the actual status of an object before they can proceed with

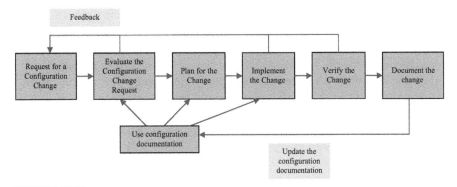

FIGURE 10.5
Steps in the configuration management process.

making a change. This reverse-engineering process is expensive in terms of resources and can be eliminated using a good configuration management system. An example of the steps in the configuration management process is demonstrated in Figure 10.5.

The configuration management process for both hardware and software configuration objects comprises five areas as established in the MIL-HDBK-61A [11] and ANSI/EIA-649 [10]. These areas are implemented as policies and procedures for establishing baselines and performing a standard configuration management process. The basic areas to be included in the process are as follows:

- *Configuration management planning and management:* A formal document and plan to guide the configuration management program that includes items such as personnel, policies, responsibilities and resources, training requirements, administrative meeting guidelines including a definition of procedures and tools, baselining processes, configuration control and configuration status accounting, naming conventions, audits and reviews, and subcontractor/vendor configuration management requirements.
- *Configuration identification:* Consists of setting and maintaining baselines that define the system or subsystem architecture components. It is the basis by which changes to any part of an information system are identified, documented, and later tracked through design, development, testing, and final delivery. Configuration items incrementally establish and maintain the inclusive and current basis for configuration status accounting of a system and its configuration items throughout their life cycle.
- *Configuration control:* Includes the evaluation of all change requests and change proposals, and their subsequent approval or disapproval. It is the process of controlling modifications to a system's components.

- *Configuration status accounting:* Includes the process of recording and reporting configuration item descriptions and all variations from a baseline during design and production.
- *Configuration verification and audit:* An independent review of hardware and software for the purpose of assessing compliance with established performance requirements and standards, as well as functional, allocated, and product baselines. Configuration audits verify that the system and subsystem configuration documentation matches their functional and physical performance characteristics before acceptance as an architectural baseline.

The critical information in a configuration management process is:

1. *Version control:* The capability to check the configuration information into a common repository, retrieve it to see any changes done by anyone, and maintain a complete version history.
2. *Baseline and release information:* Knowing when the last version was released, what the last version contained, and maintaining a baseline version to deploy at any time.
3. *Audits and review:* Conduct a periodic audit of the process to make sure that personnel are following the configuration management and versioning system correctly and consistently.
4. *Documented process:* Make sure that the documented process is agreed on by all team and committee members to guarantee compliance with the configuration management system processes.
5. *Build, integrate, and deploy software:* Utilize standard software that automates the work of building, testing, integrating, and deploying, and eliminates errors made manually from the configuration and change process. Standardization of the processes and their implementation are important.

Configuration Management Example

The example used here is for a large organization with over 100 locations, and the organization determines that it is time to upgrade the hardware and software at each location. This requires sending a team to upgrade the software and hardware, and get the systems up and running in each of the locations around the country as soon as possible.

Assume each location has its own servers that need to be upgraded to standard versions of the system components, which may or may not all be compatible with each other. The organization may have a good change management system in place that will track how changes to the requirements in terms of scope, time, cost, quality, etc. are to be managed. But the IT team will have a difficult time doing the upgrade if the organization does not implement a good configuration management system, which tracks the different versions of the hardware, software, and compatibility across the versions that are running on each server. This will enable the IT team to know what is compatible, what is not compatible, and what has been upgraded or not.

This is a large project and the IT team is going to be spread out, and no single team member will be able to remember the different versions of each server specification and its upgrade status. With a proper configuration management system, all changes to the servers would have been tracked and team members can easily find out what version is running where, on which server, its compatibility, and other attributes. This will make implementing and managing the project easier, more effective, more efficient, and less stressful for the IT team [5].

SOFTWARE CONFIGURATION MANAGEMENT

The software configuration management process is considered by many IT personnel as the best solution for handling changes to software projects. The software configuration management process identifies the functional and physical attributes of software at critical points in time, and implements procedures to control changes to an identified attribute with the objective of maintaining software integrity and traceability throughout the software life cycle.

The software configuration management process traces changes and verifies that the software has all of the planned changes that are supposed to be included in a new release. It includes four procedures that should be defined for each software project to ensure that a reliable software configuration management process is utilized. The four procedures typically found in a reliable software configuration management system are:

1. Configuration identification
2. Configuration control
3. Configuration status documentation
4. Configuration audits

These procedures have different names in various configuration management standards but the definitions are basically the same across standards.

- *Configuration identification* is the procedure by which attributes are identified that defines all the properties of a configuration item. A configuration item referred to as an object is a product (hardware and/or software) that supports use by an end user. These attributes are recorded in configuration documents or database tables and baselined. A baseline is an approved configuration object, such as a project plan, that has been authorized for implementation. Usually a baseline is a single work product or set of work products that can be used as a logical basis for comparison. A baseline may also be established as the basis for future activities. The configuration of a project often includes one or more baselines, the status of the configuration, and any measurement data collected. A current configuration refers to the current status, current audit, current measurements, and the latest revision of all configuration objects. Sometimes a baseline may refer to all objects associated with a specific project. This may include all revisions made to all objects, or only the latest revision of objects in a project, depending on the context in which the term *baseline* is used.

Baselining a project attribute forces formal configuration change control processes to be enacted in the event that these attributes are changed. A baseline may also be specialized as a specific type of baseline, such as

1. *Functional baseline*—initial specifications, contract specifications, regulations, design specifications, etc.
2. *Allocated baseline*—state of work products once requirements have been approved.
3. *Developmental baseline*—status of work products while in development.
4. *Product baseline*—contains the contents of the project to be released.
5. Others, based on individual business practices.
   - *Configuration change control* is a set of processes and approval stages required to change a configuration object's attributes and to rebaseline them.
   - *Configuration status accounting* is the ability to record and report on the configuration baselines associated with each configuration object at any point in time.
   - *Configuration audits* are divided into functional and physical configuration audits. An audit occurs at the time of delivery of a project or at the time a change is made. A functional configuration audit is intended to make sure that functional and performance attributes of a configuration object are achieved. A physical configuration audit attempts to ensure that a configuration object is installed based on the requirements of its design specifications.

Configuration Management and Information Assurance

Configuration management is closely associated with information assurance. Information assurance is typically defined as managing the risks associated with the use, processing, storage, and transmission of information or data and the systems and processes used for those purposes. Information assurance includes protection of the integrity, availability, authenticity, non-repudiation, and confidentiality of user data. In the context of information assurance, configuration management is the management of security features and assurances through the control of changes made to hardware, software, firmware, documentation, and tests throughout the life cycle of an information system [12]. This is sometimes referred to as secure configuration management (SCM), which includes baselines of performance, functional attributes of IT platforms, physical attributes of IT platforms, IT products, and the IT environment to determine the appropriate security features and assurances that are used to measure the state of a system configuration. For example, configuration requirements may be different for a network firewall that functions as part of an organization's Internet boundary versus one that functions as an internal intranet network firewall.

Configuration Management and System Maintenance

Configuration management can be used to maintain an understanding of the status of system components that can help provide a high level of serviceability at a reasonable cost. Configuration management attempts to ensure that operations are not disrupted due to a system failure by exceeding the limits of its lifespan or functioning below required quality levels. In this context, configuration management attempts to define which components of a system are available and operating up to standard. Configuration management can even be used to maintain operating system configuration files [12]. Examples of automated configuration control systems include products such as CFEngine, Bcfg2, Puppet, and Chef.

Automation of Configuration Management

A theory of configuration maintenance was worked out by Burgess [13,14, 15], with a practical implementation on present-day computer systems using the software program CFEngine, which is able to perform real-time repair as well as preventive maintenance. Its primary function is to provide automated configuration and maintenance of large-scale computer systems, including the unified management of servers, desktops, embedded networked devices, mobile smartphones, and tablet computers.

One of the main concepts in CFEngine is that changes in computer configuration should be carried out in a convergent manner. This means that each change operation made should have the characteristic of a fixed point. Rather than describing the steps needed to make a change, the CFEngine language describes the final state in which to end up. The CFEngine agent then ensures that the necessary steps are taken to end up in this policy-compliant state. Thus, CFEngine can be run many times and whatever the initial state of a system happens to be, it will end up with a predictable result. CFEngine supports the concept of statistical compliance with policy, meaning that a system can never guarantee to be exactly in an ideal or desired state, rather one converges toward the desired state by best effort, at a rate that is determined by the ratio of the frequency of environmental change to the rate of CFEngine execution. Thus, if the system environment changes one time every day (e.g., a system update) and the CFEngine is run every two days and completely accommodates the changes, the ratio is 1:2 or 0.5 as to having the system in the ideal state.

Chef is another popular configuration management software tool written in Ruby and Erlang. It uses a pure-Ruby, domain-specific language (DSL) for writing system configuration "recipes" or "cookbooks." Chef was written by Opscode and is released as open source under the Apache License 2.0. Chef is a DevOps tool used for configuring cloud services or to streamline the task of configuring a company's internal servers. Chef automatically sets up and modifies the operating systems and programs that run in data centers. Chef can be integrated with cloud-based platforms, such as Rackspace and Amazon EC2.

Traditionally, Chef is used to manage GNU/Linux and later versions run on Microsoft's Windows platform as well. The user of Chef writes recipes that describe how Chef manages server applications (e.g., Apache, MySQL, or Hadoop) and how they are to be configured. These recipes describe a series of resources that should be in a particular state, packages that should be installed, services that should be running, or files that should be written. Chef makes sure each resource is properly configured, and automatically discovers data points of the system. When used in a client-server model, the Chef client sends various attributes about a node to the Chef server. The server uses Solr to index these attributes and provides an API for clients to query this information. Chef recipes can query these attributes and use the resulting data to help configure a node.

Understanding the current state of a system and its major components is an important element in preventive maintenance. Serviceability of a system and its components is critical to an organization and is defined in terms of the level of usage a component has had since it was acquired, since it was installed, since it was repaired, over its life, and other maintenance-related factors. Understanding how near the end of its life each system component is has been a major undertaking by IT personnel involving labor-intensive record-keeping until recent developments in software that support this function. Many types of components use electronic sensors to capture data that provides live condition monitoring. This data is analyzed on board or at a remote location by computers to evaluate its serviceability, and increasingly its likely future state using algorithms that predict potential future failures based on previous examples of failure through field experience and modeling. This is the basis for predictive maintenance.

Availability of accurate and timely serviceability and maintenance data is essential for a configuration management system to provide operational value, and a lack of this data can often be a limiting factor to the usefulness of a configuration management system. The consumers of this data have grown more numerous and complex with the growth of programs offered by original equipment manufacturers (OEMs). This data is designed to offer an operator guaranteed availability of maintenance data, but makes the situation complex with the operator managing the asset but the OEM taking on the liability to ensure its serviceability. In such a situation, individual components within an asset may communicate directly to an analysis center provided by the OEM or an independent analyst.

NETWORK CONFIGURATION MANAGEMENT SYSTEM

A network configuration management system is similar to a software configuration management system but is the process of acquiring, organizing, and maintaining information about all the components of a computer network. When a network needs repair, modification, expansion, or upgrading, the network administrator can refer to the network configuration management database to determine the best course of action. This database must contain the locations and network addresses of all hardware devices, as well as information about the programs, versions, and updates installed on network computers.

Network configuration management tools are vendor neutral or vendor specific. Vendor-neutral tools, by far the more common, are designed for networks containing hardware and programs from multiple suppliers. Vendor-specific tools usually work only with the products of a single company, and can offer enhanced performance in networks where that vendor dominates. Many network configuration management tools use the Simple Network Management Protocol (SNMP) standard [16].

The major advantages of a network configuration management system include:

- Systemizing the processes of maintenance, repair, expansion, and upgrading.
- Reducing configuration errors.
- Eliminating downtime.
- Increasing network security.
- Making sure that changes made to a device, software, or system don't adversely affect other devices, software, or systems.
- Reverting to a previous configuration if change results are unsatisfactory.
- Documenting and saving the details of all network configuration changes.

CONFIGURATION MANAGEMENT DATABASE

A configuration management database (CMDB) is a storage facility of information related to the components of an IT installation. It contains details of the configuration items, sometimes referred to as objects, in the IT infrastructure. Although database facilities similar to CMDBs have been used by IT departments for some time, the CMDB stems from ITIL. In the context of ITIL, a CMDB represents the authorized configuration of all the significant components in the IT environment. A CMDB helps an organization understand the relationships between these components and track their configuration and changes made to the configuration objects. The CMDB is a basic component of the ITIL framework's configuration management process.

A CMDB contains data describing the following entities:

- Managed resources, such as computer systems and application software
- Process artifacts, such as incident, problem, and change records
- Relationships among managed resources and process artifacts

Relationships among the configuration items are of the highest importance and the most difficult to determine and create. Figure 10.6 illustrates a simple example of the types of items/objects in the CMDB and the relationships among them. All relationships are bidirectional using foreign keys in the database tables.

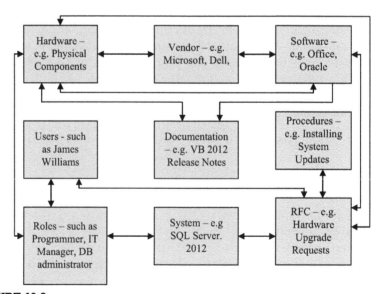

FIGURE 10.6
CMDB item relationships.

The contents of the CMDB should be managed by a configuration management process and serve as the foundation for other IT management processes, such as change and availability management. With good configuration, the CMDB is an essential part of an organization. It is essential that it be backed up regularly so that it can be recovered to the point of failure.

Concepts for building a CMDB can use the management information base (MIB) model, which also has the objective of providing logical models of the IT infrastructure and has a long history in the area of systems management [17].

CERTIFICATION

In Chapter 16 certifications for information assurance are discussed. That chapter also discusses some of the pros and cons of certification. However, there are several certifications specific to configuration management that are useful to mention here. Formal training and certification for configuration managers is available from sources such as:

- Configuration Management Process Improvement Center (CMPIC) offers configuration management training and certification (*http://cmpic.com/*)
- Configuration Management Training Foundation offers certified international configuration manager (CICM), certified international software configuration manager (CISCM), and certified configuration management professional (CCMP) certifications (*http://www.cmtf.com/*)
- Institute of Configuration Management offers five levels of certification (*http://www.icmhq.com/*)

SUMMARY

Many information security models are struggling to keep up with the changing business and technology environment due in part to the nature of today's system infrastructure. Current system infrastructures require constant change due to device customization, application enhancements, fixing security risks, cloud computing, and constant hardware and software upgrades. This forces system and network components to become context dependent and adaptive to support emerging requirements and minimize threats. Change management systems in conjunction with configuration management systems can help improve system and network security as the nature and complexity of requested changes continue to vary greatly.

The risk attributed to each change has become increasingly more important. Existing change and configuration management processes often rely on incomplete risk analysis leading to ineffective security. Patch management is part of the change management process and is highly important since patches to software at all levels occur frequently and must be considered as possible security risks. A well-defined change management process in conjunction with a highly structured configuration management plan and associated processes can improve system security and information assurance. In addition, by leveraging automated solutions that detect difficult-to-determine weaknesses in security resulting from system and network changes, organizations can move security from being reactive to proactive in mitigating risks.

REFERENCES

[1] ISO/IEC ISO 27002: 2005: information technology–security techniques—code of practice for information security management. International Organization for Standardization and International Electrotechnical Commission; 2005. Retrieved April 7, 2013, from <http://www.iso.org/iso/catalogue_detail?csnumber=50297>.

[2] PMI Practice standard for project configuration management. Newtown Square, PA: Project Management Institute; 2007.

[3] Net-Security. Change management leads to security breaches; 2011, November 17. Retrieved April 5, 2013, from <http://www.net-security.org/secworld.php?id=11966>.

[4] Rouse M. Change management; 2010, September. Retrieved April 4, 2013, from <http://searchcio-midmarket.techtarget.com/definition/change-management>.

[5] Prakash V. Configuration management and change management system: differences; 2013, March. Retrieved April 4, 2013, from <http://www.pmchamp.com/configuration-management-system-change-management-system/>.

[6] TechAmerica Standard. Configuration management standard EIA-649-B, 2011, April. Retrieved May 23, 2013, from <http://daphne.meccahosting.com/~a00070f5/EIA-649-B%20CM%20Std.pdf>.

[7] Microsoft—TechNet. Chapter 3: change and configuration management; 2001, October. Retrieved April 6, 2013, from <http://technet.microsoft.com/en-us/library/cc750253.aspx#mainSection#mainSection>.

[8] Office of the Chief Information Officer. Project management framework change management example; 2012. Retrieved April 7, 2013, from <http://www.ofm.wa.gov/ocio/pmframework/examples/changemgmt.asp>.

[9] Chan J. Essentials of patch management policy and practice; 2004, January 31. Retrieved April 10, 2013, from <http://www.patchmanagement.org/pmessentials.asp>.

[10] ANSI/EIA-649. National consensus standard for configuration management, 2011, April 1. Retrieved March 24, 2012, from <http://www.techstreet.com/products/1800866>.

[11] Department of Defense. Military handbook configuration management guidance; 2002, September 10. Retrieved April 7, 2013, from <http://www.product-lifecycle-management.com/download/MIL-HDBK-61B%20(Draft).pdf>.

[12] Schaffer R, editor. Committee on National security systems. National information assurance glossary. 2010, April 26. Retrieved April 7, 2013, from <http://www.cnss.gov/Assets/pdf/cnssi_4009.pdf>.

[13] Burgess M. On the theory of system administration. Oslo, Norway: Oslo University College; 2003, May 7. Retrieved April 8, 2013, from <http://research.iu.hio.no/papers/sysadmtheory3.pdf>.

[14] Burgess M. Configurable immunity for evolving human–computer systems. Sci Comput Program. 2004;51:197–213.

[15] Burgess M. A site configuration engine: computing systems. Cambridge, MA: MIT Press; 1995.

[16] Stallings W. Network security essentials: applications and standards, 4th ed. Englewood Cliffs, NJ: Prentice-Hall; 2011.

[17] Brenner M, Garschhammer M, Sailer M, Schaaf T. CMDB—Yet another MIB? on reusing management model concepts in ITIL configuration management (2006). In: Proceedings of 17th IFIP/IEEE international workshop on distributed systems: operations and management (DSOM 2006), 2006.

Chapter Review Questions

1. Name three things that organization security typically includes.

2. What is one thing that is typically missing in organizational security?

3. Effective change management allows organizations to introduce change into an IT environment using what two criteria?

4. What is the primary goal of change management?

5. What is configuration management?

6. What are the phases of a system life cycle?

7. Name one automated change management system.

8. What does ITIL stand for?

9. Name four types of changes that occur in an IT environment that should be managed.

10. What is an RFC?

11. What are the four general categories for grouping changes?

12. What is one of the major benefits of thorough and complete documentation of the change management processes?

13. Name three types of critical information in a configuration management process.

14. What is information assurance?

15. What is a CMDB?

16. Describe how a change in an application program could compromise the security of an entire system.

17. What security issues are involved in installing a new database management system such as SQL Server or Oracle?

Chapter Exercises

1. Describe how change and configuration management can help prevent fraud.

2. Use the forms in Figures 10.3 and 10.4 to make and log a hypothetical change request in a system that you use regularly.

PART

4

Recognition/Recovery

Network Analysis and Forensics

INTRODUCTION

This chapter begins the first of four on strategies for recognizing when an attack has penetrated the defender's resistance. This chapter focuses on human-driven network-based analysis. Chapter 12 considers automated detection in the form of network-based intrusion detection and prevention systems (NIDPSs). Chapter 13 changes focus from the network to the host and discusses both recognition and forensics after an attack has been recognized. Finally, Chapter 14 discusses data integrity and recognition based on various properties of the data that can be location-independent.

There are several benefits to network-centric recognition strategies. This is true of both manual and automated analysis; this chapter focuses on manual analysis, because every automated rule was at some point discovered and analyzed by a human, probably in response to an incident. The techniques and procedures described in this chapter are likely to be performed due to some suspicion that something is wrong, either as part of the incident response process (see Chapter 15) or due to public reporting or news coverage of a

235

common problem. This chapter describes some tools and policies necessary to enable such retrospective analysis.

Much of the preparation process for establishing a network traffic analysis and forensics capability is a set of practical trade-offs about what the defender can reasonably expect to detect with a particular detail level in their sensor architecture and inspection. Before discussing a variety of inspection and analysis options in more depth, the chapter begins with an overview of OSI-model protocol layers and what information is available at each layer to frame the discussion.

The remainder of the chapter discusses these levels of analysis, along with the practical trade-offs they include, such as processing time and storage space. This discussion echoes that in Chapter 5 regarding the resources necessary for various network-based frustration technologies, such as packet filters and proxies. Along with the details the chapter provides some example tools or uses for each specialization.

INTRODUCTION TO THE OSI MODEL

The Open Systems Interconnection (OSI) model is a way to divide up the problem of communicating between two remote computers. The abstract model has seven layers, and each layer has certain functions that should be performed by the service at that layer [1]. Further, each layer needs only know about the layer below it, and needs to only worry about providing reliable information to the layer above it. This structure makes the communication structure modular and flexible. For instance, a web application does not need to know if it is being transmitted over radio waves, fiber optics, or copper phone lines, because the application (web) is more than one layer removed from the transmission media. If the web application did need to know this, communications over the Internet would be too complicated.

In practice, the implementation of communications protocols does not strictly align with the OSI model. OSI was developed by the International Organization for Standardization (ISO) as ISO 7498, and has some support from the International Telecommunication Union (ITU) as the X.200 series. However, much of the Internet infrastructure standards have been developed by the Institute of Electrical and Electronics Engineers (IEEE) and Internet Engineering Task Force (IETF), which do not strictly abide by the OSI model in their protocol definitions. An introduction to how the Internet actually works using the IEEE and IETF protocols is covered in Chapter 3.

Nonetheless, Internet protocols are roughly arranged to follow the OSI model, and regardless, it provides a useful framework for thinking about the different layers of abstraction in Internet protocols. Once the reader has a

OSI Model -- a summary				
	Name of Data	Layer	Summary	
Processed on Host	Data, Messages	7. Application	From network process to application process	
		6. Presentation	Encryption, convert to/from host-specific representations	
		5. Session	Manage sessions between applications between hosts	
Processed on Network	Segments	4. Transport	End-to-end connections and reliability	
	Packets/Datagram	3. Network	Logical address for end-to-end delivery, routing to logical addresses	
	Frames	2. Data link	Physical address for one-hop delivery	
	Bits	1. Physical	Transmission and signals on physical medium	

FIGURE 11.1

The seven layers of the OSI model, the term for data units of that layer, and a short summary of the functions of each layer [1].

handle on these abstractions, understanding the trade-offs for network analysis at different network architecture layers is easier.

Figure 11.1 summarizes the seven layers of the OSI model. There are some features of network communications that are not explicitly represented in the model, such as management and security. Conceptually, these can be applied in different ways at each layer. This discussion will leave these aspects aside. Layer 1 deals with the physics of how to transmit information reliably on a medium, such as copper or radio waves. Layer 7 is transitioning data on the host computer to a format for the user or his or her application. The intermediate layers are steps along that process.

Each layer has some control information to accomplish its task. For example, layer 3 is responsible for logical addresses of endpoints; IP addresses can be considered the layer 3 header. Layer 2 is responsible for transmitting data between each computer along the way. So to make a layer-2 frame, the machine adds a media access control (MAC) address and some other information to the IP datagram. IP and MAC addresses are not defined in or related to the OSI model, but conceptually this is where they fit.

At each network hop, the router strips off this layer-2 information, reads the layer-3 information, decides where the next destination is to move the data toward the desired endpoint, prepends new layer-2 information, and resends it. This process of adding addressing and other information around the data is called *encapsulation*. A similar encapsulation process, with different details, happens every time data is passed from one layer to the layer above or below it. Figure 11.2 displays this process.

Through several layers of encapsulation, decoding, and reencapsulating, data is transmitted across the Internet. Different network devices and network security devices strip off different numbers of layers to do their job. A rough schematic of this process is displayed in Figure 11.3. As a general rule, the more layers a device has to read and process, the more computationally

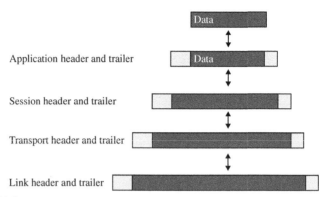

FIGURE 11.2

The general idea behind encapsulation. When each header and trailer is added or removed, the layer treats the data in the darkened area as mere data and passes it along, even though it may have header and trailer information for other layers.

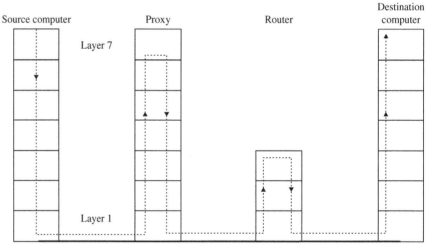

········▶ National information flow up and down layers as information is transmitted across a network, according to the OSI model

FIGURE 11.3

Sample transmission of data from one host to its destination across the network, as viewed by what OSI model layers are involved in each step. Note repeated encapsulation and processing of data units as the data traverses different layers.

expensive that process is. Switches only understand up to layer 2. Routers only need to understand up to layer 3. Application proxies need to understand all seven layers. This is also true of human analysts. If the analyst is just looking for communication between IP addresses, the task will be simpler, both cognitively for the analyst and computationally for the computer assisting, than piecing back together a whole application from what was seen on the network.

The next discussion provides starting points for those who might manage analysts. The remainder of the chapter will start the discussion of network analysis with information available at lower layers of the OSI model. This focus is perhaps unorthodox. On smaller networks, analysts can often start analyzing whole packets without too much trouble. However, the discussion will focus on structures that can help defenders find their way through a complex problem, from general (lower layers) to more specific (higher layers). This process of starting in quick broad strokes, characterizing, and drilling down when indications of specific problems are found helps analysts be successful. The appropriate technical and policy frameworks also need to be in place to support this analysis architecture. There is a cost to supporting analysis architecture, and to extract value from this expenditure it is important the rest of the organization understands the analysts' capabilities.

ANALYSIS FOR MANAGERS

Not everyone in an organization is an analyst, and more people than just the analysts need to benefit from the results of analysis. For those who will not be performing analysis but managing those who are, an important item to know is what questions one can reasonably ask an analyst and expect a useful answer. There is not one single set of reasonable questions; different questions are more or less reasonable with different classes of tools. This chapter discusses tools and what information they provide to help guide these expectations.

The following sections are roughly organized such that later sections describe techniques that use information from higher layers in the OSI model. This organization is necessarily rough because the Internet protocols do not strictly adhere to the OSI model. However, the general idea of trade-off holds: as one inspects traffic in more detail, the analyst trades precision for breadth. More detail equates to analyzing more layers of the model. On small networks, an organization might afford equipment to provide both. On larger networks, the analysts and managers must jointly decide if precision or breadth is the priority; different preferences may be possible at different levels of the organization. If these choices are made cohesively, subunits of the organization may be able to prioritize precision while an organization-wide team can prioritize breadth—both organizationally and temporally—storing multiple years of records. Such specialization provides better organizational defense.

Each analysis focus allows different questions, as the following sections describe. However, not every question can be answered, no matter what technology and sensors are deployed in the organization. Management cannot expect analysts to perform feats from Hollywood any more than Indiana Jones represents the average life of an archaeologist. A more subtle point is that Google has not only spent an unbelievable amount of money, but a decade of work from most of the leading experts and textbook authors on the topic to develop its search capability and infrastructure. Security analysts cannot be expected to answer questions or provide network situational awareness with the ease of an Internet search engine unless the organization has made a similarly intensive decade-long investment.

There are questions that no amount of engineering support can provide an answer to. The most frustrating questions are often the most simple. Perhaps the top of the list is "Who sent this?" or, relatedly, "What country did this come from?" The key to understanding why these questions are not sensible to ask is to understand that the Internet is a logical addressing scheme, not a physical one. An IP address is not bound to a computer or a country any more than a person named John must have short red hair. The method that is used to distribute IPs gives this illusion, and there are some bureaucratic structures that try to pin a certain IP to a certain locality, but none of that is built into the logical addressing structure of the Internet. As such, the Internet protocols are happy to oblige any attacker who wants to work around these bureaucratic assumptions. Furthermore, as discussed in Chapter 5, the attacker can use a previously compromised host as a proxy to anonymize his or her actions, so there is no reason to believe that the external IP in a communication is actually the final endpoint or the attacker's IP, even if we could know where this IP was located.

The people and computers who are playing by the rules and being good citizens may not evade the IP location structures, providing an illusion that Internet protocols are accurately geolocated. However, network security analysis is primarily concerned with those who are not playing by the rules. Therefore, questions about where something came from or where it went are less productive than questions about which internal resources were affected and what behavior or attacks were observed. The precision of the information about a particular attack and the breadth of information about all attacks will vary based on the analytic capability.

FLOW-LEVEL ANALYSIS

Network flow is a relatively abstract method of working with network data. It is mostly concerned with information abstracted from layer-3 and layer-4 headers (e.g., TCP/IP suite headers). Cisco created flow as a data format for routers to report high-level, condensed status information about the traffic traversing a network. The IETF eventually adopted this data format as a standard router reporting format [2].

A flow is a summary of all the packets identified by a set of properties. For example, a common method is to group all the packets in one direction from the same source IP and port to a particular destination IP and port, on an IP protocol—for example, Transmission Control Protocol (TCP) or User Datagram Protocol (UDP)—together into one flow. When the conversation is terminated, such as with a TCP FIN packet (a packet with the *finished* flag set), or after some configured amount of time, the flow is closed and the router exports it. The flow includes many statistics about the related set of packets—for example, number, total bytes, duration, and sometimes such items as a guess about what application protocol was used in the communication—but not the packets themselves.

One feature of network flow is that it can quickly and concisely tell the analyst that IP address 10.0.0.1 communicated with 10.0.0.2, sent 1 megabyte, used the port usually associated with web traffic, and did so in less than a second. If the analyst does not have any context for what IP 1 and 2 are, this may not be helpful. So the human analyst must be flexible about incorporating context from various sources to make flow data meaningful.

For example, the Swiss CSIRT (computer security incident response team) publishes IP addresses of known command-and-control (C2) servers [3,4]. Hosts in the defender's network should not communicate with these IP addresses. If complete conversations are observed, then the defender's machines are almost certainly infected; botnet C2 servers usually do not have benign uses. Network flow is a convenient resource to investigate such queries. The query is relatively fast, and the content of the communication is less important than that the communication occurred at all. Additionally, since flow condenses years of traffic, data can be stored and investigated once such malicious addresses are known. This historical perspective allows the analyst to trace back to evidence of the initial problem; it is not uncommon for compromises to go undetected for months or even years, and so such historical records are often necessary to piece together what happened [5–8].

SiLK (System for Internet-Level Knowledge) and Argus are two common open-source network flow analysis tool suites. Both are under active development and have active communities of users. Sincer 2004, there is even an annual conference focusing on open-source network flow analysis, FloCon. The interested reader can find a variety of good network flow–related material in the past proceedings at *www.flocon.org*.

METADATA ANALYSIS

Metadata is data about data [9]. This can be used to contextualize network data, or some metadata is useful to analyze in its own right. Metadata comes from a variety of sources, and one can expect to learn very different things from different metadata. Some examples of metadata include the following:

- Application label of what application seemed to be running in a flow [10].
- Domain names that were hosted on an IP address at the time traffic was captured.
- ID of intrusion detection and prevention system (IDPS) alerts triggered by network traffic or flow.
- Users logged in to a system at the time traffic was captured.
- Uniform resource locators (URLs) extracted from an email message.
- Autonomous system numbers (ASNs) offering routes to an IP address at the time traffic was captured.
- User-agent strings in an HTTP transaction.

In some ways, metadata is the result of application-level analysis applied to another context than that in which it was derived. Domain name system (DNS) information is a good example of this. To extract the name–address mapping from DNS there has to be the capability to monitor it at the application level. However, as far as metadata about IPs generally is concerned, it does not matter who sent the DNS query, just what the contents are. In this way DNS analysis can provide metadata about what domains are hosted on what IPs. DNS analysis as application-level analysis would be about what computers asked what questions, which is a different analysis and provides different insights.

One example of a rather complex analysis that provides metadata for the whole network is to do "network profiling using flow" [11]. If the organization has a flow-monitoring capability, one can do this analysis to construct a profile about how IP addresses have behaved in the past. This provides metadata for other analysis, since IPs can be tagged with labels like "DNS client" and "NAT/Gateway."

Sometimes, abstracted data is not the analyst's choice but rather the lawyer's. Some amounts of data are considered too sensitive to be collected without cause. The extent to which this is true varies by jurisdiction. For example, the U.S. Department of Homeland Security issues privacy impact assessments (PIAs) about what is acceptable for security analysts to capture on U.S. government networks. This includes network flow and passive DNS, but not full-packet capture unless there is a reason. However, a vetted intrusion detection system (IDS) signature alert is considered sufficient cause to capture a small amount of the subsequent related packets [12].

If enough metadata has been collected it can be analyzed. This is usually a task for interorganizational groups like coordination centers and information sharing and analysis centers (ISACs) since these groups are collection points for information sharing. In general, when information is collected from multiple organizations patterns can be discerned that the individual organizations would not be able to discover on their own, since they lack the context of the other organizations. Information sharing is also the only way an organization can determine if an attack was a specially targeted attack, because no one else will have seen the attack. This information is itself further metadata. It is important to determine what attacks are targeted because these represent attacks from more determined adversaries who are not merely opportunistic attackers.

Some organizations share their collected intelligence back out to the public. These resources are usually more casual blogs and websites rather than formal scholarly articles. The following are a sample of some useful (network) security context–related blogs, as of 2013, which the reader will likely find helpful to read occasionally:

- Krebs on Security (*http://krebsonsecurity.com/*)
- CERT Coordination Center blog (*http://www.cert.org/blogs/certcc/*)
- Swiss CSIRT blog (*http://www.abuse.ch/*)
- Securelist, a collaborative blog with multiple respected authors (*https://www.securelist.com/en/blog*)
- Dark Reading, cyber-security news (*http://www.darkreading.com/*)
- For more, there is a list of 20 security-related blogs at *http://www.veracode.com/blog/2012/02/top-20-security-blogs/*

In general, analysts should be encouraged to spend some time reading about current threats and security trends. The point of metadata is to help analysts contextualize the data. There is some context that cannot be fit neatly into a tag on a flow, such as what the particular exploit-of-choice of a certain organized crime group is this week. Such information does often find its way to publication through various blogs and casual postings.

Metadata is useful, especially if the analyst knows where it came from and how it was generated. In many cases, this is derived from application-level analysis, both within the organization and data shared from other organizations.

APPLICATION-LEVEL ANALYSIS

Application-level analysis is about analyzing the data transmitted by an application as the application would have interpreted it. This is a resource-intensive type of analysis in several regards. To capture it, the device has to traverse all seven layers of the OSI model, including possibly decrypting data, which requires computing time. Further, there needs to be a different application parser for each application to be analyzed. One tool, such as Wireshark, can utilize these parsers together, but this is additional overhead. The payoff for this effort depends on the application, but as mentioned in other chapters, the most popular applications are those likely to be the target of application-level analysis. The following are good candidates:

- HTTP
- DNS
- Email
- Kerberos (perhaps within Microsoft Active Directory)
- BGP (Border Gateway Protocol)[1]
- TLS (Transport Layer Security)[2] connection information and certificates

Analyzing each of these applications in detail allows the analyst to extract information that is otherwise unavailable. This approach requires appropriate monitoring at the relevant servers, network edge, or both, depending on the application and whether the goal is to collect information about internal or external computers. Selective application-level analysis can provide benefits over blanket full-packet capture since it potentially eliminates a lot of noise from the data by extracting just the features of the application that an analyst finds interesting. The other side of this coin is that if the analyst is not consulted in the development of the system, or as analytic goals change, the system may not collect the correct information.

A mature analytic group within an organization will want to ask questions of all of these applications for various reasons. Each provides some information that only it can provide. However, that does not mean that throwing all of these application data sources at a novice analyst capability will instantly provide situational awareness and actionable intelligence. The opposite is more likely—novice analysts will be overwhelmed by the avalanche of different information types. The analysis will have to be tailored to the organization itself, and the human analytic capability will also need to grow up with the organization to some extent. For this reason, organizational memory and low staff turnover are important goals; a reasonable expectation might be that it would take an analyst two to five months to understand how to fluently analyze each particular application. Each of flow, packet capture, IDS logs, and so on has a similar learning curve. Therefore, supporting people is still one of the most important steps in ensuring quality application-level analysis, and analysis in general.

---

[1] Although BGP is a method of determining how IP addresses are routed, it is also an application that runs on TCP/IP; by default it listens on TCP port 179 [13].

[2] TLS is not technically an application, but runs at what could be called layers 5 or 6 of the OSI model.

PROFILE: SURESH LAKSHMAN KONDA

Network Analysis on an Internet Scale

Suresh Konda was born in 1950 in India. Konda earned his M.S. in public policy and management from the Heinz College (then School) at Carnegie Mellon in 1975 and went on to earn his Ph.D. in 1980. He published in artificial intelligence (data mining), information portals, and vulnerability trends. Konda was one of the world's pioneering researchers in information security, and worked at Carnegie Mellon's Software Engineering Institute (SEI) for many years, often collaborating across the university.

He was recognized widely for his work on the security of large networks. To provide a quantitative basis for security decision making, he pioneered the development of large-scale collection infrastructures for network traffic summaries, ultimately resulting in the System for Internet-Level Knowledge, a network flow data collection and analysis tool suite. He received the SEI's first Angel Jordan Award for Innovation in 2002. Konda was an extremely passionate individual, eager to promote quality work in himself and in others. In turn, he provoked intense loyalty in his colleagues.

Suresh died suddenly in 2003, while living in Washington, DC. Subsequent to his death, the tool suite he pioneered was renamed SiLK, with the capitalization taken from his initials. The Heinz College also established the Konda Memorial Lecture Program and the Konda Award for outstanding Ph.D. student publication.

SIGNATURE ANALYSIS

Signature analysis is, most simply, looking for something that is already known to be suspicious or malicious. Usually the term applies to an IDS inspecting full-packet and application data and comparing it to known signatures, producing alerts. Network IDSs are the topic of Chapter 12, so we will leave that description aside for now. Human analysts can use signatures in a few ways: testing, as metadata, hunting, and campaign detection.

Before signatures are installed in an IDS, they should be tested. This process is a special case of change management, as described in Chapter 10. The producers of a signature are probably good at determining that the signature has a high true-positive rate: that it detects what it is supposed to detect. Signatures should be tested before deployment because the false-positive rate—that is, erroneous alerts—will be different for each environment. As discussed in Chapter 12, too many false positives can render a system useless.

More interesting is to use the fact that some particular trace of traffic matched a known-malicious signature as metadata for other analysis. If this capability is designed well, the analyst can ask for details such as "Show me all the traffic flows that matched the most recent flash zero-day exploit signature." Such questions help the analyst orient him- or herself faster to recognize which attacks succeeded and which the host managed to resist.

Skilled analysts will be able to go hunting for evidence of attacks that have evaded all the automated detection and recognition systems. Part of this process is the rather fuzzy process of looking for behavior that is outside the accepted normal behavior of machines on a network. This knowledge of what is unacceptable behavior is more complex than what a machine can usually bring to bear, because it depends on context and inferring intent to an extent that machines have not been able to match human capabilities. It also requires an analyst with detailed knowledge of both how the Internet protocols are intended to be used and how they are used in practice. Any one tool or monitoring capability is probably insufficient to allow an analyst to hunt down intrusions. A hunting capability within an organization is expensive, but it is an important investment if the organization is being specifically targeted by attackers. So far, persistent human attackers can always outsmart machines, so the only way to find them is with other persistent humans looking to defend the network.

Detecting campaigns against the organization is related to the task of finding persistent human attackers. If an analyst detects 50 distinct attack events, it is important to know if those attackers were by 15 different entities or 1. The organizational response to attacks by 15 distinct entities should be different than if there is 1 entity that is so tenacious and successful. The best public example of campaign identification is Mandiant's tracking of APT1 (advanced persistent threat) as an element of the People's Republic of China armed forces [5]. Campaign detection relies on certain attackers using certain signature tactics, techniques, and procedures (TTPs). Attackers cannot really avoid this; having no pattern is itself a pattern. For example, the TDSS (aka Alureon) botnet randomizes certain characteristic startup communications to avoid signature detection, which itself can be used as a signature to detect its startup communications [14].

FULL-PACKET CAPTURE

Full-packet capture is any technology that records every bit that goes over the wire for later inspection. The results are often colloquially referred to by their file extension: pcap.[3] This is the most voluminous network analysis option; even a rather modest 100-megabit link—a good and common residential connection in 2013—could fill up a terabyte of hard drive space in just 22 hours. A common corporate link of 10 gigabits could fill the same space in less than 14 minutes. As discussed before, many if not most intrusions are not detected for weeks [8]. Retention of sufficient packet capture data so that it can be analytically useful is a challenge. On the other hand, packet capture is the only way to reconstruct the exact details of an attack, which makes it an important tool.

---

[3] Various pcap files are available for free for training or research. For an index, see *http://www.netresec.com/?page=PcapFiles*.

Unfortunately, network payload traffic is often obscured. Defenders advocate network encryption, such as discussed in Chapter 8. Attackers have taken this lesson as well, and often enough it is precisely the data that would make pcap valuable that is encrypted. In some cases this encryption can be avoided, such as by forcing the hosts on the network to use a proxy and simply having the proxy record the traffic in its unencrypted state. The proxy breaks the connection into two distinct connections, and since network encryption only protects data in transit and not at the endpoints, the proxy can observe it. However, attackers can still obscure data from proxies, such as by encrypting or encoding the data twice.

Once packet capture data is stored, and assuming it has the desired data in an unencrypted format, it can still be challenging to find the important data. Searching through a large collection of pcap files has been likened to finding a needle in a needle-stack. Most of the solutions to this problem involve using one of the OSI analysis levels as an index into the pcap itself. Network flow particularly lends itself to this task, since it contains a condensed form of all the same data as full-packet capture. Broad queries can be done using flow tools, and then when more detail is needed all the packets that were part of the flow in question can be pulled out. Some flow meters provide the option to retain and index the pcap files when it processes packet capture to produce network flow [10].

Full-packet capture remains an important tool for analysts, but it needs to be filtered before it is stored. Judicious full-packet capture, rather than blanket capture, provides useful information. Do you really need a complete copy of every streaming video that the employees have watched for the past three weeks? No. Realistically, even if it becomes important to watch for some odd reason, keeping the URL should be enough to fetch the video again from the content provider. When planning a packet capture capability, it is important to allow time for optimizing what is captured and what is allowed to be summarized by other technologies. That process will be idiosyncratic to each network, but without adaptation and a focused goal, packet capture can be hard to work with.

NETWORK FORENSICS

The difference between what might be called human-driven network analysis and network forensics is not sharply drawn. One might say that network forensics is network analysis in some relation to a reactive investigation, although not necessarily a legal one. Kessler and Fasulo [15] provide a more detailed discussion of the attributes of network forensics, and its importance within digital forensics. Network forensics is a subset of digital forensics, which is a topic covered more thoroughly in Chapter 13. This section introduces some features specific to networks, but there are many aspects shared with forensics more generally as discussed in Chapter 13.

To do network forensics the network traffic must be intentionally recorded. This fact contrasts sharply with host-based forensics, since hosts generally write information to stable storage media as a matter of course. Traffic can be recorded under specific goals, in response to a warrant or other cause for concern raise by the CSIRT (see Chapter 15), or traffic can be recorded as a matter of course all the time. The level of detail about traffic that can be recorded without cause varies by legal jurisdiction. On most large networks, it is impractical to keep full-packet capture of the whole network for long periods of time anyway, and so network flow is both a reasonable technical and legal compromise. This is essentially the assessment the U.S. government has reached in regard to monitoring its own civilian networks [12], for example.

The other primary purpose of network forensics is to support root-cause analysis. The goal of root-cause analysis is to discover the initial method and manner of compromise. These results can be used to harden the organization against future attacks; for more information on this feedback process, see Chapter 15. As noted earlier, most intrusions go undetected for weeks, if not months or years [5–8]. This makes network forensics particularly challenging. It is even more difficult if only reactive network capture is used, since there is no network evidence of how the compromise began. Without general historical records (as opposed to purpose-captured traffic in response to an incident), root-cause analysis is often impossible.

A network forensics capability is an important supplement to host forensics because the traffic record provides out-of-band evidence of activity. If the adversary compromises a host, he or she may be able to erase some or all the evidence of the compromise. However, the network monitoring devices are not subject to such manipulation, and so can provide a more stable, if less precise, measure of activity in the organization. There are certainly steps that an adversary can take to avoid network detection; some are discussed in Chapter 12. All the same, most common attacks arrive on the network, and so they will leave some trace.

The tools for network forensics are largely the same as those for network analysis. As alluded to before, it is mostly the motivation that differentiates the two terms. With forensics, the motivation is more about gathering evidence to assign responsibility to specific individuals. The anonymity possible on computer networks makes attribution particularly challenging. There are a variety of special considerations that need to be made to preserve the proper legal and ethical frameworks while performing work with this motivation. These considerations are not special to network forensics, but hold more generally for digital forensics. Since these handling considerations make up the bulk of the difference between human-driven network analysis and network forensics, they are left for Chapter 12.

SENSOR NETWORK ARCHITECTURE

Where the network sensors are located in the network is important. Sensor architecture is a subset of the importance of network architecture generally, which was introduced in Chapter 5. Just as some analysis techniques are better or worse at detecting certain attacks, certain sensor placements are better suited for detecting certain attacks or gathering certain information. All of the preceding types of sensors can be located in various places on the organization's network. It is also important for analysts to understand where a sensor is located to accurately analyze the information from the sensor and its impact on the organization.

There are two broad types of sensor placement: on the edge and internal. Observing traffic as it is entering or leaving the organization is more common. There are usually a small number of Internet access points for an organization, so installing sensors on the edge is somewhat easier. The other reason for sensing on the edge is the assumption that attacks on the organization come from the outside. If this were true, then if the defenders can observe and analyze all the attacks coming in on the edge, then the defenders could see all the attacks.

Unfortunately, not all attacks come from the outside. Internal sensors are necessary to detect such problems. There are two general use cases for internal attacks that could be important. One is detecting insider attacks where the attacker is actually a member of the organization with some valid credentials and authorizations. The other would be in the case where an attacker compromises an internal resource and uses that resource to compromise other internal resources. Therefore, determining the full scope and root cause of an infection likely will involve monitoring internal communications as well as communications at the edge.

SUMMARY

Human-driven network analysis is an important part of a recognition strategy because IT systems are made by humans, for humans, and are attacked by humans, therefore, humans must also be involved in their effective defense. There are several specializations of network analysis. The OSI model can be used to conceptualize the different analysis types. One benefit of this model is the idea that as an analysis moves up to process more and higher layers, the resources required for the analysis increase. Figure 11.4 provides a rough guide for which layers are involved in which analysis type. It introduces a layer 8, for human intelligence tasks like reading blogs and campaign analysis that do not easily fit into the technical OSI model.

Network analysis and the OSI Model -- a summary					
Layer	Network analysis type				
	Flow-	*metadata*	*application-*	*signature*	*full*
"8. Human Intel"		-		-	
7. Application		-	#	-	#
6. Presentation			-	-	#
5. Session			-	-	#
4. Transport	#			-	#
3. Network	#	-		-	#
2. Data link					#
1. Physical					
Key:	# :used in analysis		- :partially used		

FIGURE 11.4

The seven layers of the OSI model and the rough usage of information from those layers in different network analysis specializations. The chart introduces a layer 8, not in the OSI model, to cover human intelligence tasks relevant to network defense.

The questions that one can expect an analyst to answer vary depending on what technology and analysis types are available to them. However, some questions are always difficult to answer based on certain features of the Internet, such as the fact that IP addresses are logical, not physical, which makes physically locating machines and attacks difficult. Yet, in most cases, the variety of analysis techniques available can be arranged in a complementary manner, such that the strengths of one support the weaknesses of the others.

For better or worse, effective human-driven analysis remains trade craft rather than science. A skilled analyst derives much benefit from familiarity with the network he or she is defending, and this specific knowledge is not easy for an organization to capture. This difficulty is not true for all analyst experiences. Chapter 12 discusses the aspects of analyst workflow that are easier to codify, and the tools and procedures used to capture those experiences and apply them to network defense at machine speed.

REFERENCES

[1] International Organization for Standardization and International Electrotechnical Commission. Open systems interconnection—basic reference model: the basic model. ISO/IEC, 1996. 7498-1:1994(E).

[2] Claise B. Cisco Systems NetFlow Services Export Version 9. RFC 3954, 2004.

[3] Abuse.ch blog. abuse.ch Palevo Tracker. Retrieved Apr 6, 2013, from <https://palevotracker. abuse.ch/>; 2013.

[4] Abuse.ch blog. abuse.ch Zeus Tracker. Retrieved Apr 6, 2013, from <https://zeustracker. abuse.ch/>; 2013.

[5] Mandiant. APT1: exposing one of China's cyber espionage units. Retrieved Apr 8, 2013, from <http://intelreport.mandiant.com/>; 2013.

[6] The Center for Internet Security. The CIS security metrics: consensus metric definitions, v1.0.0, 2009. Retrieved Apr 8, 2013, from <https://buildsecurityin.us-cert.gov/swa/downloads/CIS_Security_Metrics_v1.0.0.pdf>.

[7] Verizon. 2012 Data breach investigations report. Retrieved Apr 8, 2013, from <http://www.verizonenterprise.com/DBIR/2012/>; 2012.

[8] Verizon. 2013 Data breach investigations report. Retrieved Apr 8, 2013, from <http://www.verizonenterprise.com/DBIR/2013/>; 2013.

[9] Weinberger D. Everything is miscellaneous: the power of the new digital disorder. Times Books, New York City; 2007.

[10] Software Engineering Institute. CERT NetSA security suite—monitoring for large-scale networks. Retrieved Apr 15, 2013, from <http://tools.netsa.cert.org/>; 2013.

[11] Whisnant A, Faber S. Network profiling using flow. CMU/SEI-2012-TR-006, 2012. Retrieved from <www.sei.cmu.edu/library/abstracts/reports/12tr006.cfm>.

[12] U.S. Department of Homeland Security. Privacy impact assessment for the national cyber-security protection system, 2012. Retrieved from <http://www.dhs.gov/sites/default/files/publications/privacy/privacy-pia-nppd-ncps.pdf>.

[13] Rekhter Y, Li T, Hares S. A border gateway protocol 4 (BGP-4). RFC 4271. Updated by RFCs 6286, 6608, 2006.

[14] Jerrim J. Detecting Malware P2P traffic using network flow and DNS analysis. Flocon 2013. Software Engineering Institute, CERT Directorate. Retrieved Apr 15, 2013, from <http://www.cert.org/flocon/2013/presentations/jerrim-john-detecting-malware.pdf>; 2013.

[15] Kessler GC, Fasulo M. The case for teaching network protocols to computer forensics examiners. Proceedings of the conference on digital forensics, security and law, 2007. p. 115–137.

Chapter Review Questions

1. What are the seven layers of the OSI model? Which layers are processed by network nodes and which are processed on the host?

2. What simple questions are hard to answer using only IP address information?

3. What are some common applications that might be important to do application-level analysis of?

4. What is campaign detection and analysis?

5. How is network forensics different from human-driven network analysis?

Chapter Exercises

1. Figure out which applications are most prevalent on a network you care about, either your home network or your corporate/school network if you are authorized. How would you prioritize application-level analysis of these applications? Which are most important to the security of the network?

2. Read some of the blogs listed on page 237 and summarize a couple recent relevant posts.

CHAPTER 12

Recognition Strategies: Intrusion Detection and Prevention

INTRODUCTION

This chapter expands on the strategy for recognition. Due to the nature of the modern computer infrastructure, compromises are inevitable. Chapter 11 detailed various analysis techniques that a human analyst might use to detect evidence of a compromise on the network. This chapter discusses the natural next step in that process: reducing the workload on the human analyst by automating some of the functions. Intrusion detection and prevention systems aim to do just that.

The formal definition of an intrusion detection system (IDS) is a system that "monitor[s] the events occurring in a computer system or network and analyz[es] them for signs of possible incidents, which are violations or imminent threats of violation of computer security policies, acceptable use

253

policies, or standard security practices" [1, p. 2-1]. This National Institute of Standards and Technology (NIST) definition has also been adopted by the Internet Engineering Task Force (IETF) [2]. Intrusion prevention is directly related, for it is "the process of performing intrusion detection and attempting to stop detected possible incidents" [1].

Following NIST, this chapter will use the combined term *intrusion detection and prevention system* (IDPS) for brevity. This does not replace the terms IDS or IPS, which are well established. However, most of the functions of an IDS are shared with an IPS, and devices termed IPSs can usually be configured to disable the prevention activity and function just as an IDS can [1]. So combining the terms is convenient and generally accurate. Any exceptions will be noted.

There are several types of IDPSs, based on what the system is monitoring. The most common is a network IDS, a machine that observes traffic at a choke point in the network and inspects it for intrusions across the organization [3, p. 660]. Network-based IDPSs are also characterized by the fact that they reassemble the packets of the network communication and attempt to interpret them as the target host would. The other three types are host based, wireless, and network behavior analysis (NBA) [1]. This chapter focuses on network-based IDPSs, however, the general principles are relevant to all IDPS technologies. Anti-virus software can be considered a type of host-based IDPS, but these products have expanded to attempt to prevent exploits and have taken on many characteristics of an IDPS [4]. Wireless IDPSs are intended to detect abuse of wireless networks themselves, either interference with the radio spectrum or rogue access points.

This chapter discusses several issues related to IDPSs. First, why instrumenting an IDS is important in addition to the network resistance and frustration strategies previously discussed; also, why it should be instrumented independently of these other devices. Next, the chapter covers some common historical pitfalls of intrusion detection devices, and their fixes, to describe the uses and limitations of IDPSs. Two common modes of detection for IDPSs are then discussed: signature-based and anomaly-based detection. Finally, the modifications necessary to go from an IDS to an IPS, and the ramifications, are discussed before concluding.

It is important to note that an IDPS is a conceptual device. Just as with firewalls and proxies discussed in Chapter 5, actual devices on the market may combine features of more than one category of device. For example, application-level proxies may contain IDPS features specific to an application, or a firewall may contain IDPS features for network traffic. The defender should account for this fact when designing and purchasing a sensor architecture. Sensor architecture and some other network analysis concepts relevant to IDPSs are discussed in Chapter 11.

WHY INTRUSION DETECTION

An IDPS is one of the more important devices in an organization's overall security strategy. There is too much data for any human analyst to inspect all of it for evidence of intrusions, and the IDPS helps alert humans to events to investigate, and prioritize human recognition efforts. An IDPS also serves an important auditing function. If the machines that form the technological backbone of the frustration and resistance strategies are misconfigured, the IDPS should be positioned to detect violations due to these errors. Furthermore, some attacks will exist for a period of time before there is any available patch or mitigation. An IDPS may be able to detect traffic indicative of the new attack, either as soon as a signature is made available or if the attack traffic is generally anomalous.

An IDPS has many actions available when responding to a security event. Generating an alert for human eyes is a common action, but it can also log the activity, record the raw network data that caused the alert, attempt to terminate a session, alter network or system access controls, or some combination thereof [5]. If managed well, the different rules stratify the actions into different categories related to the severity of attack, reliability of rule, criticality of target, timeliness of response required, and other organizational concerns. Once the notifications are stratified, the human operator can prioritize response and recovery actions, which are the topic of Chapter 15.

Returning to our walled-city metaphor from Chapter 5, we already have our static defenses—moats, walls, and gates—as well as the more active defenses, such as guards who inspect people coming into the city. An IDPS is similar to a sentry posted above the city gate and/or in a tower nearby. If the guard gets overrun by a suddenly unruly mob, the guard cannot call for help. The sentry provides a basic defense-in-depth function of recognizing that a problem has occurred and an alert needs to be issued. Also like an IDPS, the sentry may have some immediate corrective actions available, such as telling the gate operator to close it temporarily or in some castles there are grates over the entryway from which a sentry could pour boiling oil to deter invaders who breached the outer defenses. But like an IDPS, while these responses may be effective stop-gap measures, they are not sustainable methods of network management. The most important functions are to alert the authorities so that a recovery of security can begin, and to keep a record of how the incident occurred so a better system can be put in to place going forward.

The three major components of an IDPS and how they interact with the relevant organizational components are summarized in Figure 12.1. The IDPS sensor infrastructure observes activity that it normalizes or processes into events, which the analyzer ingests and inspects for events of interests. The manager processes deals with the events appropriately. In the tower sentry

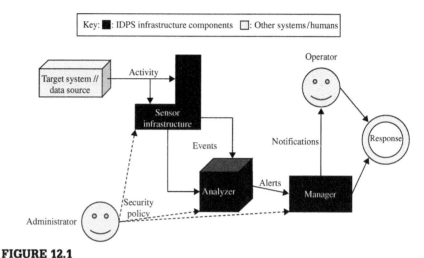

FIGURE 12.1
The basic components of an IDPS and how they interact with their environment.

metaphor, these components are all inside the one human sentry. In an IDPS, they can be part of one computer or distributed to specialized machines.

Figure 12.2 displays the internal components of an IDPS in more detail. The operator interacts with the system components through the graphical user interface (GUI); some systems use a command-line interface for administration in addition to or instead of a GUI. The alarms represent what responses to make. The knowledge base is the repository of rules and profiles for matching against traffic. Algorithms are used to reconstruct sessions and understand session and application data. The audit archives store past events of interest. System management is the glue that holds it all together, and the sensors are the basis for the system, receiving the data from the target systems.

NETWORK INTRUSION DETECTION PITFALLS

A network-based IDPS (NIDPS) has many strengths, but these strengths are also often its weaknesses. A NIDPS strength is that the system reassembles content and analyzes the data against the security policy in the format the target would process it. Another strength is that the data is processed passively, out of band of regular network traffic. A related strength is that a NIDPS can be centrally located on the network at a choke point to reduce hardware costs and configuration management. However, all of these benefits also introduce pitfalls, which will be discussed serially. Furthermore, there are some difficulties that any IDPS suffers from simply due to the fact that the Internet is noisy, and so differentiating security-related weird stuff from

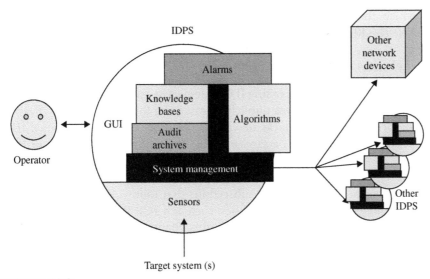

FIGURE 12.2
A more detailed view of how the internal components of an IDPS interact. If two shapes touch within the IDPS, then those two components interact directly.

general anomalies becomes exceptionally difficult. For some example benign anomalies, see Bellovin [6].

The following sections are not intended to devalue IDSs or to give the impression that an IDS is not part of a good security strategy. An IDS is essential to a complete recognition strategy. The following pitfalls are remediated and addressed to varying degrees in available IDPSs. Knowledge of how well a potential IDPS handles each issue is important when selecting a system for use. Despite advances in IDPS technology, the following pitfalls do still arise occasionally. It is important for defenders to keep this in mind: no one security strategy is infallible. Knowing the ways in which each is more likely to fail helps design overlapping security strategies that account for weaknesses in certain systems. For these reasons, we present the following common pitfalls in IDPSs.

Fragmentation and IP Validation

One of the pitfalls of reassembling sessions as the endpoints would view them is that endpoints tend to reassemble sessions differently. This is not just true of applications. This is true of the fundamental fabric of the Internet, the TCP/IP (Transport Control Protocol/Internet Protocol) protocol suite. To handle all possible problems that a packet might have while traversing the network, IP packets might be fragmented. Furthermore, if packets are delayed they might be resent by the sender. This leads to a combination of situations in which the receiver may receive multiple copies of all or part of an IP packet. The RFCs (request for changes) that standardize TCP/IP behavior are silent on how the receiver should handle this possibly inconsistent data, and so implementations vary [7, p. 280].

Packet fragmentation for evading IDS systems was laid out in detail in a 1997 U.S. military report that was publicly released the following year [8]. Evasion is one of three general attacks described; the other two attacks against IDSs are insertion and denial of service (DoS). Insertion and evasion are both caused, in general, by inconsistencies in the way the TCP/IP stack is interpreted. DoS attacks against IDPSs are not limited to TCP/IP interpretation, and are treated throughout the subsections that follow. DoS attacks are possible through bugs and vulnerabilities, such as a TCP/IP parsing vulnerability like the teardrop attack [9], but when this chapter discusses DoS on IDPSs it refers to DoS specific to IDPSs. DoS attacks such as the teardrop attack are operating system vulnerabilities, and so such things are not IDPS specific, even though many IDPSs may run on operating systems that are affected.

The general problem sketched out by the packet fragmentation issues is that the strength of the IDPS—namely, that it analyzes the data against the security policy in the format the target would process—is thwarted when the attacker can force the IDPS to process a different packet stream than the target will. This can be due to insertion or evasion. For example, if the IDPS does not validate the IP header checksum, the attacker can send blatant attack packets that will initiate false IDPS alerts, because the target system would drop the packet and not actually be compromised. This insertion attack can be more subtle. IP packets have a time-to-live (TTL) value that each router decrements by 1 before forwarding. Routers will drop an IP packet when the TTL of the packet reaches 0. An attacker could send the human responder on lots of confusing, errant clean-up tasks if the TTL of packets are crafted to reach the IDPS, but be dropped before they reach the hosts [8]. And if an attacker knows your network well enough to manipulate TTLs like this, it is technically hard to prevent. The IDPS would have to know the number of router hops to each target host it is protecting—a management nightmare.

Another result of Ptacek and Newsham's report [8] was some research into how different operating systems handle different fragmentation possibilities [10]. Some NIDPS implementations now utilize these categories when they process sessions, and also include methods for the NIDPS to fingerprint which method the hosts it is protecting use so the NIDPS can use the appropriate defragmentation method [11]. This method improves processing accuracy, but management of this mapping is not trivial. Further, network address translation (NAT) and Dynamic Host Configuration Protocol (DHCP) will cause inconsistencies if the pool of computers sharing the IP space does not share the same processing method. This subtle dependency highlights the importance of a holistic understanding of the network architecture—and keeping the architecture simple enough that it can be holistically understood.

Application Reassembly

NIDPSs perform reassembly of application data to keep states of transactions and appropriately process certain application-specific details. The precise applications reassembled by an IDPS implementation vary. Common applications like File Transfer Protocol (FTP), Secure Shell (SSH), and Hypertext Transfer Protocol (HTTP) are likely to be understood. Down the spectrum of slightly more specific applications, Gartner has published a business definition for "next-generation" IPSs that requires the system understand the content of files such as portable document format (PDF) and Microsoft Office [12]. The ability to process this large variety of applications when making decisions is a significant strength of IDPS devices, as most other centralized network defense devices are inline and cannot spend the time to reassemble application data. Proxies can, but they are usually application specific, and so lack the broader context that IDPSs usually can leverage.

The large and myriad application-parsing libraries required for this task introduce a lot of dependencies into IDPS operations, which can lead to some common pitfalls. First, IDPSs require frequent updates as applications change and bugs are fixed. If the IDPS was only purchased to fill a regulatory requirement and is ignored afterwards, it quickly becomes less and less effective as parsers fall out of date.

Even in the best case where the system is up to date, many of the variable processing decisions that were described earlier related to IP fragmentation are relevant to each application the IDPS needs to parse. The various web browsers and operating systems may parse HTTP differently, for example. This is less a problem in application handling, because as long as the IP packets are reassembled correctly, at least the IDPS has the correct data to inspect. But due diligence in testing rules might indicate that different rules are needed not just per application, but one for each common implementation of that application protocol. Bugs might be targeted in specific versions of application implementations, further ballooning the number of required rules. So far, NIDPSs themselves seem to be able to handle the large number of rules required, although rule management and tuning are arduous for system and security administrators.

Out-of-Band Problems

Although an IDPS is located on a central part of the network, it may not be in the direct line of network traffic. An inline configuration is recommended only when IPS functionality will be utilized, otherwise an out-of-band configuration is recommended [1]. When an IDS is running out of band it has some benefits, but it also introduces some possible errors. If the IDS is out of band, then if the IDS is dropping packets no network services will suffer. This is a benefit, except that the security team then needs to configure the IDS to alert them when it is dropping packets so they can take that into account. A more difficult problem to detect is if the network configuration that delivers packets to the IDS develops errors, either accidental or forced by the attacker, that result in the IDS not receiving all the traffic in the first place. There is a similar problem with other resource exhaustion issues, whether due to attacks or simply to a large network load, at the transport and application layer.

Inline architectures have to make harder decisions about what to do when the IPS resources are exhausted. Despite the best planning, resource exhaustion will happen occasionally; if nothing else, adversaries attempt to cause it with DoS attacks. Whether the IPS chooses to make network performance suffer and drop packets, or it chooses to make its analysis suffer and not inspect every packet, is an important decision. The administrator should make the risk analysis for this decision clear. This is an example of a failure control situation [2]. In general, a fail-secure approach is recommended; in this example the IPS would fail-secure by dropping packets. This approach fails securely because no attack can penetrate the network because of the failure, unlike the other option.

In either case, the resource exhaustion failure still causes damage. The IDPS cannot log packets it never reads, and if its disk space or processor is exhausted, then it cannot continue to perform its recognition functions properly. Therefore, appropriately resourcing the IDPS is important. On large networks, this will likely require specialized devices.

Centrality Problems

Since the NIDPS is centrally located, it has a convenient view of a large number of hosts. However, this central location combined with the passive strategy of IDPS also means that data can be hidden from view. Primarily this is due to encryption, whether it is IPSec [13,14], Transport Layer Security (TLS) [15], or application-level encryption like pretty good privacy (PGP) [16]. Encryption is an encouraged, and truthfully necessary, resistance strategy (Chapter 8). However, if application data is encrypted, then the IDPS cannot inspect it for attacks. This leads to a fundamental tension—attackers will also encrypt their attacks with valid, open encryption protocols to avoid detection on the network. One strategy to continue to detect these attacks is host-based detection. The host will decrypt the data, and can perform the IDPS function there. However, this defeats the centralized nature of NIDPS, and also thwarts the broad correlation abilities that only a centralized sensor can provide. And as groups like the Electronic Frontier Foundation encourage citizens with programs like "HTTPS Everywhere" [17], in addition to the push from the security community, the prevalence of encryption will only increase.

On a controlled network it is possible to proxy all outgoing connections, and thereby decrypt everything, send it to the IDPS, and then encrypt it again before it is sent along to its destination. It is recommended to implement each of these functions (encryption proxy, IDPS) on a separate machine, as each are resource-intensive and have different optimization requirements [18].

Base-rate Fallacy

The final problem that IDPSs encounter is that they are trying to find inherently rare events. False positives—that is, the IDPS alerts on benign traffic—are impossible to avoid. If there are too many false positives, the analyst is not able to find the real intrusions in the alert traffic. All the alerts are equally alerts; there is no way for the analyst to know without further investigation which are false positives and which are true positives. Successful intrusions are rare compared to the scope of how much network traffic passes a sensor. Intrusions may happen every day, but if the intrusions become common it does not take an IDPS to notice. Network performance just plummets as SQL Slammer,[1] for example, repurposes your network to scan and send spam. But that is not the sort of intrusion we need an IDPS to find. And hopefully all of the database administrators and firewall rule sets have learned enough from the early 2000s that the era of worms flooding whole networks is passed [19]. It also seems likely criminals realized there was no money in that kind of attack, but that stealing money can be successful with stealthier attacks [20]. Defenders need the IDPS to recognize stealthy attacks.

Unfortunately for security professionals, statistics teaches us that it is particularly difficult to detect rare events. Bayes' theorem is necessary to demonstrate this difficultly, but let's consider the example of a medical test. What we are interested in finding is the false-positive rate—that is, the chance that the medical test alerts the doctor the patient has the condition when the patient in fact does not. We need to know two facts to calculate the false-positive rate: the accuracy of the test and the incidence of the disease in the population. Let's say the test is 91% accurate, and 0.75% of the population actually has the condition. We can calculate the chance that a positive test result is actually a false positive as follows: Where Pr is the probability of the event

---

[1] Structured Query Language (SQL) is a common database language. SQL Slammer is so named because it exploits a vulnerability in the database and then reproduces automatically through scanning for other databases to exploit.

in brackets ([ ]) and the vertical bar (|) between two events can be read as "given," it means that calculating an event is dependent on, or given, another. For example, the probability that the patient does not have the condition given the test result was positive could be written $Pr[healthy|positive]$. This is the probability the test result is an incorrect alert. Therefore:

$$Pr[healthy|positive] = \frac{Pr[positive|healthy] \times Pr[healthy]}{Pr[positive|sick] \times Pr[sick] + (Pr[positive|healthy] \times Pr[healthy])}$$

There will be a subtle difference here. We are not calculating the false-positive rate. That is simply $Pr[positive|healthy]$. We are calculating the chance that the patient is healthy given the test alerted the doctor to the presence of the condition. This value is arguably much more important than the false-positive rate. The IDPS human operator wants to know if action needs to be taken to recover security when the IDPS alerts it has recognized an intrusion. That value is $Pr[healthy|positive]$, what we're trying to get to. Let's call this value the alarm error, or AE. Let's simplify the precding equation by calling the false-positive rate FPR, and the true-positive rate TPR. The probabilities remaining in the equation will be the rate of the condition in the population, represented by the simple probability that a person is sick or healthy:

$$AE = \frac{FPR \times Pr[healthy]}{TPR \times Pr[sick] + (FPR \times Pr[healthy])}$$

Let's substitute in the values and calculate the AE in our example. The test is 91% accurate, so the FPR is 9% or 0.09, and the TPR is 0.91. If 0.75% of people have the condition, then the probability a person is healthy is 0.9925, and sick is 0.0075. Therefore:

$$AE = \frac{0.09 \times 0.9925}{0.91 \times 0.0075 + (0.09 \times 0.9925)}$$
$$AE = \frac{0.089325}{0.006825 + (0.089325)}$$
$$AE = 92.9\%$$

Therefore, with these conditions, 92.9% of the time when the test says the patient has the condition, the patient will in fact be perfectly healthy. If this result seems surprising—that with a 9% false-positive rate that almost 93% of the alerts would be false positives—you are not alone. It is a studied human cognitive error to underestimate the importance of the basic incidence of the tested-for condition when people make intuitive probability evaluations [21,22]. One can bring intuition in line with reality by keeping in mind that if there are not very many sick people, it will be hard to find them, especially if the test for something is relatively complicated (like sickness or computer security intrusions). It is the proverbial needle-in-a-haystack problem.

There has been some research into the technical aspects of the effects of the base-rate problem on IDPS alarm rates [23]. The results are not very encouraging—the estimate is that the false-positive rate needs be at or below 0.00001, or 10^{-5}, before the alarm rate is considered "reasonable," at 66% true alarms. However, in the context of other industrial control systems, the studies of operator psychology indicate that in fields such as power plant, paper mill, steel mill, and large ship operations, the operator would disregard the whole alarm system as useless if the true alarm rate were only 66%.

The base-rate fallacy provides two lessons when considering an IDPS. First, when an IDPS advertises its false-positive rate as "reasonable," keep in mind that what is reasonable for a useful IDPS is much lower than is intuitively expected. Second, the base-rate problem has a lot to do with why signature-based operation is the predominant IDPS operational mode. It has much lower false positives, and so even though signatures may miss many more events, they can achieve sufficiently low false-positive rates to be useful. Given how noisy the Internet is, anomaly-based detection is still largely a research project, despite the alluring business case of a system that just knows when something looks wrong. The following two sections describe these two modes of operation.

An additional important point is that a grasp of statistics and probability is important for a network security analyst. For a treatment of the base-rate fallacy in this context, see Stallings [24, ch. 9A]. For a good introductory statistics text that is freely available electronically, see Kadane [25].

PROFILE: MARTIN ROESCH

The Father of Snort

As the story goes, one weekend in 1998 Marty Roesch sat down and wrote a little Linux program for traffic analysis, and after those two days he shared his creation with the open-source community [26]. Roesch was amazed at the positive response from the project, and how many people downloaded the code. This was how one of the most influential open-source projects of the current era was born: the Snort IDS. This led to a quick set of developments for a man who had just graduated from Clarkson University in 1992, a smaller technical school in upstate New York. In early

2001, Roesch hired four employees and founded Sourcefire, a network defense company. While Sourcefire sells a lot of commercial products to enhance Snort's capabilities, they still maintain the core Snort IDS engine as an open-source product.

In 2009, InfoWorld included Snort in their Open-Source Hall of Fame [27]. It was one of only three security-related tools included in the 36-item list. It's hard to accurately convey the impact Snort has had on the network defense community. Reading the academic literature about intrusion detection systems before 1998, there is a tangible undercurrent of depression in the academic literature. The implementations up to that time were expensive, bulky, and, despite the cost, ineffective. Snort was not only free, but it consumed fewer computational resources than many of the commercial counterparts. Furthermore, it ran well in software and did not require special equipment purchases for smaller networks, unlike most IDSs at the time that did require special hardware.

In 2013, it is expected as a matter of course that you have NIDS defending your network. In 1998 a single NIDS was a luxury item. Snort and Marty Roesch are the primary forces that have bridged that gap. Roesch is still the CTO of Sourcefire, overseeing the technical development of Snort and all the other software components that enhance it. He also occasionally spends stints as the interim CEO, demonstrating a management and salesman skill that is rare in people who can write a functional piece of software in a weekend. Although Sourcefire is best known for its technology, Roesch says that his real goal and vision are to make Sourcefire "instrumental in transforming the way organizations manage and minimize their risks" [26].

MODES OF INTRUSION DETECTION

In broad strokes, NIDPSs can operate with signature-based or anomaly-based detection methods. Practically, both modes are used because they have important benefits and uses. However, it is useful to understand the different benefits, and limitations, of each style of detection, even though a single IDPS that is purchased will likely possess both signature-based and anomaly-based detection capabilities to some extent. For example, Snort (an open-source IDS, see the preceding sidebar) has been extended to perform some anomaly detection capabilities in various ways [28]. This categorization is similar to the reason to understand NIDPSs as a separate kind of device from the various types of firewalls as described in Chapter 5, even though devices on the market often do not strictly adhere to any category. Categorizing is helpful for the network defender to conceptualize and plan a coordinated defense strategy.

Network Intrusion Detection: Signatures

Signatures are one of two modes that IDPSs use to detect intrusions. The idea is that the NIDPS detects a known pattern, or signature, of a specific malicious activity that is exhibited within the traffic. Signature-based detection is simpler to implement than anomaly-based detection, and a good signature will have a lower, more consistent false-positive rate. However, signatures can be easy to evade and require the attack to be known before they can be written and the attack detected. Rules can usually be written fairly quickly once an attack is known, but someone, somewhere, must first detect it without a signature.

Signatures are quite flexible. A NIDPS aims to inspect the content of all the traffic that traverses the network. This is opposed to firewalls, which tend to only inspect the headers for the packets. This increased scope is arduous, and

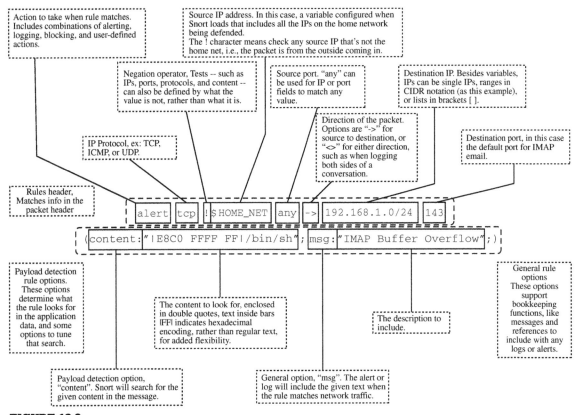

FIGURE 12.3

An example snort rule. The different features and fields of the rule are labeled. Source: *Roesch et al. [30].*

partly explains why NIDPSs can have performance issues. It also is the reason that they are such a useful tool.

To understand what a signature can accomplish, it may be helpful to understand the anatomy of a rule. The de facto standard format for a signature is its expression in a Snort rule. Snort is an open-source NIDPS that began development in 1998, and is primarily signature based. Due to its popularity, many other NIDPSs accept or use Snort-format rules. A rule is a single expression of both a signature and what to do when it is detected. Figure 12.3 displays a sample text Snort rule and annotates the components.[2] For a complete rule-writing guide, see the Snort documentation [29].

Figure 12.3 is not as complex as it may appear at first glance. There are three sections in this rule: one for what kind of rule this is and packets to look at, one for

---

[2] Compiled Snort rules exist, and these are in binary format, unreadable by humans. They have a different format than this text rule, which will not be discussed here, but the function is essentially the same.

what to look for in the packets, and a third for what to say once the rule finds a match. These sections are enclosed in light-gray dashed lines. The first section is the rules header, which is the more structured of the three. This section declares the rule type. Figure 12.3 is an "alert," one of the basic built-in types.

Rule types define what to do when the rule matches, which we'll return to later. The rest of the rule header will match against parts of the TCP/IP headers for each packet. This essentially performs a packet-filter, like a firewall access control list (ACL; see Chapter 5), even though the syntax and capabilities are different than a firewall. IP addresses can be matched flexibly, either with variables or ranges. Although not demonstrated in this rule, ports can also be specified with ranges or variables. IP addresses can also be specified as "any," for any value matches. The arrow indicates direction, and < > (not pictured) means either direction matches. Although the first versions used to allow it to be either →or←, that soon became confusing. Now only → is allowed, so the source IP is always on the left and the destination is always on the right.

The contents of the rule all go inside parentheses, with different parts separated by semicolons. This is where the flexibility of an IDPS rule can really be leveraged. Figure 12.3 demonstrates two of the simpler sections—payload detection and general—each with only their quintessential option demonstrated. Payload detection dictates what to look for in packet payloads, and it also offers some options to describe how and where to look for the content, which are not demonstrated in the figure. The content field is the quintessential option, as it defines the string that the signature will look for. In the example, there is a particular sequence of bits that can be used to inject malicious data into a particular email process in a known way, and this rule looks for that sequence of bits. Since this sequence is in the application data, it is clear why such signatures can be easily evaded with encryption—encrypting the payload would change these bits while in transit. The general section includes descriptors about the rule whenever an alert is sent or packets logged, so that the analyst does not have to remember that the hex sequence E8C0FFFFFF is particular to a buffer overflow in the Internet Message Access Protocol (IMAP), for email.

As the amount of available software has grown, so have the number of vulnerabilities. At the same time, older vulnerabilities do not go away—at least not quickly. If a vulnerability only afflicts a Windows 98 machine, most IDPSs in 2013 do not still need to track or block it. The basic premise is that if a vulnerability does not exist on the network the IDPS is protecting, it does not need signatures to detect intrusions resulting from it. But this in practice provides little respite, and the number of signatures that an IDPS needs to track grows rapidly.

There is a second way to view this threat landscape, and that is to ask what vulnerabilities attackers are commonly exploiting, and preferentially defend against them. There is always the chance that a targeted attack will use an unknown, zero-day vulnerability to still penetrate the system undetected, but that is a different class of attacker. There is a set of common, lucrative criminal malicious software that exploits a small set of known vulnerabilities, and these are the attacks that are all but guaranteed to hit an unprepared network. There are only about 10 vulnerabilities of this mass-exploit quality per year, against only a handful of applications [31]. The best way to defend against such common exploits may not be an IDPS, however, an IDPS should be a device that helps the defenders decide what exploits are most common on their network, and thus which exploits deserve the special attention to prevention, such as the steps described in Guido [31].

Network Intrusion Detection: Anomaly Based

Anomaly-based detection generally needs to work on a statistically significant number of packets, because any packet is only an anomaly compared to some baseline. This need for a baseline presents several difficulties. For one, anomaly-based detection will not be able to detect attacks that can be executed with a few or even a single packet. These attacks, such as the ping of death, do still exist [32], and are much better suited for signature-based detection. Further difficulties arise because the network traffic ultimately depends on human behavior. While somewhat predictable, human behavior tends to be changeable enough to cause NIDPS anomaly detection trouble [33].

While signature-based detection compares behavior to rules, anomaly-based detection compares behavior to profiles [1]. These profiles still need to define what is normal, like rules need to be defined. However, anomaly-based profiles are more like white lists, because the profile detects when behavior goes outside an acceptable range. Unfortunately, on most networks the expected set of activity is quite broad. Successful anomaly detection tends to be profiles such as "detect if ICMP (Internet Control Message Protocol) traffic becomes greater than 3% of network traffic" when it is usually only 1%. Application-specific data is less commonly used. This approach can detect previously unknown threats, however, it can also be defeated by a conscientious attacker who attempts to blend in. Attackers may not be careful enough to blend in, but the particularly careful adversaries are all the more important to catch. In general, adversaries with sufficient patience can always blend in to the network's behavior. Therefore, anomaly detection serves an important purpose, but it is not a panacea, especially not for detecting advanced attackers.

NETWORK BEHAVIOR ANALYZERS

A network behavior analyzer (NBA) is an IDPS device that does not inspect the full packet data [1, p. 6-1]. Since anomaly detection often works on packet headers and dynamics, much of this value can be realized in a NBA without the overhead of a full-fledged IDPS. There are many advantages to using such a lightweight device for anomaly detection, in which the payload data is much less useful. It is possible to custom build a NBA, however, there are already several existing data formats that store partial network traffic data, and these can be leveraged more easily. One such common format is network flow, which is introduced in Chapter 11.

There are several open-source tools for working with network flow data, such as SiLK [34]. This tool suite includes a NBA called Analysis Pipeline [35]. Since a NBA using network flow only has to process about 5% of the volume of data as an IDPS processing the full-packet capture, it can be a bit more scalable. This savings can be most felt when data from multiple sensor points needs to be aggregated. If full-packet capture needs to be rebroadcast from a monitoring point to a central location, bandwidth to and from that monitoring point needs to be double what it would be without the rebroadcast. The traffic needs to be sent to its intended location and the central anomaly detector, so it needs to be sent twice, doubling the bandwidth. If only flow is aggregated at the anomaly detector, bandwidth only needs to increase about 5%. A 5% increase instead of a 100% increase for full-packet capture makes back-haul more feasible.

WIRELESS IDPS

A wireless IDPS focuses on preventing abuse of the wireless access point and medium in the first place. According to the OSI model layers described in Chapter 11, a wireless IDPS only analyzes up to layer-2 data. Since this data is only useful in point-to-point communications, not end-to-end communications, a wireless IDPS must collect data from the wireless access points. This fact means that the sensor architecture needs to be distributed, unlike a NIDPS or NBA.

Wireless IDPSs monitor the radio waves for abuse or attacks on the wireless access points. They can also detect attempts to establish rogue access points for subversive communication. A wireless IDPS has its own radio antennae that it uses to scan the radio waves and issue commands to devices to correct abuse. The types of events that a wireless IDPS can detect include the following [1, p. 5–8]:

- Unauthorized wireless local area networks (WLANs) and WLAN devices
- Poorly secured WLAN devices
- Unusual usage patterns
- The use of wireless network scanners
- DoS attacks and conditions (e.g., network interference)
- Impersonation and middle-person attacks

Entities attacking a wireless device need to be physically close to the device, unlike most network attacks. Thus, the impact of these events is different than those detected by other IDSs. If an adversary can gain access via a wireless device, the adversary can often evade other defensive technologies, such as those described in Chapter 5. A wireless IDS is helpful in detecting attempts at such attacks.

NETWORK INTRUSION PREVENTION SYSTEMS

A network intrusion prevention system (NIPS) acts like a NIDS, except that it must process packets quickly enough to respond to the attacks and prevent them, rather than merely report the intrusion. This is much easier if the NIPS can enforce a choke point in the traffic flow. Therefore, a NIPS is recommended to be deployed inline, whereas a NIDS is recommended out of band [1]. This decision has several ramifications. It determines what risks the NIPS brings to the system and what remediations are feasible.

There are dangers associated with putting the NIPS inline, namely that it can become a single point of failure for the network. This possibility raises a question of what the NIPS should do when it can no longer keep up with traffic: Does it drop the packets, or pass them along without inspecting them for possible intrusions? If a device has the property that when it fails it maintains the security of the system, it is said to be fail-secure. The fail-secure operation option for an overloaded NIPS is to drop packets, because packets that are not routed cannot damage the system, whereas uninspected packets passed on may. This fail-secure operation may make the network fragile, and if it occurred would cause a DoS condition on that network link, and thus possibly the whole organizational network. Since an IDPS consumes a lot of computational resources, a NIPS will reach this overloaded condition more quickly than other network devices. Therefore, it is important to ensure that a NIPS is sufficiently provisioned before deploying it.

There are prevention attempts that a NIDPS can make either inline or out of band. As a general rule, out-of-band remediations are less effective than inline remediations. Inline remediations include performing a firewall action on the traffic, throttling bandwidth usage, or sanitizing malicious content. These three actions are unique to inline systems. The three actions available out of band are attempting to end TCP sessions, usually by spoofing TCP RST packets (packets with the reset flag set); changing the configuration of other network security devices to block future traffic; and executing some arbitrary program specified by the administrator to support functionality the IDPS does not natively support [1, p. 4–12ff]. Out-of-band actions are also available to inline systems, but inline systems do not usually use them because out-of-band actions are less effective. The six available remediations, both inline and out of band, can be summarized as follows:

- *Perform a firewall action (inline only):* Dynamically create a rule to drop, reject, or log the packet. This rule might be only for the packet in question, or may apply to packets for some period of time into the future.
- *Throttle bandwidth (inline only):* Reduce the bandwidth available to a certain type of activity while it is evaluated further.
- *Sanitize malicious content (inline only):* Remove or overwrite certain parts of the packets before forwarding them along. Some proxies naturally do this by normalizing traffic, such as collecting all fragments of a packet and writing them back in a predictable format before forwarding, which will sanitize any fragmentation attacks.
- *Reset TCP session:* Spoof a packet to both the source and destination as if the IDPS is the other party in the communication, with the RST flag of the TCP header set. This flag is used to represent a forcible end to the TCP session, or a reset. A well-behaved host should abandon the connection, however, this is not guaranteed.
- *Reconfigure other network security devices:* Insert or change rules in devices, such as those described in Chapter 5, to affect future transactions and prevent further damage.
- *Execute a program:* If the IDPS cannot perform a certain action, the data can be passed to another program that can. An example might be to make a domain name system (DNS) or WHOIS (pronouced as "who is") query to include that data in a log file.

The superiority of inline remediations can be captured by discussing race conditions. Race conditions are a situation in which the outcome of the process is unpredictable due to two or more processes occurring in an unpredictable order. The term originates in software engineering [36], however, the concept applies to network behavior as well. At the risk of oversimplification, out-of-band remediations are race conditions and inline remediations are not. Therefore, out-of-band remediations are less reliable because the order in which operations occur is not stable or predictable. The condition is so named because, for example, the adversary and the IDPS are in a race as to which entity can execute its commands to affect the target host first.

There is one large-scale example of using TCP reset packets as a NIPS system. TCP resets are one of the methods used by the censorship system of the People's Republic of China (mainland China), commonly called the "Great Firewall of China." This method is less prone to overblocking and false positives than other methods at such a scale, such as DNS poisoning or dropping packets. On the other hand, it is also easy to evade a TCP-RST NIPS, such as demonstrated in Clayton, Murdoch, and Watson [37], so long as both end-points ignore the resets. Therefore, if both parties to a communication are intent on persisting, such as a bot and its command and control server, the defender should assume that a TCP-RST-based defense will be insufficient.

SUMMARY

This chapter discusses automated intrusion detection and prevention, primarily via the network. Intrusion detection and prevention systems are valuable tools in recognizing adversarial attacks on the network and initiating an appropriate response programmatically. Properly configuring an IDPS is a challenge, and the devices must be properly resourced. Problems detecting events with a low base-rate fallacy of occurrence also present a significant challenge to making use of IDPS alerts. Despite these challenges, IDPSs can provide crucial value to the network defender. No defensive strategy should be considered complete without a network IDPS to assist in recognition.

IDPSs operate in two general detection modes: signature based and anomaly based. These modes have different strengths and weaknesses that should be used to complement each other. A network behavior analyzer can leverage the strengths of anomaly detection with less overhead than a full NIDPS. Automatic prevention and remediation mechanisms can be enacted for rules or profiles that indicate particularly dangerous attacks or are particularly certain to be accurate. The available mechanisms vary based on the NIDPS architecture. Chapter 13 continues to discuss recognition strategies, in the context of host-based recognition and forensics.

REFERENCES

[1] Scarfone K, Mell P. Guide to intrusion detection and prevention systems (IDPS). NIST Special Publication 800-94, 2007.

[2] Shirey R. Internet security glossary, Version 2. RFC 4949, 2007.

[3] Anderson RJ. Security engineering: a guide to building dependable distributed systems, 2nd ed. New York: Wiley; 2008.

[4] Abrams SJR, Ghimire D. Corporate AV/EPP comparative analysis—exploit protection 2013. NSS Labs, Inc.; 2013. Retrieved from <https://www.nsslabs.com/reports/corporate-avepp-comparative-analysis-exploit-protection-2013>. Retrieved Feb 4, 2013.

[5] Wood M, Erlinger M. Intrusion detection message exchange requirements. RFC 4766, 2007.

[6] Bellovin SM. Packets found on an internet. *ACM SIGCOMM* Comput Commun Rev 1993;23(3):26–31.

[7] Cheswick WR, Bellovin SM, Rubin AD. Firewalls and internet security: repelling the Wily Hacker. Reading, MA: Addison-Wesley Professional; 2003.

[8] Ptacek TH, Newsham TN. Insertion, evasion, and denial of service: eluding network intrusion detection. Defense Technical Information Center; 1998.

[9] CERT Coordination Center. IP denial-of-service attacks. CERT Advisory CA-1997-28. Carnegie Mellon University, Pittsburgh, PA. Retrieved from <http://www.cert.org/advisories/CA-1997-28.html>; 1997.

[10] Shankar U, Paxson V. Active mapping: resisting NIDS evasion without altering traffic. In: Security and privacy. Proceedings of the 2003 Symposium on IEEE; 2003. p. 44–61.

[11] Novak J. Target-based fragmentation reassembly. Sourcefire Vulnerability Research Team; 2005. Retrieved from <http://www.snort.org/assets/165/target_based_frag.pdf>. Retrieved Feb 4, 2013.

[12] Pescatore J, Young G. *Defining next-generation network intrusion prevention*. Gartner, Stamford, CT; 2011.

[13] Kent S, Seo K. Security architecture for the internet protocol. RFC 4301. Updated by RFC 6040, 2005.

[14] Briscoe B. Tunneling of explicit congestion notification. RFC 6040, 2010.

[15] Dierks T, Rescorla E. The transport layer security (TLS) Protocol Version 1.2. RFC 5246. Updated by RFCs 5746, 5878, 6176, 2008.

[16] Callas J, Donnerhacke L, Finney H, Shaw D, Thayer R. OpenPGP Message Format. RFC 4880, 2007. Updated by RFC 5581.

[17] Electronic Frontier Foundation. HTTPS everywhere FAQ. Retrieved from <https://www.eff.org/https-everywhere/faq>; 2013. Retrieved Feb 4, 2013.

[18] Sourcefire. The case for the next-generation IPS. Whitepaper, 2011.

[19] Travis G, Balas E, Ripley D, Wallace S. Analysis of the SQL slammer worm and its effects on indiana university and related institutions. Indiana University; 2004. Retrieved from <http://paintsquirrel.ucs.indiana.edu/pdf/SLAMMER.pdf>. Retrieved Feb 4, 2013.

[20] Anderson R, Moore T. The economics of information security. Science 2006;314(5799):610–3.

[21] Kahneman D, Tversky A. On the psychology of prediction. Psychol Rev 1973;80(4):237.

[22] Bar-Hillel M. The base-rate fallacy in probability judgments. Acta Psychologica 1980;44(3):211–33.

[23] Axelsson S. The base-rate fallacy and the difficulty of intrusion detection. ACM Trans Inf Syst Secur (TISSEC) 2000;3(3):186–205.

[24] Stallings W. Network security essentials: applications and standards, 4th ed. Englewood Cliffs, NJ: Prentice-Hall; 2011.

[25] Kadane JB. Principles of Uncertainty. Boca Raton, FL: Chapman & Hall; 2011. Retrieved from <http://uncertainty.stat.cmu.edu/wp-content/uploads/2011/05/principles-of-uncertainty.pdf>.

[26] Hopkins S. From Snort to sourcefire to Nasdaq. *Clarkson University Magazine*; 2009, Summer. Retrieved from <http://www.clarkson.edu/alumni_magazine/summer2009/cyber-security_roesch.html>. Retrieved Feb 4, 2013.

[27] Dineley D, Mobley H. The greatest open-source software of all time. *InfoWorld Magazine*; 2009, August 17. Retrieved from <http://www.infoworld.com/d/open-source/greatest-open-source-software-all-time-776>. Retrieved Feb 4, 2013.

[28] Szmit M, Weżyk R, Skowroński M, Szmit A. Traffic anomaly detection with snort Information systems architecture and technology. Information Systems and Computer Communication Networks, Wydawnictwo Politechniki Wrocławskiej, Warsaw; 2007. p. 181–87.

[29] Roesch GC. Martin, Sourcefire 3: writing snort rules. In: SNORT Users Manual 2.9.4. Sourcefire, Inc. Columbia, MD. Retrieved from <http://manual.snort.org/node27.html>; 2013. Retrieved Feb 24, 2013.

[30] Roesch M, et al. Snort-lightweight intrusion detection for networks. Proceedings of the 13th USENIX conference on system administration, Seattle, 1999. p. 229–38.

[31] Guido D. The exploit intelligence project. iSEC Partners; 2011. Retrieved from <http://www.trailofbits.com/resources/exploit_intelligence_project_2_slides.pdf>. Retrieved Apr 4, 2013.

[32] Keizer G. Microsoft patches 1990's-era "Ping of Death". ComputerWorld 2011, August 9.

[33] Uddin M, Rahman AA. Dynamic multilayer signature-based intrusion detection system using mobile agents, arXiv:1010.5036 2010. <http://arxiv.org/abs/1010.5036>. Retrieved Sept 20, 2013.

[34] Software Engineering Institute. CERT NetSA security suite—monitoring for large-scale networks. Retrieved from <http://tools.netsa.cert.org/>; 2013. Retrieved Jul 4, 2013.

[35] Ruef D. Analysis pipeline—streaming flow analysis U.S. government forum of incident response and security teams. Nashville, TN: US-CERT; 2011. Retrieved from <http://www.us-cert.gov/sites/default/files/gfirst/presentations/2011/Analysis_Pipeline.pdf>. Retrieved Feb 4, 2013.

[36] Netzer RHB, Miller BP. What are race conditions? some issues and formalizations. ACM Letters on Programming Languages and Systems 1992, March(1):74–88. Retrieved from <http://doi.acm.org/10.1145/130616.130623>.

[37] Clayton R, Murdoch S, Watson R. Ignoring the Great Firewall of China Privacy enhancing technologies. In: 6th Workshop on Privacy Enhancing Technologies. Cambridge, UK. June 28–30, 2006. p. 20–35.

[38] McDonald M. Adding more bricks to the Great Firewall of China IHT rendezvous. New York Times; 2012. Retrieved from <http://rendezvous.blogs.nytimes.com/2012/12/23/adding-more-bricks-to-the-great-firewall-of-china/>. Retrieved Feb 27, 2013.

Chapter Review Questions

1. What is IP fragmentation? How can it be used to evade an IDPS?

2. What is the base-rate fallacy? What challenge does it present to utilizing IDPS alerts?

3. How does an IDPS signature work?

4. What are two major differences between signature-based detection and anomaly-based detection?

5. Imagine a medieval king trying to test for poison in his food. He has a different food-tester taste each dish before he eats it (this is extravagantly many food-testers, but let's just go with it because it makes the math easier). Let's say the king eats 10 different dishes per day. If a food-tester eats a poisoned dish, there is a 95% chance that person dies within the testing window, before the king eats the food. Due to poor sanitation and food preparation conditions, two food-testers die every 30 days of natural causes during the testing time. If there are two attempts

to kill the king with poisoned food per 360 days, over 5 years (360-day cycles—they have bad calendars), how many food-testers actually died from poisoned food? What is the expected probability if a food-tester died that the food destined for the king was actually poisoned?[3]

Chapter Exercises

1. Use [1, ch. 9] to evaluate an IDPS product. If you need an open-source product to consider, Bro-IDS (*http://www.bro.org/documentation/*) or Snort (*http://snort.org/*) would probably be suitable.

2. Using available reporting, try to determine the top 5 to 10 crucial vulnerabilities that are being exploited right now on the Internet at large.

3. The "Great Firewall of China" has been modernizing to resist evasive users [38]. Can you think of, or find, any methods to circumvent these new additions? Have there been further updates since the end of 2012 that also would need to be evaded?

---

[3] Answer: If there are 10 attempts to poison the king in 5 years, if the food-testers are 95% effective, then 10×0.95 food-testers should die. During the same course of time, 120 testers will die of natural causes ($2\,(testers/month) \times 12\,(months/year) \times 5\,(years/sample\_period)$). The alarm error rate can be calculated with Bayes' theorem as follows:

$$AlarmError = \frac{FPR \times Pr[no\,poison]}{TPR \times Pr[poison] + (FPR \times Pr[no\,poison])}$$

$$AE = \frac{2/300 \times 3598/3600}{.95 \times 2/3600 + (2/300 \times 3598/3600)}$$

$$AE = \frac{0.00666296296}{0.0005277777778 + (0.00666296296)}$$

$$AE = 92.66\%$$

Therefore, if a food-tester died, there is a 92.66% chance the food was not poisoned. Therefore, the chance that the food was actually poisoned is $1 - 0.9266 = 7.44\%$.

CHAPTER 13

Digital Forensics

J. Sammons
Marshall University, West Virginia, USA

INFORMATION IN THIS CHAPTER

- Forensic fundamentals
- Digital forensics process
- Properties and characteristics of digital evidence
- Storage media technology
- Dealing with volatile memory
- Potential evidence

INTRODUCTION

Today's adversaries' tactics, techniques, and procedures (TTPs) are constantly evolving, becoming more complex and sophisticated. Understanding how our enemies attack and what their objectives are can provide the information we need to effectively defend our networks. Digital forensic processes, principles, and procedures give us the tools we need to gather this understanding and combat these challenging attacks.

USES OF DIGITAL FORENSICS

Because of the world's heavy dependence on technology, digital forensics plays a key role in a wide variety of situations. Criminal cases at the local, state, and federal levels now rely heavily on a wide variety of digital evidence. The sources of this evidence include, but are not limited to, single computers, networks, cell phones, tablets, gaming platforms, and global positioning system (GPS) units. With the pervasiveness of technology in our society, almost every crime can involve some type of digital evidence. Network security and incident response receive tremendous benefit from the application of sound forensic procedures, processes, and methods. Forensic techniques can help locate the breach, establish the scope and method of the compromise, and the reconstruction of security-related events.

Digital evidence also plays a significant role in civil litigation. Companies no longer exchange massive amounts of paper documents (memos, reports, and the like) as part of the legal discovery process. Digital evidence is just as legitimate as paper documentation in a legal context, and its admissibility relies heavily on forensics.

Digital evidence has found its way onto the battlefield. It is routine practice today for cell phones and computers to be seized during raids and then rapidly analyzed to provide actionable intelligence to the battlefield commander [1].

Furthermore, digital forensics can play a significant role in the investigation of administrative violations of company policies. Behavior that may not be criminal may still be in direct violation of established company rules. For example, using company computers for personal gain or to view pornography could be violations of company policy. These violations could result in the discipline or termination of the employee(s) involved. Digital forensics could be used to uncover and prove these violations.

FORENSIC FUNDAMENTALS

Digital forensics goes by several different names, depending on if the process is emphasized or the term is more general. It is commonly referred to as digital forensics, computer forensics, network forensics, postmortem forensics, and digital and multimedia forensics, among others.

The definitions for digital forensics vary as well. The National Institute of Standards and Technology (NIST) defines digital forensics as follows: "Generally, it is considered the application of science to the identification, collection, examination, and analysis of data while preserving the integrity of the information and maintaining a strict chain of custody for the data" [2]. The Scientific Working Group on Digital Evidence (SWGDE) uses the term *computer forensics*, and defines it as "a sub-discipline of Digital & Multimedia Evidence, which involves the scientific examination, analysis, and/or evaluation of digital evidence in legal matters" [3].

General Forensic Principles

There are certain broad forensic principles that underpin the entire forensic process. They are designed and implemented with the singular goal of reaching a reliable and accurate result. These general principles can provide a decision-making framework for any exigent circumstances that may arise.

Preserve the Original Evidence

Classic forensic thought dictates that any potential modification to the original evidence is of major concern and should absolutely be avoided. Any change to an original evidentiary item calls the integrity of that item into question. Once the item's integrity has been compromised, it is no longer reliable. For example, items in a crime scene such as the murder weapon should remain completely undisturbed until its location, description, condition, etc. have been fully documented.

Once documentation is complete, evidence must be collected in a manner to preserve any blood, DNA, or fingerprints that may be present. Digital evidence must be treated with this same level of care. The evidence should remain in its original pristine condition. With digital evidence, however, this is often easier said than done. The volatile nature of digital evidence has created both significant challenges and exceptions to its preservation and collection. Sometimes situations arise that necessitate tampering with the original state of the evidence. Nothing illustrates this issue better than a running computer.

Interacting with a running machine, even in a very minimal way, will cause changes to the system. The traditional response to collecting data from a running computer was to pull the power from the back of the machine, with the thought that this was the cleanest way to power down the computer without making changes to the state of the evidence. Today, pulling the plug in every situation is unrealistic. There is simply too much potential evidence in volatile memory, known as random access memory (RAM), to ignore, not to mention other associated risks. In fact, some evidence may only exist in RAM and may never touch the hard drive. The only way to acquire such volatile evidence is by tampering with the running computer. As such, digital forensic philosophy has begun to evolve—interaction with a running computer is no longer the taboo action it once was.

Forensic science as a whole can be very slow to change. Thus, this relatively new approach is not fully accepted by all courts and agencies. A major hurdle is ensuring that first responders are properly trained and equipped to successfully collect evidence in volatile memory.

There is a significant amount of evidence that can be found in the RAM of a host that is powered on. This very fragile data will disappear when power is lost. As we know, any interaction with a running machine will cause changes to the system. However, these changes may have zero impact on the evidence that is relevant to the investigation.

Documentation

Complete, detailed, and thorough documentation underpins any forensic process. Documentation provides a record of what was done, who did

Table 13.1 Example Forensic Data Acquisition Documentation

Category	Description	Example
Dates and times	The date and time particular actions or events took place.	"08/11/13, 1432 hrs" "August 11, 2013, 2:32 PM"
Names	Who performed specific actions, such as collected evidence, conducted an examination, etc.	"Tim Smith"
Actions taken	What was done? What tool was used?	"…collected hard drive from office computer…" "…conducted examination …"
Descriptions and observations	What did you see? What did you find? Descriptions of locations and devices. Device description should include make, model, serial number, condition (damage observed, etc.), size, etc.	"… Dell Optiplex 9010, service tag #123456 …" "User observed dialog box with anti-virus warning…"
Photos and video	Record of scenes and specific evidentiary items. Should start with general shots of the scene.	Photos of room, desk, hard drive, cell phone, etc. that show makes, models, and serial numbers.

it, when they did it, and the condition and location of any evidence upon discovery. Documentation should enable others to recreate the steps taken so that they may reach the same results and conclusions about the collected evidence.

Documentation can take many forms, including written notes, photographs, sketches, and video. Good documentation covers the entire forensic process from start to finish. The value of the documentation is directly related to the level of detail. Proper notes should include details such as who, what, where, when, and how. See Table 13.1 for an example.

Chain of Custody

As part of the documentation, a detailed record of who had care, custody, and control of specific evidentiary items should be maintained. This record starts from the very beginning of evidence collection. It continues through the examination and analysis process, and should only conclude when the case or incident is officially closed. A well-documented chain of custody can be very helpful in case questions arise about where a particular item came from, how it was handled, and who collected it. Secure storage plays a key role in the chain of custody. Evidence should be secured at all times so that it cannot be altered, stolen, or destroyed, either intentionally or accidently. Storing the evidence in a fireproof data safe is one way to achieve this level of security.

Validation

Validation ensures that a particular tool, technique, or procedure performs as intended, and produces reliable and consistent results. The SWGDE defines validation as the "process of performing a set of experiments, which establishes the efficacy and reliability of a tool, technique or procedure or modification thereof" [3].

Take, for example, a specific tool that is used to make a forensic clone of a hard drive. Prior to its use in the field, it should be put through a validation process. A known sample drive should be used to test the tool and verify that it indeed captures everything on the drive including both the allocated and unallocated space. This validation process should be well documented and a record kept for future reference. In addition, the process must be repeated every time a tool or procedure is upgraded or changed.

Quality Assurance

For any process that must yield reliable, highly accurate results, quality assurance is a must. The SWGDE defines quality assurance (QA) as a set of "planned and systematic actions necessary to provide sufficient confidence that an agency's/laboratory's product or service will satisfy given requirements for quality"[3].

Attention must be paid to all of the individual factors that come together to achieve accurate and reliable results. Proper QA encompasses every facet of any forensic process. At a minimum, the QA program should address:

- Personnel qualifications and training
- Personnel competency testing
- Validation procedures
- Required documentation
- Policies and procedures

Locard's Exchange Principle

Dr. Edmond Locard's exchange principle states that whenever two objects come in contact, a transfer of material occurs. For example, when a killer enters and subsequently departs a crime scene, the attacker could leave blood, DNA, latent prints, hair, and fibers [4], or pick up such evidence from the victim.

Locard's exchange principle also applies to a digital environment. Registry keys and log files can serve as the digital equivalent to hair and fiber [5]. Like DNA, our ability to detect and analyze these artifacts relies heavily on the technology available at the time. Look at the numerous cold cases that are now being solved due to the significant advances in DNA science. Viewing a device or incident through the "lens" of Locard's exchange principle can be very helpful in locating and interpreting not only physical but also digital evidence.

Digital Forensic Process

Just as there are several ways to define digital forensics, there are also multiple schemes used to describe the forensic process. The NIST breaks down the process into four distinct phases: collection, examination, analysis, and reporting [2].

During the collection phase, data is identified, labeled, and recorded from potentially relevant sources. A well-devised plan prior to collection is highly beneficial. It reduces mistakes and saves time. As always, maintaining the integrity of the evidence is of paramount importance throughout the process.

The examination phase forensically processes the data collected, seeking to separate out data that is most relevant to the investigation. One of the major objectives of this phase is to reduce the volume of data to be analyzed. Reducing the "noise" helps save time and money. For example, much, if not all, of the operating system code has no forensic value. Therefore, it serves no purpose in our analysis. These files can be automatically excluded (removed) during the examination phase using their digital fingerprint (hash value). The data elements are either processed by hand or through some automated means. Throughout the process, pieces of data are assessed for relevance, and are also extracted into a format that will enable analysis. As always, care is taken not to compromise its integrity.

After the information has been examined, it is then analyzed to develop information that can be useful to the investigation. The data produced during the examination phase is evaluated and the results are validated using different tools and possibly different examiners.

Lastly, the results of the analysis are reported. The report can take many forms and its depth and detail will vary depending on the situation, as well as the policies and procedures of the organization producing the report. The report should detail the actions taken, and how the data was collected, examined, and analyzed. It should also contain the results of the analysis, the chain of custody, etc. Figure 13.1 depicts the four-phase process as defined by NIST.

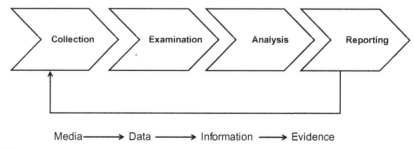

FIGURE 13.1
Four phases of the digital forensic process. *Source: Kent et al. [2].*

HASHING

How do we know our clone is an exact duplicate of the evidence drive? The answer comes in the form of a hash value, which is the result of a hash function. Hash functions are introduced in Chapter 8 and further discussed in Chapter 14. One use of hash functions is evidence integrity; this is a special case of data integrity as discussed in Chapter 14. Hash values are commonly referred to as a "digital fingerprint" or "digital DNA." Any change to the hard drive, even by a single bit, will result in a different hash value, making any tampering or manipulation of the evidence readily detectable as long as the original hash value is securely stored.

Types of Hashing Algorithms

There are multiple types of hashing algorithms, but the most common are Message Digest 5 (MD5) and Secure Hashing Algorithm (SHA) 1 and 2. The slightest change in the data will result in a dramatic difference in the resulting hash values. Let's hash a short phrase to demonstrate what happens with only a minor change. For this exercise we'll use part of the book title.

Phrase: Introduction to Information Security

MD5 hash value: `d23e 5dd1 fe50 59f5 5e33 ed09 e0eb fd2f`

Now let's make one small alteration, changing the "t" in "to" from lowercase to uppercase:

Phrase: Introduction To Information Security
MD5 hash value: `0b92 f23e 8b5b 548a aade bd1b 40fa e2a3`

Note the complete change in the resulting hash values. Here they are stacked for an easier comparison:

```
d23e 5dd1 fe50 59f5 5e33 ed09 e0eb fd2f
0b92 f23e 8b5b 548a aade bd1b 40fa e2a3
```

As you can see, small changes make a big difference. If you would like to try this yourself, it is easy to do. For example, go to *www.wolframalpha.com* and enter the hash function you would like to use (MD5, SHA1, etc.), followed by a space and then the phrase.

Uses of Hashing

Hash values can be used throughout the digital forensic process. They can be used to identify specific files. In this application, they can identify files of interest like malware, or files to exclude like most operating system files. Hash values can be used after the cloning process to verify that a forensic image is indeed an exact duplicate. Examiners often have to exchange forensic images

```
Created by AccessData® FTk® Imager 3.0.1.1467 110406
Case Information:
Acquired using: ADI3.0.1.1467
Case Number: 1
Evidence Number:1
Unique Description:
Examiner:
Notes:

- — — — — — — — — — — — — — — — — — — — — — — — — — — — — — — -

Information for D:\book hash:

Physical Evidentiary Item (Source) Information:
[Deive Geometry]
 Cylinders: 5,874
 Heads: 255
 Sectors per Track: 56
[Physical] Drive Information]
 Drive Interface Type: buslogic
[Image]
 Image Type: VMWare Virtual Disk
 Source data size: 40960 MB
 Sector count:  83226080
[Computed Hashes]
 MD5 checksum: 4963c323e507b2db85d4ec7bc93d54b1
 SHA1 checksum: 5b9f88d9247f50c42267bc3e481c5985409c0701

Image Information:
 Acquisition Started:  Tue Sep 06 05:47:17 2011
 Acquisition finished: Tue Sep 06 06:04:13 2011
 Segment list:
  D:\book hash.001
Image verification Results:
 Verification started:  Tue sep 06 06:04:15 2011
 Verification finished: Tue sep 06 06:14:37 2011
 MD5 checksum: 4963c323e507b2db85d4ec7dc93d54b1 : verifed
 SHA1 checksum: 5b9f88d9247f50c42267bc3e481c5985409c0701 : verified
```

FIGURE 13.2

A text file containing the hash verification for a piece of evidence. This example is generated by AccessData's FTK Imager. Note the MD5 and SHA1 hash values and the "verified" confirmation for each.

with the opposing examiner. A hash value is sent along with the forensic clone so that it can be compared with the original to ensure its integrity.

The relevant hash values that were generated and recorded throughout the case should be kept and included with the final report. These digital fingerprints are crucial to demonstrating the integrity of the evidence and ultimately getting them before the jury. Figure 13.2 shows an example of a hash verification.

TECHNOLOGY

Any real understanding of digital forensics must start with the technology, specifically how data is created, stored, transmitted, and processed. This underlying knowledge provides a basis to determine what will be searched, what will be collected, how evidence is handled, and more. Since the focus of this chapter is on a single networked computer or host, we will concentrate on the data, hardware, and software that comprise these systems. This is similar to the fact that technical expertise is required for network analysis, as discussed in Chapter 11. It is important to understand the technology so that one can understand what questions are reasonable to ask of digital forensics.

Characteristics of Digital Evidence

It is important to recognize the unique characteristics or properties of digital evidence. Failure to understand or appreciate them can lead to trouble. Take volatility, for example: digital evidence is very susceptible to change. It can be changed without any human interaction, via an automated process such as a virus scan, backup routine, purge, etc. Even "stable" digital data can be easily wiped away—for example, some credit cards' magnetic strips can be disrupted simply by being too close to electrical devices like a cell phone. Failing to recognize the threat to potential evidence can result in the destruction of evidence. Potentially damaging processes must be recognized and stopped as soon as possible.

Data Types

Data can be divided into three distinct categories: active, latent, and archival. Data from each of these categories could yield evidence that would be helpful to an investigation.

Active data is the data that is tracked by the computer's file system. It is readily accessible by the user and the operating system. The files you can see and open through Windows Explorer are examples of active data.

In contrast to active data is latent data, which is not tracked by the file system, nor is it readily accessible to the user. Latent data cannot be accessed by the operating system. A deleted file (emptied from the recycle bin) is one example of a latent data element. When the operating system deletes the file it removes links and pointers to the start of the file, but the file information remains on the drive until it is physically overwritten, which may take quite a long time if left to chance.

Archival data elements are backups located on other storage devices, such as backup tapes, hard drives, USB devices, servers, and cloud storage.

Volatility

Digital evidence is extremely volatile. The nature of digital evidence should be a primary concern at the start of an investigation. Changes can be easily made with or without human interaction. For example, a scheduled anti-virus scan can change the last accessed date of a particular file. This will impact not only how the evidence is preserved and collected, but also the order in which it is collected.

Some digital evidence is more volatile than others. This differentiation is known as the order of volatility, and it lists the locations of potential evidence in order from the most volatile to the least. The order of volatility will be discussed in more detail later in the chapter.

Persistence

It is a bit of a contradiction, but digital evidence can be both persistent and volatile. Digital evidence can be hard to destroy. Many actions, such as deleting a file or reformatting a hard drive, might seem to destroy the data. In reality, these events can be very ineffective at destroying data. Even if a file is successfully destroyed, there could be multiple copies in other locations. These additional sources could include network devices like servers and tapes, as well as mobile devices and home computers. Responders should keep this in mind when setting the scope of the evidentiary sources to be collected and examined.

Volume

The sheer volume of potential digital evidence is staggering. Host machines alone can store terabytes of data. A terabyte is equivalent to 1,099,511,627,776 bytes of data. A single terabyte of data would equal approximately:

- 65,536,000 pages of text in a Microsoft Word document
- 333,333 MP3 songs
- 20 high-definition Blu-ray films

The volume of data in a case to be forensically processed is a major concern. While care must be taken not to exclude relevant data, all reasonable steps to "whittle down" the mountain of potential evidence should be taken. Many forensic tools provide the functionality needed to efficiently reduce the "noise" in a case and examine the files of most interest to the examiner. Failing to adequately address the volume of data in a case can exact significant costs in terms of time and money.

Computing Environments

There are substantial differences between various computing environments. An accurate clarification of the environment is useful to have right from the start of an investigation, even before an investigator responds to the scene. We can encounter individual computers, networks of various sizes, or even more complex systems. These disparities will have an impact on the collection process, such as where to look for data, the tools used, and the level of complexity. In today's hyperconnected world, few machines operate in a true vacuum. Environments can be broken down into four categories: standalone, networked, mainframe, and the cloud:

- A *standalone* machine is one that is not connected to another computer. These are the easiest of the four environments to deal with. Any potential evidence is reasonably contained, making locating, preserving, collecting, and analyzing less complicated than other environments.
- A *networked* computer is connected to at least one other computer and potentially many, many others. This escalates the complexity of the investigation, as well as the number of places evidence could be found. In such a situation, files and artifacts normally found on the local machine have spread out to servers or network devices.
- Unlike a standalone machine, a *mainframe* system centralizes all of the computing power into one location. Processors, storage, and applications can all be located and controlled from a single location. This environment, like the cloud, can significantly raise the complexity of any forensic process.
- The *cloud*, a remote and heavily virtualized environment, is rapidly gaining popularity with individuals and enterprises alike. Cloud providers offer not only storage but software as a service (SaaS), platform as a service (PaaS), and infrastructure as a service (IaaS). Forensically, the environment is highly challenging from both technical and legal perspectives. Forensic tools and techniques for virtualized systems are still being developed. The transient and cross-border nature of cloud-stored data often creates complex legal problems that must be solved just to get access to the data.

Inside the Host Machine

Intimate knowledge of the inner workings of a computer and, more specifically, how data is created, stored, transmitted, and processed, is a necessity. It is this knowledge that permits us to work through the digital forensics process and render an accurate opinion. It is important to note that not all processes and hardware hold the same forensic value. While memory and storage play major roles in almost any examination, the central processing unit (CPU) plays little, if any, role.

Storage and Memory

Where and how data elements are stored and written is one of the major fundamental concepts that must be learned to get a full grasp of digital forensics. There is more than one way to write data. Today, data is generally created using three different means: electromagnetism, microscopic electrical transistors (flash), and reflecting light (CDs, DVDs, etc.). Storage locations inside a computer serve different purposes. Some are for the short term, used to temporarily hold data that the computer is using at the moment. Others are for more permanent, long-term storage.

Magnetic Disks

Most drives in today's host computers read and write data magnetically. They will render each particle either magnetized or not magnetized. If the particle is magnetized, it is read as a 1; if not, it is read as a 0. The drives themselves are usually made up of aluminum platters coated with a magnetic material. These platters spin at very high speeds. The platters spin in the neighborhood of 7,000 rpm to 15,000 rpm. The speed could even be greater for high-end drives. These heavy-duty drives are typically found in servers or professional-grade workstations. From a forensic standpoint, faster drive speeds can result in faster acquisitions.

A standard magnetic drive is comprised of several components. The platter revolves around a small rod called a spindle. The data is physically written to the platter using a read–write head attached to an actuator arm, which is powered by the actuator itself. The actuator arm moves the head across the platter, reading and writing data. The read–write head floats on a cushion of air. The read–write head, as it is called, is barely floating above the platter surface, at a height less than the diameter of a human hair. Figure 13.3 shows the inside of a typical magnetic drive. We can clearly see the platters, actuator arm, and the read–write head.

Flash Memory

Flash memory is used in a wide range of devices including thumb drives, memory cards, and solid-state hard drives. Unlike RAM, flash memory retains data without electricity. Flash is made up of transistors. Each transistor is either carrying or not carrying an electric charge. When the transistor is charged, it is read as a 1; without a charge it is read as a 0.

Flash-based hard drives are starting to become more and more common. They are referred to as solid-state drives (SSDs). Unlike magnetic drives, flash drives are solid state, meaning they have no moving parts. They offer several significant advantages, including increased speed, less susceptibility to shock, and lower power consumption.

The use of SSDs will continue to grow. While these devices offer improved performance, they also present a major challenge to digital forensics. It certainly appears that recovering deleted files, the "bread and butter" of digital forensics, is in serious jeopardy.

FIGURE 13.3
The inside of a typical magnetic drive.

Solid-State Drives

Magnetic drives have been a mainstay in personal computers for years. Forensically, they afford examiners the ability to potentially recover significant amounts of user-deleted data, including data that has been partially overwritten. That easy accessibility may very well be coming to an end. These traditional magnetic drives are increasingly being replaced by SSDs.

How SSDs Store Data

Traditional magnetic drives have multiple moving parts, including platters and the actuator arm, which moves the read–write head. As the name implies, solid-state drives do not. SSDs are similar to RAM and USB thumb drives, storing data in tiny transistors. Unlike RAM, SSDs are nonvolatile and can store data even without power. To keep charge over long periods of time without power, SSD transistors employ an additional gate, called a floating gate, which is used to contain the charge [6].

If you recall, magnetic drives break up the storage space into smaller units. These units include sectors, clusters, cylinders, and tracks. SSDs also separate the storage space into smaller units. The base units are called blocks and are normally 512 kilobytes in size. Blocks are then subdivided into even smaller units called pages; each page is typically 4 kilobytes in size.

Wear is a concern with SSDs. Each block can only withstand a certain number of writes. Some estimates put that number somewhere between 1,000 and 10,000 times. Given this limitation, you would want the drive to avoid writing to the same block over and over. Writing to the same space repeatedly will cause it to wear out faster than others. Manufacturers solved the issue by instituting a wear leveling process performed by the SSD.

MORE ADVANCED

File Translation Layer

On a SSD, where the computer thinks the data is stored is not really where it is physically located. An SSD uses a file translation layer to ensure that the computer isn't writing to the same block over and over. If the SSD detects this is occurring, it will "translate" the new writes to a less used location [6].

Magnetic drives have the ability to instantly overwrite data to any sector that is located in the unallocated space of a hard drive. SSDs do not. Each transistor must be "reset" (erased) before it can be reused. This reset process can slow down the drive as it writes. To speed things up, SSD manufacturers have configured the drive's controller to automatically reset unused portions of the drive. This process is known as garbage collection.

Taking Out the Trash: A Game Changer

SSDs have a mind of their own. Many drives initiate this garbage collection routine completely on their own, without any prompting by the system at all. This process can start in a matter of seconds once the drive is powered up. Forensically, this is both problematic and troubling. First, verifying the integrity of the evidence becomes extremely difficult and jeopardizes its admissibility in court. More difficult to cope with is the fact that SSDs routinely automatically destroy potentially relevant data. If the garbage collection routine is run during or after the drive's acquisition, validation becomes more difficult because the hash values are changed after garbage collection. Even though the file's content is not changed, it moves, and this change in location information changes the hash.

Volatile versus Nonvolatile Memory

Memory and *storage* are two terms that are somewhat synonymous when it comes to computers. They both refer to internal places where data is kept. Memory is used for short-term storage, while storage is more permanent. No matter what you call it, there is a significant difference between the two, especially from a forensic perspective. That difference lies in the data's volatility. Data in RAM exists only as long as power is supplied. Once the power is removed (i.e., the machine is turned off), the data starts to disappear. This behavior makes this kind of memory volatile. In contrast, files saved on a hard drive remain even after the computer is powered down, making it non-volatile. RAM stores all the data that is currently being worked on by the CPU. Data is fed from the RAM to the CPU where it is executed. Traditionally, forensic analysis of a host computer focuses on the hard drive since much of the evidence can be found there. Today, we are finding that that is not always the case. Many types of malware clean up after themselves and might only be visible in RAM while the machine is running. Therefore, RAM should be captured from a running machine whenever possible. There is more on this later in the chapter.

File Systems

With all the millions or billions of files floating around inside a computer, there has to be some way to keep things organized. This indispensable function is the responsibility of the file system. The host file system determines how files are named, organized, and stored. The file system tracks all of the files on the volume noting their location and size, along with markers for the created, accessed, and modified dates and times.

There are many different types of file systems. Some of the most commonly encountered by forensic examiners include FAT, NTFS, and HFS+:

- The File Allocation Table (FAT) is the oldest of the common files system. It comes in four types: FAT12, FAT16, FAT32, and FATX. Although not used in the latest operating systems, it can often be found in flash media and the like.
- The New Technology File System (NTFS) is the system used currently by Windows 7, Windows 8, Vista, XP, and Windows Server. It is much more powerful than FAT, and capable of performing many more functions.
- The Hierarchical File System (HFS +) and its relatives HFS and HFSX are used in Apple products. HFS+ is the upgraded successor to HFS.

Allocated and Unallocated Space

Generally speaking, the file system categorizes all of the space on the hard drive in one of two ways. The space is either allocated or unallocated (there are a few exceptions; see the sidebar). Put another way, the space is either being used or it is not. Windows cannot see data in this unallocated space. To the operating system, files located in unallocated space are essentially invisible. It is important, however, to understand that "not used" does not always mean "empty." Unallocated space can contain files that have been deleted or disk space that has yet to be used. It is also known as drive-free space.

Remember, the file system's job is to keep track of all files and storage space. Think of a file system as an index in the back of a book. When looking up a particular subject, we flip through the index until we find the term we are looking for. The index then gives us the page number, which allows us to find each iteration of the term in the book. The file system works basically the same way. Using the book analogy again, deleting a file would be akin to removing the entry from the book's index. Although our subject is no longer referenced in the index, the page and all of its contents are still in the book, intact and untouched.

The file system tracks the locations of the separate clusters so they can be reassembled the next time you open a specific file. Clusters can get spread out throughout the drive. Moving them closer together speeds things up for your computer. The closer they are, the faster they can be put together and made available to you. Defragmenting the drive moves these disparate pieces as close together as possible.

Files that are overwritten are generally considered to be unrecoverable. It is possible that the new file assigned to that space will not require as much space as its predecessor. If that is the case, the original file is only partially overwritten. The piece that remains can be recovered and could contain information we can use. This remaining space is called slack space.

How Magnetic Hard Drives Store Data

To further our understanding of how the computer stores files, we must understand drive geometry. Computers store data in defined spaces called sectors. Think of sectors as the smallest container a computer can use to store information. Each sector holds up to 512 bytes of data as illustrated in Figure 13.4. It can hold less, but it cannot hold more.

1. A file, test1.doc, is created and saved to our example hard drive. Test1.doc is 2,075 bytes. The file system, using a best-fit algorithm, assigns the file to clusters 5245 and 5246. The file system now shows these two clusters as allocated. The file will occupy all of 5245 and only 27 bytes of the first sector of 5246. See Figure 13.5.
2. That leaves 485 bytes in the first sector of 5246. The system will automatically fill those remaining bytes with 0 s. See Figure 13.6.
3. The first file, test1.doc, is deleted. Note that the data is still there. It hasn't been erased. The file system now shows that clusters 5245 and 5246 are unallocated and available to store data. Note that even though in unallocated space, these clusters are not empty. See Figure 13.7.
4. A new file is created, test2.doc. This file is 546 bytes in size. The file system assigns the new file to cluster 5245. Since the file is less than 2,048 bytes, it is assigned to a single cluster. It just happens to be assigned to

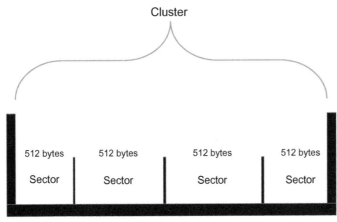

FIGURE 13.4

One 2,048-byte cluster comprised of four 512-byte sectors.

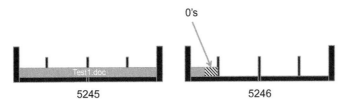

FIGURE 13.5

File test1.doc as assigned to clusters 5245 and part of 5246.

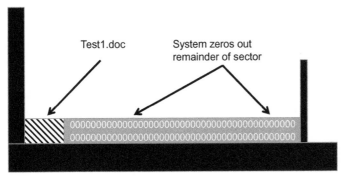

FIGURE 13.6

Note the remainder of the first sector of 5246 (the second cluster) is filled with zeros and the remaining three sectors are free.

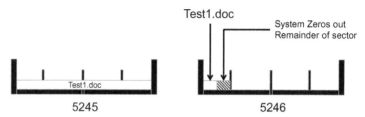

FIGURE 13.7
File test1.doc is deleted but still occupies the same space it did before deletion.

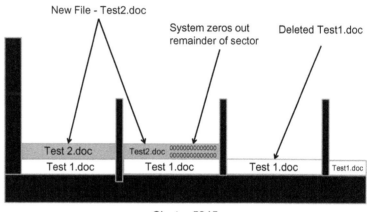

FIGURE 13.8
A new file, test2.doc, is saved to cluster 5245. The new file only overwrites part of the original file, test1.doc. Note the zeros that fill the void in unused portion of the second sector. Also note the portion of test1.doc that is not overwritten.

cluster 5245, one of the clusters recently marked as unallocated. File test2.doc will occupy the entire first sector and 34 bytes of the second sector. The remaining 478 bytes in the second sector will be overwritten with 0s by the system See Figure 13.8.

5. Note that the original data from test1.doc still resides in the second two clusters. The data is located in the slack space and can be recovered with forensic tools. See Figure 13.9.

We can recover fragments of the previous file out of the slack space. It may or may not be of any use, however. It could be part of an incriminating spreadsheet, email, or picture. These fragments could contain just enough of an email to identify the sender or the sender's IP address. A partial picture of the victim could link them to the suspect. Slack space cannot be accessed by the user or the operating system. As such, this evidence exists unbeknownst to the suspect.

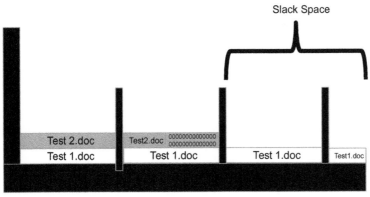

Cluster 5245

FIGURE 13.9
Note the data that remains after part of the original file, test1.doc, has been overwritten. The remaining data contained in the slack space can be recovered.

Virtual Memory or Page File

The page file is used when all of the computer's RAM has been exhausted. This virtual memory is called the page file or swap space. The page file is not a function that is used on a consistent basis. The RAM holds everything your computer is working on at the moment. All of the data and instructions (programs, etc.) must move from the main memory to the CPU, where it is processed. Every computer comes with a limited amount of RAM. When the RAM runs out, the computer is going to need an additional temporary space to hold the extra data that needs to be in RAM. To alleviate this situation, the computer will swap data in and out of the RAM, writing data to the page file to free up room in the RAM. The great thing about the page file is that it can contain files and file fragments that no longer exist anywhere else on the drive. Even suspects who are successful in deleting and overwriting their files will overlook the swap space, leaving this evidence for later recovery.

ONSITE COLLECTIONS

At the scene, examiners could be confronted with a variety of devices and storage media. They could find one or more running computers and wireless devices like cell phones. Together, these devices present some unique challenges for the investigator. All the following onsite collections must follow a chain of custody as described previously in the chapter.

Actions during the collection process must be well documented. Notes, photos, video, and sketches record actions and refresh investigators' recollections.

As digital evidence is extremely volatile, preservation is paramount. If at all possible, a forensic image or clone (which is an exact bit-for-bit copy) is made from the original media. The examination and analysis is conducted on the clone rather than the original.

Documenting the Incident

Any time evidence is collected, documentation is a vitally important part of the process. There are several different types of documentation. Photographs, written notes, and video are the most common methods for documenting evidence.

This documentation process begins the moment investigators arrive at the scene. Typically, investigators start by noting the date and time of their arrival along with all the people at the scene. The remainder of the notes consists of detailed descriptions of the evidence collected, its location and condition, the names of who discovered and collected it, and how it was collected. It is also a good idea to note the items' condition, especially if there is visible damage.

Accurately and precisely describing the evidence is of critical importance. A piece of digital evidence is described by make, model, serial number, or other similar descriptors. It is also important to note whether a device is on or off or if it is connected to other devices, such as printers, or a network, such as the Internet. Virtually everything investigators see, find, and do should be documented.

In contrast, a scene with digital evidence presents an entirely new dimension of access. Most computers and digital devices are connected to the Internet, cellular, or other kinds of networks. It is this connection that permits remote access and puts the evidence at risk. Computers and wireless devices must be made inaccessible as soon as the investigators are sure that no volatile data would be lost [7]. For computers, it may be a matter of removing the Ethernet cable or unplugging a wireless modem or router. With wireless devices such as cell phones, investigators must take steps to isolate the phone from network signals.

After securing the evidence, a survey of the scene will give the investigators an accurate sense of what is ahead. Several questions need to be answered, such as:

- What kinds of devices are present?
- How many devices need to be dealt with?
- Are any of the devices running?
- What tools will be needed?
- Is the necessary expertise on hand?

Once these questions are answered, the real work begins. It is a good idea to prioritize the evidence to be collected, which will in turn assist responders.

Evidence that is most at risk is collected first, while evidence denoted as least volatile is collected last. The order of volatility is [8]:

1. CPU, cache, and register content
2. Routing table, Address Resolution Protocol (ARP) cache, process table, kernel statistics
3. Memory
4. Temporary file system/swap space
5. Data on hard disk
6. Remotely logged data
7. Data contained on archival media

Photography

Next, the entire scene should be photographed. Photos should be taken of the scene before anything is disturbed, including the evidence. It is helpful to think of the photos as telling a story. Remember: at some point, the investigator may have to revisit this scene weeks, months, or even years later.

Photographs are used to depict the scene and the evidence exactly as it was found to help supplement the notes. However, photographs do not replace notes. Notes capture personal observations that would, and could, not be recorded in a photo. They are used to refresh investigators' recollections weeks, months, or even years later.

Notes

As someone photographs the evidence, someone else should take detailed notes of actions and any potential evidence. There is no set standard for note taking. It is really up to the individual on how to document findings at the scene. Chronological order is common groundwork. Note things such as the arrival time, who was present at the scene, who took what action, who found and collected which piece of evidence, etc. Detailed notes are important not just for others, but for oneself (months or years later, perhaps in court), and should be sufficiently detailed for someone who was not present to reconstruct the event accurately.

Marking Evidence

The first "link" in the chain of custody in any case is the person collecting the evidence. An organization's IT staff is often the first link in this chain. The evidence is marked as it is collected. Typically, evidence items are marked with initials, dates, and possibly case numbers. Permanent markers are best to ensure markings are not smudged or removed altogether. Marking the evidence is also essential to keep it from being lost or confused with other cases or items.

Purpose of Cloning

A forensic clone is an exact bit-for-bit copy of a piece of digital evidence. Files, folders, hard drives, and more can be cloned. A forensic clone is also known as a bit-stream image or forensic image. A forensic image of a hard drive captures everything on the hard drive, from the physical beginning to the physical end. Performing a "copy and paste" via the operating system is not the same as a forensic clone. A true forensic image captures both the active and latent data. That is a key difference between the two and the primary reason why a forensic image is preferred.

We know from earlier in the chapter that digital evidence is extremely volatile. As such, one should never conduct an examination on the original evidence unless there are exigent circumstances or no other options.

If possible, the original drive should be preserved in a safe place and only brought out to clone again if needed. Sometimes that is not an option, especially in a business setting wherein the machine and drive must be returned to service.

Hard drives are susceptible to failure. Having two clones gives an investigator one to examine and one to fall back on. Ideally, all examinations are done on a clone as opposed to the original.

Cloning Process

Typically, one hard drive is cloned to another forensically clean hard drive. The drive being cloned is known as the source drive, and the drive being cloned to is called the destination drive. The destination drive must be at least as large (if not slightly larger) than the source drive. While not always possible, knowing the size of the source in advance is quite helpful. Having the right size drive on hand will save a lot of time and aggravation.

As the first step in the cloning process, the drive we want to clone (the source) is normally removed from the computer. It is then connected via cable to a cloning device of some kind or to another computer. To safeguard the evidence, it is critical to have some type of write-blocking device in place before starting the process. A write block is a crucial piece of hardware or software that is used to preserve the original evidence during the cloning process. The write block prevents data from being written to the original evidence drive. The hardware write block is placed between the cloning device (PC, laptop, or standalone hardware) and the source. Using this kind of device eliminates the possibility of inadvertently compromising the evidence.

A forensically clean drive is one that can be proven to be devoid of any data at the time the clone is made. "Clean" here is analogous to being sterile before use in surgery. It is important to prove the drive is clean, because comingled data is inadmissible data. Drives can usually be cleaned with the same devices used to make the clones.

The cleaning process overwrites the entire hard drive with a particular pattern of data, such as 1111111111111[9]. Most, if not all, forensic imaging tools will generate some type of paper trail proving that this cleaning has taken place. This paperwork becomes part of the case file.

The end result of the cloning process is a forensic image of the source hard drive. The finished clone can come in a few different formats. The file extension is the most visible indicator of the file format. Some of the most common forensic image formats include EnCase (extension .E01) and Raw dd (extension .001).

There are differences in the formats, but they are all forensically sound. Some, like DD, are open source, while others are proprietary. Choosing one format over the other can simply be a matter of preference, however, compatibility and interoperability should be considered when choosing a format. Most forensic examination tools will read and write multiple image formats.

Live System versus Dead System

Additional volatile information can be gathered from a "live" system, or one in which the power is still on. Keeping a system live has the potential risk of modifying or corrupting data that could otherwise be safely collected from a powered-down machine. The following are examples of the kinds of data that can only be gathered from a live machine.

Live System Forensic Benefits

Network connections (i.e., IP address and port) can lead investigators to the source of an intrusion, the command and control server for malware, or the destination of exfiltrated data. Ports could shed light on the type of traffic that was used in the attack. More detail on investigating network traffic is covered in Chapter 11. Usernames and passwords can be found in the clear in RAM. We have all seen the "dots" that populate the login fields as we enter our password. The letters, numbers, and special characters "underneath" the dots are stored in the clear in RAM. Recovering the password for an encrypted file in this manner could constitute a huge investigative break.

When looking at a running machine, we can see the open windows and use the task manager to view the running processes. That information is very helpful, but it does not tell the full story about all the activity on the machine. Identifying the running processes in RAM will give a much more complete picture of the device's data. Using the task manager and noting the open windows will not reveal rootkits, key loggers, or other stealthy malware.

The dynamically linked libraries (DLLs) loaded into memory are also of interest. A malicious DLL could have inserted itself into a running process that would result in the system becoming compromised. Data that has been keyed into an open window can also be recovered from RAM. This could include chats, form data, email contents, etc.

Malware is getting more and more sophisticated, and many specimens go to great lengths to avoid detection. Malware may reside on disk in a packed or encrypted state, making it very difficult to detect. The malware must decrypt or unpack itself to run. It is in RAM that we can find it in this state. Some types of malware only exist in RAM. Therefore, a live acquisition provides the only opportunity to collect and identify it. Additionally, tying a malicious process to a specific registry key can help investigators determine the malware's functionality and potentially lead to the user account (via the security identifier, or SID) that initiated the process [10].

An alternative approach is to capture the data in RAM and fully document all open files, as well as all running processes and applications. Up until fairly recently, capturing RAM was not a realistic option. The solutions that existed were impractical for field work. In contrast, present-day examiners have some forensically sound alternatives. There are several commercial and open-source tools that can be used to collect this volatile data. Unlike the older lab-bound approaches, these tools are very simple to use. So simple, in fact, they are being marketed to nontechnical folks like most first responders.

A sudden loss of power could damage the data, rendering it unreadable. Lastly, some evidence may not get recorded on the drive unless and until the computer is properly shutdown. A proper shutdown is simply closing all open applications and following the normal shutdown procedure used every day.

Live System Forensic Detriments

The argument in favor of pulling the power centers around preventing changes to the system. Pulling the plug eliminates the need to interact with the running machine. Interacting with a running computer in any way causes changes to the system, and, as a general principle, any changes to the system should be avoided. These changes can call the integrity of the evidence into question. When a computer is just sitting powered on, things are actually changing. When a person interacts with a running machine, even more things are changing. Knowing that change is a forensic faux pas, it is easy to see why pulling the plug is an attractive option. Even though these changes may have no impact on the artifacts relevant to the case, changes are frowned upon nonetheless.

Encryption is another compelling argument against pulling the power. The system or files may be unencrypted while the machine is powered on.

Abruptly pulling the plug could return them to an encrypted state, potentially putting that evidence out of reach for good. Encryption available today is extremely powerful. If used properly, it can essentially put the data out of reach for parties without the encryption keys.

Conducting and Documenting a Live Collection

When interacting with a live machine, its best to always choose the least-invasive approach possible. This will require thinking before clicking. Haste is not helpful in this situation. Collect the most volatile information first, by the order of volatility.

Properly conducting a live collection requires focus and attention detail. Once started, one must work uninterrupted until the process is complete. To do otherwise only invites mistakes. Before getting underway, gather all required tools such as report forms, pens, and memory capture tools. Detailed documentation is essential for a complete record of each and every interaction with the system. These details can be used to determine what if any changes were made to the system during the process. Every interaction with the system (and its response) should be noted.

The Association of Chiefs of Police Officers (ACPO) [7] offers the following advice regarding the capture of live data:

> By profiling the forensic footprint of trusted volatile data forensic tools, an investigator will be in a position to understand the impact of using such tools and will therefore consider this during the investigation and when presenting evidence. A risk assessment must be undertaken at the point of seizure, as per normal guidelines, to assess whether it is safe and proportional to capture live data which could significantly influence an investigation.

> Considering a potential Trojan defense, investigators should consider collecting volatile evidence. Very often, this volatile data can be used to help an investigator support or refute the presence of an active backdoor.

> The recommended approach towards seizing a machine whilst preserving network and other volatile data is to use a sound and predetermined methodology for data collection. It may be worthwhile considering the selected manual closure of various applications, although this is discouraged unless specific expert knowledge is held about the evidential consequences of doing so.

> For example, closing Microsoft Internet Explorer will flush data to the hard drive, thus benefiting the investigation and avoiding data loss. However, doing this with certain other software, such as KaZaA, could result in the loss of data.

It is important to realize that the behaviors of specific applications are subject to change at any given time. Just because a specific version of a web browser, for example, will flush data to the drive when closed, does not mean the next version will do the same.

MORE ADVANCED FORENSIC TOOLS

There are a wide variety of forensic tools available today that can increase the efficiency of the entire forensic process. These tools can come in the form of hardware and software. There are open-source and commercial tools available on the market. There are advantages and disadvantages to both. Cost is one factor. The cost of commercial forensic hardware and software can be quite high. In addition to the purchase price, most tools require an annual license fee for maintenance and support. Open-source fees are attractive from a cost perspective, but the support will likely be less than that provided with commercial tools.

There are general forensic tools that provide a wide range of functionality and there are tools that perform a more specific function. More targeted tools can provide better functionality. General tools can be compared to Swiss Army knives, as they have multiple functions. Two of these most widely used general exam and analysis tools are Guidance Software's EnCase and AccessData's Forensic Toolkit (FTK). The SANS Investigative Forensic Toolkit (SIFT) is a widely used open-source tool.

With the wide array of potential evidentiary sources, specialized collection tools are often needed. Cell phones are an excellent example. Specialized commercial hardware is available that greatly enables and enhances the forensic analysis of cellular phones. Cellebrite manufactures one of the most widely used commercial tools for the forensic analysis of cell phones.

FINAL REPORT

At the conclusion of the analysis, the examiner may be asked to generate a final report. The report should detail what was done, what was found, and any interpretations. Ideally, final reports need to be crafted with the intended audience in mind. Many reports are filled with jargon and code, rendering them nearly useless to nontechnical readers. It is important to remember that the audience must be able to understand it, and the audience is probably partly, if not largely, nontechnical.

The major commercial forensic tools like EnCase and FTK have very robust reporting features, generating quite a bit of customizable information. However, as helpful as these reports are, they are just not adequate to stand on their own. Important information may be lacking (e.g., specific actions taken). Furthermore, they tend to be overly complicated for the average lay person. A professional report will consist of much more than the standard report generated by these tools. The final report should include a detailed narrative of all the actions taken by the examiner, starting at the scene if he or she was present. The examination should be documented with sufficient detail so that another examiner can duplicate the procedure.

ORGANIZATIONAL PREPAREDNESS

Digital forensics is a vital part of an overall incident response strategy. As such, it should be addressed by the organization through its policies, procedures, budgets, and personnel. All applicable policies and procedures should be drafted in such a way that it maximizes the effectiveness of the digital forensic process. Specific policies should be drafted covering digital forensic procedures and concerns. The budget should reflect the importance of digital forensics by dedicating funds for the tools and training needed to support an incident response. An adequate number of personnel should be trained in forensic fundamentals, as well as certified with the specific tools they will use. Validation is a fundamental principle of digital forensics. Maintaining both trained and certified personnel is essential to meeting that objective. More details on response policies and contingency planning are provided in Chapter 15.

SUMMARY

This chapter discusses digital forensic processes, principles, and procedures, and their overall value to an organization as they defend their network. Understanding how the enemy attacks provides vital information to the defenders, greatly enhancing their overall effectiveness.

REFERENCES

[1] United States Army Army techniques, tactics, and procedures: site exploitation operations. Washington, DC: U.S. Army Training and Doctrine Command; 2010.

[2] Kent K, Chevalier S, Grance T, Dang H. Guide to integrating forensic techniques into incident response. Gaithersburg, MD: National Institute of Standards and Technology; 2006:ES-1.

[3] Scientific Working Group on Digital Evidence and Scientific Working Group on Imaging Technology. Digital and multimedia evidence glossary, v2.7. Retrieved June 24, 2013, from <https://www.swgde.org/documents/Current%20Documents/2013-04-08%20SWGDE-SWGIT%20Glossary%20v2.7>; 2013, April 8.

[4] Saferstein R. Criminalistics: an introduction to Forensic Science (College Edition), 9th ed. Upper Saddle River, NJ: Prentice-Hall; 2006.

[5] Carvey H. Locard's exchange principle in the digital World: windows incident response, 2005, January 27. Retrieved February 23, 2011, from <http://windowsir.blogspot.com/2005/01/locards-exchange-principle-in-digital.html>.

[6] Bell GB, Boddington R. Solid state drives: the beginning of the end for current practice in digital forensic recovery. J Digit Forensics Security Law 2010;5:1–20.

[7] Association of Chiefs of Police Officers. Good practice guide for computer-based electronic evidence. London: Association of Chiefs of Police (ACPO); 2011.

[8] Henry P. Best practices in digital evidence collection. Retrieved October 15, 2011, from <http://computer-forensics.sans.org/blog/2009/09/12/best-practices-in-digital-evidence-collection/>; 2009, September 12.

[9] Casey E. Digital evidence and computer crime: forensic science, computers, and the internet, 3rd ed. Boston: Academic Press; 2011.

[10] Wade M. Memory Forensics: where to start: DFI News; 2011, June 12. Retrieved June 23, 2013, from <http://www.dfinews.com/articles/2011/06/memory-forensics-where-start#. UcxrXj7F1ah>.

Chapter Review Questions

1. Define the following terms and describe their importance to digital forensics:
   a. Active data
   b. Allocated space
   c. File system
   d. Hash value
   e. Latent data
   f. MD5
   g. Registry
   h. Swap space
   i. Validation

2. Define Locard's exchange principle and explain how it can be applied to the investigation of a network intrusion.

3. Compare and contrast volatile and nonvolatile memory. Give examples of each.

4. What are the four phases of digital forensics?

5. Compare and contrast each of the four computing environments described in the chapter. What are the forensic challenges presented by each?

6. Compare and contrast how magnetic drives store data versus a solid-state drive.

7. What is the biggest forensic challenge presented by solid-state drives?

8. What role does a write-blocking device play in the cloning process?

9. What is the order of volatility? Why should data in RAM be collected before evidence on the hard drive?

10. The MD5 hash value of an evidence drive you removed from the vault no longer matches the hash value obtained when it was collected three months earlier. What does that tell you? What are some possible explanations?

Chapter Exercises

1. Find reporting on a legal takedown of malicious activity, such as that of the DNSchanger botnet in 2012. What forensic evidence was obtained from the seized machines? How was it obtained?

2. How can network forensics and host-based digital forensics be used to complement one another?

CHAPTER 14

Recognition Strategies: Integrity Detection

INTRODUCTION

The final subject group of recognition strategies center around the concept of recognizing when something has changed. This process is called checking the integrity of the data. There are several different aspects of the data that can be checked for changes, and there are several different methods for each aspect. The first integrity detection methods were not developed against attackers, but simply against the random errors computers happen to make during their operation. This chapter begins with these more simple methods, and builds to more robust methods for checking data that use cryptography to detect not only accidental but purposeful changes. The focus of integrity detection is *data* generally, which can mean important or system-critical data such as software executables, configuration files, or file permissions. Maintaining the integrity of such data from accidental or intentional alteration is critical for the operation of all other security strategies.

The second part of the chapter discusses a different aspect of integrity detection than simply if the data has been altered. These aspects are more relevant to databases and such applications, and so have become more important as databases have become more popular. One method in this area is based on rules for the data, and the second method focuses on the content of the data. Finally, an example instantiation of integrity detection in the global positioning system (GPS) ties these different aspects together in a real-world application.

CHECKSUMS

Simple integrity detection is as old as electronic computers. Computers, as well as electric transmission and storage, are far from perfectly reliable. Therefore, to even make computers useful there needs to be some basic integrity detection, otherwise random errors are introduced that ruin calculations. Checksum is the general term for this basic integrity detection, because you *check* the integrity of the bits by adding them up and making sure the *sum* has the correct properties. For example, every IP packet that traverses the Internet has a checksum to protect the integrity of the header [1].

Checksums are a safety mechanism, not a security mechanism. That is, they protect against random environmental changes to data—safety. However, they do not prevent an intelligent actor from purposefully subverting the data—security. However, checksums are an important basis for understanding secure integrity detection, and there are shared principles between the two. In the following subsections, parity bits and repetition codes will be discussed in preparation for the discussion about the 1940's breakthrough, Hamming codes, which are still widely employed to this day.

This section is not a comprehensive survey of all important integrity check methods. For example, Berger codes, cyclic redundancy check (CRC) codes, Fletcher checksums, and a variety of noncryptographic hashing algorithms are all practically useful but not covered here. The topics covered are intended to adequately cover the concepts of safety integrity checks; the reader interested in more encoding algorithms could start with Pless [2] and Peterson and Weldon [3].

Parity Bits

A parity bit is part of an encoding that is designed to detect a single error in a set of binary bits. When sending a string of bits, say 1111010, the ASCII encoding for the lowercase z, there will be noise on the transmission channel. If there is enough disturbance in the transmission the receiver may not receive the same bits as what were sent. This is true even if the transmission channel is just the wire from the keyboard to the computer.

A naive method of detecting errors would just be to send every string twice. Thus, to encode a lowercase z one could send 11110101111010. However, if the receiver reads 11110101111011 it can detect an error, but cannot tell if the error was in the first version, second version, or some combination. Further, this method is inefficient, as it cuts throughput in half to send double the symbols. A more efficient method of detecting a single error is to add a single bit that indicates some property of the string. An even parity bit is 1 if the number of 1s in the string is odd, and 0 if the number of 1s is even. Another way to say this is that we add a bit to the message, and force the number of 1 symbols to be even [2, p. 3]. So z could be encoded as 11110101, where the last bit is the parity bit. This is easy to check, because the receiver just checks that every 8-bit block has an even number of 1s. Otherwise, there is an error, which also detects an error in the check bit itself.

There are several limitations to this encoding. Most importantly, it can only detect an odd number of errors, where errors are assumed to be flipping a single bit from 1 to 0 or vice versa. If z is sent as 11110101, but 01010101 is received, then it passes the parity check and the receiver erroneously records a capital R.

Bar codes (universal product code, or UPC) use a parity check to ensure integrity, although the UPC parity check is not in the binary but in the regular decimal (0–9) number system. UPCs have 12 digits. The first 11 digits carry the information about the product. The twelfth digit is used to make sure that a function of all the digits is a multiple of 10 [4], just like a parity bit is used to make sure that the sum of the bits in a string is a multiple of 2. In this way, errors when entering or reading a UPC can be detected and the sales clerk can re-enter the information, rather than charging the customer for the wrong product accidentally.

Repetition Codes
To detect more errors, more bits are generally required. An alternative code would be to repeat each bit twice. Under this scheme, each 1 or 0 would actually be sent as 111 or 000. Not only can this encoding detect errors, it can also automatically correct them. This is because if the receiver reads 110 or 011 or 101, it is more probable that the original message was 111 than 000, since the former only would require one bit to flip instead of two.

A common notation for codes is to write how many total bits are sent, n=error detection + data, with how many bits k represent just data. This is written in pairs, (n,k) [3]. The repetition code in this example is a $(3,1)$ code, because there are three bits transmitted total, one of which contains the data to be communicated, per block. Seven-bit ASCII with parity bits, as described in the previous subsection, is a $(8,7)$ code. A $(3,1)$ code is inefficient. There are theoretical limits that describe the best possible encoding given certain desired properties, such as single-error detecting, double-error detecting, or the ratio between k and n. While the repetition code can correct single errors, it is not the best code that can do so.

Hamming Codes

A Hamming code is an example of a perfect code. A perfect code is an encoding that can be mathematically demonstrated to be the best possible code for its length and a set of error detection and correction properties [3, pp. 89, 117]. Hamming code actually denotes a family of codes created in a formulaic manner, because the code can have an arbitrarily long block size and it is always a perfect code for that block size if the block length is a power of 2. The formal definition of Hamming codes is best done with matrices [3, p. 118ff], however, a more colloquial definition follows.

Hamming code uses parity bits in an overlapping manner. Each parity bit is calculated as to whether the number of 1s is even or odd. Overlapping manner means each parity bit is only calculated on a subset of the data bits. However, each data bit is checked by a unique combination of parity bits. This way, if a data bit is in error, it can be uniquely identified by the combination of parity bits that fail the parity check. If a parity bit itself is flipped and in error, this is also detectable and identifiable based on the particular method of overlapping the parity check bits used in Hamming codes. To achieve this proper overlapping configuration, every bit position that is exactly a power of 2 is a parity bit, and other bits are data bits [5].

Hamming codes can correct single errors with much better data rates than repetition codes. The redundancy rate of a code is the ratio k/n, or the number of data bits over the total number of bits. A (7,4) Hamming code redundancy rate is about 57%, compared to the repetition code's 33% rate. A (31,26) Hamming code would have a redundancy rate of nearly 84%.

Hamming codes such as (7,4) can correct single errors, but they would fail to detect a double error in which two bits are flipped. To detect a second error, one more parity bit can be included over the whole block, just as in the ASCII (8,7) encoding, which will allow a second error in the block to be detected. Such a code would be termed single-error correcting, double-error detecting (SEC DED). Hamming codes, albeit with larger block lengths, have a long history of application. Hamming codes are used in modern hardware, such as flash drives, for error correction and detection [6]. They are also used in communications with long transmission delays, where it is infeasible to simply retransmit the correct code; it is important for the receiver to be able to correct the error without retransmission. Space missions like the Mariner Mars Probe took advantage of this feature, using a (32,26) encoding.

CRYPTOGRAPHIC INTEGRITY DETECTION

Cryptographic integrity detection takes the principles learned through a few decades of doing integrity detection for safety and applies them to security—preventing intentional subversions of the data. Some of the properties of these techniques will be familiar from the last section on checksums, but since the goals of safety and security are surprisingly different, the design of cryptographic integrity detection is significantly different. In practice, checksums are used in combination with cryptographic integrity detection because neither supplies the services of the other. For a short introduction to the differences between the concepts in safety and security, see Schneier [7].

The basic idea is that the author includes a secret in the checksum or other integrity check algorithm. As with encryption described in Chapter 8, this secret is called the key. The method for including the key in the calculations, and all the calculations themselves, are not secret. If the key is secret, only those entities that know the key can have produced the integrity check value. This certifies that one of the key holders produced the message, and that it has not been altered. When this is accomplished with symmetric (secret key) cryptography it is called a keyed hash function, and sometimes a message authentication code [8, p. 331].

The most common method of performing cryptographic integrity protection is with asymmetric (public key) cryptography, which is introduced in Chapter 7. Asymmetric key cryptographic integrity detection is best exemplified in digital signatures. A different, but related, approach is to use a one-way function instead of a cryptographic function, which is two-way, meaning reversible. One-way functions are called hash functions, which are introduced in Chapter 8. There are a variety of uses for cryptographic hash functions, however, the general principles can be captured with a discussion of digital signatures. For a more complete discussion of the uses of hash functions, see Stallings [8, part3]. Whatever method is being used, there needs to be a secret key. Otherwise the adversary can modify the message and recompute the integrity check value. Keys in this context carry all the difficulties of key management, just as in encryption, as discussed in Chapter 8.

Digital Signatures

The first rigorous description of a robust digital signature scheme and what it means to attack it was published in 1988 [9], although it drew heavily from Diffie and Hellman's initial public key work [10]. The two predominant digital signature schemes in use are RSA (for its inventors, Rivest, Shamir, and Adleman) [11] and Digital Signature Standard (DSS) [12]. There are some differences between them in the math they use, and for the fact that RSA can be used more flexibly to also provide confidentiality as well as a digital

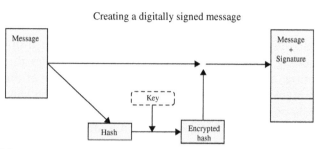

FIGURE 14.1

One common method of creating a digitally signed message. First, the message is hashed; the resulting hash is then encrypted with the signer's private key. The encrypted hash also includes a date or nonce to prevent the same message from being replayed; it is then appended to the original message.

signature. However, this section will only be concerned with the digital signature aspects, and in this regard the two schemes are conceptually similar. Therefore, this section will discuss digital signatures, and group the two together, because at the provided level of detail it is not important to distinguish between the two.

Although there are many ways of applying a digital signature, Figure 14.1 demonstrates an elegant method for providing integrity and authentication, but not confidentiality. The method, used in RSA and DSS, involves the creation and signing of a hash of the message. Hashing algorithms, the output of which is a hash, were introduced briefly in Chapter 8. Hashing is fundamentally different from encryption because a hashing algorithm is not intended to be reversible. The requirements for a cryptographic hashing algorithm are summarized in Table 14.1

The hash provides the integrity protection. It takes in a piece of data of any length, and outputs a fixed length of data. But given the unique properties of sensitivity to change and collision resistance (see Table 14.1 for definitions), it provides a high degree of assurance that a given message actually correlates to that hash. The size of the fixed output has similar requirements to the key size in encryption—if it is too small, the attacker can try enough of the possible values to find a match and break the defense. But with a properly defined hash, the chances of finding two messages with the same hash (i.e., collisions) are small enough as to be negligible. Collisions are always possible; with a properly sized hash the chance of finding them is computationally infeasible. This principle of computational security is also the principle used in key size of encryption algorithms, as described in Chapter 8.

A hash provides integrity protection just like a checksum—if one bit in the message changes, the hash does not match and an error is detected to be

Table 14.1 Seven Required Properties of a Cryptographic Hash Function (call it H) and Their Purposes

Requirement	Definition	Purpose
variable input size	H works on any size of input data	We want to compare all possible data sources, so we need to accept data of any size
fixed output size	The output of H is always the same length	Will make all outputs easily and soundly comparable
efficiency	H is reasonably easy to compute	H needs to be practical or no one will use it.
preimage resistant (one way function)	Given only the output of H, it is infeasible to guess any input that would produce that output. "Infeasible" generally means about 50 billion years at current computing power, or longer than the universe is likely to exist.	That H is one-way is what makes it different from encryption. This is important because it allows a system to check the accuracy of an input without storing a copy of that input. This is particularly important for passwords, for example.
second preimage reisistant (weak collision resistance)	Given a input block, it is computationally infeasible to find a different input value which produces the same output	A digital signature is not very useful if after you sign a message the attacker can find another message that would have the same hash and exchange the two messages.
(strong) collision resistance	It is computationally infeasible to find any pair of different inputs that produce the same output	This stronger version is required if the adversary can choose a message that will be signed, because then no two message can collide or the adversary can choose the signature of one message and then substitute the other.
psuedorandom output	The output appears to be a statistically random string of bits	If the output is predictable then the adversary will be able to make predictions based on it.

somewhere in the message. In this case, the message is arbitrarily long, but the hash cannot determine where the error was. In this sense, it is inferior to a Hamming code for safety-related integrity detection.

There does not need to be a key involved with the hashing function itself. As Figure 14.1 shows, the hash is encrypted. This encryption provides the cryptographic integrity protection. Only the message actually sent can produce the hash, but anyone could make a new message and a new hash if they were attacking the message. The essential step is to tie that hash to someone by his or her private key. Only the private key could make a hash recoverable by the public key, and in this way the hash cannot be modified. So if the message is modified, the hash cannot be tampered with afterwards. Therefore, the algorithm can guarantee that the message is the one that the person created and/or sent. Cryptographic hash functions also exist, which incorporate a key directly; the strategic result and use is essentially the same between these two methods.

The application to recognition strategies is straightforward. The defender may not always be able to prevent the adversary from modifying the contents of a message or file. So in case the adversary modifies the contents, it is important to be able to recognize the change in reference to some data incorporated in the content but that the adversary cannot readily forge. This can be used for files transferred over the network, as well as for files stored locally.

PROFILE: RICHARD HAMMING

Father of Coding Theory

Although Richard W. Hamming (1915–1998) wanted to study engineering, he studied mathematics for both his undergraduate (University of Chicago, 1937) and doctorate (University of Illinois at Urbana-Champaign, 1942) degrees. This degree was already an accomplishment for someone who grew up modestly on the south side of Chicago during the Great Depression, but it was just the beginning. He was recruited into the Manhattan Project in 1945, and with his wife, Wanda, moved to Los Alamos, NM. Hamming's primary task during the project included running the computers the physicists used for their calculations in designing the atomic bomb [13].

This time at Los Alamos was formative for 30-year-old Hamming for two reasons. First, he came into contact with renowned scientists such as Enrico Fermi, Edward Teller, and Robert Oppenheimer, and became envious of their greatness and captivated by the question of what made them so good at what they did [14]. Second, the Manhattan Project gave Hamming confidence and responsibility that would give him the clout and confidence to do "unconventional things in unconventional ways and still [get] valuable results" [15 p. 61].

It was much in this way that Hamming pioneered the field of coding theory at Bell Labs. Hamming worked at Bell from 1946–1976. Since Claude Shannon also worked at Bell Labs during these formative years, much of the theoretical basis for modern computing and telephony was laid in those walls within a remarkably short period of time. Hamming had a strong personality; he was always direct and was not afraid to challenge his colleagues or friends. Despite his harshness, Hamming was a genuine person and displayed an unflagging respect for hard work.

After retiring from Bell, Hamming quit researching but took a position as a professor at the Naval Postgraduate School in Monterey, CA. He focused on teaching and writing, especially textbooks. He shifted his intellect from coding theory to mathematics pedagogy, attempting to modify teaching methods by supplying innovative textbooks. He also remained interested in what made great scientists great, a theme still carried over from his encounters with Fermi and Oppenheimer but seeded now with his own experience with success. He had several recommendations, but besides the rather obvious hard work—sensibly directed—and cleverness, he singled out the ability to tolerate ambiguity such that one can work within a theory but also question it enough to expand it [14].

Hamming taught in Monterey for 21 years as an adjunct professor. He accepted emeritus status in December 1997, but despite this change he continued to come in daily. A month later he passed away. He left quite a legacy, not only in the various aspects of information theory that carry his name, but in the impression he made on his students and colleagues. He has also been memorialized in many awards, scholarships, and namesakes, including the observatory at Cal State. A group of his former students at the Naval Postgraduate School have reconstructed his capstone course, including video of his presentations, available at *https://savage.nps.edu/hamming/HammingLearningToLearnRecovered/*.

RULE-BASED INTEGRITY CHECKING

Rule-based integrity checking is most commonly associated with database systems or other structured data formats. Whenever a process reads data in, it should check that the data adheres to the rules it is expecting, otherwise serious errors can occur. Both SQL injection and buffer overflow attacks, two of the three most common and damaging software programming errors ever, are a failing to check that data adheres to the expected rules [16]. Recognition of these violations is a key aspect of a good security strategy.

Like intrusion detection systems discussed in Chapter 12, integrity checking sometimes blurs the line between recognition and resistance. A sufficiently accurate and fast intrusion detection system (IDS) can begin to perform preventative measures, and then it may be called an intrusion prevention system (IPS). Likewise with integrity checking, some processes are suitable to prevent the erroneous entry from being stored, whereas others are only suitable for recognition afterwards. Preventative integrity checking may be particularly useful during human data entry, where the computer will have enough time to keep up with the relatively slow human input rate and give feedback.

There are many different types of integrity rules. In general, any arbitrary rule can be made about the format and content of the data. When a program specifies that a field must be filled by an integer, or a date, this is specified by a rule about the type of data. Tax calculation documents contain a lot of good examples of arbitrarily complex integrity rules. For example, "If box 2 is greater than 4,000 and you checked yes in box 5, then enter the contents of box 2 in box 9; otherwise, enter the difference between box 3 and box 2, unless it is less than 0, then enter 0." Such a statement specifies a relation between different fields, in addition to simple rules like the value in the field is an integer. In database systems, arbitrary integrity rules can be specified using table constraints and assertions [17, p. 69]. The types of integrity rules that usually get special attention in database systems are entity, referential, and domain integrity.

Entity Integrity

Entity integrity is a constraint on the uniqueness of the entity. In a postal system, it may be a constraint that within one zip code there cannot be two streets with the same name. There can be differently defined constraints for different relevant realms. Within the whole country, there may be allowed to be multiple streets with the same name. However, there should probably be a constraint that no two buildings share the same address. Entity integrity is maintained by uniqueness constraints in a database system, which are technically called primary key constraints [17, p. 64].

When specifying the rules for a primary key constraint, it is important to specify the minimal subset that is of interest. Considering houses again, some features of the house could be confusing when specifying a unique house. We do not care what color the house is or if it is made of cement or wood when we specify the unique address. The address alone can make up the primary key of the building, whereas a set of information {address, red, brick} would not help specify uniqueness. Such a set is a superset of the primary key.

In a file system, the unique entities are files as specified by their file path. One form of entity integrity checking is to see if there is already a file by the requested name before writing to it. If there is, the operating system often prompts for verification before overwriting the file, which is a form of integrity check.

Referential Integrity

Referential integrity is verifying that the relationships between different entities meet certain standards. For example, if we keep track of students enrolled in a course by their student ID numbers, there should be a referential integrity check on those IDs of students enrolled in the course to ensure that they are IDs of students who attend the school and have paid their tuition. Referential integrity is maintained by foreign key constraints in a database system [17, p. 66].

Domain Integrity

Domain integrity is a constraint on the possible values for an entity. This is perhaps the most basic integrity constraint. However, it can become rather complex. A shopkeeper might want to ensure all the items being sold in the "cameras" section are cameras. But what makes an item a camera versus a cell phone may need to be carefully defined, with no clear borders. As an aside, digital shopkeepers can solve this issue by giving items multiple types, and thus multiple legal locations [18]. Domain integrity is maintained by domain constraints in a database system [17, p. 61].

Failing to sanitize input data, or make sure that data accepted from users does not contain system commands, remains one of the most common computer exploits [16]. Input sanitization can be viewed as a special case of domain integrity. For a comical illustration of the importance of domain integrity, see *http://xkcd.com/327/*.

CONTENT COMPARISONS

Another possible integrity checking mechanism is to inspect the content of the file or container and compare it, either to a reference file or just to an older version to look for changes. This is more than just comparing the hash values of the files to see if they trivially differ, as is done with most cryptographic integrity detection. Content comparison is more interested in where and how two files differ. This has uses in change and version management, as well as integrity detection. It also allows for making decisions about what changes are allowed. Certain changes to a file may not violate organizational policy, but others might, and so a content comparison tool is necessary to pull out changes before it can be determined if they are appropriate.

The Unix `diff` command-line utility is the quintessential content comparison tool. The `diff` algorithm is specified in Hunt and McIlroy [19], and the algorithm has not changed much since 1976. The underlying problem is a computationally difficult one—the least common subsequence problem. But the `diff` algorithm has proven to be a practically good solution, in lieu of a theoretically optimal one. The output of `diff` specifies what changes are necessary to convert file 1 into file 2. This is listed as a series of insertions and deletions, by line numbers, necessary to make the conversion. Figure 14.2 displays some sample output.

If the defender has a reference copy of files on the file system, they can use content comparison to highlight possible material for further inspection. If one assumes that the system yesterday or last week was in a good state (a dangerous assumption, but we have to start somewhere), then one could use a content comparison to prioritize resources. Both directories and files could be inspected. The contents of new and old directories can be compared to look for new files. The contents of files that existed both last week and now can be checked for changes.

Further, the defender can prioritize the new files and changes in the files for a possible scan to recognize malicious changes. The previously mentioned (see Chapter 5) host-based tool Tripwire is one example of a tool that provides

	Original text	Edited text
	18. All warfare is based on deception. 19. Hence, when able to attack, we must seem unable; when using our forces, we must seem inactive; when we are near, we must make the enemy believe we are far away; when far away, we must make him believe we are near. 20. Hold out baits to entice the enemy. Feign disorder, and crush him. 21. If he is secure at all points, be prepared for him. If he is in superior strength, evade him. 22. If your opponent is of choleric temper, seek to irritate him. Pretend to be weak, that he may grow arrogant.	17. According as circumstances are favorable, one should modify one's plans. 18. All warfare is based on deception. 19. Hence, when able to attack, we must seem unable; when using our forces, we must seem inactive; when we are near, we must make the enemy believe we are far away; when far away, we must make him believe we are near. 21. If he is secure at all points, be prepared for him. If he is in superior strength, evade him. 22. If your opponent is of hyperbolic temper, seek to irradiate him. Pretend to be weak, that he may grow arrogant. 23. If he is taking his ease, give him no rest.
diff output	0a1 > 17. According as circumstances are favorable, one should modify one's plans. 6d6 < 20. Hold out baits to entice the enemy. Feign disorder, and crush him. 9c9 < 22. If your opponent is of choleric temper, seek to irritate him. --- > 22. If your opponent is of hyperbolic temper, seek to irradiate him. 10a11 > 23. If he is taking his ease, give him no rest.	

FIGURE 14.2

The output of `diff` on two sections of Sun Tzu's *Art of War* [20]. The right side has been edited. The `diff` output consists of a encoding followed by a hunk of changes. The encoding is line numbers in the first file, a single letter for addition, deletion, or change [*a, d, c*], and line numbers in the second file. The lines are reproduced that were added, changed, or deleted, with > indicating the line was in the right file, and < in the left file. This is the default format; `diff` can also be used to simply state if the files differ, for example.

some of this functionality. This kind of local integrity check tool could also be termed a kind of host-based intrusion detection and prevention system (IDPS; see Chapter 12).

AN EXAMPLE: GPS

The global positioning system contains a practical and important example of integrity detection. The GPS is used by a receiver device to determine the receiver's position on Earth. The receiver does this by measuring its distance from several satellites and triangulating its position. Synchronizing clocks between the satellite array and the receiver is also important, because the distance is measured by how long it takes a radio signal to reach the receiver. Since radio waves travel at the speed of light, this is a constant[1] and simply knowing the time difference is enough to calculate the distance.

If one of the satellite signals is wrong, the navigator wants to know. Especially if they are flying a 747 plane. This is an integrity detection problem. GPS uses receiver autonomous integrity monitoring (RAIM) to detect faulty satellites. GPS needs four satellites to determine position while flying: one to sync the clocks and one each for latitude, longitude, and altitude. These distances are continuous numbers, rather than discrete bits; however, the math works similarly to Hamming code and SED or SEC DED codes. If the receiver wants to detect an error it needs five satellites. To both detect an error and determine which signal is in error, discard it, and compute the correct value automatically, the receiver needs six satellites [21].

The algorithm for detecting when a satellite is in error uses statistics and a specified error threshold, unlike Hamming codes, which are discretely either right or wrong. The position is calculated using several combinations of the satellites, since only four of the available ones are necessary per calculation. If all the results are close enough together, as defined by the threshold, the measurement is considered accurate. The chance that two satellites would be wrong in the same way is considered sufficiently low that this is not a concern; such an error would be similar to the way that a double error in electronic transmission can avoid detection by parity bits.

In the United States, the FAA considers RAIM important enough that it requires aviators to check for the availability of RAIM before flying [21], such as on *http://www.raimprediction.net/*. This is application-level integrity, and is

---

[1]Technically, it is not quite constant. It is affected by gravity, as per Einstein's theory of relativity. Furthermore, the clocks on the satellites do not count at the same speed as the receiver, since the satellites are orbiting enough faster than the receiver device for relativity to be relevant. However, both of these deviations are predictable and included in the calculations the receiver makes based on the timing difference.

much more specific than the IP packet header checksum or a Hamming code used to maintain accurate storage on a hard drive. However, the principles of all these safety-related integrity detection mechanisms are similar. And like most good services, the average consumer does not know they exist as long as they are working.

SUMMARY

This concludes the last of four chapters on recognition strategies. We have discussed network-based, host-based, and data-based recognition. In this chapter, methods of integrity detection are explored, beginning with simpler safety-related checksums and Hamming codes, followed by more robust cryptographic checksums capable of detecting intentional changes by an adversary.

This chapter also discusses higher-level integrity detection methods that do more than just check that the information received is the information that was input. Rule-checking integrity mechanisms verify that the data meets formatting, size, and style requirements. Failure to enforce certain integrity rules, such as input size, is still one of the most common sources of coding errors exploited by attackers. Content comparisons look for changes between versions of a file or data element. Finally, measurement integrity in the GPS is discussed.

Chapter 15 discusses perhaps the most important aspect of a security strategy: how to recover when a security violation is detected. Recognition strategies are not much use without a valid plan on what to do with the information that a violation has been recognized. And since one primary tenet of the book is that the defender will not be able to deceive, frustrate, or resist all attacks, it is essential that the defender be able to recover gracefully from successful attacks.

REFERENCES

[1] Postel J. Internet Protocol. RFC 791. Updated by RFCs 1349, 2474, 1981.

[2] Pless V. Introduction to the theory of error-correcting codes, John Wiley and Sons, New York. 1982.

[3] Peterson WW, Weldon EJ. Error-correcting codes, rev. ed. Cambridge, MA: MIT Press; 1972.

[4] Barnes S, Michalowicz KD. Now & then: from cashier to scan coordinator; from stones to bones to pc clones. Math Teach Middle School 1994;1(1):59–65.

[5] Hamming RW. Error detecting and error correcting codes. Bell Syst Tech J 1950;29(2):147–60.

[6] Kim J, Jee Y. Hamming product code with iterative process for NAND flash memory controller 2010 second International Conference on Computer Technology and Development (ICCTD). : IEEE; 2010. p. 611–615.

[7] Schneier B. Beyond fear: thinking sensibly about security in an uncertain World. Berlin: Springer; 2003.

[8] Stallings W. Cryptography and network security, 5th ed. Upper Saddle River, NJ: Pearson Education; 2011.

[9] Goldwasser S, Micali S, Rivest RL. A digital signature scheme secure against adaptive chosen-message attacks. SIAM J Comput 1988;17(2):281–308.

[10] Diffie W, Hellman M. New directions in cryptography. IEEE Trans Inf Theory 1976;22(6):644–54.

[11] Jonsson J, Kaliski B. Public-Key cryptography standards (PKCS) #1: RSA cryptography specifications version 2.1. RFC 3447, 2003.

[12] Federal Information Processing Standard Publication 186-4: Digital Signature Standard (DSS). Gaithersburg, MD: United States Department of Commerce, National Institute of Standards and Technology; 2013.

[13] O'Connor JJ, Robertson EF. Richard Wesley Hamming. Retrieved Mar 18, 2013, from <http://www-history.mcs.st-andrews.ac.uk/Biographies/Hamming.html>; 2012.

[14] Hamming RW. Retrieved Mar 19, 2013, from <http://www.paulgraham.com/hamming.html> You and your research. : Bell Labs; 1986.

[15] Lee J. Richard Wesley Hamming: 1915–1998. IEEE Ann Hist Comput 1998;20(2):60–2.

[16] Brown M, Kirby D, Martin B, Paller A. 2011 CWE/SANS Top 25 most dangerous software errors. MITRE Corporation. Retrieved Mar 19, 2013, from <http://cwe.mitre.org/top25/>; 2011.

[17] Ramakrishnan R, Gehrke J. *Database management systems*, 3rd ed. Osborne: McGraw-Hill, New York; 2003.

[18] Weinberger D. Everything is miscellaneous: the power of the new digital disorder. New York: Times Books; 2007.

[19] Hunt JW, McIlroy MD. An algorithm for differential file comparison. Bell Laboratories, Murray Hill, NJ.

[20] Sun Tzu. The art of war. Giles L, editor. Retrieved from <http://www.gutenberg.org/ebooks/132>; 1910.

[21] Volchansky L. Predictive RAIM for RNAV 1 and RNAV 2 operations using TSO-C129 GPS ICAO SAM Implementation Group. Lima, Peru: FAA; 2009. Retrieved Mar 9, 2013, from <http://www.lima.icao.int/meetprog/2009/SAMIG4/presentation\%20ICAO_SAM_IG_RAIM_Volchansky_v4.pdf>.

Chapter Review Questions

1. What is a checksum?

2. How does a parity bit check the integrity of a block of data?

3. What is a digital signature for and how does it work?

4. What is the difference between a hashing algorithm and an encryption algorithm?

5. What are two common rule-based integrity rules?

Chapter Exercises

1. In the following block of data, the Hamming code integrity check bits are replaced with x. Fill in the correct values: xx1x010 × 1101001. What is the data encoding rate of this (15,11) code?

2. Classify the top 25 software weaknesses described in Brown et al. [16] as to whether or not integrity recognition methods could prevent them, and if so what methods.

Recovery of Security

INTRODUCTION

In previous chapters we discussed various aspects of a robust security strategy: deception, frustration, resistance, and recognition. The theme so far is to have a layered approach and fall back on later aspects of the strategy for support. If the adversary cannot be deceived, frustrate him or her. If the adversary cannot be frustrated, then resist him or her. We have also emphasized that the defender cannot hope to frustrate every adversary—a sufficiently skilled and patient adversary will get past any frustration strategies deployed. And so on with resistance and recognition.

There is no such further bulwark with recovery. Furthermore, since compromises are inevitable, enacting recovery plans is inevitable. A recognition event will kick off the recovery phase; however, the initial indicator of compromise will invariably be just the tip of the iceberg. A good recovery plan will interact with and draw from processes from each of the other four strategy aspects to perform a sufficient response. In this regard, responding to an information assurance incident is highly technical. These technical details can be found throughout the reference materials cited in the chapter, therefore, this chapter omits them.

Only a few aspects that differentiate a good recovery from a lackluster recovery are technical. A good recovery is an organizational wherewithal to accept that incidents happen and respond to them with appropriate care. There is a significant body of work on disaster recovery and incident response in the physical world. The goal of this chapter is not to reproduce that body of work—that would take a book in its own right. This chapter points to related existing strategic documents for incident response, and highlights how these strategies can be adapted to provide a good grounding for cyber-incident response.

One last point is important to bear in mind before we begin. Since 2005, the security community has seen extensive evidence of adversaries routinely evading even diligent, intelligent defenders [1]. There have also been demonstrations of malicious software tenaciously penetrating physically separated, high-value systems [2]. An integrated recovery plan has been advocated for some time as part of a robust network [3,4], and in light of such persistent attacks, the practical benefits of such a recovery plan are evident. A good recovery plan will help differentiate a robust organization from a hapless organization.

This chapter covers several topics that could be considered rather diverse. First, we discuss planning for emergencies, as cyber-incident response and recovery share some similar features with emergency handling. Specifically, recommendations for building a response policy are covered as they vary relatively little. Next, continuity of operations is discussed and contrasted with recovery from malicious events. This captures the difference between strategies when dealing with safety events versus security events, which is a theme that has been discussed in regards to other strategies in this book as well. Recommendations for cyber-incident handling and surrounding policy are covered once this background is established, through the target step of restoring a cleaned system back into operations. The final section covers a critical but difficult operation—incorporating lessons learned back into the overall security strategies.

Contingency planning is the umbrella term that covers business continuity, continuity of operations, critical infrastructure protection, security incident response, disaster recovery, and other resiliency fields [5]. All of these operations and plans are important, but they have key differences. One reason this chapter treats several aspects of contingency planning, rather than just computer security incident response, is to better place incident handling in comparison to other contingency planning disciplines. This approach promotes a clearer understanding of what incident response can do, and when other specialization is needed.

EMERGENCY MANAGEMENT

Emergency management includes all aspects of an organization. Work in emergency planning has been driven in large part by local, regional, and federal government needs to plan for natural disasters and terrorist attacks.

This has created a whole emergency management discipline, and many universities now offer doctoral, master's, and bachelor's degrees specifically in emergency management. For a list see the report by the Federal Emergency Management Agency [6].

Emergency management is part domain knowledge and part skills specific to managing emergencies. These skills translate across disciplines. So while it might be unwise to have the same person in charge of responses to tornadoes as well as successful phishing emails, the two positions do have a lot to learn from one another. Some organizations have realized this to the extent that they bring all of these management roles under one operational resilience office, rather than have the chief information officer (CIO) be responsible for information technology (IT) emergency management, the chief information systems officer (CISO) responsible for information assurance breach management, the chief operations officer (COO) responsible for supply chain resiliency, etc. [7]. This consolidation reduces duplication of effort and allows different departments to share the expertise of those (few) trained in emergency management.

The steps of emergency management preparedness are planning, training, and exercises. These three steps make executing a recovery much smoother. The U.S. Federal Emergency Management Agency (FEMA) supports an Emergency Management Institute (EMI) that provides free training in emergency management via a remote-learning, independent study program. The following courses may be of use to anyone who is involved in planning a recovery capability in an organization. It is not possible for this chapter to reproduce the useful knowledge in these courses, so it is highly recommended that the recovery planner take advantage of these free resources:

- IS-1.A: Emergency Manager: An Orientation to the Position
- IS-100.B: Introduction to Incident Command System
- IS-120.A: An Introduction to Exercises
- IS-139: Exercise Design
- IS-235.B: Emergency Planning
- IS-241.A: Decision Making and Problem Solving
- IS-293: Mission Assignment Overview
- IS-454: Fundamentals of Risk Management
- IS-523: Resilient Accord: Exercising Continuity Plans for Cyber Incidents
- IS-547.A: Introduction to Continuity of Operations

Links to all of these courses and their materials are available from FEMA [8].

RECOVERY PRIORITIES

The first step on the long road of emergency planning is to know what needs to be protected. This aspect—the need for a principled risk assessment—is shared between emergency planning and security incident planning. The recovery plan should contain priorities for what systems are treated first. If 10 systems go out at once, or more likely a compromise is discovered that impacts 10 disparate systems, the response teams should not have to prioritize on-the-fly. The plan should prioritize what systems are the most important for the organization. This provides predictability for everyone in the organization when an incident occurs, and saves the responders time so that they can do their job as efficiently as feasible, which is critical to successful responses.

Inventorying assets and determining areas of greatest risk are both difficult tasks. They require strong organizational policies and the will to execute them. There are also several methods of considering which risks are greatest, and unfortunately these methods generally produce different results. An insurance company might like to look at actuarial tables to determine past incidence, cost per incident, and so on. The U.S. Social Security Administration keeps such data for life expectancy, for example [9], and so life insurance companies can use this to determine the risk of a 25-year-old male or 65-year-old female dying, and therefore how much to charge for insurance.

An actuarial approach based on incident occurrence and cost is insufficient in cyber-incident risk determination and response planning for two reasons. First, there is insufficient public reporting of cyber-security incidents to construct frequency models, and what reporting exists is insufficiently detailed to construct incident costs. Second, organizational structure, technology, software, architecture, core competencies, and services provided are too idiosyncratic, so it is unclear if the experiences of one organization generalize to those of other organizations.

In light of this difficulty, a more productive recovery planning strategy is likely to identify critical success factors (CSFs) for the organization and analytically determine key risks to them [10, p. 123ff]. This approach is advocated by the CERT[1] Resilience Management Model (RMM). There is more detail on the RMM in Caralli et al. [11]. CSFs are closely related to mission-essential functions (MEFs) as described by FEMA's EMI courses referenced earlier. This thread also runs through the Survivable Network Analysis method, because the method's definition of "survivable" is the ability to maintain mission-essential functionality in the presence of attacks and accidents [4]. This method provides a rather more practical approach than the RMM or FEMA models, but its scope is also more focused. In any case, this risk assessment function is separate from the incident response function; there are several business units involved in building a response policy.

---

[1] CERT officially is no longer an acronym, although it formerly expanded to Computer Emergency Response Team.

Perceptions of risk will likely be adjusted as the organization responds to incidents. Critical success factors should also be reevaluated occasionally, perhaps annually, to determine if new technological structures have been introduced into the organization that may affect the critical functions, or if the organization has new critical success factors. Learning from recovery events is a feature of good recoveries, and is described in more detail later in this chapter.

The process of identifying critical success factors—and the technological systems and data that support them—is a human-intensive and policy-driven process. Technology can assist this process, but it cannot automate it. There are several industry reports available on existing technology to support data discovery, such as Chuvakin's [12]. However, deciding what is important to the organization is a human function. Once the emergency management team has decided on what systems are important and what attacks are likely, they can better construct a response policy and set of plans.

BUILDING A RESPONSE POLICY

An organizational response team policy is the set of organizational policies detailing how the organization responds to incidents, what incidents are handled by whom, the standards for an acceptable response, responder code of conduct, organizational information disclosure policy, evidence handling procedures, eliciting lessons learned, and integrating feedback into the security strategies. There are several guides on how to plan and design a response policy or some part of it [4,11,13–19]. Unfortunately, no one of these guides completely covers the whole complex policy. Recovery strategies touch on many aspects of an organization, so perhaps this is not surprising. RMM is the most comprehensive, but it is one level of abstraction above implementation [11]. The National Institute of Standards and Technology's (NIST) guide on incident handling provides a more practical, focused starting point [19]. NIST also has recommendations for contingency planning [5].

There is a large list of guidance documents on creating and managing computer security incident response teams (CSIRTs) available from the CERT/CC at *http://www.cert.org/csirts/resources.html*. A quality CSIRT is the heart of a good recovery policy. Building a CSIRT is discussed in more detail in subsection "CSIRTs" under "Incident Handling". How a CSIRT interacts with the rest of the organization is part of a good response policy that is not covered by simply having a quality CSIRT; this section will focus on the CSIRT's place in the organization.

How each organization defines these various policy choices depends on their abilities, perceived threats, and priorities. A good response policy has to strike a balance between being comprehensive and being sufficiently concise so the incident responders do not waste their time re-reading the response policy to determine their responsibilities and procedures. Some aspects that a comprehensive response policy ought to address are the following:

- The goals of the response team [14, p. 3].
- How an investigation begins [13, p. 7].
- Who is in charge of the investigation.
- How and under what circumstances staff members escalate incident priority.
- How and under what circumstances incident responses and responsibility are reported to other members of the organization, including upper-level management.
- When the response team will clean infected systems and when they will observe the infection to gather information, either for intelligence or litigation [13, p. 9].
- Organizational priorities in an emergency, such as critical success factors [11] or mission-essential functions [20, p. 3.8ff].
- Who is responsible for various response functions, including but not limited to, incident command, operations, planning, logistics, and finance and administration [16, p. 4.3].
- Incident handling procedures (see "Incident Handling" section later in chapter).
- What information is disclosed to what parties under what circumstances [13, p. 10ff]. Furthermore, who is responsible for information dissemination [16, p. 5.23].
- Who collects and archives information for internal recordkeeping and process improvement [15].
- When lessons-learned data is collected, how [15] and when possible process improvements are reintegrated into the organization [11].

Building this policy is not an overnight task. It will take concerted organizational input, as several independent elements of the organization may have to share input to create the plan. This is one reason why a central, high-level management position for operational resilience helps move the policy forward. The policy will also always be evolving, so it is okay if it does not emerge fully formed from the first iteration. Although some of these policy aspects draw from response to natural disasters, there are important differences between plans for responses to accidents and responses to attacks. These differences will be highlighted in the following two sections.

Disaster recovery and incident management are both functions within an organization that partly or wholly fall under IT operations. These are not the only two functions of the IT department. Security management involves an overlapping set of business functions, not all of which are IT functions. This

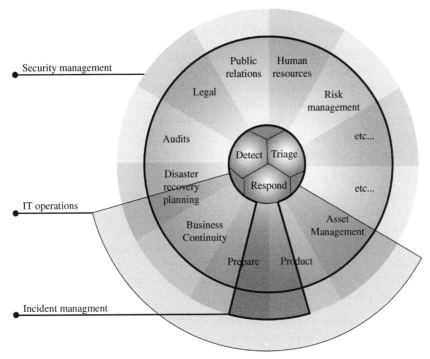

FIGURE 15.1
Notional overlap of business functions involved in incident management, IT operations, and security management, including the difference between disaster recovery planning and incident management.
Source: Reprinted with permission from Alberts et al. [17].

situation creates a complex set of relationships, since each business function has its own priorities, and personnel in each role require different, specialized training. Figure 15.1 displays the relationship between IT operations, incident management, disaster recovery, security, and other important organizational functions.

RECOVERY FROM ACCIDENTS: CONTINUITY OF OPERATIONS

Continuity is an important subject in resiliency. The plan may be embodied in a continuity of operations plan (COOP) [21] or service continuity process area improvements in RMM [11, SC area]. These plans are about more holistic concerns than just IT. As part of these holistic plans, IT plays an important supporting role and thus is part of the plan. More and more, digital services are essential functions in themselves, and so maintaining continuous service is not a supporting role but a goal. Despite the plans' broad applicability, this section will focus on IT resources. This focus produces some dissenting advice, different from a broader COOP.

With some notable exceptions, these plans largely describe reactions to random hazardous events. These may be a local earthquake that a local government must respond to, or an earthquake half the world away that disrupts an organization's supply of an essential component for its business. In the context of a large computer system, the primary advice would be to have at least two data processing centers, and keep those two centers in geographically disparate locations. Several businesses learned this the hard way after Hurricane Sandy [22].

Sometimes COOP and business continuity plans do need to change to adapt to changing services, such as in the face of greater appreciation of the severity of a disaster like Hurricane Sandy or the 2011 Tohoku, Japan, earthquake. However, there is a fundamental difference between plans that react to accidents like these and computer security incident response plans. The next time there is an earthquake, the quake will not have observed how the city responded last time and adjust the way it shakes the earth to most effectively defeat that response.

Consider this concrete IT example. If the defenders lose access to a mail server because the room it is in catches fire, it is entirely appropriate to bring an exact copy of that mail server online in another building. On the other hand, if the defender realizes an adversary has administrative access to the mail server, it is not appropriate to immediately bring an exact copy of the mail server online—the adversary will just compromise it too. Therefore, recovery personnel from security events need to carefully examine which COOP steps are appropriate for responding to a malicious event, and which need to be different. This is particularly true with IT, because attacks can be deployed against redundant IT resources automatically by the attacker at machine speed, faster than humans can respond.

RECOVERY FROM MALICIOUS EVENTS

This section discusses features of a security recovery versus a safety-based recovery. More detail on incident handling steps for a recovery of security is the subject of the following section.

Recovering from a malicious attack means the system needs to be taken down, possibly analyzed forensically to figure out what happened and what other systems need to be investigated, rebuilt, and reinstated. The act of taking the system offline is precisely the opposite of the objective for COOP. Thus, there is a tension between the two types of responses. This is further complicated by the fact that there are some systems that simply cannot come down for five minutes, let alone a day.

In the situation where a critical system is infected the recovery needs to incorporate some aspects of safety and security responses. When recovering from accidents, a copy of the affected system can be activated in a different location. When maintaining continuity while investigating a malicious event, the recovery strategy should include a system that provides the same essential functionality but eliminates nonessential functions that may be exploitable. The backup system should also operate under stricter security device configurations, as discussed in the frustration and resistance strategy chapters of this book. It is possible, depending on the adversary's skill level and persistence, that there is an exploitable, unknown vulnerability within the code for the essential functionality of the service. But limiting services until the system's shortcomings are diagnosed should help; the responder needs to keep in mind that compromises are rarely limited to one machine and may include various computers and network devices within the organization.

Having this added-security configuration of essential services prepared before the incident is part of recovery planning. Yet, the organization cannot have such backup systems for essential functions if they have not yet identified the essential functions. In most environments there are some systems that are likely to be critical and targeted by the adversary precisely for this reason. This includes the active directory or Kerberos server, email server, file server, domain names system (DNS) server, and network management server. These services cannot be brought down to be fixed; they must remain online.

Being ready for a malicious event recovery is not just a matter of having reduced-functionality, high-security backup plans for critical IT services. The organizational IT infrastructure has to be planned such that switching to a different service on short notice is possible. Executing practice exercises during less busy times is a good way to test this readiness. However, there may be some subtle changes that need to be made to enable an effective recovery operation to keep a resilient network running. For example, the critical services should be discovered by internal hosts through an internal DNS, and the time to live (TTL) on those DNS records should be on the order of minutes, so that internal hosts can be redirected to the backup services quickly by changing the DNS configuration. Then the infected systems can be taken offline without service disruption.

This is only one example; there are many possible methods to organize a resilient network with this in mind. But most of them are not likely to happen by accident—the network as a whole must be planned such that recovery strategies are possible and efficient. This is related to the RMM technology management (TM) and resilient technical solution engineering (RTSE) process areas [11].

PROFILE: THOMAS LONGSTAFF, PH.D.
SECURITY, SURVIVABILITY, AND SCIENCE

Tom Longstaff studied math and physics at Boston University before going on to earn a doctorate in the relatively new field of computer science in 1983. Soon after finishing his degree at University of California–Davis, Tom joined the maturing CERT Coordination Center® in 1992. In his 15 years at CERT, Tom had a hand in many of the projects and initiatives that have shaped CERT into a renowned cyber-security center, including network survivability [4], insider threat analysis [23], security evaluation of computer code [24], and critical infrastructure [25]. In addition, he served as the manager of the network situational awareness group as it formed, and eventually became the deputy director for technology of the CERT program.

Tom has also been instrumental in making the security process more rigorous and well defined, such as providing a high-level taxonomy for incident description [26]. This thread has been strengthened as Tom took leadership roles, first as chief scientist for the Cyber Missions Branch

of the Applied Physics Laboratory (APL), and then as technical director of the Systems Behavior office within the U.S. Department of Defense National Security Agency starting in 2012. He has been one of the few people questioning the lack of "science" in cyber security, why this is true, if it is important, and how to correct it [27,28].

This academic history demonstrates a versatility to address the salient problems of the day in most areas of cyber security. Besides contributing directly in a variety of fields, Tom serves as the editor of one of the premier security magazines, *IEEE Security & Privacy*. Although he keeps a lower profile than some of the more eccentric security-related academics like Richard Hamming or Whit Diffie, Tom has at many subtle turns influenced the direction of cyber security in many of the strategic areas discussed in this book; notable recovery-related contributions are the incident taxonomy and the network survivability analysis model.

INCIDENT HANDLING

A security incident is a group of attacks on computers and networks that have some distinctive unifying characteristics, such as likely being performed by one attacker [26, p. 15]. However, defining what counts as an incident, and how to describe its various parts, is a slippery task. The interested reader will find 10 pages of clarifications and definitions in Howard and Longstaff [26] before a suitable definition of *incident* is described, let alone the following discussion of parts of an incident. There is generally no completely agreed-on terminology or taxonomy, although Howard and Longstaff [26] do provide an oft-cited starting point.

Incidents are usually handled by a specialized team within an organization: the computer security incident response team (CSIRT). For each incident the team handles, we can describe five handling steps [13]:

1. Identification
2. Containment
3. Eradication
4. Recovery
5. Lessons learned

There are various other specifications that have slightly different steps than this, or different terms, but the steps all describe the same essential process [17]. NIST's guide breaks the process into four similar sections: preparation; detection and analysis; containment, eradication, and recovery; and post-incident activity [19]. This section is organized similarly to the SANS guide [13], but the SANS guide is more condensed. The NIST guide [19] and CERT/CC recommendations [17] are more detailed, and the interested reader should consult these guides for a detailed treatment.

This section has two subsections. The first briefly discusses CSIRTs, with an emphasis on external resources for further learning, especially if the reader needs to help establish a CSIRT within an organization. The other subsection discusses the steps in handling a single incident.

CSIRTs

This subsection provides a skeleton of the process of building a CSIRT, to introduce the whole concept at a high level. Some extra details are fleshed out in particularly important areas.

One of the first CSIRTs was formed when the CERT program was formed at the Software Engineering Institute at Carnegie Mellon University. The CERT program was initiated in 1988, as part of the response to the first major Internet outage due to malicious software: the Morris Worm [29]. The program since has become a repository for the lessons learned in building and operating CSIRTs, and has helped establish and coordinate many influential CSIRTs, such as US-CERT, the CSIRT and coordination point for the United States federal civilian government [30]. The other primary resource for information on response teams is the Forum of Incident Response and Security Teams (FIRST), founded in 1990 [31]. Both of these resources can provide guidance to organizations establishing CSIRTs.

CERT recommendations identify 19 action items for an organization establishing a CSIRT. It is worth quoting this list in its entirety to present a sense of the diversity of tasks required. The action items, with more details and further resources for more detailed reading, are available from the Software Engineering Institute [32].

1. Identify stakeholders and participants.
2. Obtain management support and sponsorship.
3. Develop a CSIRT project plan.
4. Gather information [from all stakeholders on policies, compliance, history, etc.].
5. Identify the CSIRT constituency.
6. Define the CSIRT mission.
7. Secure funding for CSIRT operations.

8. Decide on the range and level of services the CSIRT will offer.
9. Determine the CSIRT reporting structure, authority, and organizational model.
10. Identify required resources such as staff, equipment, and infrastructure.
11. Define interactions and interfaces.
12. Define roles, responsibilities, and the corresponding authority.
13. Document the workflow.
14. Develop policies and corresponding procedures.
15. Create an implementation plan and solicit feedback.
16. Announce the CSIRT when it becomes operational.
17. Define methods for evaluating the performance of the CSIRT.
18. Have a backup plan for every element of the CSIRT.
19. Be flexible.

This is neither a short nor easy process. However, the road has been traveled many times before. As long as the organization creating the incident response capability can leverage the existing lessons and documentation from past CSIRT creation, it should be able to proceed successfully.

The end result is a CSIRT—a person or persons who will be tasked with responding to computer security incidents within the organization. Although these are technically capable staff, they are not merely IT staff. Incident response requires not just special technical skill but also breadth to understand how systems interact. Since no one can be proficient on every IT system, the CSIRT staff will potentially need access to documentation about all the systems in the organization. There is one more helpful ability for these staff members: detective skills, or the ability to think like an adversary. A common problem in staffing CSIRTs is that staff members are overspecialized and are not cross-trained in each other's skills [32]. When this happens, if one key staff member leaves, the team is crippled.

The response team also has some material needs. It needs a secure place to store and investigate evidence, and the equipment to do so. The CSIRT needs a defined interface with constituents, whether it is a phone hotline, email address, physical desk, or otherwise.

At the heart of its function, the CSIRT is a service part of the organization—to provide incident response expertise. However, there are some tensions with this characterization, because one of the most useful outcomes of an incident is lessons on how to manage the systems better. However, advice or requirements on system changes is not what the "customers" of the CSIRT requested. Resolving this tension is key to success. If there is no structure for CSIRT recommendations to be implemented, and the culture does not provide support for this function, the CSIRT will be stuck chasing their tail, always resolving the same incidents over again as the underlying problems are not addressed.

Incidents

This subsection will cover the identification, containment, eradication, and recovery steps of an incident. Since incidents are complex, it is probable that while investigating or containing one incident another incident may be discovered. Adversaries can also use noisy incidents, such as distributed denial of service (DDoS), to cover up for stealthier attacks. Figure 15.2 displays one comprehensive description of the incident response process, including steps for taking lessons from the response and applying them to the prepare and protection processes in Alberts et al. [17], as discussed in the next section.

In any incident, the first stage is that the response team detects or otherwise is notified of a security violation. This step is generally before containment begins—incidents and the systems affected must be triaged [17]. *Triage* is a term for a prioritization step initially used by military field medics. The medics would group the wounded into three groups: those who will probably survive without aid, those who will probably die even with aid, and those who will only survive if given aid. Priority is given to the last group. During an incident, the response team should try to categorize events similarly, and first try to contain damage where their efforts are most effective.

The essence of triage is a quick, rough categorization of what to work on first. If it takes too long, nothing gets done. Since computer incidents are harder to diagnose than bodily injuries, because most of the evidence is invisible, evaluation criteria for responders should reflect the difficulty of the process.

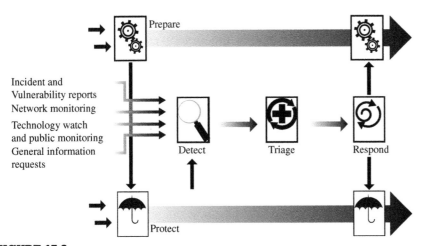

FIGURE 15.2

Comprehensive flow of the incident management process. Notice that protection and preparedness are ongoing processes that learn from the response process. It is possible to further divide the response process into three steps: containment, eradication, and recovery. *Source: Reprinted with permission from Alberts et al. [17].*

The outputs of triage are the priority aspects of the incident for the responders to manage. The CERT model calls this next step response, while the SANS models breaks up response into containment, eradication, and recovery steps [13,17]. However, the overall process described in both of these guiding documents is largely the same; as noted in the CERT document itself there is a variety of terminology from over a dozen sources that covers essentially the same process [17, p. 21ff]. The CERT model emphasizes the continuous interaction of the incident handling process with the rest of the organization's preparations and protections. Breaking up response into substeps emphasizes the stages of response and its complexity. Both are valuable contributions.

Containment is essentially stabilizing the situation. The response team needs to keep the situation from deteriorating further before improvements can be made [13, p. 19]. There is also a key decision to be made just before beginning to respond. If litigation is likely, there are special evidence handling procedures that need to be followed. These will be specific to the defender's jurisdiction, but responding to an incident with the intent of prosecuting the perpetrators will almost always require more care while trying to restore the systems. During containment, in particular, evidence may be erased or contaminated in the fervor to improve defenses. For example, storing malicious code artifacts is more difficult than simply erasing the computer. Some of these handling requirements are discussed in Chapter 13; however, for a full plan the organization should consult a local legal expert.

Probable actions within the containment stage include the following [17, p. 128; 13, p. 19]:

- Apply patches.
- Change passwords and other authentication credentials.
- Scan for malicious software.
- Disconnect affected resources from the network.
- Modify the infrastructure.
- Modify network access control rules, such as any of those discussed in Chapter 5, to prevent malicious communications. This includes blocking specific:
  - IP addresses
  - Ports
  - Services

Once the malicious activity is contained, it can be rooted out and eradicated. Eradication is removal of all malicious software from defender-owned computers. For nonessential hosts, this is relatively easy if the organization is prepared. The hosts can be removed from the network, the storage media can all be completely erased, and a known-good copy of the operating system can be restored from read-only media. This is the only way to verify the hardware is not still infected.[2] As discussed earlier, there are always mission-essential functions that cannot simply be disconnected from the network. Eradication of malicious software from these resources is more difficult. Hardened versions of the service need to be activated before the compromised machines are disconnected for repair. This transition adds logistic and operational difficulties, in addition to the difficulties of incident response.

Eradication of malicious software from large, distributed systems is a further difficulty. If the entire network file server (NFS), for example, is compromised, then the logistical details of guaranteeing every malicious data bit is removed from the system are daunting. Duplicating the data and scanning it may be implausible due to sheer scale. Furthermore, the adversary evaded the defender's scans previously, and so probably could again. The method of erasing the data and starting over, which works for individual clients, does not scale to be applied to an organization's whole knowledge base. This fact means that once the adversary has sufficiently penetrated the infrastructure, it is always possible for the adversary to retain some foothold within the network, since as a matter of practicality the whole IT infrastructure of the organization cannot be taken down and rebuilt from scratch. The purpose of the eradication step is to make this as unlikely as is feasible. The lessons-learned step includes, but is not limited to, watching for indicators of this specific compromise recurring, as discussed later in the chapter.

The final stage in the response process is recovery. Recovery is marked by bringing the cleaned systems back into the production environment, usually after some preliminary testing within the business unit [13, p. 21]. The recovery phase is marked by increased monitoring and vigilance to ensure that the eradication stage was successful. After some time period, the intensified monitoring period comes to a close and the computer is considered healthy again.

These are only the technical phases of the response process. There are also managerial and legal response processes [17, p. 129]. Management responses include decisions such as when to escalate the importance of the incident, public relations, and other management functions that may be necessary on a case-by-case basis. Several of these functions are similar to the incident command system (ICS) defined by FEMA for emergency management [16]. An example of a managerial response occurs if, for example, the incident investigation determines personally identifiable information (PII) was disclosed. This fact must be escalated to higher-level management if the incident is in

---

[2] There is some indication that hard drive firmware can be infected with malicious firmware. This would completely evade erasing the hard drive itself and restoring the operating system. Keep in mind that eradication measures are a key step that malicious actors would like to avoid, so there is always a chance that technical advances will be made that require updates to the response procedures generally, and eradication in particular.

a jurisdiction that legally requires the organization to notify individuals of PII disclosures. Then the management and legal responses must coordinate to notify the relevant parties.

INCORPORATING LESSONS LEARNED

As the old proverb goes, "Fool me once, shame on you; fool me twice, shame on me." Literary references to this sentiment abound in one form or another. For example, "Those who cannot remember the past are condemned to repeat it," as attributed to George Santayana. Learning from one's mistakes is clearly not a new idea. Yet it remains important, as well as difficult.

Many of the guides on incident handling contain the assertion that learning from mistakes is important. For example, Proffitt [13, p. 21] and Alberts et al. [17, p. 140ff] both provide overviews of a lessons-learned process. However, these do not provide sufficient practical guidance in eliciting effective information from weary responders, which is a significant leadership challenge.

To address this need, the U.S. Army developed a process called the after-action review (AAR), targeted at commanders of smaller groups to provide such guidance [15]. Other groups have since recognized the utility of this process, and adapted it to nonmilitary situations [33,34]. After handling a computer security incident, an AAR seems like a reasonable process for collecting the data required as input for feedback into preparation and protection; this feedback process is recommended, as described earlier.

An AAR has a few key features and steps of its own: planning, logistics, execution, and results from the AAR. It is generally recommended that a facilitator who was not directly involved in the incident lead the AAR. This means that the facilitator has to meet with the team leader prior to the AAR to learn enough about the incident that he or she is able to facilitate and not hinder the process. Logistically, it is highly recommended to perform the AAR in person. There are some other functions during the meeting that should be prepared ahead of time, such as a note keeper and a time keeper, who may be the same person, and may be domain specialists, but ideally are not members of the team that is participating in the AAR.

The facilitator proceeds through the AAR with a standard set of questions, operating by an established set of rules. These ground rules need to be established at the beginning of the meeting to help the participants stay on track. It is also important for the facilitator to give context and provide purpose at the beginning of the AAR. Some useful items to start out with include:

- The goal is to collect information to improve future operations.
- Success and failure are not determined or judged within an AAR.

- There will always be aspects of the response that could be improved.
- There will always be aspects of the response that were performed well.
- The goal is to collect objective observations, not praise or blame.
- Encourage openness and a culture of sharing rather than fear or blame.[3]

Once these introductions are established, the facilitator needs to guide the AAR discussion itself and keep it focused on the goals using the established ground rules. Having a small, limited number of clear, established questions promotes this function. If time permits, the facilitator could gather short written responses first and use the meeting to elaborate on a summary of these written responses.

The ultimate goal of an AAR is a useful and succinct report of the information to learn from the incident. The military version of what qualifies as useful and succinct is a little bit out of sync with CSIRT needs. Even so, since there is much organizational experience in the U.S. Army with learning from AARs, it is still instructive to consider what the Army considers to be the contents of an outstanding AAR as a starting point [15, ch. 4]:

- Commander's executive summary
- Task organization to include attached units
- Chronology of key events
- Number of soldiers deployed
- Summary of casualties during deployment
- Discussion of each phase in the deployment cycle
- Participation in major operations
- Discussion of stability operations

Many of these structural elements are immediately transferable to what a CSIRT team AAR might hope to produce. The team lead's executive summary, what different elements of the team were tasked to accomplish, chronology of events as actually occurred, and discussion of primary phases of the incident handling operation are all applicable. "Number of soldiers deployed" needs to be modified to "incident responders," and "casualties" needs to be modified to language regarding malicious software penetration into the infrastructure; however, this is not a difficult conceptual shift.

By adapting these aspects of the AAR to the defender's organization, lessons learned can be more effectively captured. This, in turn, means that lessons can be more effectively applied to the protection and prevention phases of organizational management [17]. In terms of defensive strategies, effective

---

[3] One example method of achieving this is that summaries to management should not include names or details usable in personnel evaluations.

lessons learned means that deception, frustration, resistance, and recognition strategies can all be improved by judicious updates culled from the lessons learned after responding to incidents.

SUMMARY

Recovery from computer security incidents is a complicated process that relies on technology but is driven by good organizational planning and procedures. A recovery strategy integrates aspects of the other four strategies discussed in the previous chapters for two reasons. First, an organization can only recover from events it has recognized. Second, part of recovery involves changing strategies in response to a failed strategy.

Emergency management is a mature field of academic study and organizational management, and computer security shares aspects with it. There is also a sufficient existing literature covering computer security incident response. This chapter summarizes the key aspects from both of these fields and attempts to demonstrate how they interact and how they are different. The summary presented here is particularly dense with references to other documents that the interested reader should pursue.

REFERENCES

[1] Mandiant. APT1: exposing one of China's cyber espionage units. Alexandria, VA. Retrieved from <http://intelreport.mandiant.com/>; 2013.

[2] Falliere N, Murchu LO, Chien E. W32. Stuxnet Dossier. Symantec Corp. Mountain View, CA, 2011.

[3] Fisher D, Linger R, Lipson H, Longstaff T, Mead N, Ellison R. Survivable network systems: an emerging discipline. Pittsburgh: Carnegie Mellon University, Software Engineering Institute. CMU/SEI-1997-TR-013. Retrieved from <http://www.sei.cmu.edu/library/abstracts/reports/97tr013.cfm>; 1998.

[4] Mead N, Ellison R, Linger R, Longstaff T, McHugh J. Survivable network analysis method. Pittsburgh: Carnegie Mellon University, Software Engineering Institute. CMU/SEI-2000-TR-013. Retrieved from <http://www.sei.cmu.edu/library/abstracts/reports/00tr013.cfm>; 2000.

[5] Swanson M, Bowen P, Wohl Phillips A, Gallup D, Lynes D. Contingency planning guide for federal information systems (revision 1). NIST Special Publication 800-34, 2010.

[6] Federal Emergency Management Agency. Colleges, Universities and Institutions offering emergency management courses. Retrieved Apr 4, 2013, from <http://training.fema.gov/emi-web/edu/collegelist/>; 2012.

[7] Mehravari N. Principles and practice of operational resilience. In: IEEE conference on technologies for homeland security, IEEE 2012. Retrieved Apr 6, 2013, from <http://www.cert.org/podcast/pdf/IEEE-HST-2012.pdf>; 2012.

[8] Federal Emergency Management Agency. Independent Study Program (ISP) Course List0. Retrieved Apr 6, 2013, from <http://training.fema.gov/IS/crslist.aspx?all=true>; 2013.

[9] Felicitie C, Bell MLM. Retrieved Apr 6, 2013, from <http://www.ssa.gov/oact/NOTES/as120/LifeTables_Body.html> Life tables for the United States Social Security Area 1900–2100. U.S. Social Security Administration; 2005.

[10] Allen JH, Curtis PD, White DW, Young LR. CERT: resilience management model, Version 1.0. Pittsburgh: Carnegie Mellon University, Software Engineering Institute. CMU/SEI-2010-TR-012. Retrieved from <http://www.sei.cmu.edu/library/abstracts/reports/10tr012.cfm>; 2010.

[11] Caralli RA, Allen JH, White DW. CERT resilience management model (CERT-RMM): a maturity model for managing operational resilience. Reading, MA: Addison-Wesley Professional; 2010.

[12] Chuvakin A. Enterprise Content-Aware DLP architecture and operational practices. Gartner, Stamford, CT; 2013.

[13] Proffitt T. Creating and managing an incident response team for a large company. SANS Institute; 2007. Retrieved Apr 16, 2013, from <http://www.sans.org/reading_room/whitepapers/incident/creating-managing-incident-response-team-large-company_1821>.

[14] Smith D. Forming An Incident Response Team. Proceedings of the FIRST annual conference, University of Queensland, Brisbane, Australia, July 1994.

[15] U.S. Army Center of Military History. Commander's guide to operational records and data collection. 09-22. Retrieved from <usacac.army.mil/cac2/call/docs/09-22/09-22.pdf>; 2009.

[16] Federal Emergency Management Agency. Introduction to the Incident Command System (ICS 100): Student Manual. Retrieved Apr 6, 2013, from <http://training.fema.gov/EMIWeb/IS/IS100b/SM/ICS100b_StudentManual_Aug2010.pdf>; 2010.

[17] Alberts C, Dorofee A, Killcrece G, Ruefle R, Zajicek M. Defining incident management processes for CSIRTs: a work in progress. Pittsburgh, PA. Carnegie Mellon University Software Engineering Institute, CERT Coordination Center; 2004. Retrieved from <www.cert.org/archive/pdf/04tr015.pdf>.

[18] Brownlee N, Guttman E. Expectations for Computer Security Incident Response. RFC 2350, 1998.

[19] Cichonski P, Millar T, Grance T, Scarfone K. Computer security incident handling guide (revision 2). NIST Special Publication 800-61, 2012.

[20] Federal Emergency Management Agency. Emergency Planning Independent Study 235.b: Student Manual. Retrieved Apr 16, 2013, from <http://training.fema.gov/EMIWeb/IS/IS235B/IS235B.pdf>; 2011.

[21] U.S. Department of Homeland Security. Federal continuity directive 1: Federal executive branch national continuity program and requirements. Retrieved from <http://www.fema.gov/library/viewRecord.do?id=6888>; 2012.

[22] Thibodeau P. Hurricane Sandy leaves wounded servers in its wake. Computer World. 2012, November 19. Retrieved Apr 6, 2013, from <http://www.computerworld.com/s/article/9233754/Hurricane_Sandy_leaves_wounded_servers_in_its_wake>.

[23] Maybury M, Chase P, Cheikes B, Brackney D, Matzner S, Hetherington T, et al. Analysis and detection of malicious insiders. MITRE; 2005. Retrieved Apr 6, 2013, from <http://www.dtic.mil/cgi-bin/GetTRDoc?Location=U2&doc=GetTRDoc.pdf&AD=ADA456356>.

[24] Walton G, Longstaff T, Linger R. Technology Foundations for Computational Evaluation of Software Security Attributes. Pittsburgh: Carnegie Mellon University, Software Engineering Institute. CMU/SEI-2006-TR-021. Retrieved from <http://www.sei.cmu.edu/library/abstracts/reports/06tr021.cfm>; 2006.

[25] Ellis J, Fisher D, Longstaff T, Pesante L, Pethia R. Report to the President's commission on critical infrastructure protection. Pittsburgh: Software Engineering Institute, Carnegie Mellon University; 1997.

[26] Howard JD, Longstaff TA. A common language for computer security incidents. Sandia National Laboratories, SAND98-8667. Received from <http://www.cert.org/research/taxonomy_988667.pdf>; 1998.

[27] Longstaff T, Balenson D, Matties M. Barriers to science in security Proceedings of the 26th annual computer security applications conference, ACSAC. p. 127–129. New York: ACM; 2010. Retrieved from <http://doi.acm.org/10.1145/1920261.1920281>.

[28] Maxion RA, Longstaff TA, McHugh J. Why is there no science in cyber science? a panel discussion at NSPW 2010. Proceedings of the 2010 Workshop on New Security Paradigms, NSPW 2010. New York: ACM, p. 1–6. Retrieved from <http://doi.acm.org/10.1145/1900546.1900548>; 2010.

[29] Pethia R, Allen J. CERT lessons learned: a conversation with Rich Pethia, Director of CERT. Software Engineering Institute, CERT Program. Retrieved from <http://www.cert.org/podcast/show/20061031pethia.html>; 2006.

[30] Software Engineering Institute. U.S. Department of Homeland Security Announces Partnership with Carnegie Mellon's CERT Coordination Center. Press Release. Retrieved Apr 9, 2013, from <http://www.sei.cmu.edu/newsitems/uscert.cfm>; 2003.

[31] FIRST. About FIRST. Retrieved Apr 21, 2013, from <http://www.first.org/about>; 2013.

[32] Software Engineering Institute, CERT Program. Action List for Developing a Computer Security Incident Response Team (CSIRT). Retrieved Apr 6, 2013, from <http://www.cert.org/csirts/action_list.html>; 2013.

[33] Salem-Schatz S, Ordin D, Mittman B. Guide to the After Action Review. U.S. Deptatment of Veterans Affairs. Retrieved Apr 20, 2013, from <www.queri.research.va.gov/ciprs/projects/after_action_review.pdf?>; 2010.

[34] Glass I, Calhoun B. This American Life 487: Harper High School, Part One. Transcript. Chicago Public Media. Retrieved Apr 22, 2013, from <http://www.thisamericanlife.org/radio-archives/episode/487/transcript>; 2013.

Chapter Review Questions

1. How is effective incident response a technical process?

2. How is effective incident response a nontechnical process?

3. What are critical success factors? What are mission-essential functions?

4. What are some key aspects of a good incident response policy?

5. How is COOP different from computer security incident response?

6. How is COOP the same as computer security incident response?

7. What five steps can be used to summarize the computer security incident handling process?

8. What is a CSIRT?

9. What is FIRST?

10. In the context of incident response, what is "triage"?

11. What are some key features of a good AAR?

Chapter Exercises

1. Using one of the references for this chapter, find a different categorization of the computer security incident handling process you described in review question 7 above. How are the two summaries related?

2. Outline a possible computer security incident response policy for your organization, school, or local government. Try to indicate who would be responsible for certain high-level tasks, and, if possible, name the individuals. Include some general idea of who would be in charge of various tasks. Some templates may be available on the Internet, such as at *security.ucdavis.edu/pdf/iet_irp.pdf*.

3. Outline a possible AAR for a computer security incident in your organization, school, or local government, given the plan described in exercise 2.

CHAPTER 16

Professional Certifications and Overall Conclusions

INTRODUCTION

This book presents a series of strategies for protecting information in an organization, and a number of technologies for implementing each strategy. The strategies do not exist independently of the culture of organizations or of each other. Understanding how the culture of security has been codified in specific security certifications provides a viewpoint on how strategic principles may be applied in that culture. Understanding how the strategies relate to one another to form a cohesive and balanced approach to address specific threats provides a viewpoint on the value of multiple strategies. All of this leads to an ongoing need to improve one's skills and knowledge to meet the shifting demands on security professionals.

PROFESSIONAL CERTIFICATIONS

In a field as complex and technical as information security, managers prefer professionals with documented expertise. This preference has led to the emergence of a large number of security certifications. Some of these certifications have been mentioned in this book, particularly in Chapter 10, which listed several for change management certifications. This section deals with more general information security certifications, and with the strengths and limitations of each, and with certification in general (see Figure 16.1).

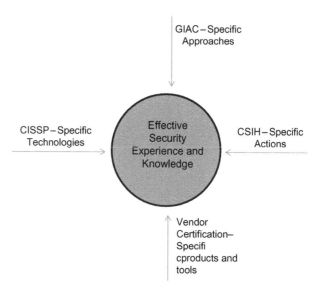

FIGURE 16.1
Certification overview.

Certified Information Systems Security Professional

One of the most widely cited information security certifications is the Certified Information Systems Security Professional (CISSP), offered by the International Information Systems Security Certification Consortium (ISC)² [1]. This certification covers individuals who have five years or more experience and covers multiple aspects of security. The certification requires a thorough exam, and normally preparatory course work.

The CISSP certification centers on 12 security domains [2]:

- Access control
- Telecommunications and network security
- Information security governance and risk management
- Software development security
- Cryptography
- Security architecture and design
- Operations security
- Business continuity and disaster recovery planning
- Legal
- Regulations
- Investigations and compliance
- Physical (environmental) security

Certified professionals are expected to have demonstrated knowledge in each domain (via the certification exam) and have at least five years' experience covering 2 of the 12 domains. This structure allows certified professionals to have documented breadth of knowledge, plus some degree of focus in their professional expertise. Further information on the types of knowledge expected of a CISSP certified professional may be obtained by examination preparation guides, including the *CISSP Study Guide* [3].

Depending on the experience factor, individuals with CISSP certification serve in multiple roles [2], ranging from consultants and security engineers to a variety of management and executive positions. The consortium cites a survey [4] indicating that certified professionals earn about 30% more than noncertified compatriots, although that survey is sponsored by the consortium and weighted to respondents who had certification (at least 66%) and were employed in large, established industries (information technology and telecommunications only account for 20% of the total). The comparison in the survey was against averages, and was not normalized for amount of experience—that is, the survey did not compare salaries of similar individuals, but rather compared averages against averages.

$(ISC)^2$ also offers a range of other certifications [1]. The Certified Authorization Professional is largely for U.S. Department of Defense systems authorization personnel—staff tasked with ensuring systems meet requirements and granting systems the authority to operate. The Systems Security Certified Professional is for individuals with limited experience. The Certified Secure Software Life-cycle Professional is for software developers working on security-critical systems. In addition, the consortium also offers add-on concentrations for the CISSP to document more specific expertise.

Global Information Assurance Certifications

The Global Information Assurance Certification (GIAC) is offered by the SANS (derived from sys-admin, audit, networking, and security) Institute [5]. This set of over 20 certifications closely connects to the SANS training offerings, but extends the content with requirements for a more in-depth examination, practicum, and report generation. A timespan of approximately four months is cited as the level of effort associated with a GIAC. In general, the topics of this certification are more hands-on, direct activity associated with secure administration, forensics, audit, and management. The SANS courses have a strong reputation in the field, and these certifications derive their respect (and the advantage of possessing them) from the affiliated SANS courses.

One difficulty with the GIAC is the breadth of certification available. While the certifications allow a range of individuals to be certified at the skill levels they possess, the large number of them makes it difficult for any one certification to be widely recognized. As such, employers may find it more difficult to connect these certifications to the required expertise of candidates or current personnel.

CERT Computer Security Incident Handler

The Computer Security Incident Handler (CSIH) is a certification offered by the CERT[1] Directorate at Carnegie Mellon's Software Engineering Institute (SEI). Incident handling is a systematic set of recovery tactics for the restoration of organizational security. Given that adversaries have already damaged the organization's security, this recovery is always time-critical and often stressful. To promote methodical application of these tactics, CERT provides training on incident handling, and certification derived from that training [6]. This certification requires only an examination, not the connected training, allowing for cost-effective certification of expertise. The certification is valid for a period of three years, and may be renewed by application.

Since this certification has no experience component, it is less comprehensive than CISSP or GIAC. It certifies knowledge, but not skill in practice. This certification is not as widely recognized or required by employers as CISSP or GIAC.

Certified Ethical Hacking

Certified Ethical Hacker (CEH) is a certification provided by the International Council of E-Commerce Consultants (EC-Council) [7]. This certification focuses on very current network intrusion methods, trained via hands-on exercises and classroom instruction. Expertise is verified via the CEH exam. The methods profiled are those observed in practice as used by adversaries against organizations. The underlying approach is that to be effective in protecting security, one needs to think like an adversary and proactively assess the organization's network using methods like an adversary would. While this viewpoint is true to a certain extent, the details of making an attack work (or a sufficient sequence of attacks) may require a substantive effort that may not result in overall improvements in information security.

Vendor-specific Certifications

A large number of vendors offer completion certificates for training in their products. These certifications may or may not be associated with demonstrated proficiency in the products involved. Often, the vendor provides some examination prior to awarding the certificate, but the overwhelming majority of participants pass such examinations. This type of certification rarely provides significant advantages to the participants, beyond the underlying training in the products involved. However, there are a few exceptions to the low value of vendor-specific certifications. Specifically, two of the more widely respected vender certifications are from Microsoft and Cisco Systems.

---

[1] CERT originally stood for computer emergency response team, however, like IBM and KFC, the acronym is now trademarked as-is, and officially does not have an expansion.

As Microsoft has become dominant in the operating system (and, to an extent in the browser) markets, demand for expertise in their products likewise grew. This has been reflected in courses and certification standards [8]. The courses mix very product-oriented information (the configuration of specific Microsoft components, services, and systems) with explanation of the underlying (and more general) protocols and methods used in the products. The exams walk through the same mix of specific components and underlying protocols and methods. This mix allows certified professionals to apply the specific technologies (as configured in current products) to provide for secure operations. One weakness of such certification is that, since it is tied to specific configurations of specific products, new certifications will be required as the products evolve. Recertification is required every two to three years for most Microsoft certifications, and requires either retaking the exams or becoming qualified as a trainer [8].

Cisco Systems is a major networking equipment manufacturer. They also provide training in their products and a range of associated certifications [9]. Cisco arranges these certifications in career tracks, going from entry-level through expert rankings on a four-step scale. For security, this range starts with the Cisco Certified Entry Technician, which covers fundamentals of networking and initial device configuration. This entry certification feeds into the Cisco Certified Network Associate level, which focuses on security policies and their enforcement via network devices. The associate level in turn feeds into the Cisco Certified Network Professional Security, which focuses on specific security components along with how those components are associated with network devices, such as firewalls, IDSs, and VPNs. The expert range for security certifications is the Cisco Certified Internet Expert Security. At the expert level, this includes overview of industry best practices and standards associated with security. As a whole, these certifications are more concept centered and less product centered than the Microsoft certifications. In general, the certifications require an examination, which covers topics taught in the recommended training. These training courses are five days of combined lectures and exercises, which could be criticized for lack of depth. Cisco requires recertification every three years by taking a recertification exam.

Other Certifications
There are a variety of other certifications that are less often cited in relation to security, but may be useful in the course of a security career:

- ISACA[2]—security audit (see *http://www.isaca.org/CERTIFICATION/Pages/default.aspx*), for example, Certified Information Systems Auditor (CISA), Certified Information Security Manager (CISM), Certified in

---

[2] ISACA stood for Information Systems Audit and Control Association, however, like CERT, it now officially does not have an expansion.

the Governance of Enterprise IT (CGEIT), and Certified in Risk and Information Systems Control (CRISC).

- IEEE (Institute of Electrical and Electronics Engineers)—security engineering (see *http://www.ieee.org/education_careers/education/professional_ certification/index.html*)
- BSI—business security standards (see *http://www.bsigroup.com/en-GB/ our-services/certification/*)

Critiques of Certification

Certification has become a frequently cited feature on many professional resumes, but due to the specifics of information security, there is reason for concern regarding such certifications. First, the security field is always changing, with new technologies and applications to protect, new threats to address, and emerging means of protection. The way organizations use networks today differs from five years ago. The forms of threat that were of high concern five years ago are not as high currently—new forms have emerged. The security tools available to protect organizations have also matured in the last five years. With this high a pace of change, it is very difficult to establish a fixed curriculum and examination that indicates a professional is current and productive in the protection of information.

Second, it is not clear that the effort (and cost) demanded to obtain certification results in commensurate reward. Many certifications are closely tied to specific products or methods. If those products and methods age too rapidly, the productivity of a certified professional will not benefit an organization as much as a noncertified, but current, professional.

Third, there are lingering concerns of bias in the examination process. While several certifications do not demand preparatory coursework (only recommend it), it may not be simple to understand the specialized vocabulary used in the examination (which derives from the courses). Such vocabulary shifts widely from vendor to vendor, so a similar course taken from another vendor may cover similar concepts, but not produce a passing score on the certification examination. Certifications often focus on specific products, and require some knowledge of configurations that might not be gained from even longterm exposure to the products. Some of this may be intentional, as the vendors typically want to sell training in addition to selling certification examinations.

Fourth, certification is a for-profit enterprise for many of the certifying bodies. As such, the success rate of the certification examination must be carefully managed: too high a success rate and the value of the certification is disputable; too low and individuals are discouraged from attempting certification. These concerns are quite outside the issue of how specific certification actually improves the productivity of an organization, and may produce certified professionals who are not, in fact, productive.

Fifth, security in general, and especially information security, is characterized by adversarial relationships between intelligent actors. Network defenders are acting to deceive, frustrate, resist, and nullify adversaries. Network aggressors are acting to deceive, evade, control, and nullify network defenses. The interplay between these adversaries will rapidly adjust to changes in the skill or knowledge level of either side. On the other hand, the certification process, by its very nature, demands a large amount of stable knowledge and common practice of certified professionals. This stability of knowledge and methods on the part of the defenders will likely produce blind spots that are opportunities for dedicated and persistent adversaries. Preventing such blind spots requires a degree of preparation and flexibility that is far beyond most, if not all, current certification programs.

Last, the certification itself may form a vulnerability. As managers focus on a set of certifications (rather than a record of accomplishment) as a hiring or promotion justification, they are ceding a certain degree of judgment to an outside body that inherently does not have the same view of security as their own organization. As such, managers may trust individuals to perform certified actions that they, in fact, may be unprepared to perform in the context of the organization.

While certification is likely to remain an important feature of the security field for some time to come, the critiques noted here recommend that organizations exercise a degree of caution in how they view such certifications and certified professionals. Particularly for product-tied certifications, a balanced approach may produce better results for the organization.

ADVANCED PERSISTENT THREAT

Systematic Strategic Hacking

Since the middle of the 2000s, a series of long-term, high-value attacks against computer networks have been observed [10]. These attacks have spanned months and years of ongoing activity (with a cited average length of activity greater than 10 months). These attacks have occurred despite diligent network defenses, although the adversaries rapidly exploited lapses in security. Commonly, the aggressors establish a command-and-control infrastructure on compromised third-party networks, and then use that infrastructure for a series of attacks on a range of organizations. While there appear to be key individuals among the adversaries, there is apparently a large number of staff members engaged in the aggressor activity. The adversaries rapidly adopt (and discard) technologies to establish an initial point of presence on a targeted network, then propagate from this point of presence internally on the network to identify and export information of interest. The scope of the identified activity and the value of the assets compromised speak to the preparation and focus associated with these adversaries. In some cases, where the targeted network could not be compromised directly, subsidiary organizations or vendors (particularly of security solutions) were attacked to progressively gain access to the main target.

Dealing with such a focused, resourced, and aggressive adversary is a daunting challenge. It requires careful planning as to a series of protective measures operating in a supportive fashion. It requires a balance of protective features deployed across the organization's network, and usually a certain degree of luck.

TYING THE PIECES TOGETHER

The strategies of deception, frustration, resistance, recognition, and recovery do not stand alone, fragmented, and independent. Choices in one strategy should inform choices in another. Effective defense in depth requires coordinated strategies, both in the original military description [11] and the computer security metaphor as explained in Chapter 2. As described in the previous chapters, there are quite a few areas with which an architect of an overall security strategy needs to be familiar. There are some tools and models that can assist in crafting a coordinated, cohesive strategy.

There is no easy or magic solution to the problem of coordinating strategies. People in decision-making positions need some domain knowledge to make appropriate choices; managers cannot quite be abstracted away from the technical details. There is organization guidance on how to cohesively manage these strategies. For example, the Resiliency Management Model (RMM) [12] and the Operationally Critical Threat, Asset, and Vulnerability Evaluation (OCTAVE®) [13] provide organizational guidance. Although the models are always developing, guidance such as RMM and OCTAVE, as well as many other models, have been under development since the 1990s and draw from experience prior to that. The field of computer security is not as raw and experimental as it once was. As discussed and cited throughout the book, guidance exists for an organization to improve the accuracy of assessments of risk related to computer systems and, in most any area, improve the security of those computer systems if needed.

One method of visualizing the coverage of security programs for an organization against certain threats is with a coverage diagram [14], as introduced in chapter 2. A partially filled example coverage diagram is shown in Figure 16.2. The concentric circles of the diagram represent different layers of the defense strategies. We have presented five strategic layers, with one circle for each. The three sectors in the diagram represent three distinct threats: denial of service (DoS), malicious software, and data theft. Each technology or policy that helps defend against each threat goes in the segment of the circle at the layer of defense. If there are multiple items at one layer for one threat, the segment is shaded darker. This provides a visualization of the weak points for the organization, as they are white. The DoS attack sector is filled in with examples from the book. If there are more protections at a strategic layer, the segment is darker. The other two sectors are left as an exercise.

One of the common properties of complex systems is that small changes can have large, unexpected consequences. One euphemism for this is the "butterfly effect," the image that whether or not there is a storm in North America may depend on whether or not a butterfly flaps its wings in Asia a

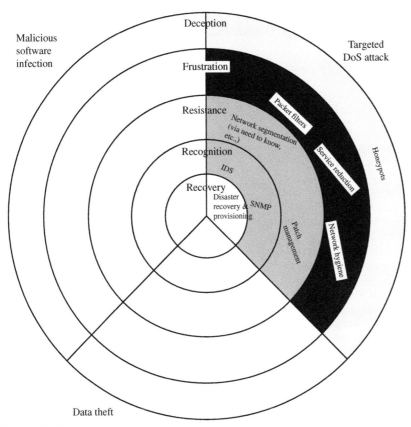

FIGURE 16.2

An expanded coverage diagram following Butler [14]. The DoS attack sector is filled in with examples from the book. If there are more protections at a strategic layer, the segment is darker. The other two sectors are left as an exercise.

few months prior. Security and security engineering definitely are attempts to manage a complex system [15]. Perrow [16] and others have studied accidents in complex systems, and have found that tightly coupled complex systems (with extensive intercommunications, requiring behavior to span across components, and with large interdependencies among components for successful operation) have systemic properties that inherently lead to accidents.

Healy [17] described a range of options for the future of networking as an international domain of either cooperation or conflict—anticipating that continued systemic weakness would lead to a balkanization of the network, but systematic and globally informed improvements in security could lead to increased cooperation. Bringing together all the pieces will help manage the complex system of organizational computer security. However, the external environment is constantly changing. New exploits and technology are constantly being created. The defender must remain flexible, adaptive, and continue to learn.

PROFILE: SUN TZU

The First Strategist

Sun Tzu (traditional Chinese: 孫子; simplified: 孙子; pinyin: Sūnzǐ), born Sun Wu, was a general, strategist, and philosopher just before the Warring States period in China [18]. His birth and death are generally put at c. 544–496 BCE, although the two great histories of China disagree as to his birthplace. In any event, he was an important strategist for the state of Wu. After his military successes, he codified his strategic ideas in *The Art of War*. To this day, *The Art of War* [11] is still required reading in many military officer training programs, although a suitable translation did not find its way into the Western training regimen until World War II [11]. The next oldest is probably Julius Caesar's *Gallic Wars*, not written until 500 years after *The Art of War* (and widely judged as much more limited application than Sun Tzu). Macchiavlli's *The Prince* and Clausewitz's *On War* are equally widely cited, but written about two millennia after *The Art of War*. Sun Tzu's treatise has truly stood the test of time.

Sun Tzu provides strategic advice that cuts across technologies and eras. Whenever two commanders are vying for strategic victory, it can apply. This is as true of a defender and attacker in a digital conflict as in the state of Wu. Sun Tzu focuses on planning, careful study of one's opponent, constructing careful strategy with fluidly changing applications to meet the opponent's action, and readiness to exploit circumstances as they arise, to the advancement of one's goals. While not laying out a specific organization, Sun Tzu characterizes aspects (and rewards) of effective leadership in conflict.

Military-grade determination is most present in so-called advanced persistent threats (APTs), where adversaries have specifically selected targets, and the defenders would know there is a specific enemy commanding the attack with whom the defenders must deal. With the advent of such adversaries, information security is shifting from dealing with the bandit-like hacker groups of the 1980s through the early 2000s, to something closer to organized military forces. This transition is precisely what Sun Tzu faced in his military career. The state of Wu had historically been irritated by roving groups of bandits, striking opportunistically. Sun Tzu noted that in addition to these bandits, addressing the newly emerging organized forces required systematic understanding of conflict—the motivation for *The Art of War*.

Some of Sun Tzu's more practical comments, such as observing birds and dust patterns to infer enemy movements, may not be applicable. However, there are many salient passages, such as "all warfare is based on deception" [11, ch. 1, no. 18], and the resulting recommendations for deceiving one's opponent. Another example is Sun Tzu's opening characterization of success in combat, starting with understanding the purpose and moral justification of the conflict (as in, why specifically is this organization's information worthy of defense and what larger values are threatened) before engaging in it.

WHERE TO GO FROM HERE

This book provides a broad, accurate overview of the computer security discipline. This means we have covered (almost) everything, and in so doing, covered nothing in as much detail as a specialist from any information security field might like. If a particular area has struck the reader's interest, follow the citations in the chapter and read the more detailed treatments therein. Many of the resources are available electronically, and any resources not available electronically are cited because the information in the book is worth a trip to the library. As a reminder, some of the textbooks cited often throughout are [15,19–21]. NIST's Special Publication series, the IETF's Request for Comments (RFC) series, and guidance from Carnegie Mellon's Software Engineering Institute, as well as other government-funded research labs, make up another large portion of more detailed guidance on particular topics.

For more breadth of knowledge, there is a substantial catalog of information security–related books available from Syngress. The Syngress imprint of Elsevier [22] focuses on cutting-edge technology and provides a large amount of information on topics of immediate use to the professional and to the student. Specific works that are relevant to the material in this book include Evan Wheeler's *Security Risk Management*, John Sammon's *Basics of Digital Forensics*, and *Data Hiding* by Michael Raggio et al.

In a field as applied and fluid as information security, a range of experience is essential. Serious students should deliberately diversify their career across industries and organizations of varying sizes. By understanding, at a practitioner's level, the driving factors in security improvements and organizational risk management, the need for new skills and new knowledge will emerge naturally. This experience will also allow professionals to accurately assess the utility of strategies, methods, and security products in protecting the information for the organization with which they are associated. It is extremely difficult (if not impossible) to gain such an understanding from academic study alone. On the other hand, it is difficult to effectively apply such understanding, without knowledge of the basic principles and trade-offs involved, which is often most efficiently gained via academic study.

At an extremely practical level, anyone involved in computer security would be well served to become familiar with the basic UNIX-like command-line interface (CLI). This is less useful on Windows machines, since there are fewer applications for Window's PowerShell, but it is still helpful. Mac OSX includes a full-featured "terminal" similar to the UNIX-like CLI. A command line has a notoriously steep initial learning curve, because the user has to remember the basic commands, and even the help command can be overwhelming initially. To make use of the CLI, the user has to be a moderately skilled typist, which also requires practice, but this is an important skill in its own right. There are several CLI tutorials available online. A friendly neighborhood search engine may turn up better results, as these may change often; however, some places to start for introductory tutorials include:

- *http://www.ee.surrey.ac.uk/Teaching/Unix/*
- *https://help.ubuntu.com/community/CommandlineHowto*
- *http://www.tuxfiles.org/linuxhelp/cli.html*
- *http://linuxcommand.org/learning_the_shell.php*

Although it takes some practice, effort on the command line is rewarded by the fact that one can accomplish more tasks, and more complicated tasks, more easily than one can with a standard graphical user interface (GUI; pronounced as "gooey"). Certain applications are better suited to GUIs, but no computer security professional would be disserviced by a familiarity with a CLI.

One ongoing challenge to improving security skills is finding relevant data on which to practice. There is no widely available reference data on which to perform analysis and understand security trade-offs. This lack of data is due to a number of factors: the large variability between organizations, legal ramifications involved in disclosure of organizational information, repeated failure to successfully remove identifying characteristics from data while preserving its utility, and the rapid shifting of technologies on both the aggressive and defensive sides.

There is still no replacement for practical experience. Thinking critically about unique practical situations will provide novel insights that no book can quite predict. Do not be afraid to ask questions. To this end, if readers have a difficult problem, the authors are always happy to offer some help, time permitting. The authors can be reached at InfoSecurityFeedback@elsevier.com. This offer is in part standing behind the claim that there is still some tradecraft and apprenticeship in becoming a quality security professional—everything has not been codified and written down yet.

REFERENCES

[1] International Information Systems Security Certification Consortium. (ISC)2—IT Certification and Security Experts. Retrieved May 20, 2013, from <https://www.isc2.org>; 2013.

[2] International Information Systems Security Certification Consortium. CISSP Information. Retrieved May 20, 2013, from <https://www.isc2.org/uploadedFiles/Credentials_and_Certifcation/CISSP/CISSP-Information.pdf>; 2013.

[3] Conrad E, Misenar S, Feldman J. CISSP study guide, 2nd ed. Boston, MA: Syngress; 2012.

[4] Frost & Sullivan Corporation. The 2013 ISC2 global information security workforce study. Retrieved May 20, 2013, from <https://www.isc2.org/GISWSRSA2013/>; 2013.

[5] SANS Institute. GIAC Forensics, Management Information, IT Security Certifications. Retrieved May 20, 2013, from <http://www.giac.org/>; 2013.

[6] Software Engineering Institute. CERT-Certified computer security incident handler. Retrieved May 20, 2013, from <http://www.sei.cmu.edu/certification/security/csih/>; 2013.

[7] EC-Council. CEH: Certified Ethical Hacking Course from EC-Council. Retrieved May 20, 2013, from <http://www.eccouncil.org/Certification/certified-ethical-hacker>; 2013.

[8] Microsoft. IT certifications: microsoft learning. Retrieved May 20, 2013, from <http://www.microsoft.com/learning/en/us/certification-overview.aspx#fbid=jAnXZaJMwuQ>; 2013.

[9] CISCO Systems. CCNP security—IT certifications and career paths. Retrieved May 20, 2013, from <http://www.cisco.com/web/learning/certifications/professional/ccnp_security/index.html>; 2013.

[10] Mandiant   Retrieved May 20, 2013, from <http://intelreport.mandiant.com/Mandiant_APT1_Report.pdf> APT1: exposing one of China's cyber espionage units. Mandiant Corporation; 2013.

[11] Sun Tzu. (6th century BC). The art of war. [Giles L, Trans.]. Project Gutenberg, transcribed from original, 1910. Retrieved May 20, 2013, from <http://www.gutenberg.org/ebooks/132>.

[12] Caralli R, Allen J, White D. CERT resilience management model (CERT-RMM): a maturity model for managing operational resilience. Reading, MA: Addison-Wesley Professional; 2010.

[13] Alberts C, Dorofee A. OCTAVE Criteria. Software Engineering Institute, Carnegie Mellon University; 2001. Technical Report CMU-SEI-TR-01-16. Retrieved May 20, 2013, from <www.cert.org/archive/pdf/01tr016.pdf>.

[14] Butler S. The security attribute evaluation method. Ph.D. Dissertation. School of Computer Science. Carnegie Mellon University; 2003. SCS Tech Report CMU-CS-03-132. Retrieved May 20, 2013, from <http://reports-archive.adm.cs.cmu.edu/anon/anon/home/ftp/usr/ftp/2003/CMU-CS-03-132.pdf>.

[15] Anderson R. Security engineering: a guide to building dependable distributed systems, 2nd ed. New York: Wiley; 2008.

[16] Perrow C. Normal accidents. New York: Basic Books; 1984.

[17] Healy J. The Five Futures of Cyber Conflict and Cooperation. Georgetown Journal of International Affairs. Special Issue: International Engagement on Cyber; 2011. Retrieved May 20, 2013, from <http://journal.georgetown.edu/wp-content/uploads/cyber-Healy.pdf>.

[18] Sawyer R. The seven military classics of ancient China. New York: Basic Books; 2007.

[19] Cheswick W, Bellovin S, Rubin A. Firewalls and internet security: repelling the Wily Hacker. Reading, MA: Addison-Wesley Professional; 2003.

[20] Katz J, Lindell Y. Introduction to modern cryptography: principles and protocols. Boca Raton, FL: Chapman & Hall/CRC; 2008.

[21] Stallings W. Network security essentials: applications and standards, 4th ed. Englewood Cliffs, NJ: Prentice-Hall; 2011.

[22] Syngress. Syngress: An Imprint of Elsevier". Retrieved May 20, 2013, from <http://store.elsevier.com/Syngress/IMP_76/>; 2013.

Chapter Review Questions

1. Briefly explain at least one reason why certifications have become important as job requirements.

2. Briefly explain at least one of the reasons why overdependence on certifications may contribute to organizational vulnerability.

3. Define the following terms, and briefly explain their relevance to information security:
   a. Deception strategy
   b. Logical semantics
   c. Frustration strategy
   d. Algebraic semantics
   e. Resistance strategy
   f. Access control list
   g. Recognition/recover strategy
   h. Access control matrix

       i. Tranquility principle
       j. Incident handling
       k. Verification
       l. Certification
       m. Validation

4. What is one reason why the lack of "typical" security incident information is a barrier to improving information security practices?

5. What are two options available to build on the information in this book?

6. Which of the topics addressed in this book are of specific interest to you? Why?

7. Of the personality profiles identified in this book, which is most relevant to you? Why?

Chapter Exercises

1. What is one option, other than the coverage diagram shown in Figure 16.2, for summarization of information security protections in an organization?

2. Fill in the blank sectors for "data theft" and "malicious software infection" in Figure 16.2 with strategies and technologies from the book.

Index

Note: Page numbers followed by "*f*" and "*b*" refers to figures and boxes respectively.

Printed and bound by CPI Group (UK) Ltd, Croydon, CR0 4YY

03/10/2024

01040341-0011